um Crazy!

tales of a

tiger-striped cat 1

story & art by

HOSHINO NATSUMI

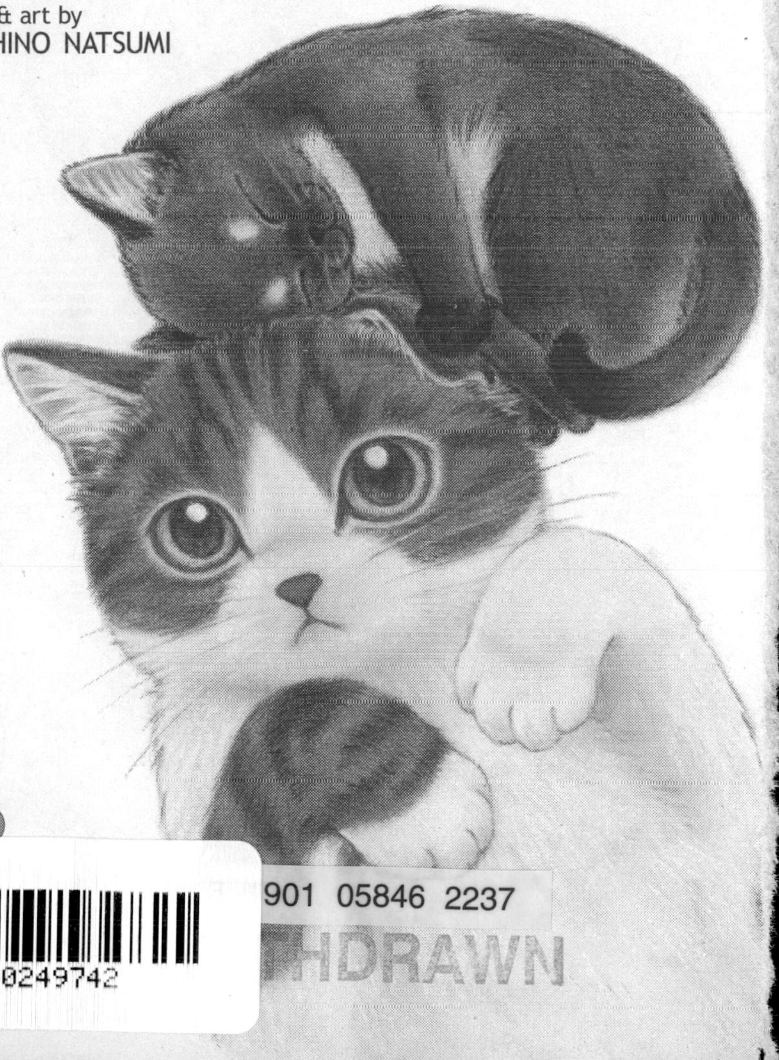

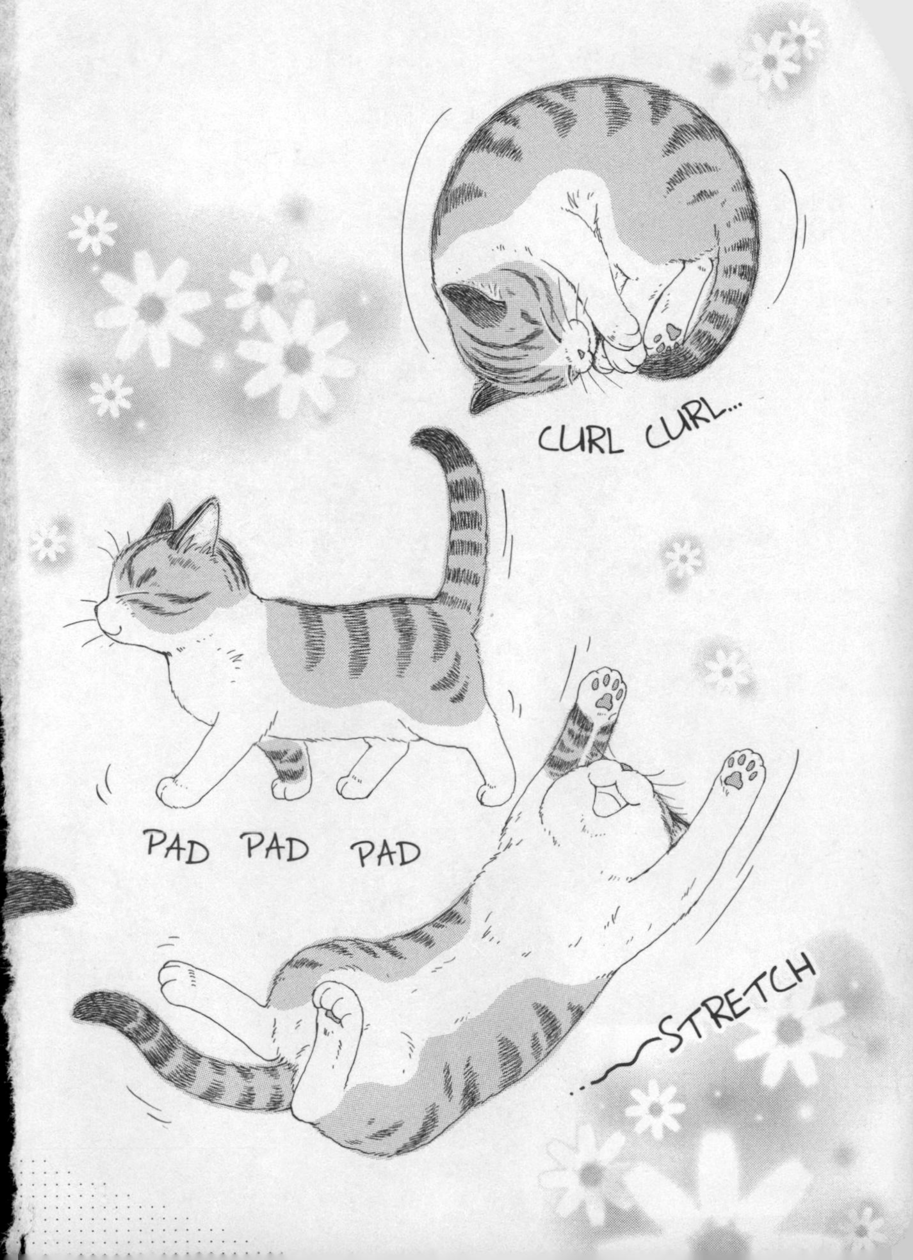
CURL CURL...
PAD PAD PAD
...~~~STRETCH

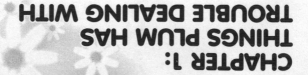

CHAPTER 1: THINGS PLUM HAS TROUBLE DEALING WITH

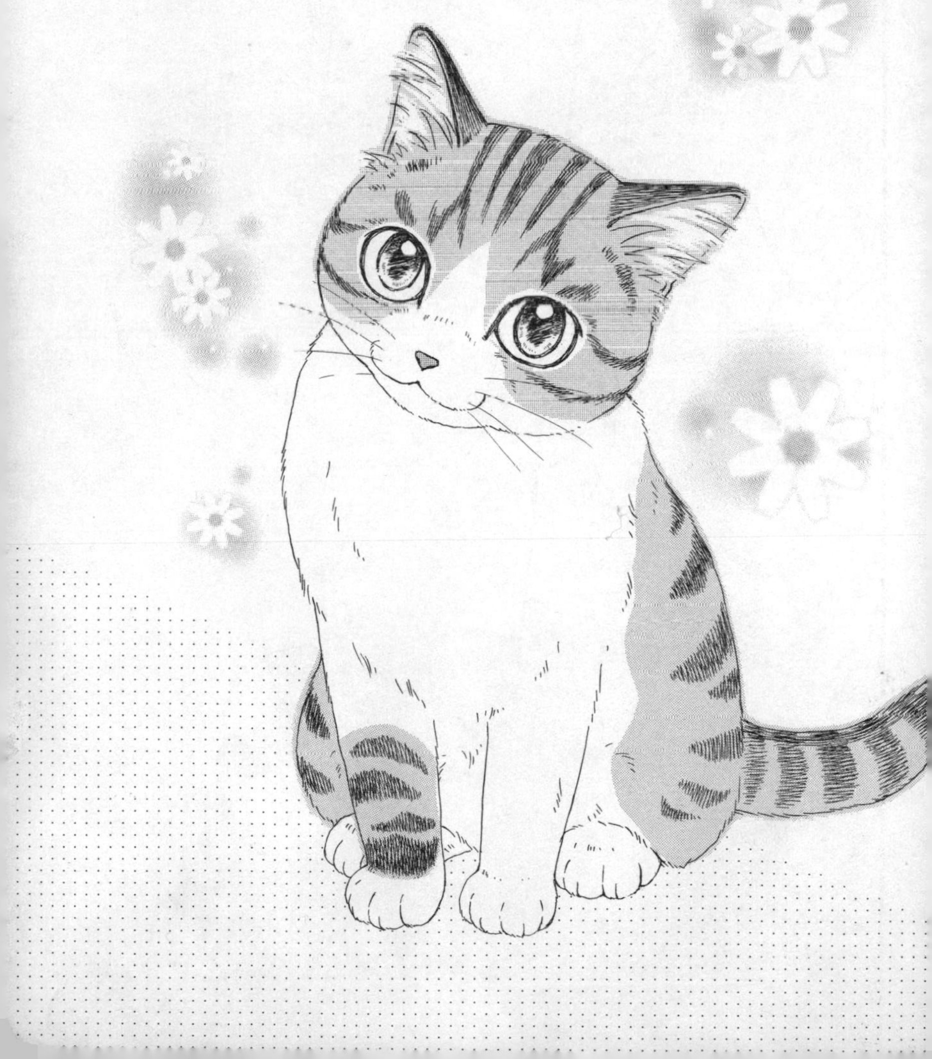

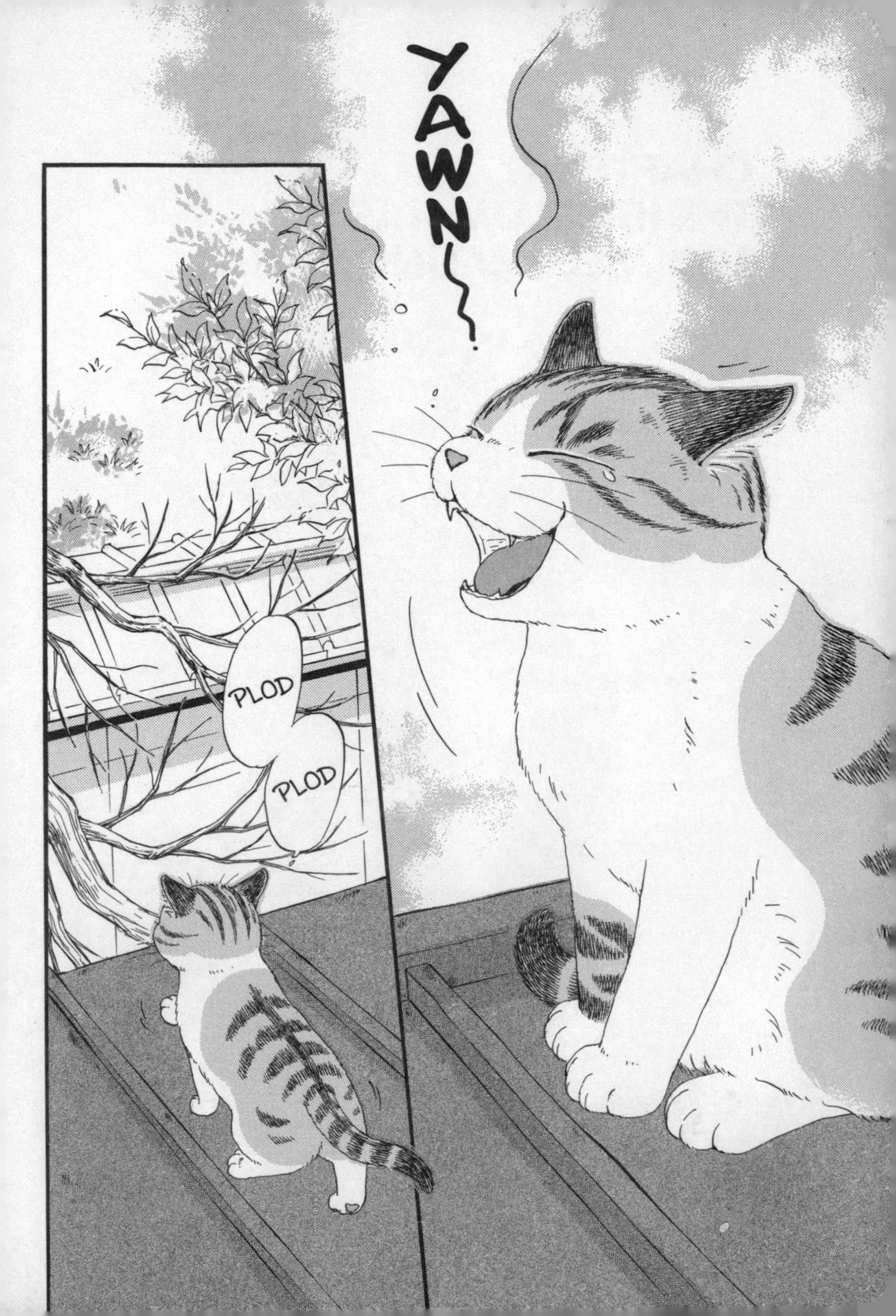
YAWN
PLOD
PLOD

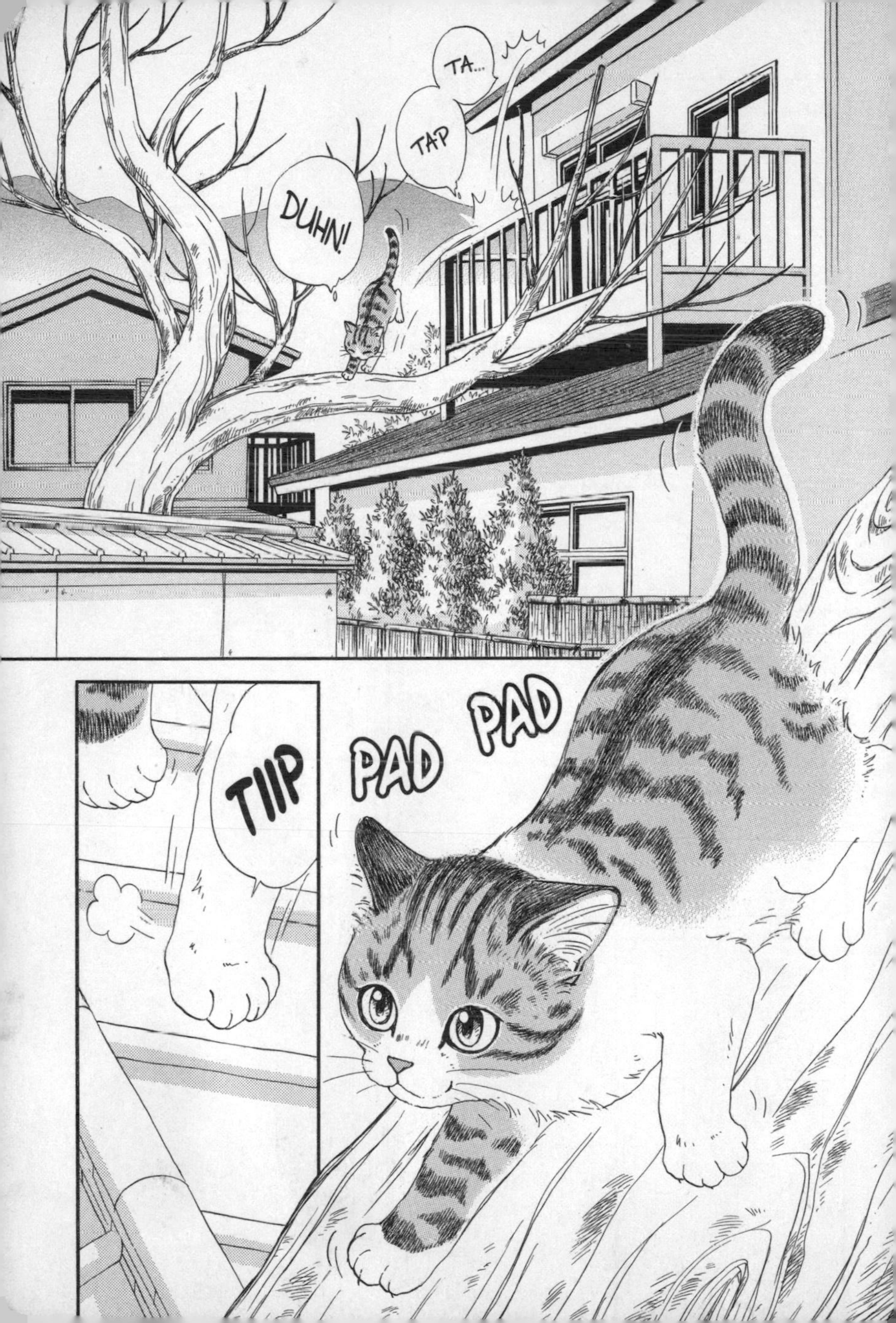
TA...
TAP
DUHN!
TIP
PAD
PAD

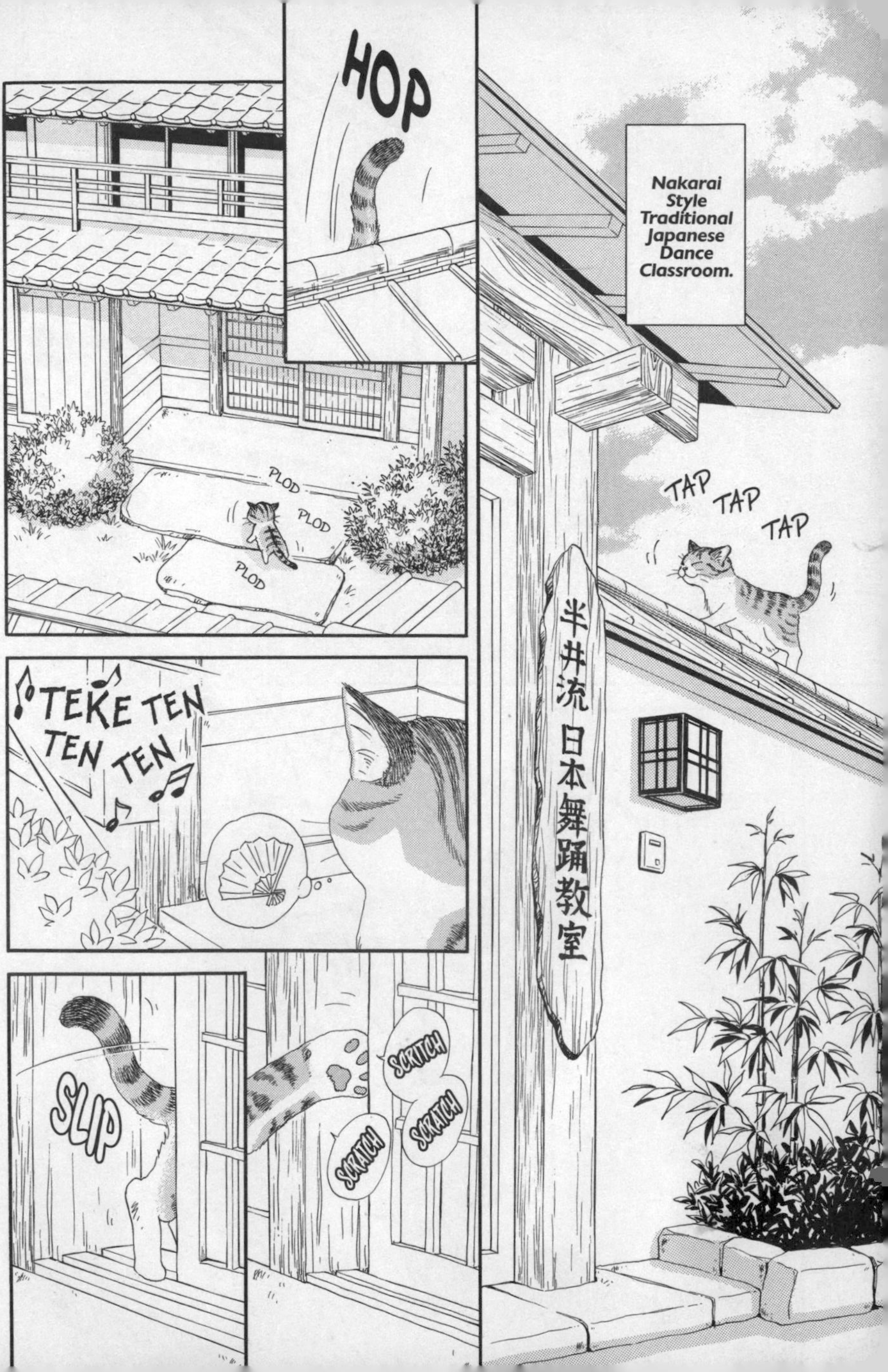
Nakarai Style Traditional Japanese Dance Classroom.
半井流 日本舞踊教室
TAP
TAP
TAP
HOP
PLOD
PLOD
PLOD
TEKE TEN
TEN TEN
SCRITCH
SCRATCH
SCRATCH
SLIP

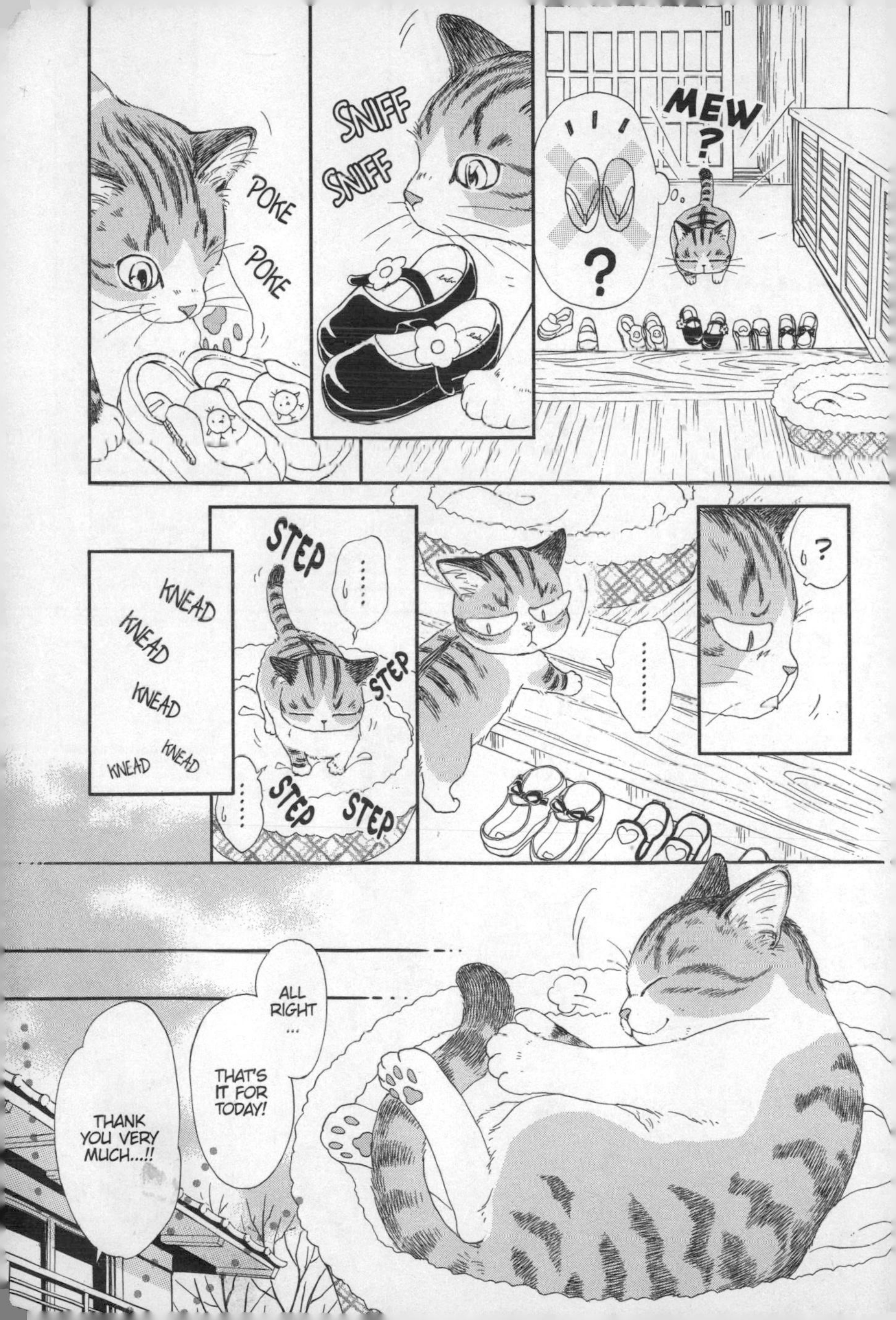
MEW?
?
SNIFF
SNIFF
POKE
POKE
?
......
STEP
......
STEP
STEP
STEP
......
KNEAD
KNEAD
KNEAD
KNEAD
KNEAD
ALL RIGHT ...
THAT'S IT FOR TODAY!
THANK YOU VERY MUCH...!!

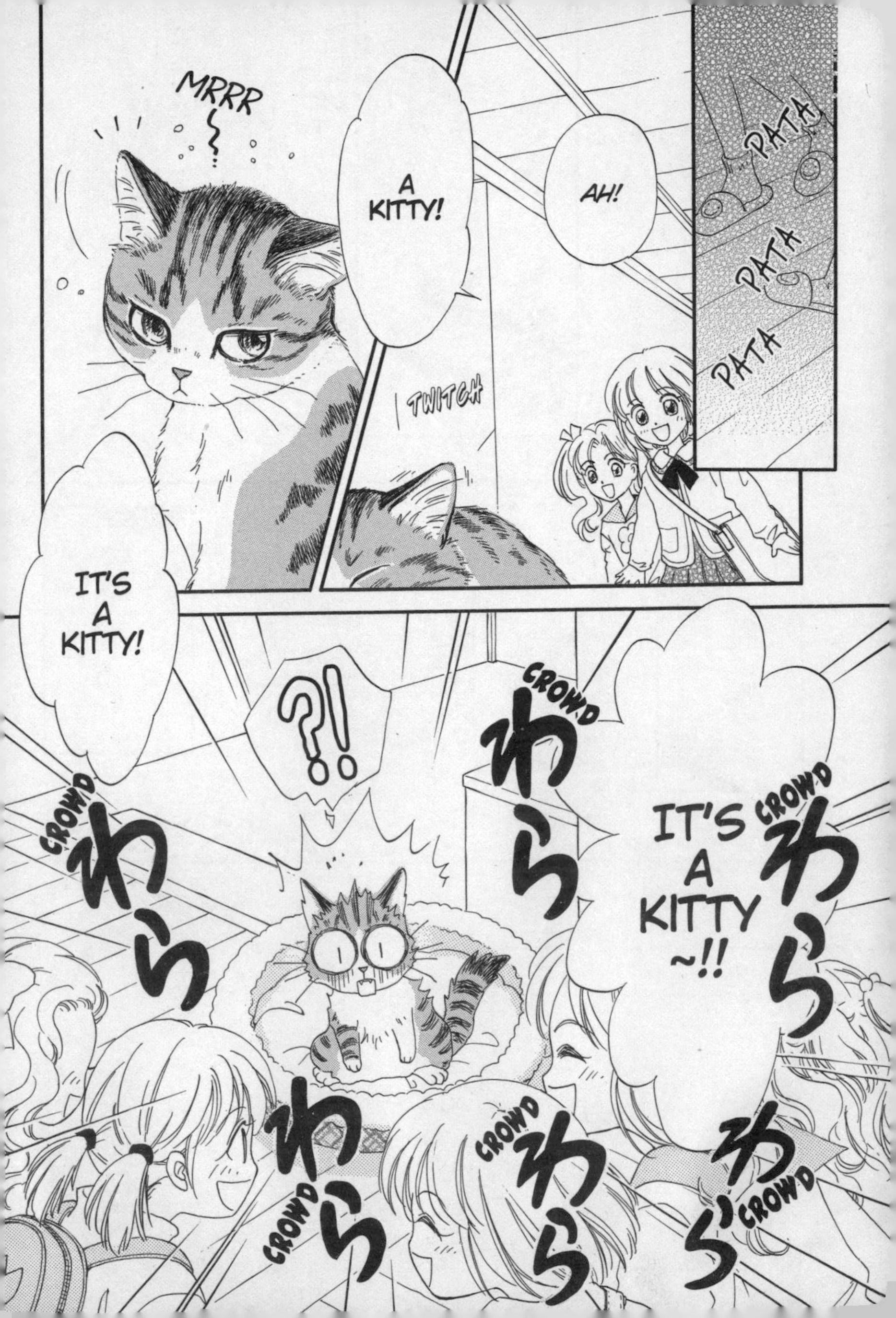
PATA PATA PATA
AH!
A KITTY!
TWITCH
MRRR
CROWD わら
IT'S A KITTY ~!!
CROWD わら
CROWD わら
CROWD わら
CROWD わら
CROWD わら
?!
CROWD わら
IT'S A KITTY!

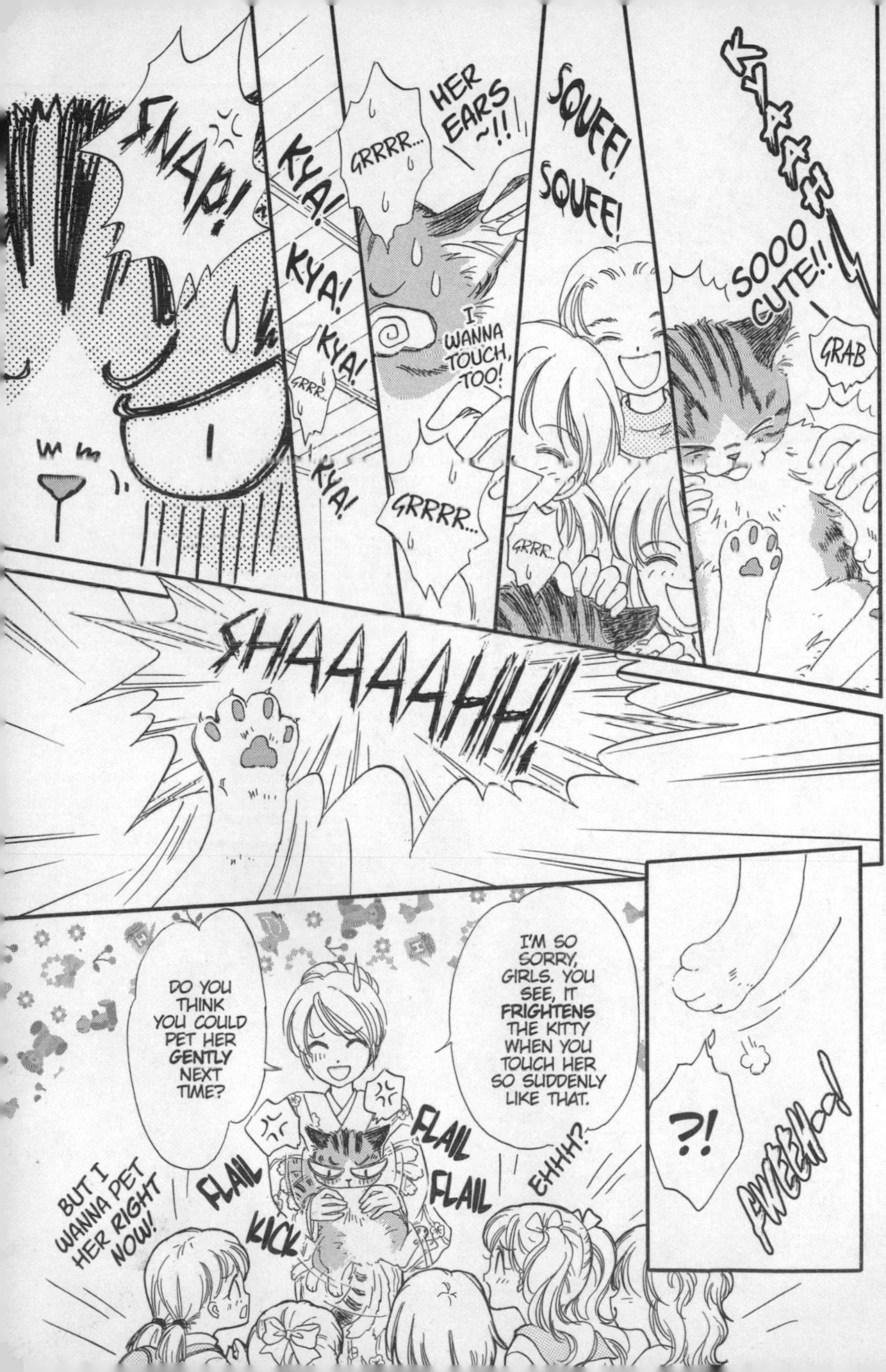
KYAAA
GRAB
SOOO CUTE!!
SQUEE! SQUEE!
HER EARS ~!!
GRRRR...
GRRR...
GRRRR...
I WANNA TOUCH, TOO!
KYA! KYA! KYA! KYA!
GRRR...
SNAP!
SHAAAAAHH!
?!
I'M SO SORRY, GIRLS. YOU SEE, IT FRIGHTENS THE KITTY WHEN YOU TOUCH HER SO SUDDENLY LIKE THAT.
EHHH?
FLAIL
FLAIL
DO YOU THINK YOU COULD PET HER GENTLY NEXT TIME?
FLAIL
KICK
BUT I WANNA PET HER RIGHT NOW!

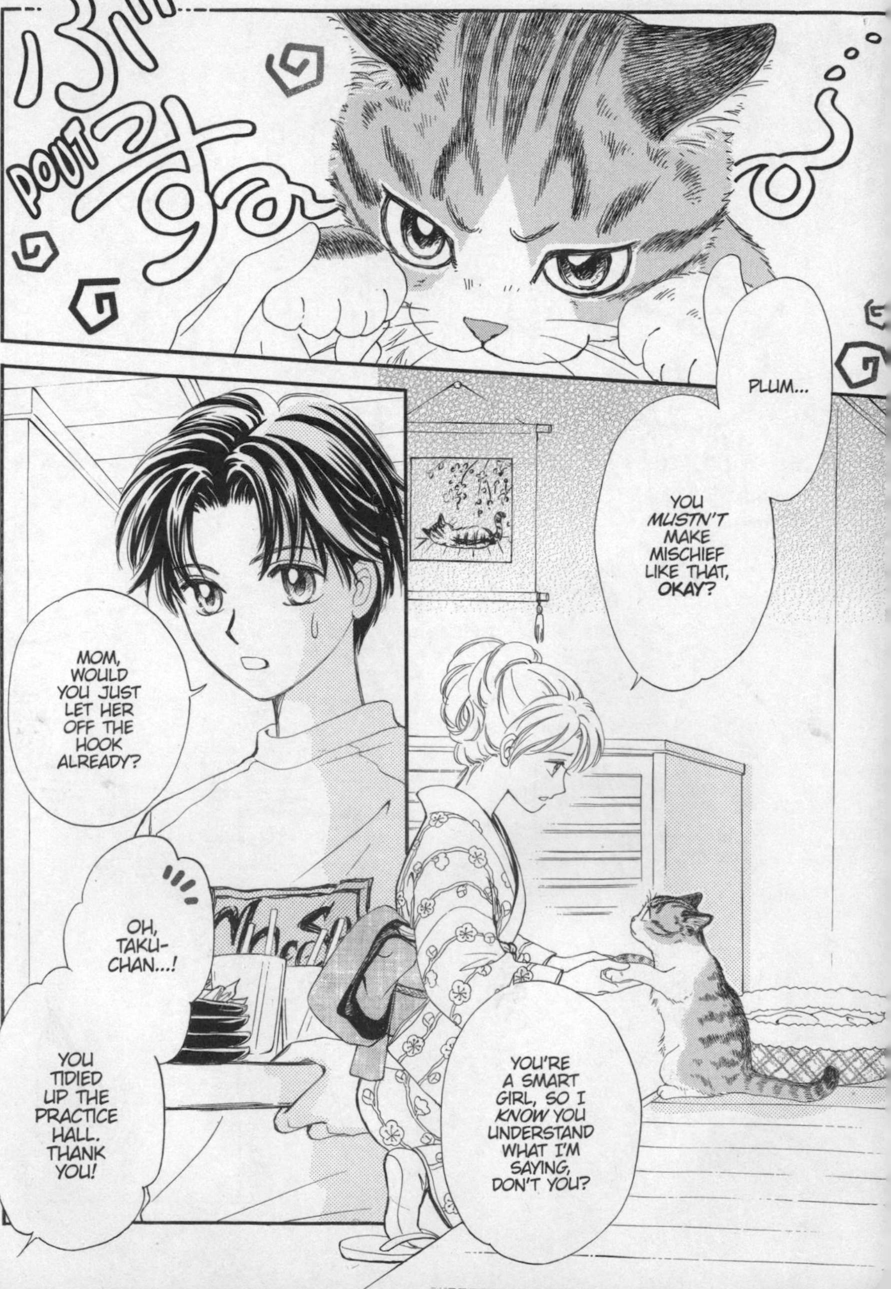
POUT
PLUM...
YOU MUSTN'T MAKE MISCHIEF LIKE THAT, OKAY?
YOU'RE A SMART GIRL, SO I KNOW YOU UNDERSTAND WHAT I'M SAYING, DON'T YOU?
MOM, WOULD YOU JUST LET HER OFF THE HOOK ALREADY?
OH, TAKU-CHAN...!
YOU TIDIED UP THE PRACTICE HALL. THANK YOU!

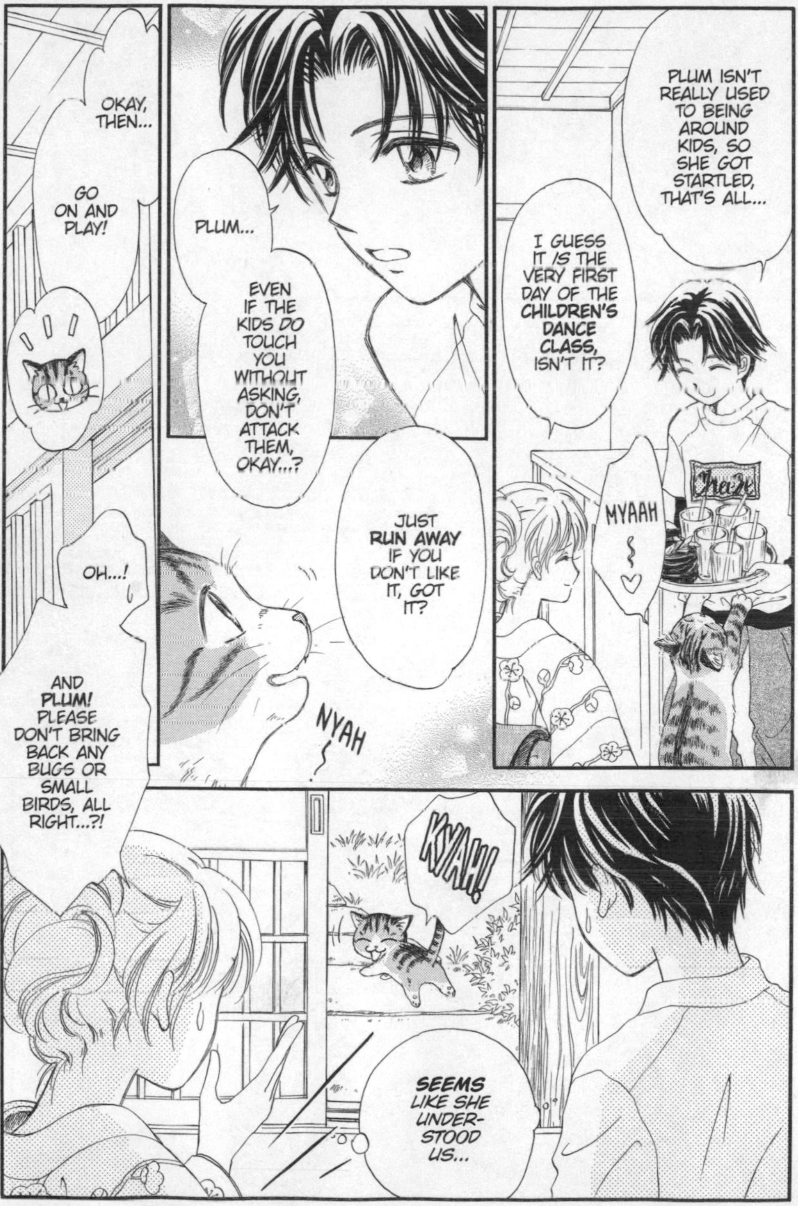
PLUM ISN'T REALLY USED TO BEING AROUND KIDS, SO SHE GOT STARTLED, THAT'S ALL...
I GUESS IT IS THE VERY FIRST DAY OF THE CHILDREN'S DANCE CLASS, ISN'T IT?
MYAAH
PLUM...
EVEN IF THE KIDS DO TOUCH YOU WITHOUT ASKING, DON'T ATTACK THEM, OKAY...?
JUST RUN AWAY IF YOU DON'T LIKE IT, GOT IT?
NYAH
OKAY, THEN...
GO ON AND PLAY!
OH...!
AND PLUM! PLEASE DON'T BRING BACK ANY BUGS OR SMALL BIRDS, ALL RIGHT...?!
KYAH!
SEEMS LIKE SHE UNDER-STOOD US...

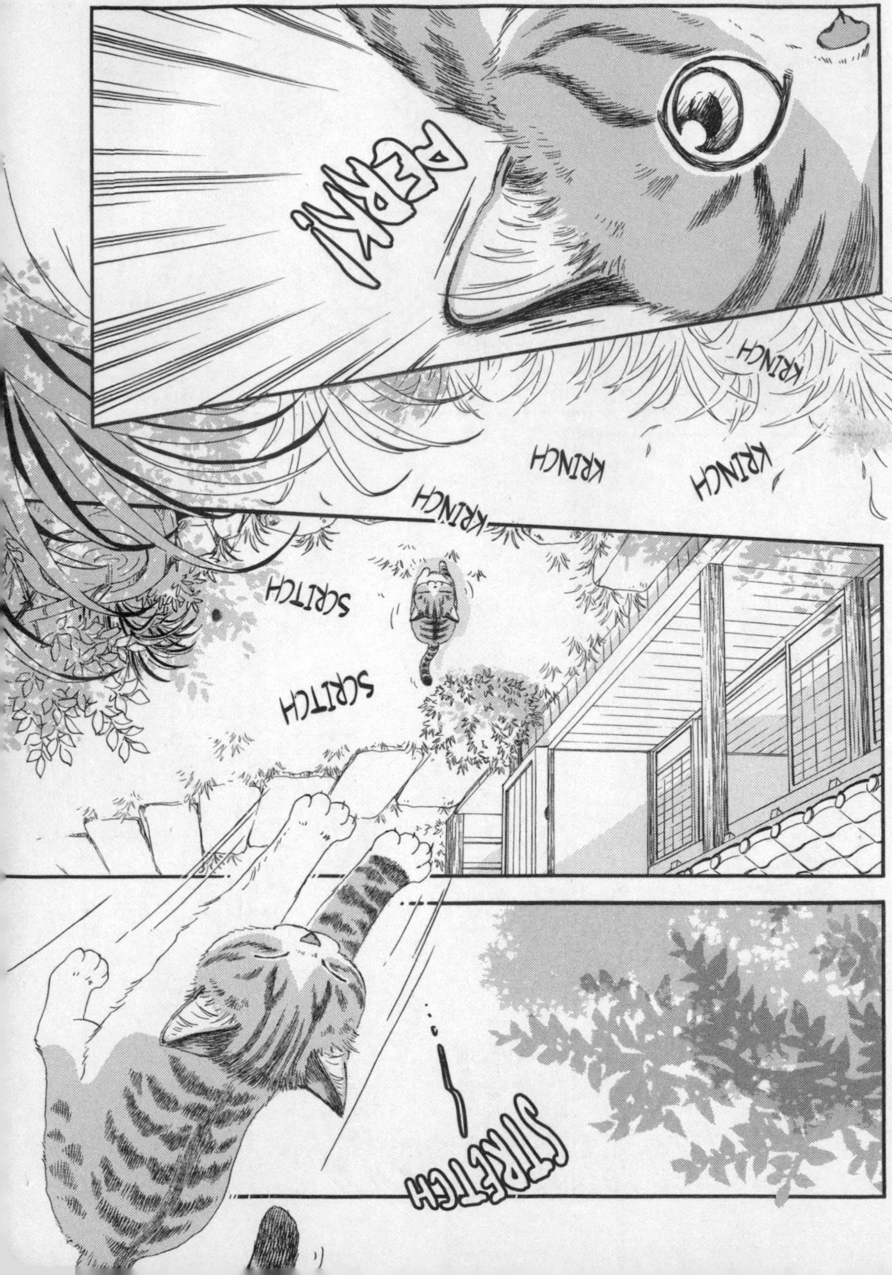
PERK!
KRINCH
KRINCH
KRINCH
KRINCH
SCRITCH
SCRITCH
STRETCH

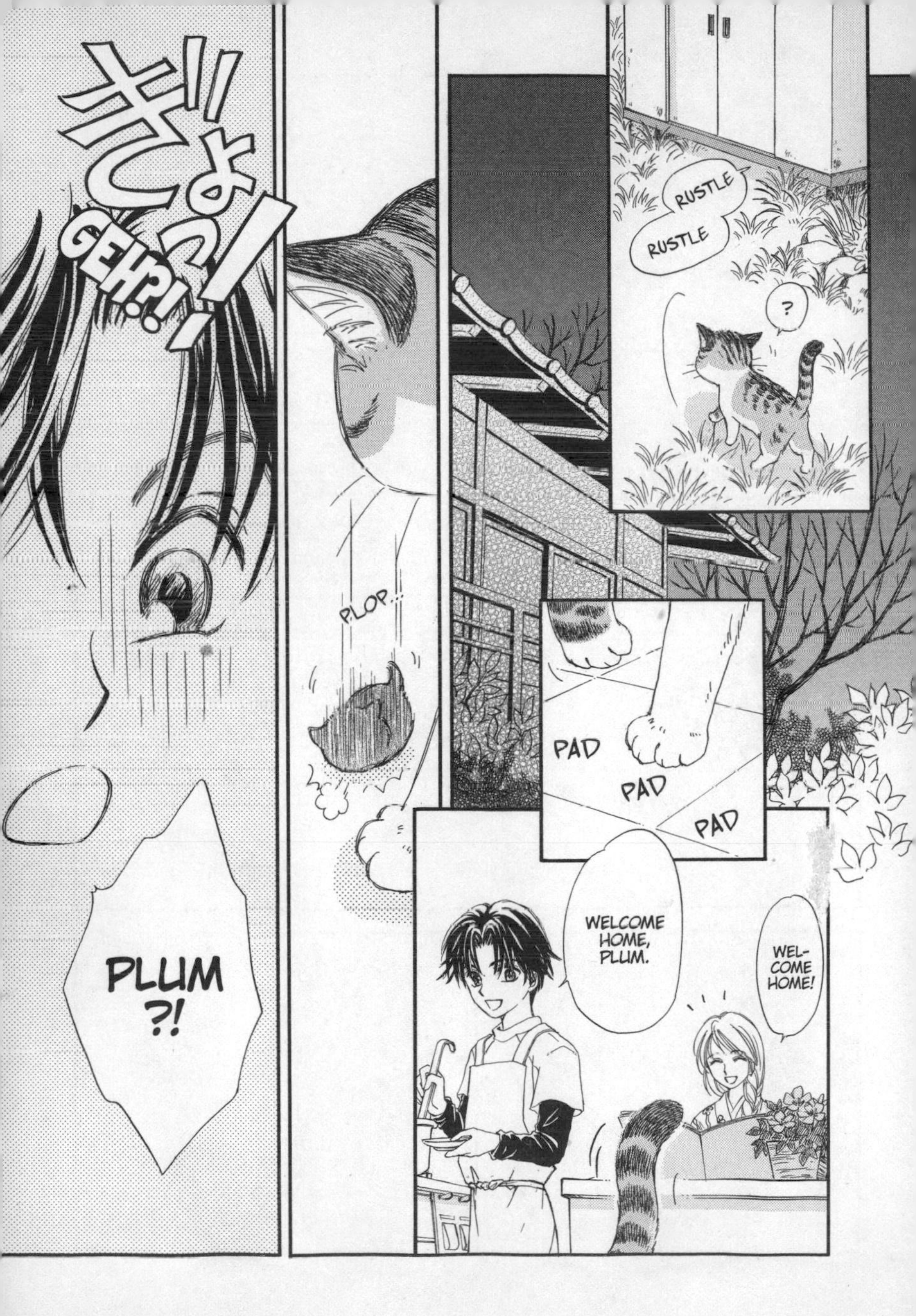
RUSTLE
RUSTLE
?
PAD
PAD
PAD
WELCOME HOME, PLUM.
WEL- COME HOME!
PLOP...
ぎょっ!
GEH?!
PLUM ?!

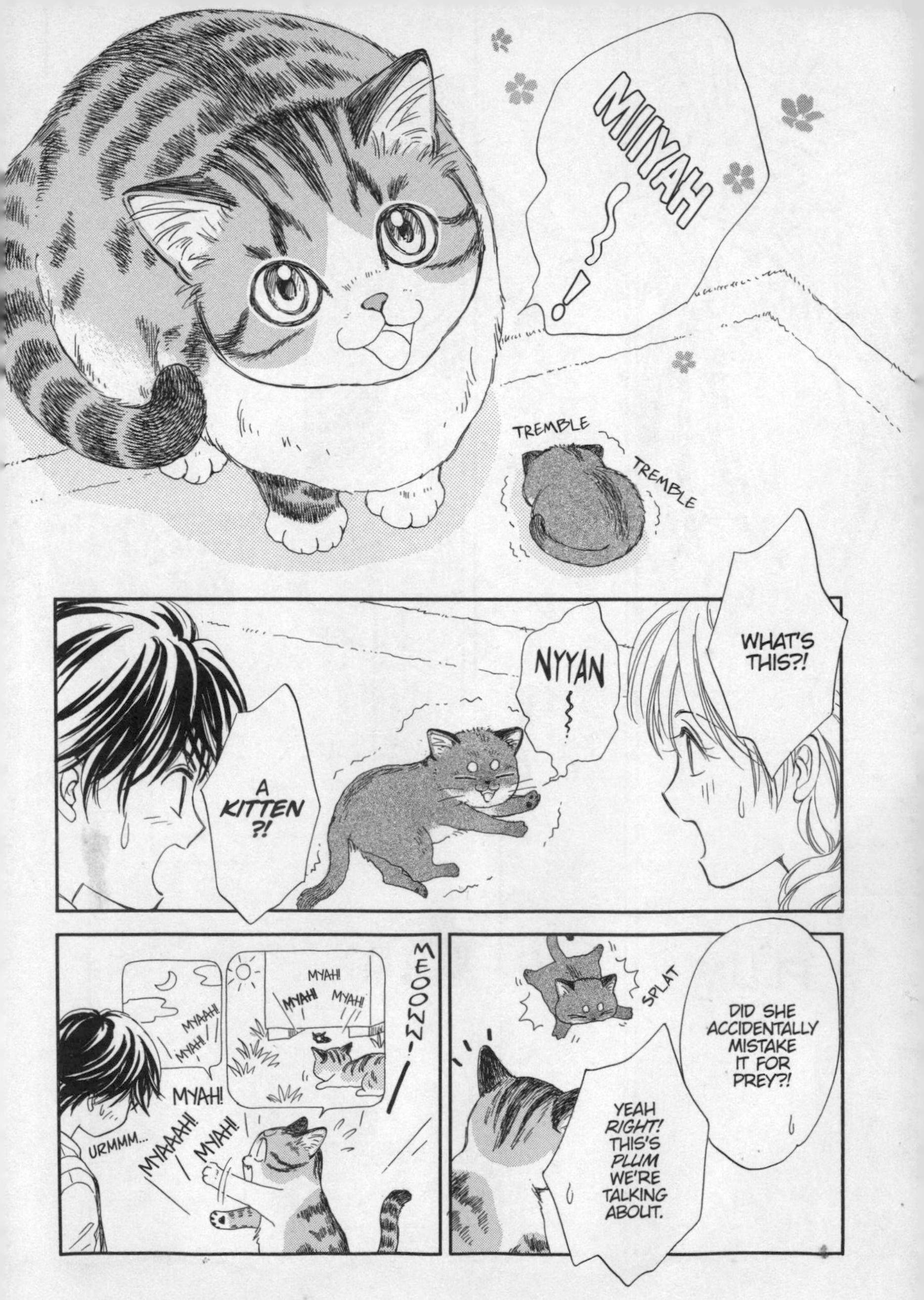
MIIYAH ~~!
TREMBLE
TREMBLE
WHAT'S THIS?!
NYYAN ~~
A KITTEN ?!
DID SHE ACCIDENTALLY MISTAKE IT FOR PREY?!
SPLAT
YEAH RIGHT! THIS'S PLUM WE'RE TALKING ABOUT.
MEOOWN--!
MYAH!
MYAH!
MYAH!
MYAAH!
MYAH!
MYAH!
URMMM...
MYAAAH!
MYAH!

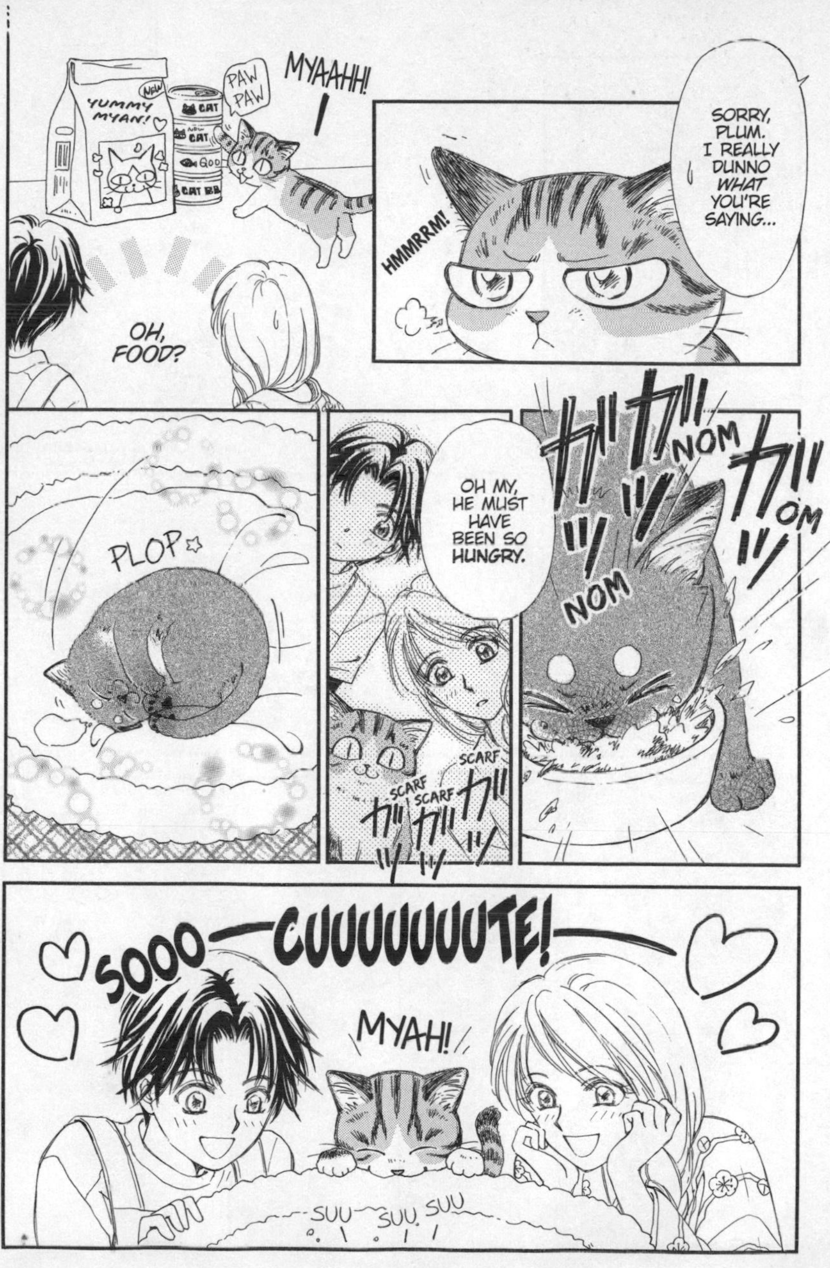
SORRY, PLUM. I REALLY DUNNO WHAT YOU'RE SAYING...
HMMRRM!
MYAAHH!
PAW PAW
YUMMY MYAN!
NEW
CAT
CAT
GOOD
CAT
OH, FOOD?
NOM
OM
NOM
OH MY, HE MUST HAVE BEEN SO HUNGRY.
SCARF
SCARF
SCARF
PLOP
SOOO—CUUUUUUUTE!
MYAH!
SUU SUU SUU

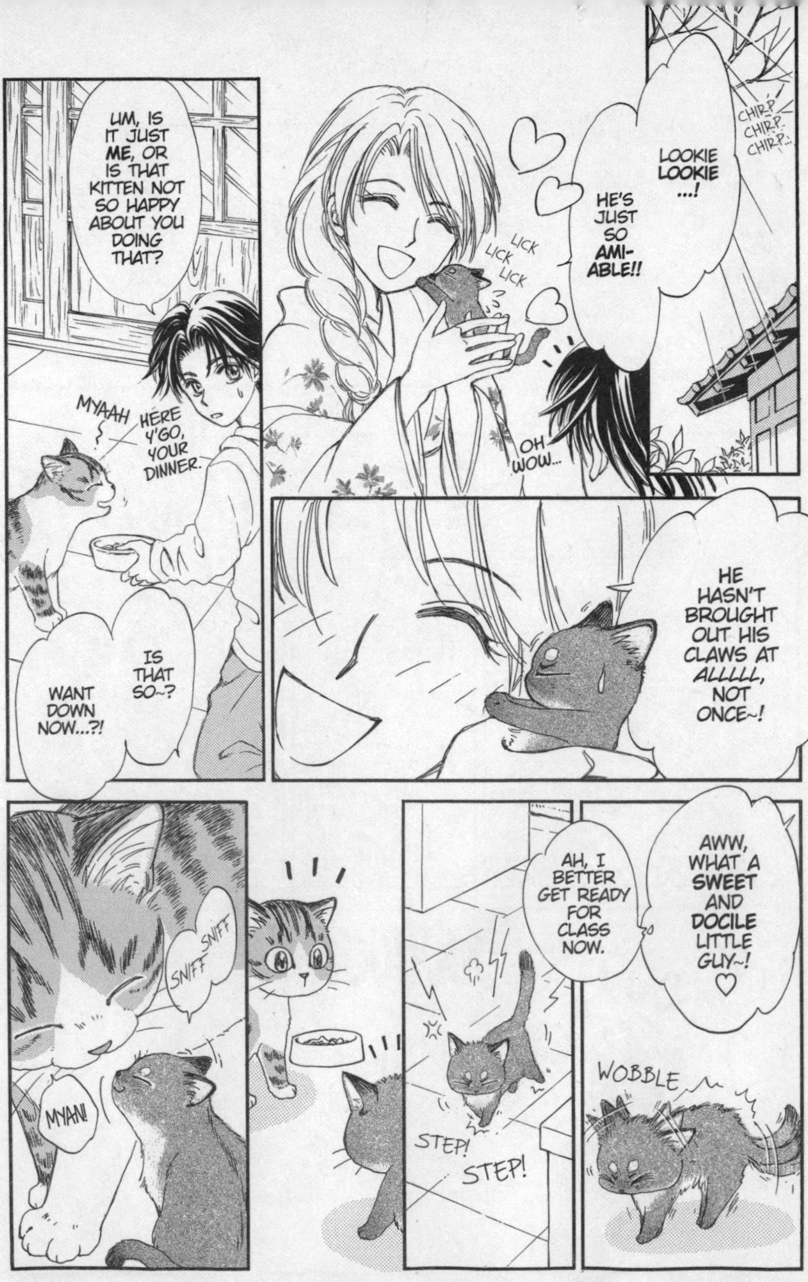
CHIRP CHIRP CHIRP...
LOOKIE LOOKIE ...!
HE'S JUST SO AMI-ABLE!!
LICK LICK LICK
OH WOW...
UM, IS IT JUST ME, OR IS THAT KITTEN NOT SO HAPPY ABOUT YOU DOING THAT?
HE HASN'T BROUGHT OUT HIS CLAWS AT ALLLLL, NOT ONCE~!
HERE Y'GO, YOUR DINNER.
MYAAH
IS THAT SO~?
WANT DOWN NOW...?!
AWW, WHAT A SWEET AND DOCILE LITTLE GUY~! ♡
WOBBLE
AH, I BETTER GET READY FOR CLASS NOW.
STEP!
STEP!
SNIFF SNIFF
MYAN!

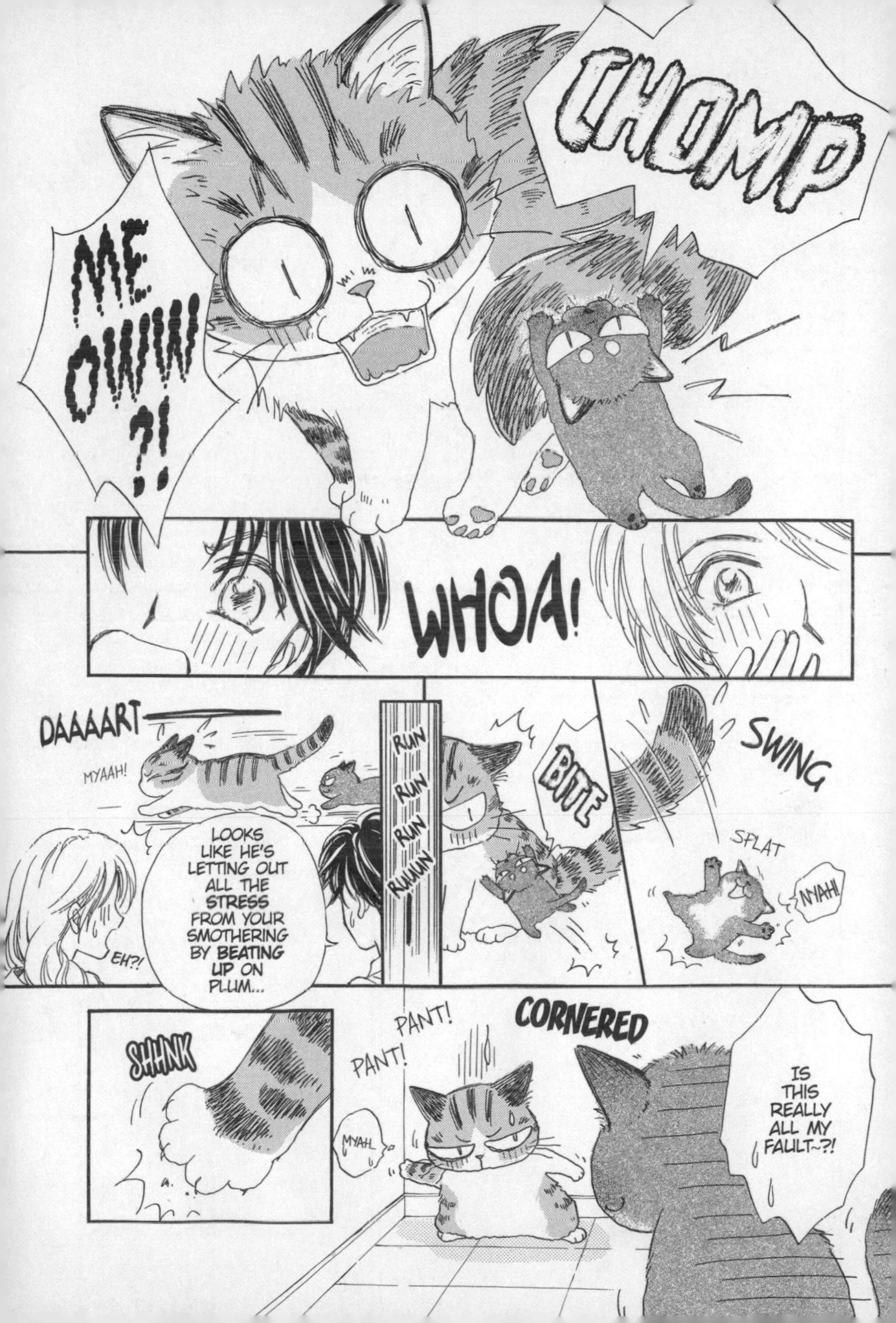
CHOMP
ME OWW ?!
WHOA!
SWING
SPLAT
NYAH!
BITE
RUN RUN RUN RUUUN
DAAAART
MYAAH!
LOOKS LIKE HE'S LETTING OUT ALL THE STRESS FROM YOUR SMOTHERING BY BEATING UP ON PLUM...
EH?!
IS THIS REALLY ALL MY FAULT~?!
CORNERED
PANT! PANT!
MYAH...
SHHNK

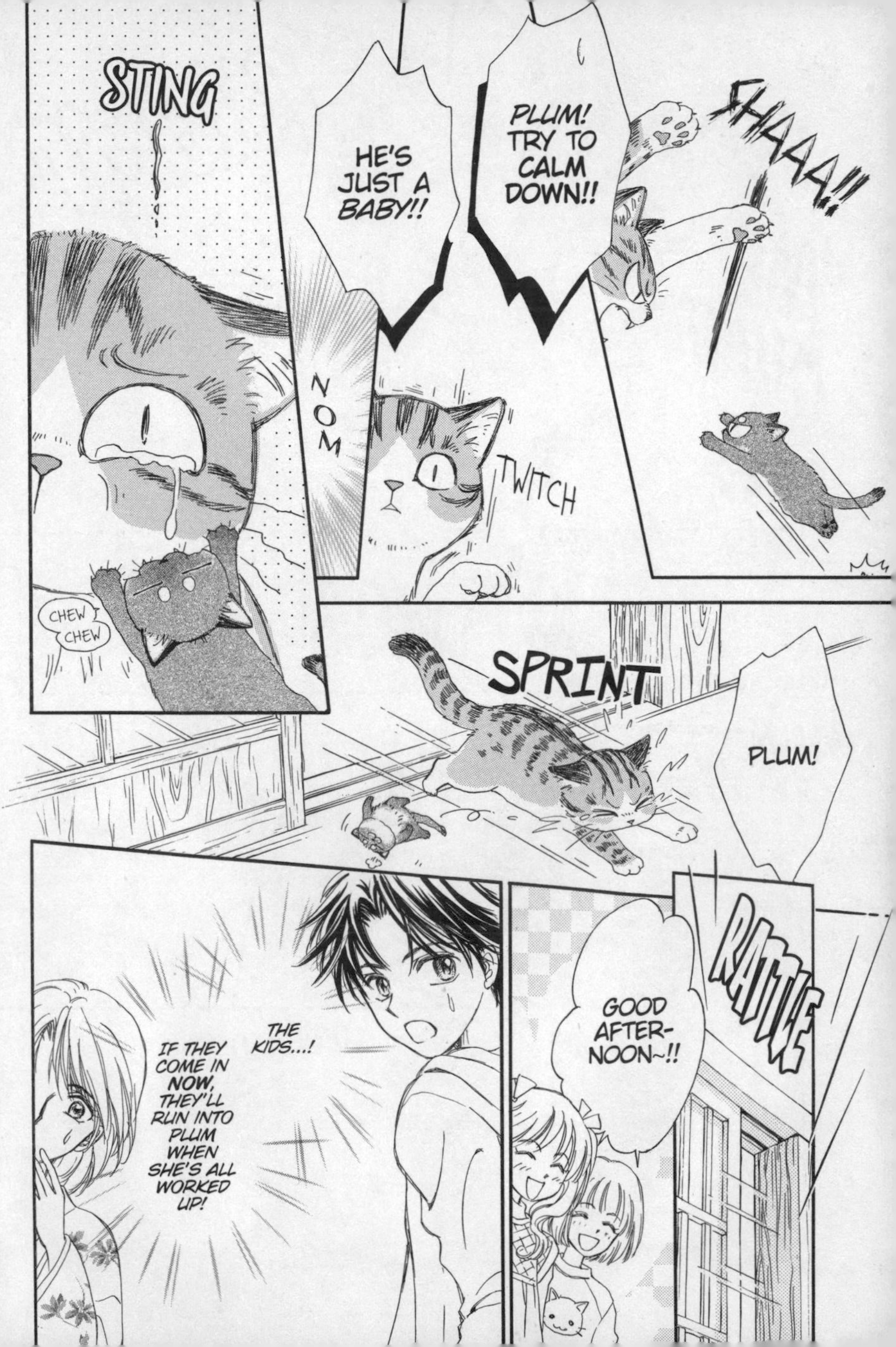
SHAAAA!!
PLUM! TRY TO CALM DOWN!!
HE'S JUST A BABY!!
TWITCH
NOM
STING
CHEW CHEW
PLUM!
SPRINT
RATTLE
GOOD AFTER-NOON~!!
THE KIDS...!
IF THEY COME IN NOW, THEY'LL RUN INTO PLUM WHEN SHE'S ALL WORKED UP!

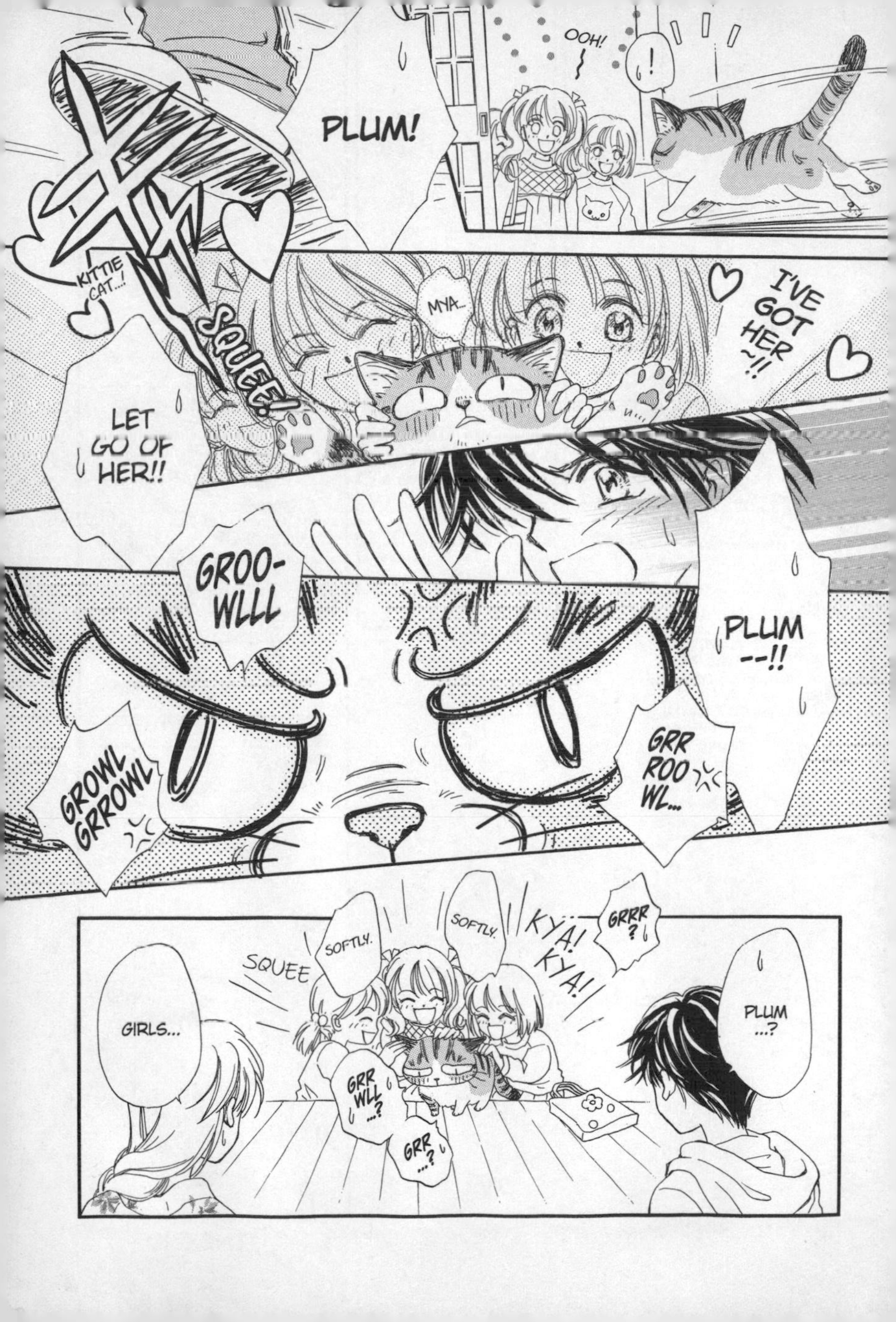
!
OOH!
PLUM!
I'VE GOT HER ~!!
MYA...
SQUEE
KITTIE CAT...!
LET GO OF HER!!
PLUM --!!
GROO-WLLL
GRR ROO WL...
GROWL GRROWL
PLUM ...?
GRRR ?
KYA! KYA!
SOFTLY.
SOFTLY.
SQUEE
GRR WLL ...?
GRR ...?
GIRLS...

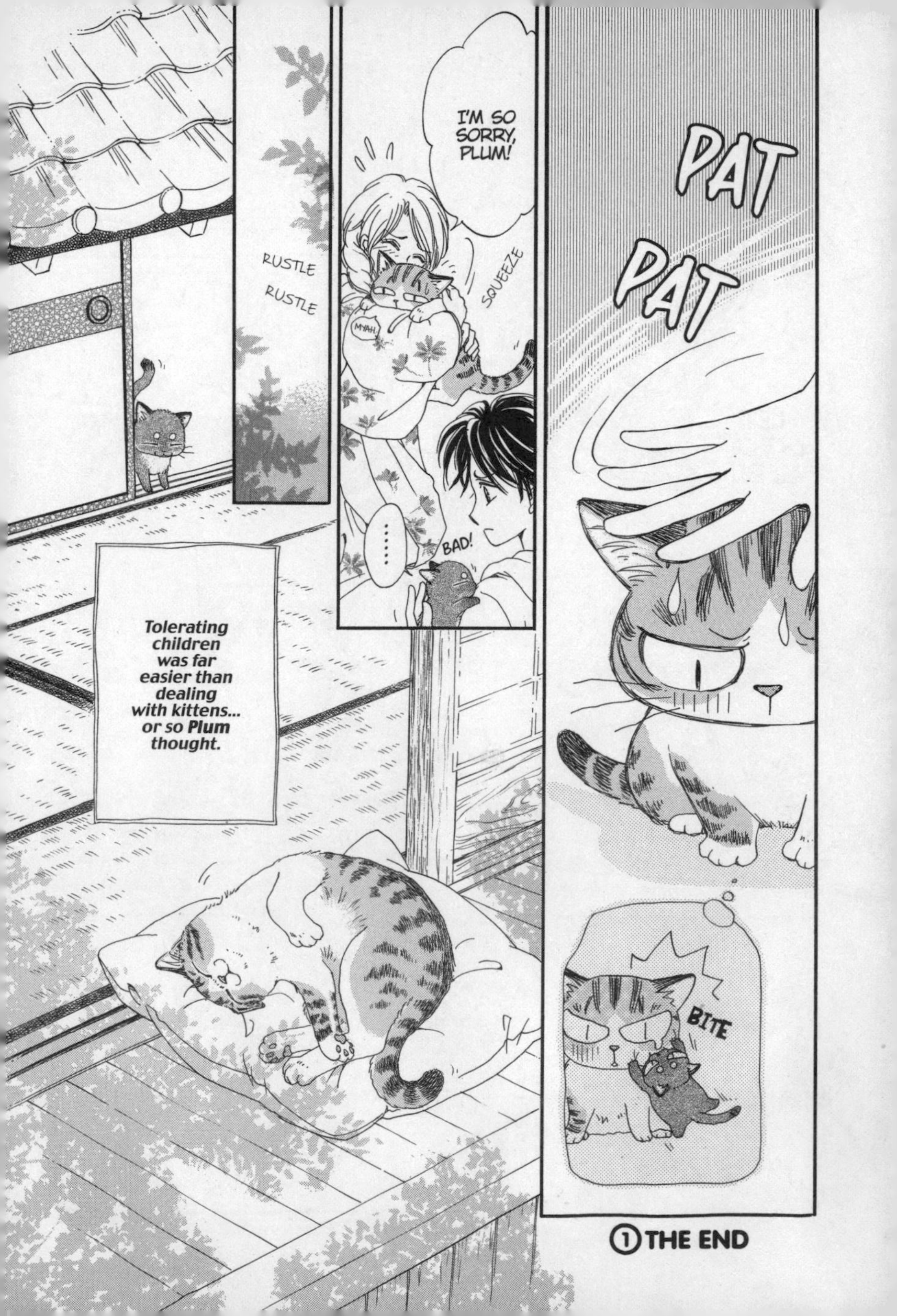
PAT
PAT
BITE
I'M SO SORRY, PLUM!
SQUEEZE
MYAH
......
BAD!
RUSTLE
RUSTLE
Tolerating children was far easier than dealing with kittens... or so Plum thought.

① THE END

STORIES ABOUT MY CAT

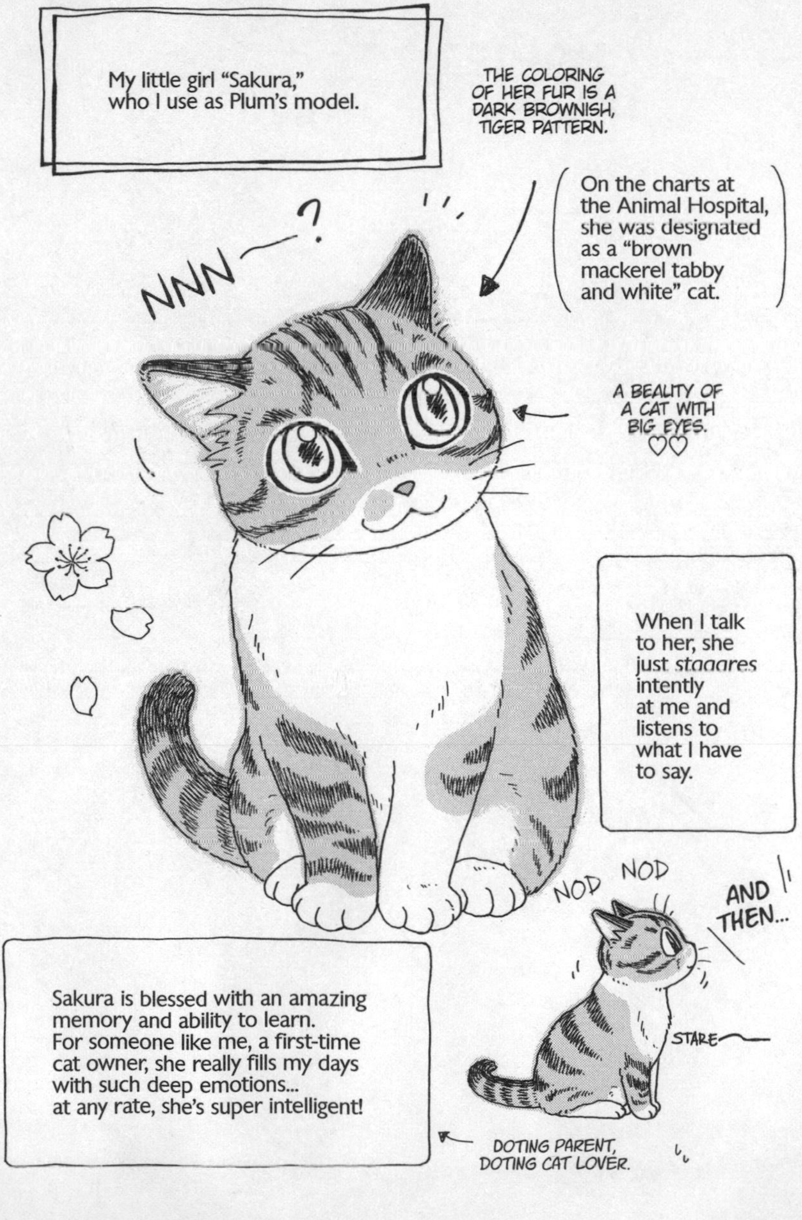
My little girl "Sakura," who I use as Plum's model.
THE COLORING OF HER FUR IS A DARK BROWNISH, TIGER PATTERN.
On the charts at the Animal Hospital, she was designated as a "brown mackerel tabby and white" cat.
NNN—?
A BEAUTY OF A CAT WITH BIG EYES. ♡♡
When I talk to her, she just *staaares* intently at me and listens to what I have to say.
NOD NOD
AND THEN...
STARE—
Sakura is blessed with an amazing memory and ability to learn. For someone like me, a first-time cat owner, she really fills my days with such deep emotions... at any rate, she's super intelligent!
DOTING PARENT, DOTING CAT LOVER.

CHAPTER 2: PLUM AND THE KITTEN

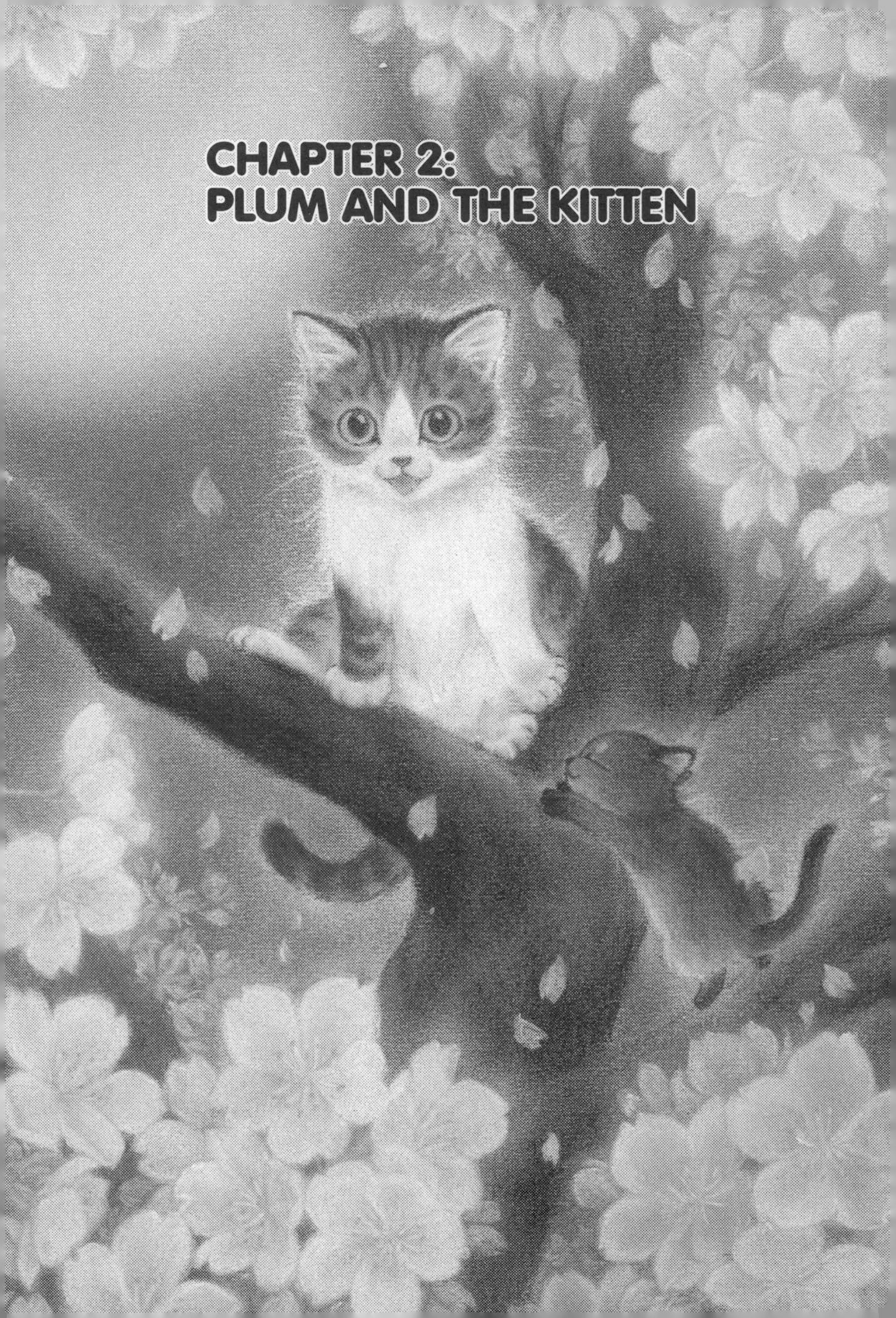

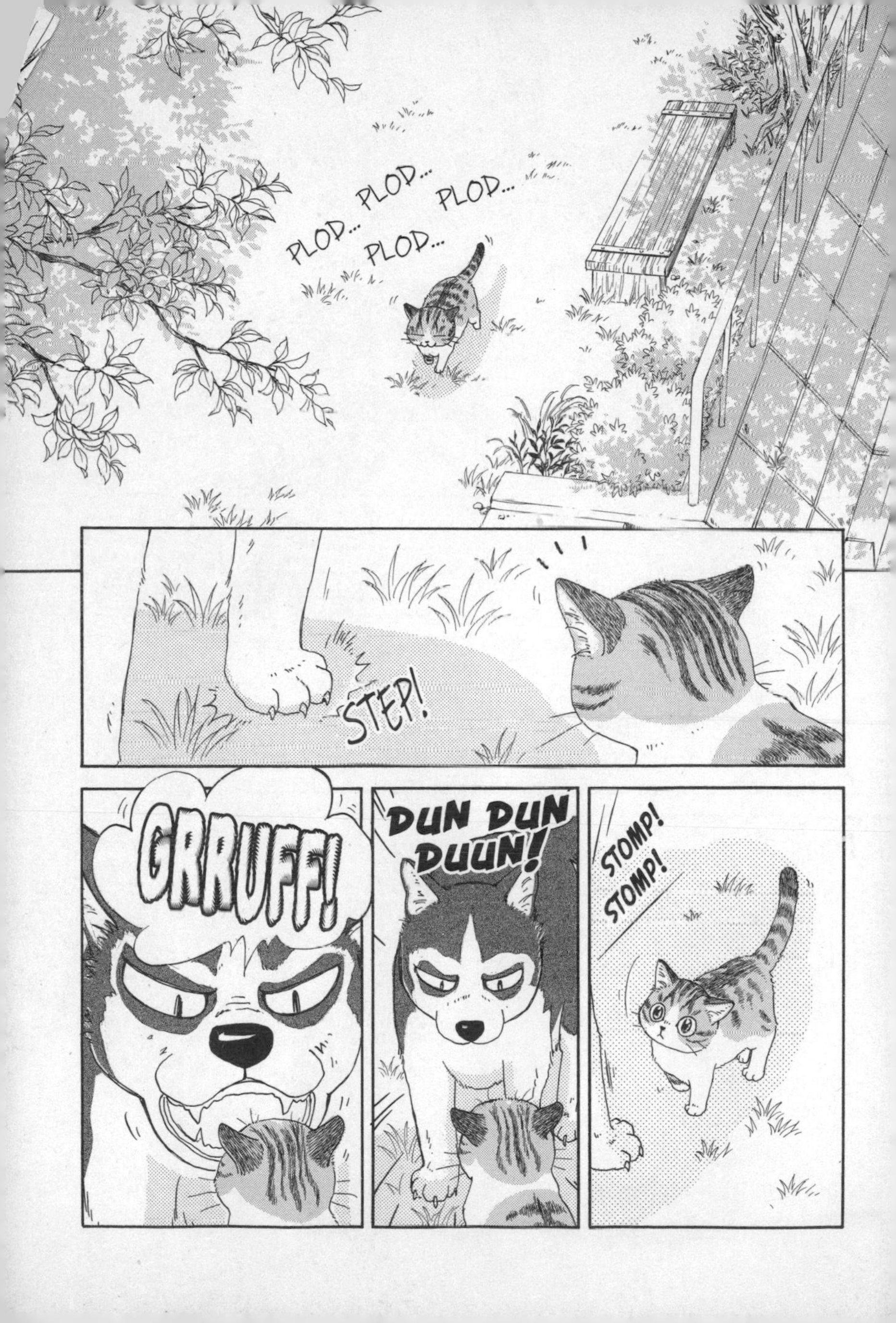
PLOD... PLOD... PLOD... PLOD...
STEP!
STOMP! STOMP!
DUN DUN DUUN!
GRRUFF!

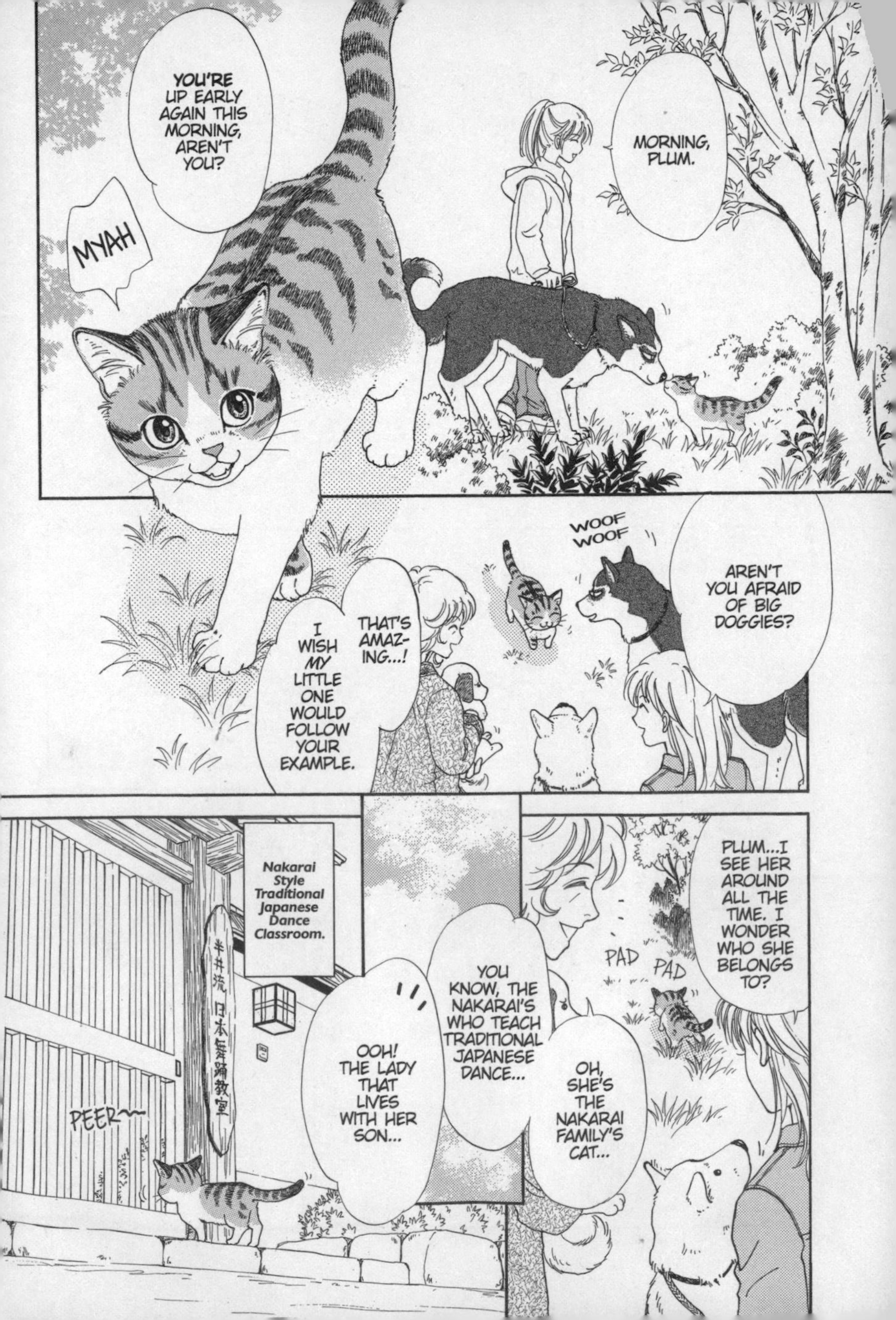
MORNING, PLUM.
YOU'RE UP EARLY AGAIN THIS MORNING, AREN'T YOU?
MYAH
AREN'T YOU AFRAID OF BIG DOGGIES?
WOOF WOOF
THAT'S AMAZING...!
I WISH MY LITTLE ONE WOULD FOLLOW YOUR EXAMPLE.
PLUM...I SEE HER AROUND ALL THE TIME. I WONDER WHO SHE BELONGS TO?
PAD PAD
OH, SHE'S THE NAKARAI FAMILY'S CAT...
YOU KNOW, THE NAKARAI'S WHO TEACH TRADITIONAL JAPANESE DANCE...
OOH! THE LADY THAT LIVES WITH HER SON...
Nakarai Style Traditional Japanese Dance Classroom.
半井流 日本舞踊教室
PEER~~

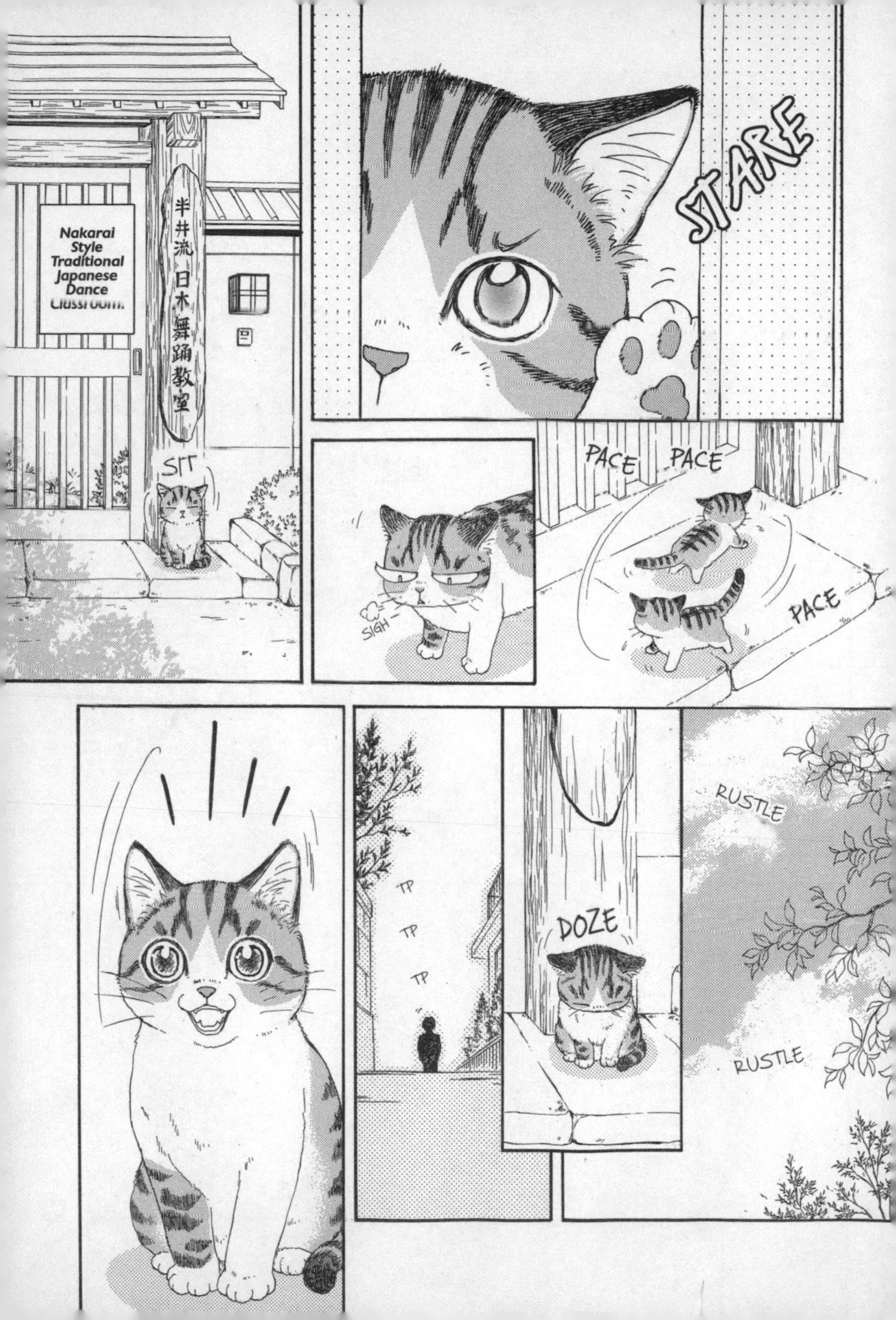
STARE
PACE
PACE
PACE
SIGH
SIT
半井流日本舞踊教室
Nakarai Style Traditional Japanese Dance Classroom
RUSTLE
RUSTLE
DOZE
TP
TP
TP

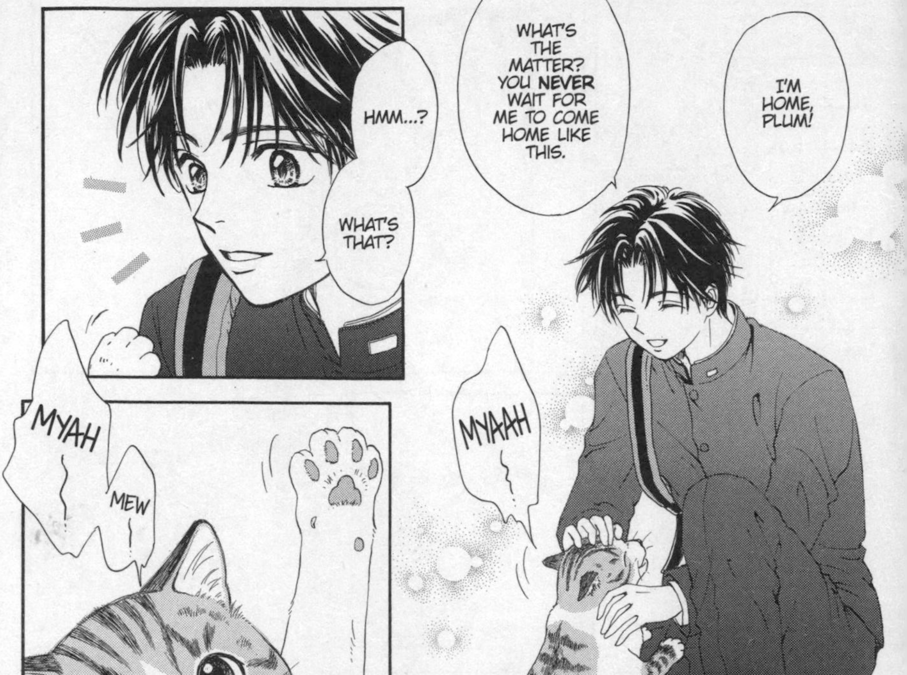
I'M HOME, PLUM!
WHAT'S THE MATTER? YOU NEVER WAIT FOR ME TO COME HOME LIKE THIS.
MYAAH
HMM...?
WHAT'S THAT?
MYAH
MEW
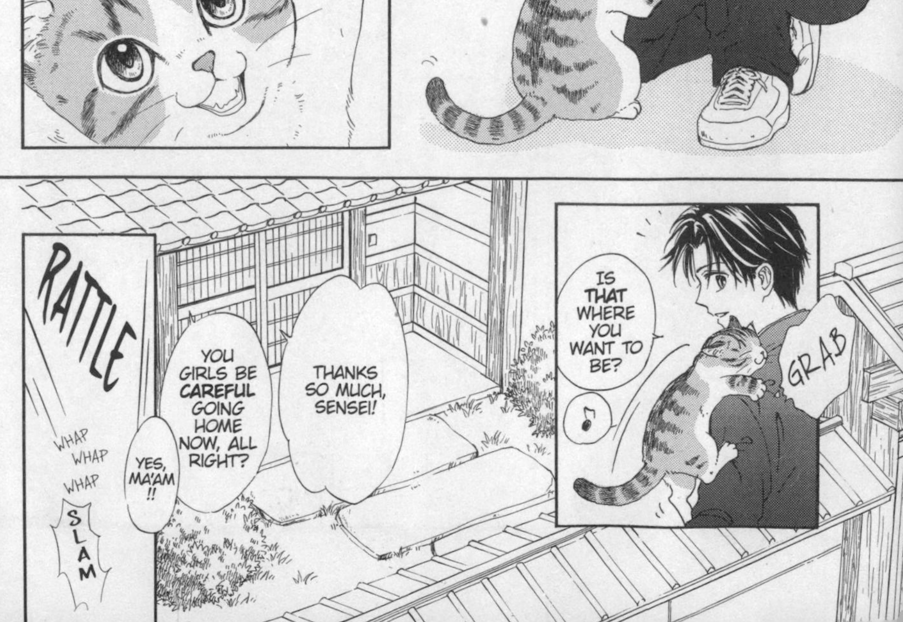
IS THAT WHERE YOU WANT TO BE?
GRAB
THANKS SO MUCH, SENSEI!
YOU GIRLS BE CAREFUL GOING HOME NOW, ALL RIGHT?
YES, MA'AM !!
RATTLE
WHAP WHAP WHAP
SLAM

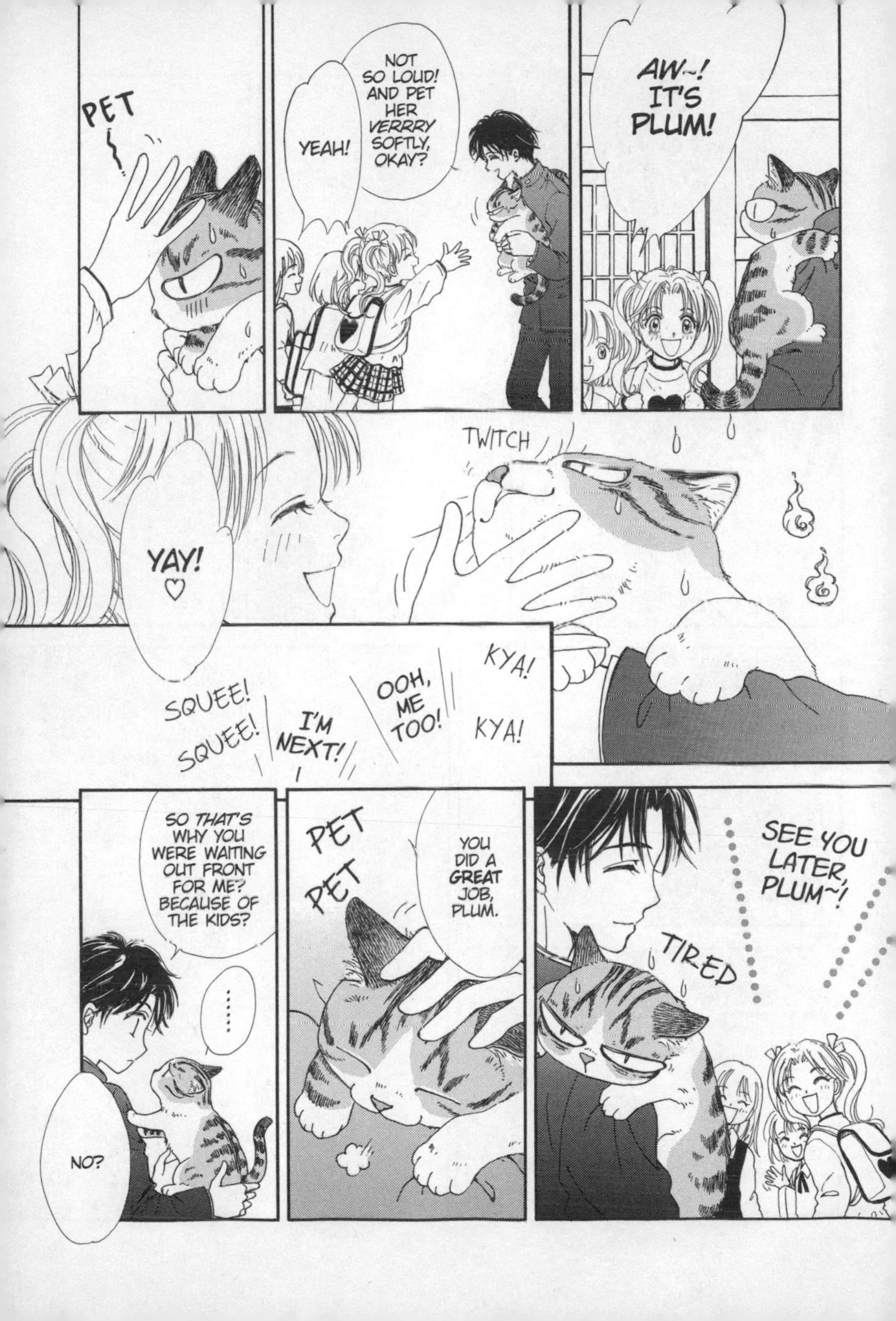
AW~! IT'S PLUM!
NOT SO LOUD! AND PET HER VERRRY SOFTLY, OKAY?
YEAH!
PET
TWITCH
YAY! ♡
KYA!
KYA!
OOH, ME TOO!
I'M NEXT!
SQUEE!
SQUEE!
SEE YOU LATER, PLUM~!
TIRED
YOU DID A GREAT JOB, PLUM.
PET
PET
SO THAT'S WHY YOU WERE WAITING OUT FRONT FOR ME? BECAUSE OF THE KIDS?
......
NO?

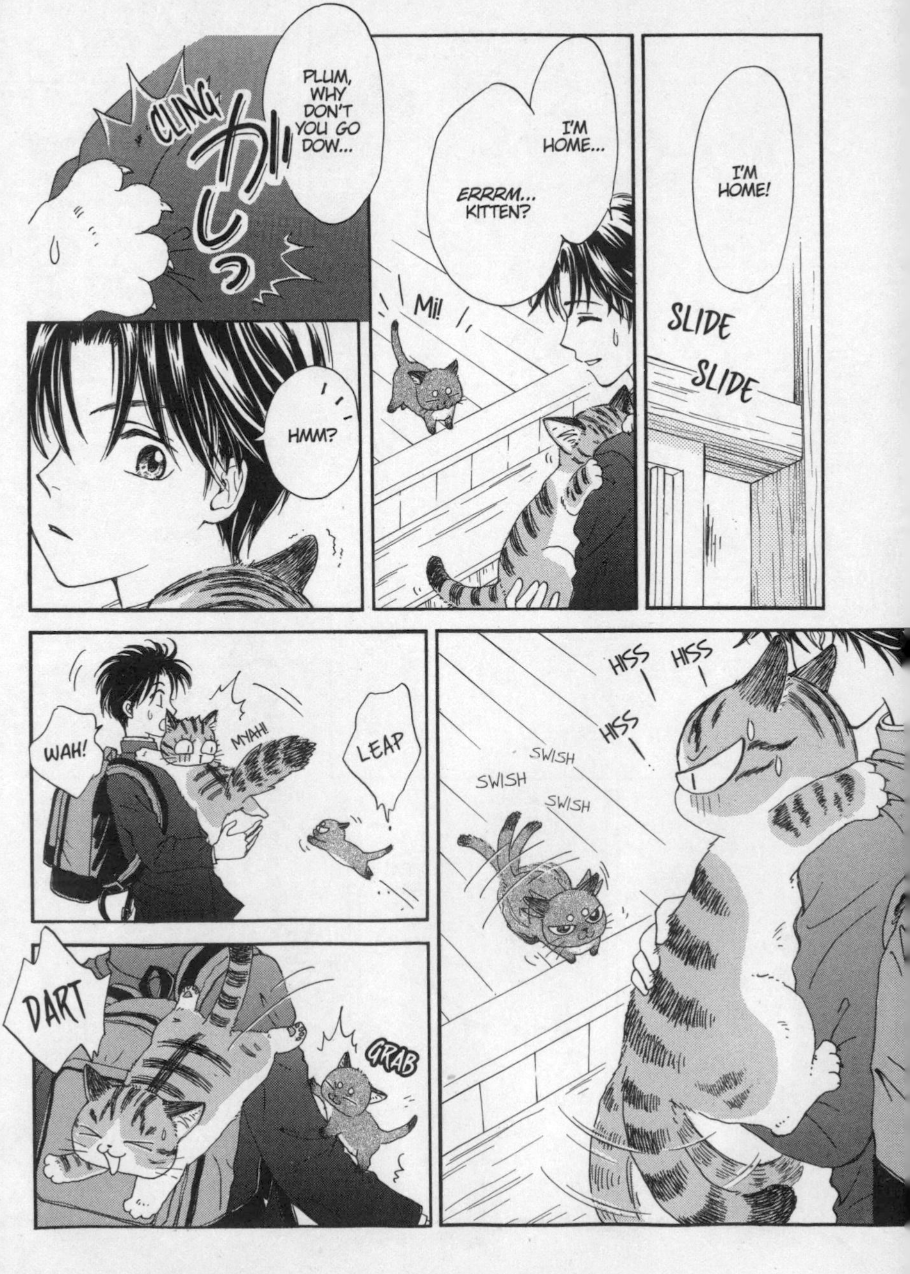
SLIDE
SLIDE
I'M HOME!
I'M HOME...
ERRRM... KITTEN?
Mi!
HMM?
PLUM, WHY DON'T YOU GO DOW...
CLING
HISS
HISS
HISS
SWISH
SWISH
SWISH
LEAP
MYAH!
WAH!
GRAB
DART

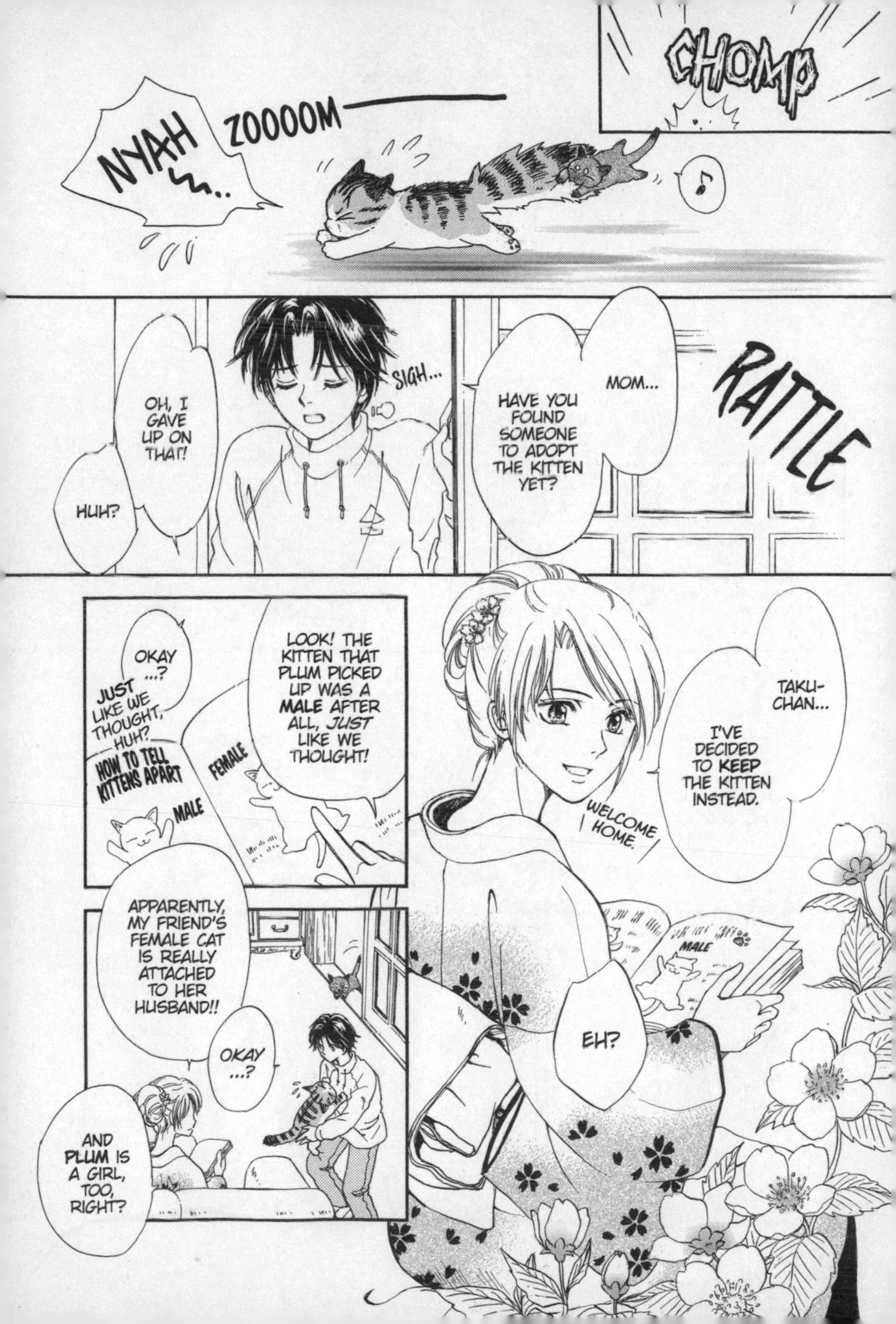
CHOMP
♪
ZOOOOM
NYAH...
RATTLE
MOM...
HAVE YOU FOUND SOMEONE TO ADOPT THE KITTEN YET?
SIGH...
OH, I GAVE UP ON THAT!
HUH?
TAKU-CHAN...
I'VE DECIDED TO KEEP THE KITTEN INSTEAD.
WELCOME HOME.
EH?
MALE
LOOK! THE KITTEN THAT PLUM PICKED UP WAS A MALE AFTER ALL, JUST LIKE WE THOUGHT!
FEMALE
MALE
HOW TO TELL KITTENS APART
OKAY ...?
JUST LIKE WE THOUGHT, HUH?
APPARENTLY, MY FRIEND'S FEMALE CAT IS REALLY ATTACHED TO HER HUSBAND!!
OKAY ...?
AND PLUM IS A GIRL, TOO, RIGHT?

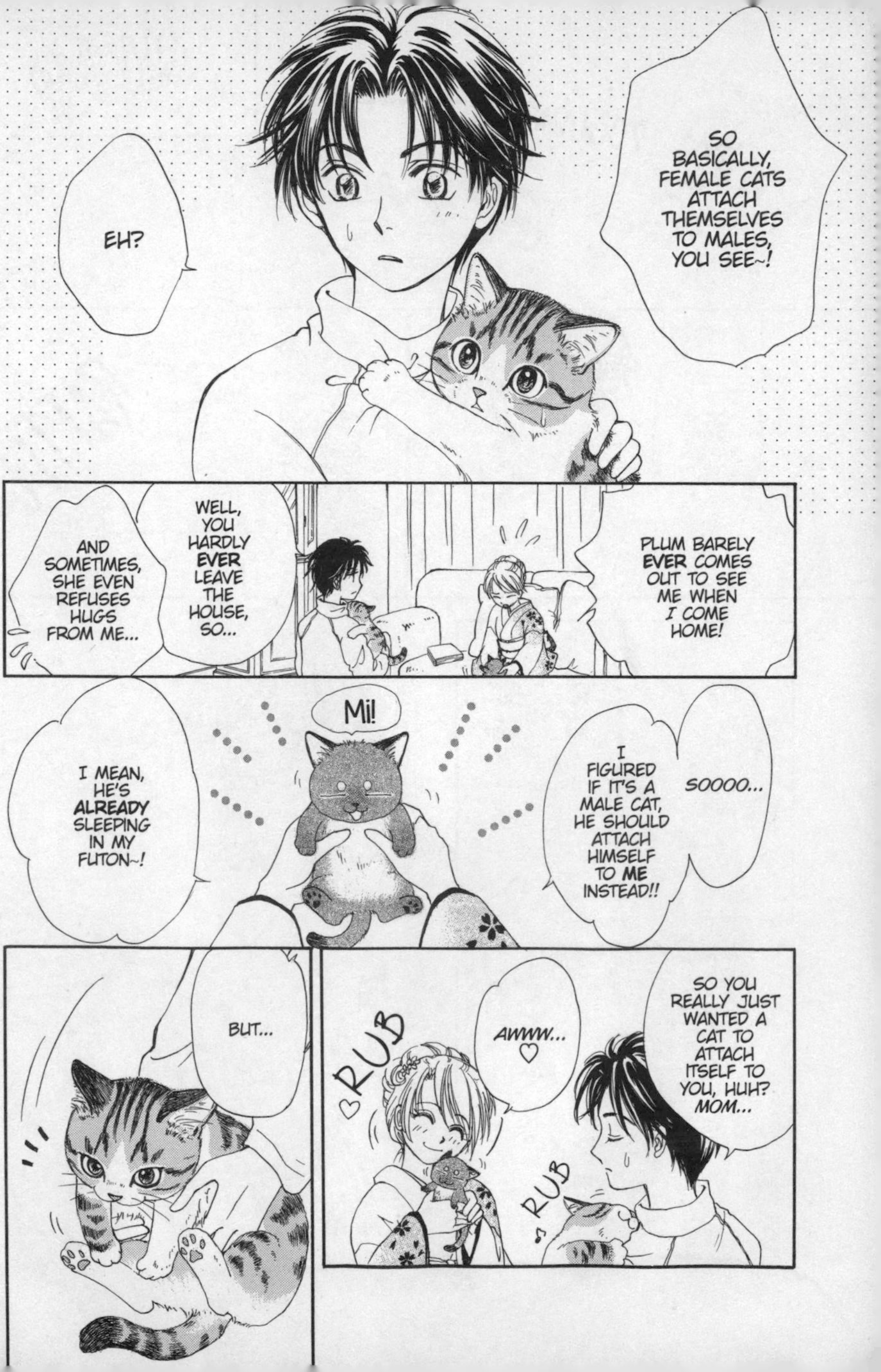
SO BASICALLY, FEMALE CATS ATTACH THEMSELVES TO MALES, YOU SEE~!
EH?
PLUM BARELY EVER COMES OUT TO SEE ME WHEN I COME HOME!
WELL, YOU HARDLY EVER LEAVE THE HOUSE, SO...
AND SOMETIMES, SHE EVEN REFUSES HUGS FROM ME...
SOOOO...
I FIGURED IF IT'S A MALE CAT, HE SHOULD ATTACH HIMSELF TO ME INSTEAD!!
Mi!
I MEAN, HE'S ALREADY SLEEPING IN MY FUTON~!
SO YOU REALLY JUST WANTED A CAT TO ATTACH ITSELF TO YOU, HUH? MOM...
AWWW... ♡
RUB ♡
RUB ♪
BUT...

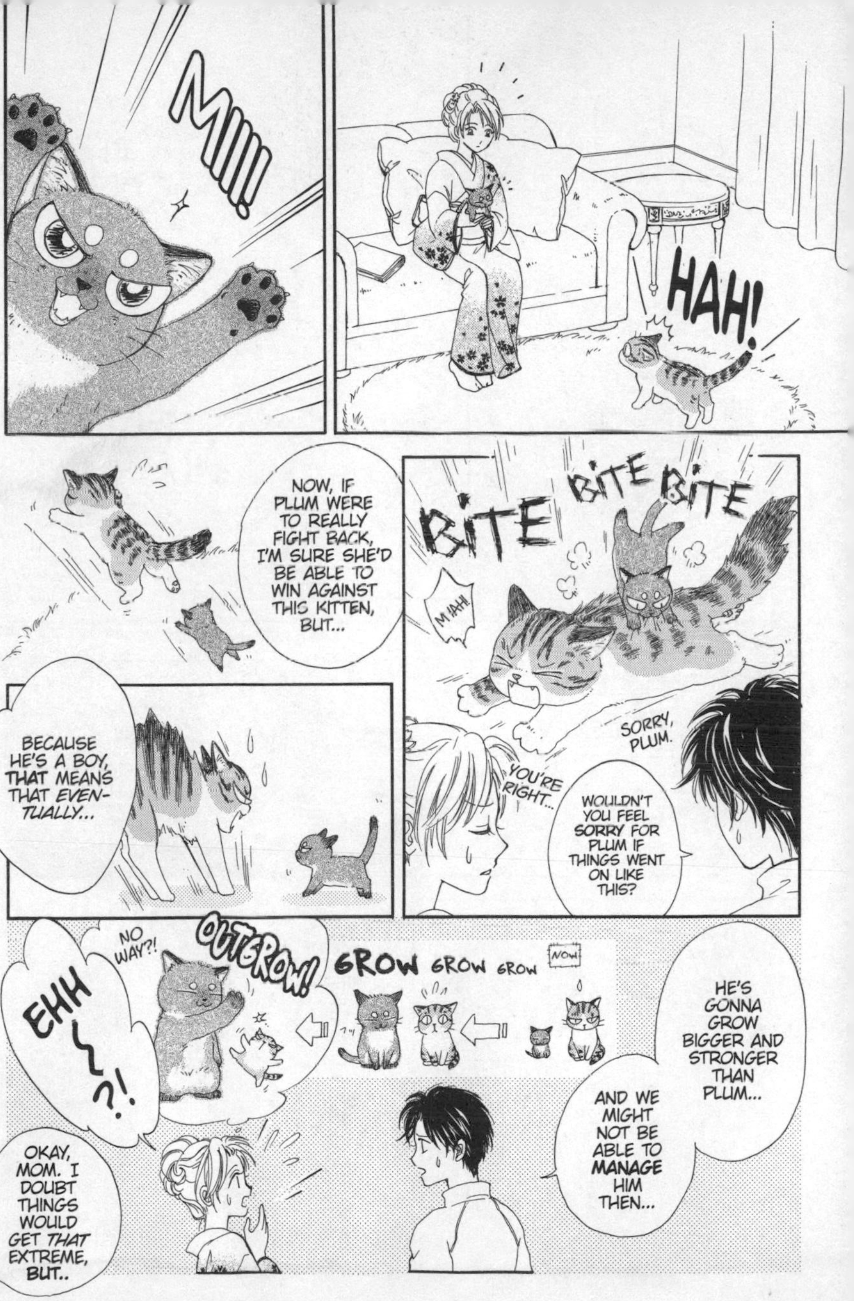
HAH!
MIII!
BITE BITE BITE
MIAH!
NOW, IF PLUM WERE TO REALLY FIGHT BACK, I'M SURE SHE'D BE ABLE TO WIN AGAINST THIS KITTEN, BUT...
SORRY, PLUM.
WOULDN'T YOU FEEL SORRY FOR PLUM IF THINGS WENT ON LIKE THIS?
YOU'RE RIGHT...
BECAUSE HE'S A BOY, THAT MEANS THAT EVEN-TUALLY...
HE'S GONNA GROW BIGGER AND STRONGER THAN PLUM...
AND WE MIGHT NOT BE ABLE TO MANAGE HIM THEN...
NOW
GROW GROW GROW
OUTGROW!
NO WAY?!
EHH~~?!
OKAY, MOM. I DOUBT THINGS WOULD GET THAT EXTREME, BUT..

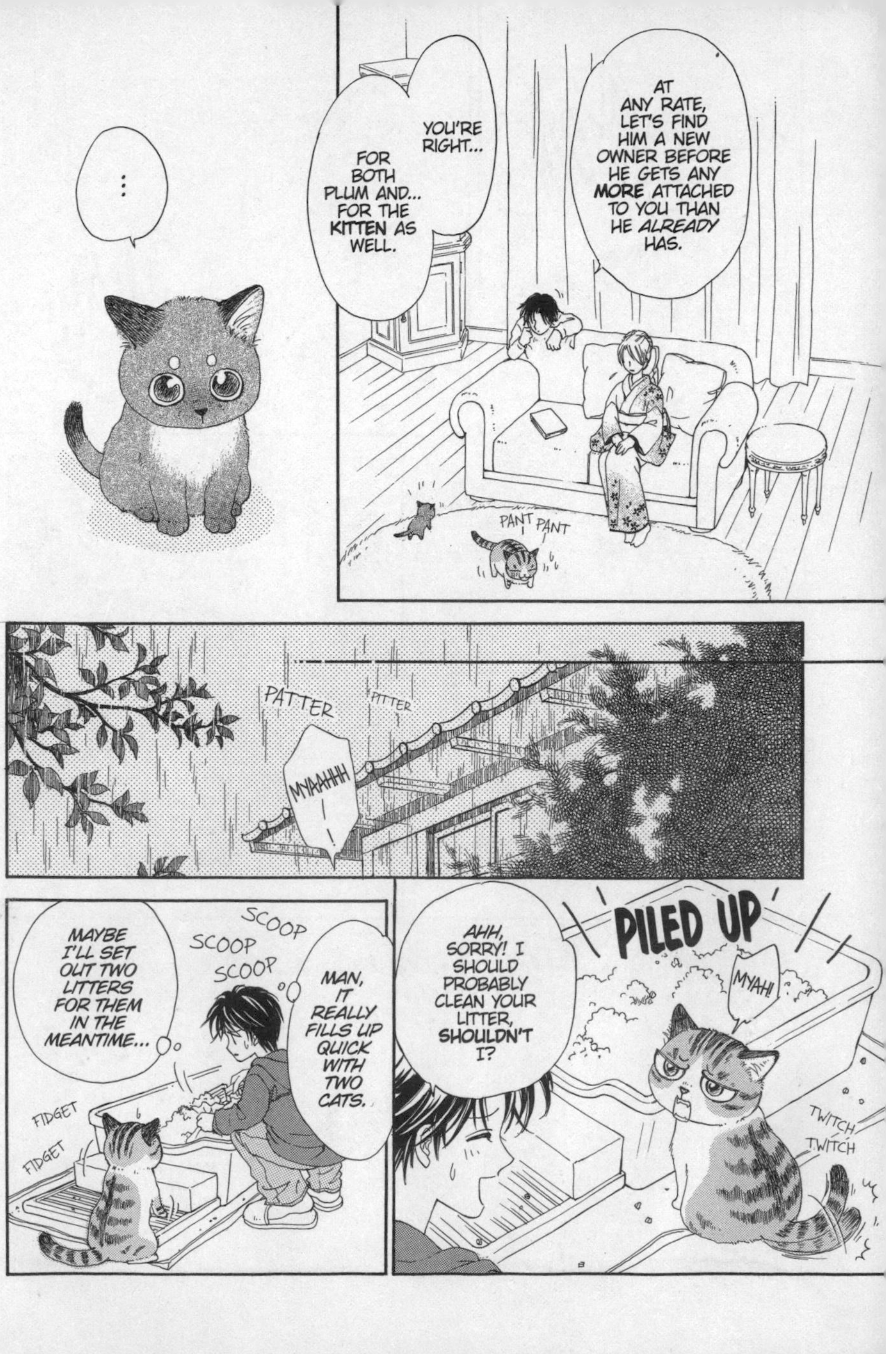
AT ANY RATE, LET'S FIND HIM A NEW OWNER BEFORE HE GETS ANY MORE ATTACHED TO YOU THAN HE ALREADY HAS.
YOU'RE RIGHT...
FOR BOTH PLUM AND... FOR THE KITTEN AS WELL.
PANT PANT
...
PITTER
PATTER
MYAAHHH!
PILED UP
MYAH!
TWITCH TWITCH
AHH, SORRY! I SHOULD PROBABLY CLEAN YOUR LITTER, SHOULDN'T I?
SCOOP SCOOP SCOOP
MAN, IT REALLY FILLS UP QUICK WITH TWO CATS.
MAYBE I'LL SET OUT TWO LITTERS FOR THEM IN THE MEANTIME...
FIDGET FIDGET

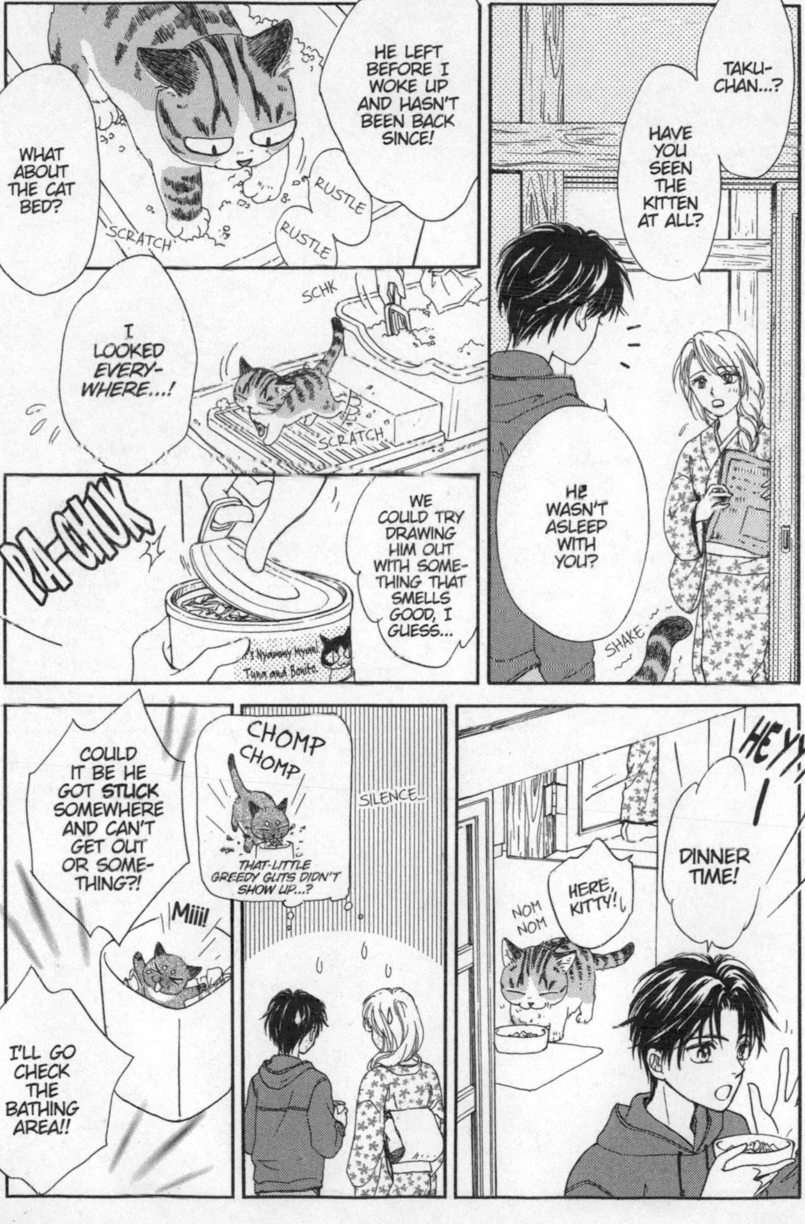
TAKU-CHAN...?
HAVE YOU SEEN THE KITTEN AT ALL?
HE WASN'T ASLEEP WITH YOU?
SHAKE
HE LEFT BEFORE I WOKE UP AND HASN'T BEEN BACK SINCE!
WHAT ABOUT THE CAT BED?
RUSTLE
RUSTLE
SCRATCH
I LOOKED EVERY-WHERE...!
SCHK
SCRATCH
WE COULD TRY DRAWING HIM OUT WITH SOME-THING THAT SMELLS GOOD, I GUESS...
PA-CHUK
Tuna and Bonito
HEYYY!
DINNER TIME!
HERE, KITTY!
NOM NOM
SILENCE...
CHOMP CHOMP
THAT LITTLE GREEDY GUTS DIDN'T SHOW UP...?
COULD IT BE HE GOT STUCK SOMEWHERE AND CAN'T GET OUT OR SOME-THING?!
Miii!
I'LL GO CHECK THE BATHING AREA!!

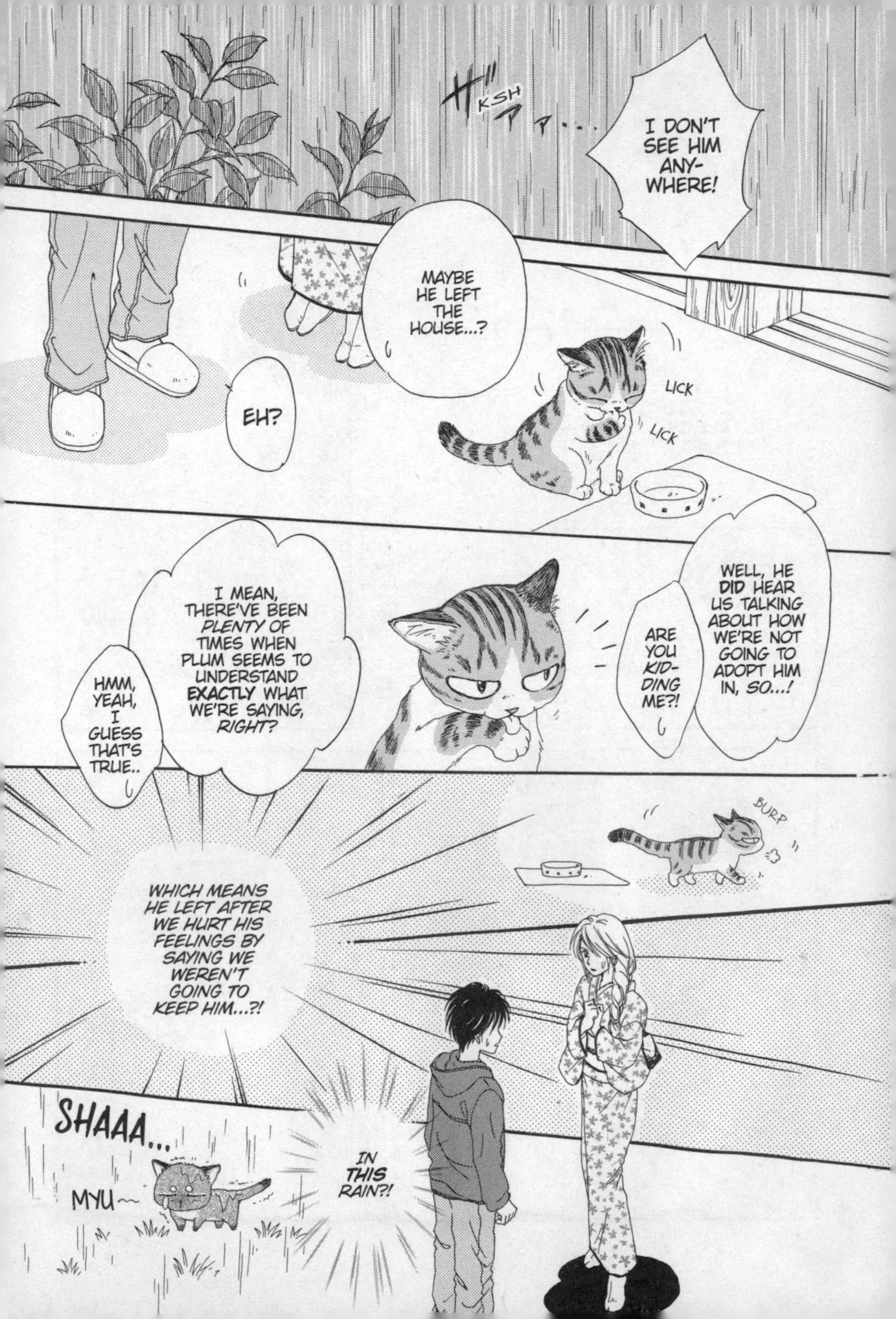
I DON'T SEE HIM ANY-WHERE!
KSH
MAYBE HE LEFT THE HOUSE...?
EH?
LICK
LICK
WELL, HE DID HEAR US TALKING ABOUT HOW WE'RE NOT GOING TO ADOPT HIM IN, SO...!
ARE YOU KID-DING ME?!
I MEAN, THERE'VE BEEN PLENTY OF TIMES WHEN PLUM SEEMS TO UNDERSTAND EXACTLY WHAT WE'RE SAYING, RIGHT?
HMM, YEAH, I GUESS THAT'S TRUE..
BURP
WHICH MEANS HE LEFT AFTER WE HURT HIS FEELINGS BY SAYING WE WEREN'T GOING TO KEEP HIM...?!
IN THIS RAIN?!
SHAAA...
MYU~~

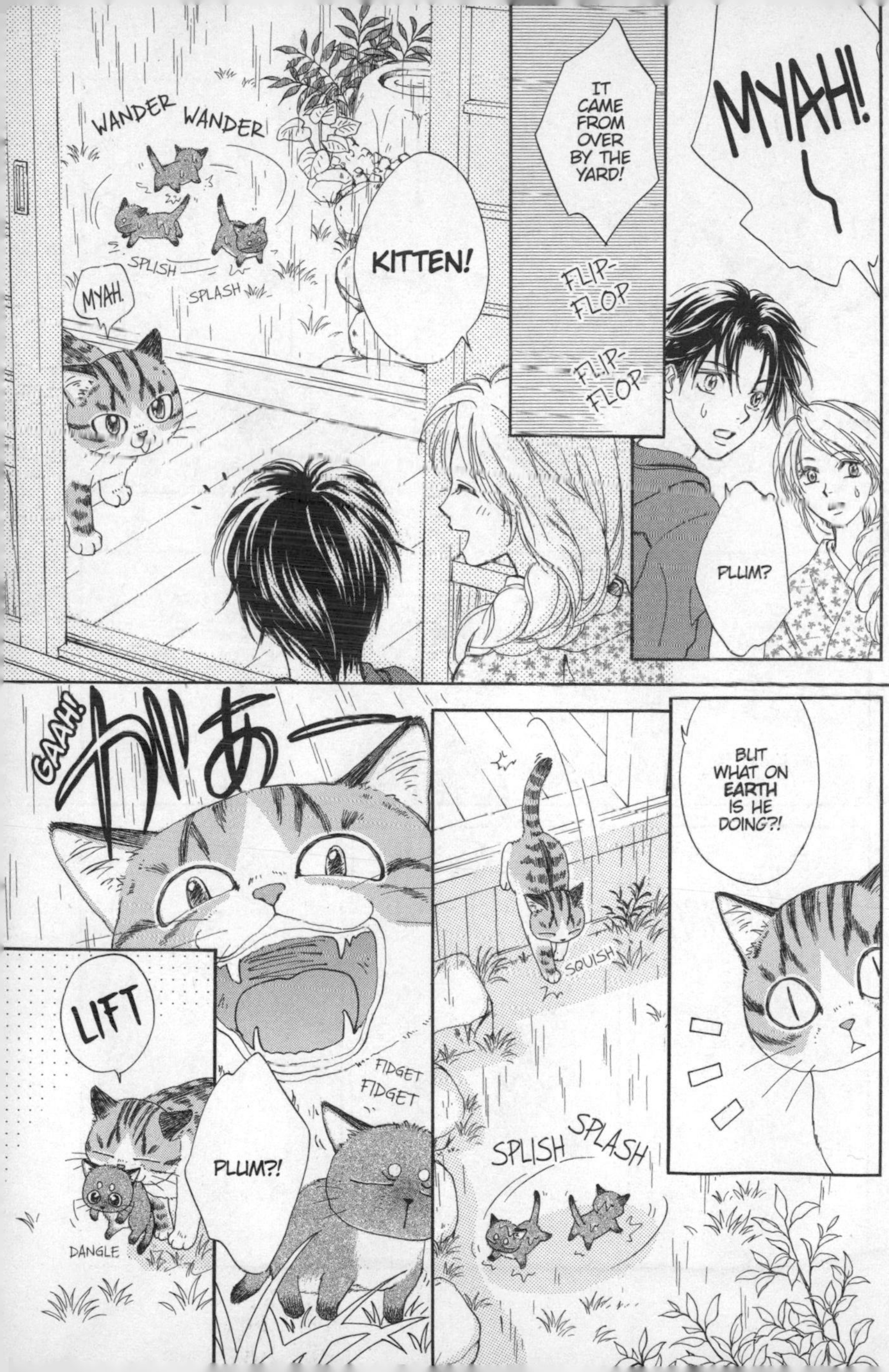
MYAH!
IT CAME FROM OVER BY THE YARD!
FLIP-FLOP
FLIP-FLOP
PLUM?
KITTEN!
WANDER WANDER
SPLISH
SPLASH
MYAH.
BUT WHAT ON EARTH IS HE DOING?!
SQUISH
SPLISH SPLASH
GAAH!
わぁー
LIFT
FIDGET FIDGET
PLUM?!
DANGLE

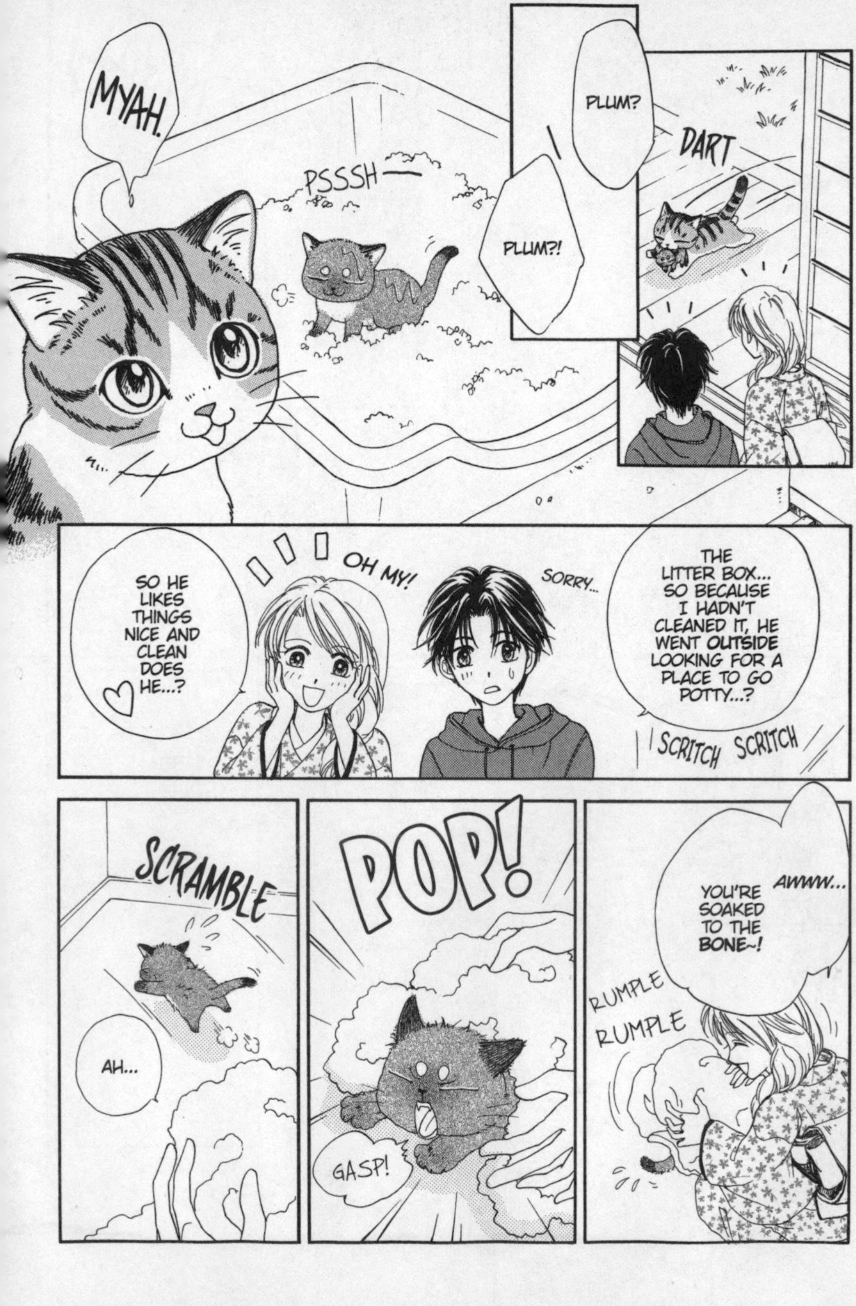
DART
PLUM?
PLUM?!
PSSSH—
MYAH.
THE LITTER BOX... SO BECAUSE I HADN'T CLEANED IT, HE WENT OUTSIDE LOOKING FOR A PLACE TO GO POTTY...?
SCRITCH SCRITCH
SORRY...
OH MY!
SO HE LIKES THINGS NICE AND CLEAN DOES HE...?
AWWW...
YOU'RE SOAKED TO THE BONE~!
RUMPLE RUMPLE
POP!
GASP!
SCRAMBLE
AH...

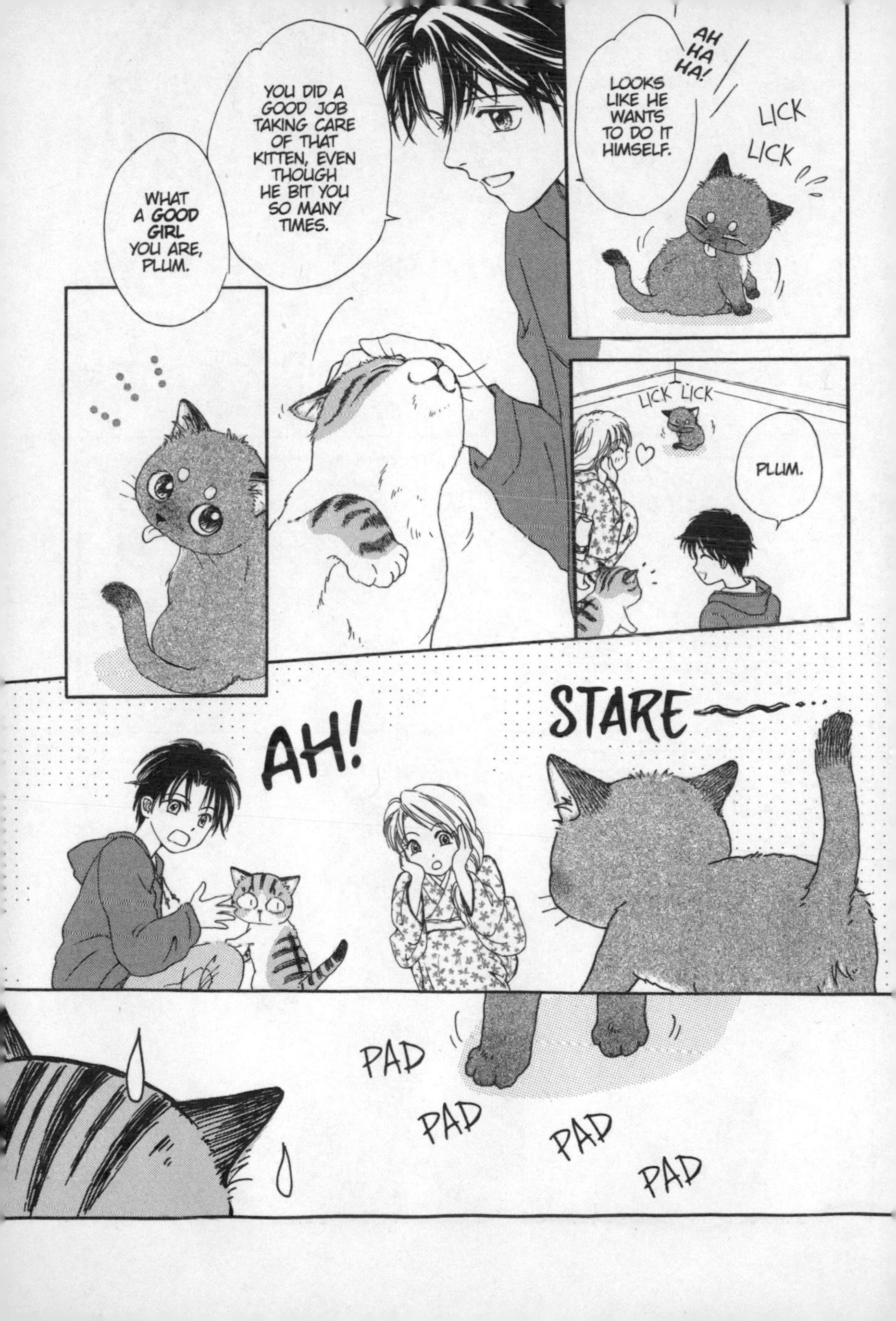
AH HA HA!
LOOKS LIKE HE WANTS TO DO IT HIMSELF.
LICK
LICK
LICK LICK
PLUM.
YOU DID A GOOD JOB TAKING CARE OF THAT KITTEN, EVEN THOUGH HE BIT YOU SO MANY TIMES.
WHAT A GOOD GIRL YOU ARE, PLUM.
STARE...
AH!
PAD
PAD
PAD
PAD

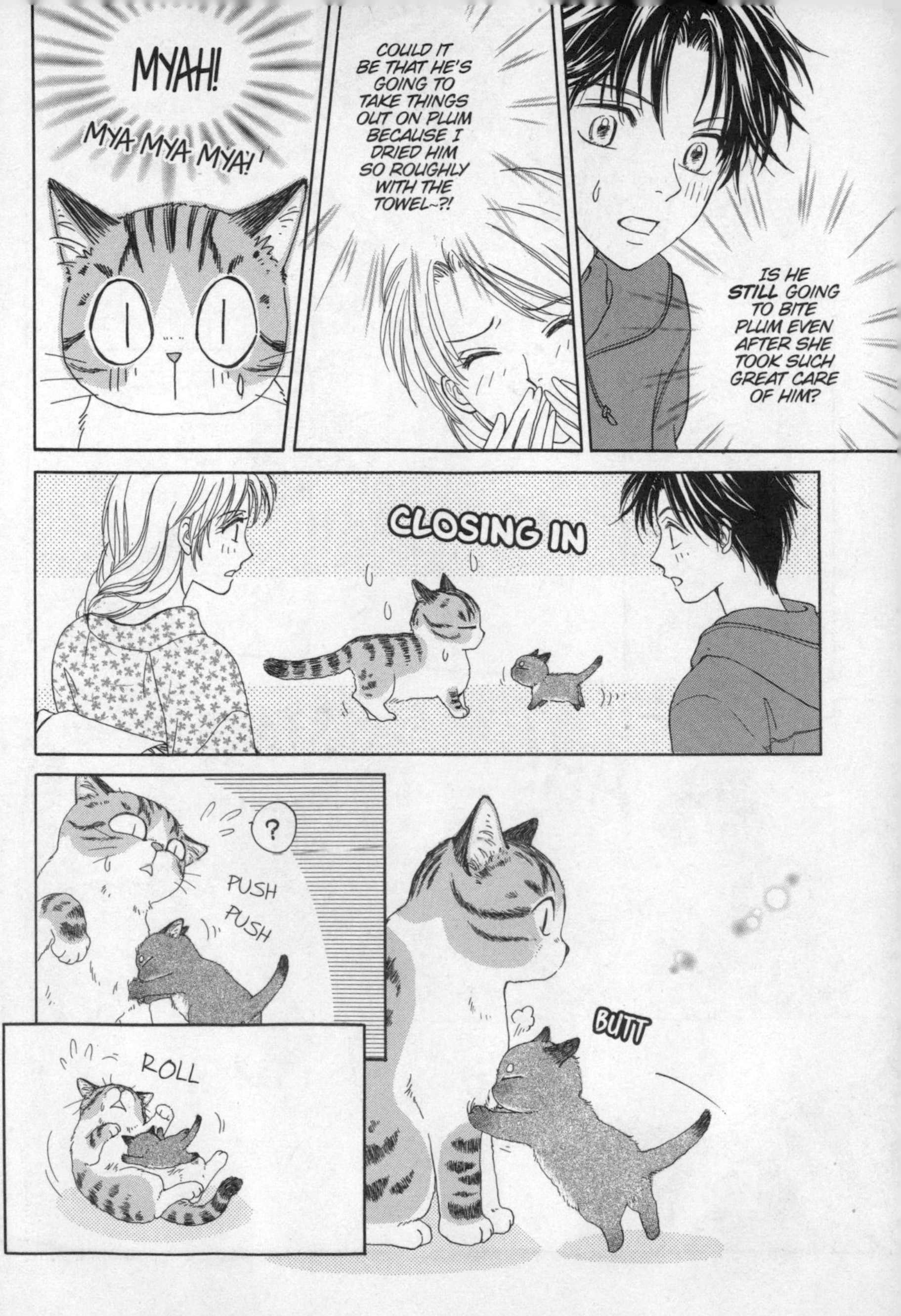
IS HE STILL GOING TO BITE PLUM EVEN AFTER SHE TOOK SUCH GREAT CARE OF HIM?
COULD IT BE THAT HE'S GOING TO TAKE THINGS OUT ON PLUM BECAUSE I DRIED HIM SO ROUGHLY WITH THE TOWEL~?!
MYAH!
MYA MYA MYA!
CLOSING IN
BUTT
?
PUSH PUSH
ROLL

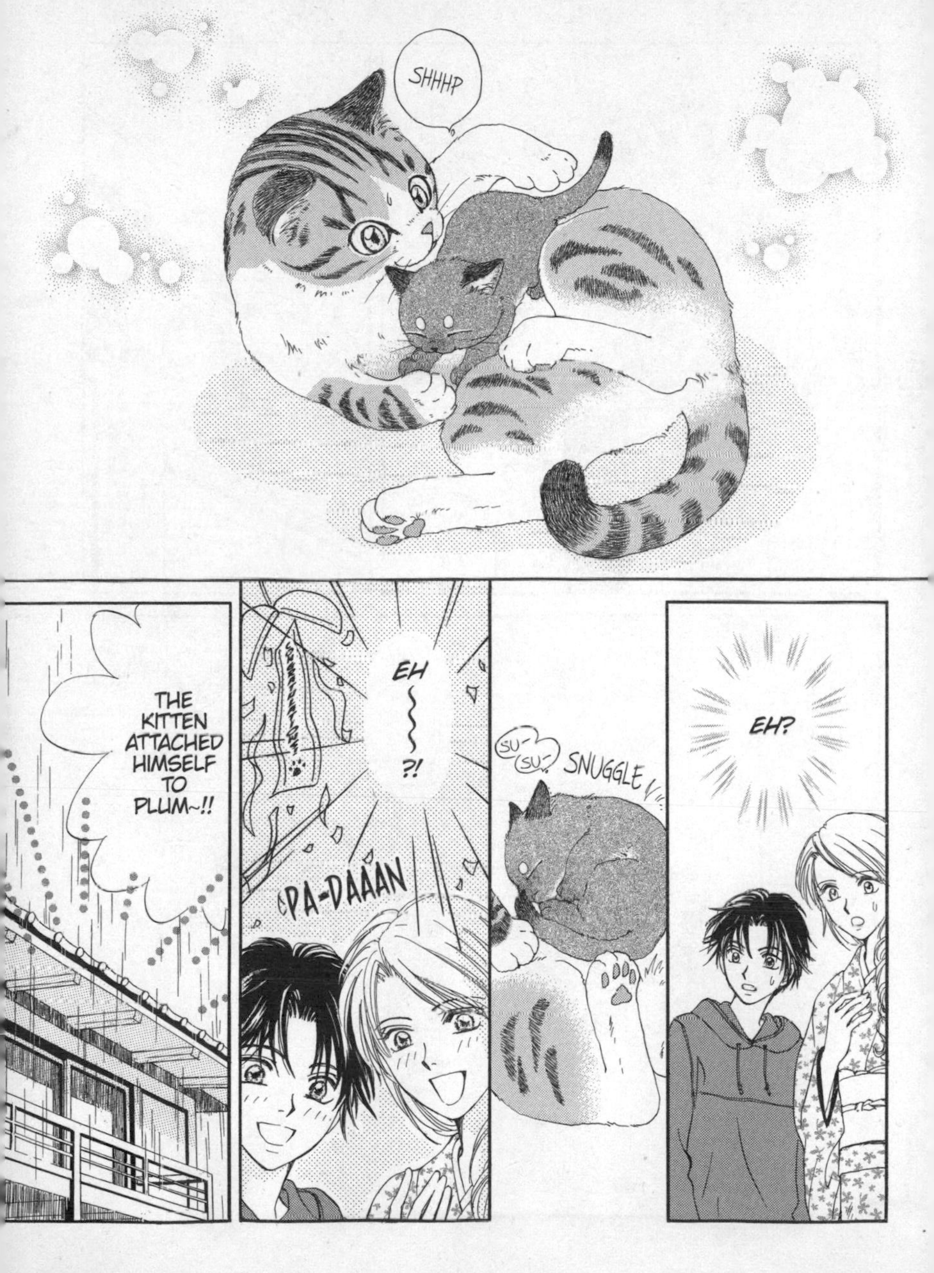
SHHHP
EH?
SU- SU-
SNUGGLE
EH~~~?!
PA-DAAAN
THE KITTEN ATTACHED HIMSELF TO PLUM~!!

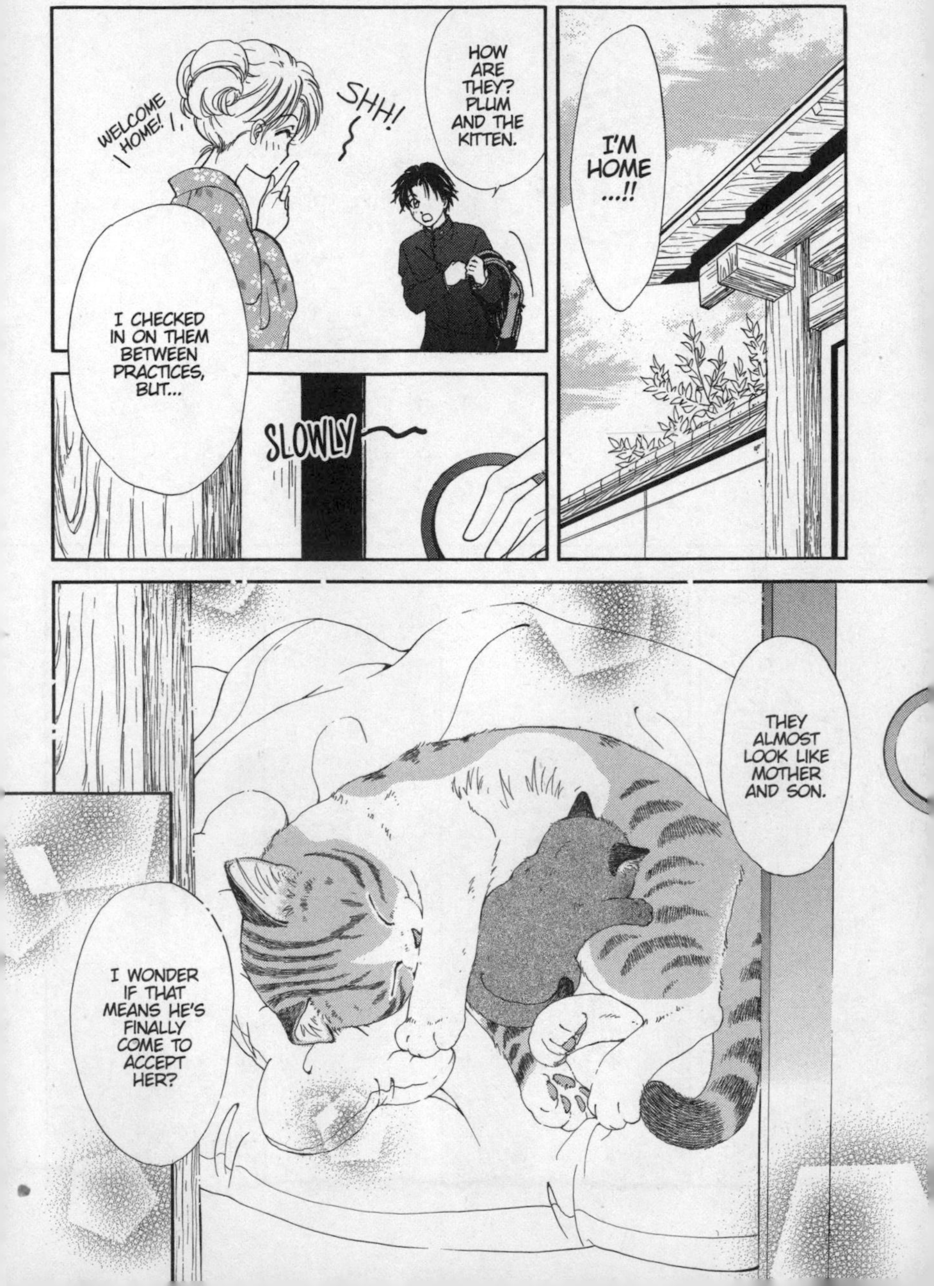
I'M HOME ...!!
HOW ARE THEY? PLUM AND THE KITTEN.
SHH!
WELCOME HOME!
I CHECKED IN ON THEM BETWEEN PRACTICES, BUT...
SLOWLY
THEY ALMOST LOOK LIKE MOTHER AND SON.
I WONDER IF THAT MEANS HE'S FINALLY COME TO ACCEPT HER?

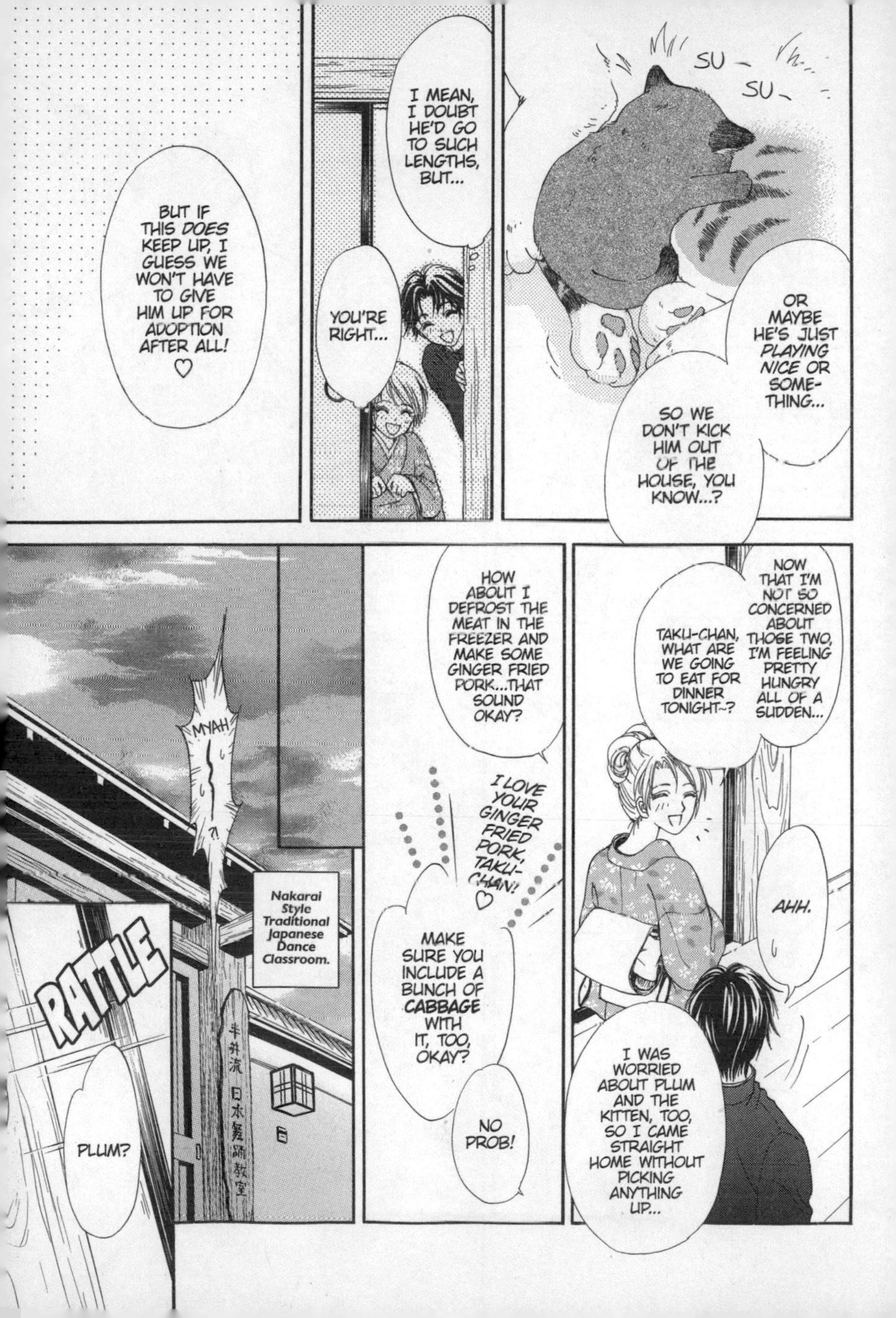
SU - SU -
OR MAYBE HE'S JUST PLAYING NICE OR SOME-THING...
SO WE DON'T KICK HIM OUT OF THE HOUSE, YOU KNOW...?
I MEAN, I DOUBT HE'D GO TO SUCH LENGTHS, BUT...
YOU'RE RIGHT...
BUT IF THIS DOES KEEP UP, I GUESS WE WON'T HAVE TO GIVE HIM UP FOR ADOPTION AFTER ALL! ♡
NOW THAT I'M NOT SO CONCERNED ABOUT THOSE TWO, I'M FEELING PRETTY HUNGRY ALL OF A SUDDEN...
TAKU-CHAN, WHAT ARE WE GOING TO EAT FOR DINNER TONIGHT~?
AHH.
I WAS WORRIED ABOUT PLUM AND THE KITTEN, TOO, SO I CAME STRAIGHT HOME WITHOUT PICKING ANYTHING UP...
HOW ABOUT I DEFROST THE MEAT IN THE FREEZER AND MAKE SOME GINGER FRIED PORK...THAT SOUND OKAY?
I LOVE YOUR GINGER FRIED PORK, TAKU-CHAN! ♡
MAKE SURE YOU INCLUDE A BUNCH OF CABBAGE WITH IT, TOO, OKAY?
NO PROB!
MYAH
Nakarai Style Traditional Japanese Dance Classroom.
牛井流 日本舞踊教室
RATTLE
PLUM?

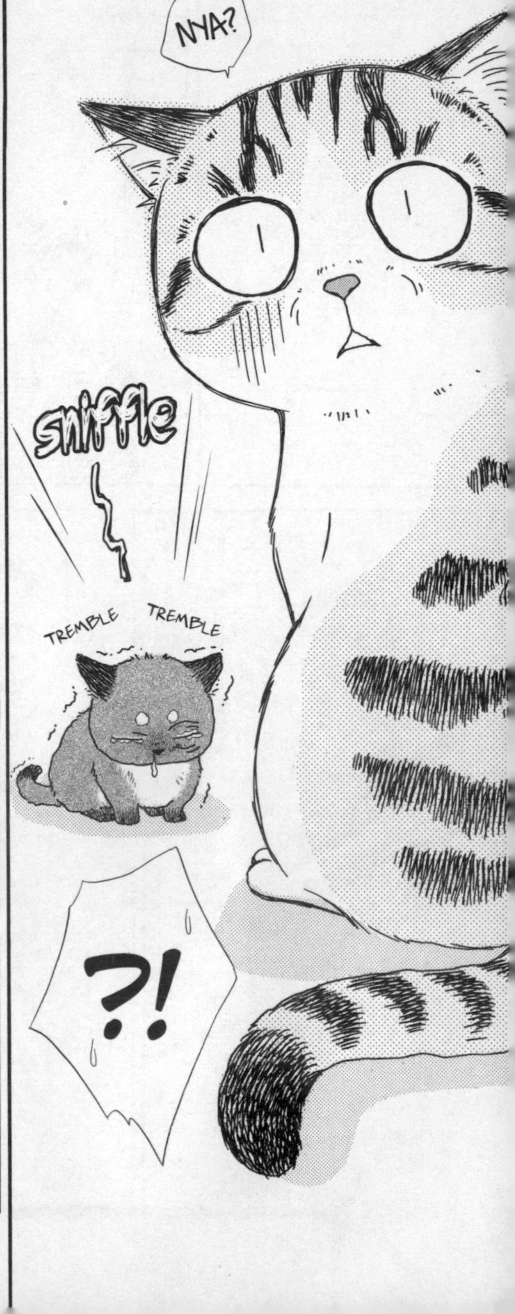
NYA?
sniffle
TREMBLE TREMBLE
?!

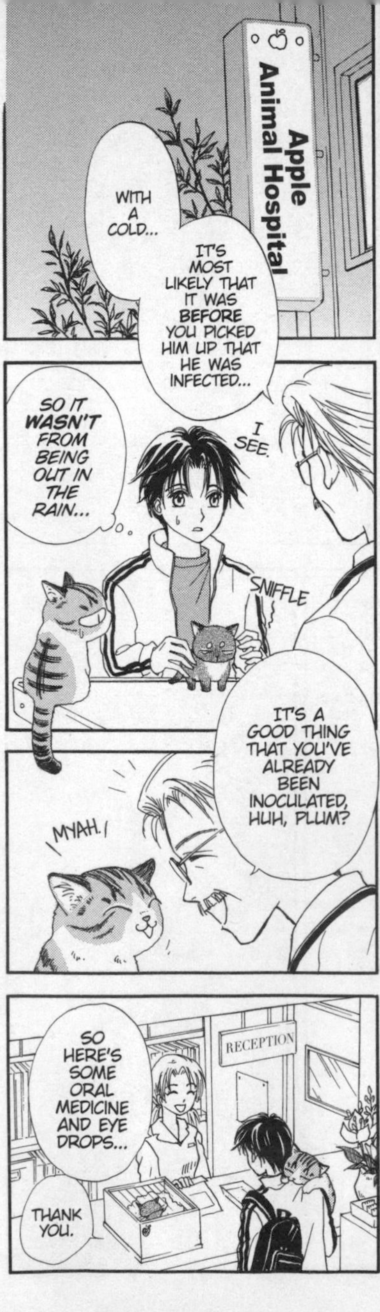
Apple Animal Hospital
IT'S MOST LIKELY THAT IT WAS BEFORE YOU PICKED HIM UP THAT HE WAS INFECTED...
WITH A COLD...
I SEE.
SO IT WASN'T FROM BEING OUT IN THE RAIN...
SNIFFLE
IT'S A GOOD THING THAT YOU'VE ALREADY BEEN INOCULATED, HUH, PLUM?
MYAH.
RECEPTION
SO HERE'S SOME ORAL MEDICINE AND EYE DROPS...
THANK YOU.

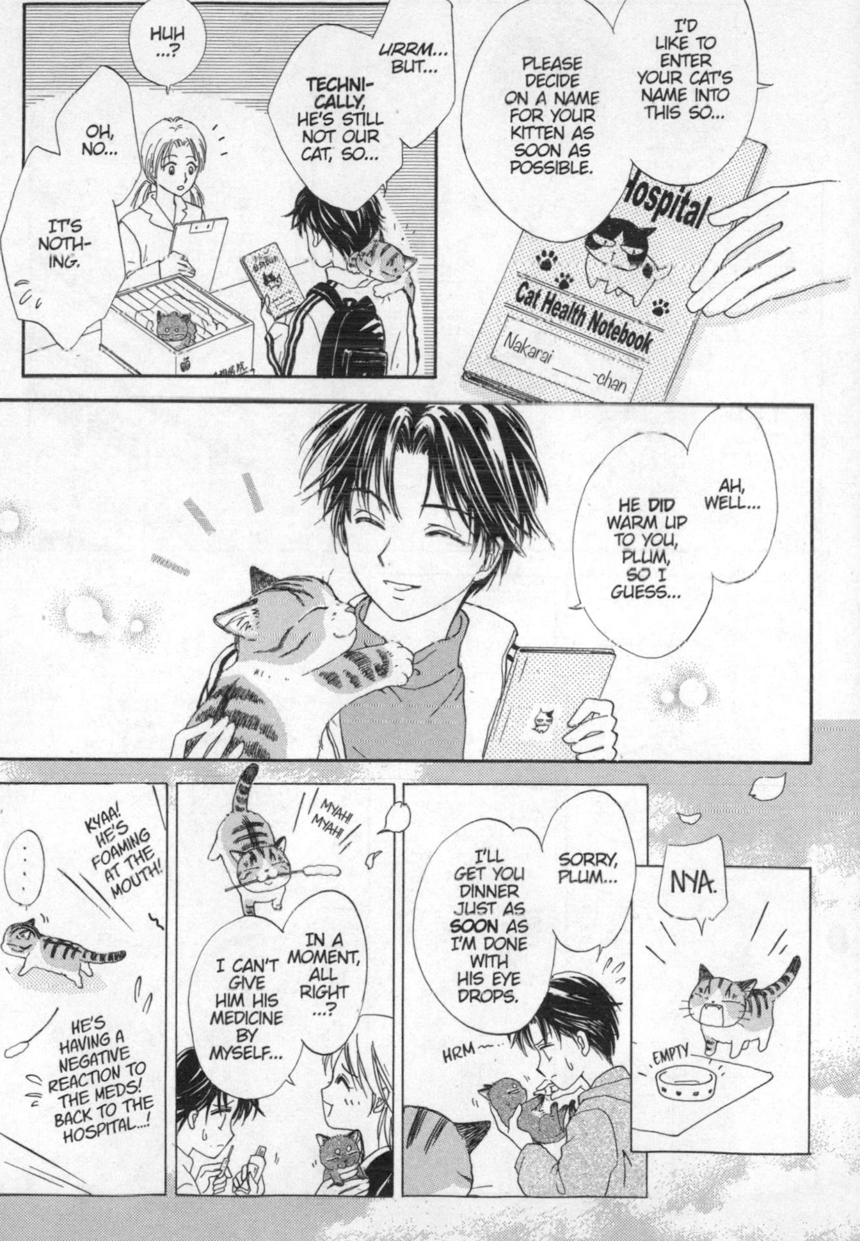
I'D LIKE TO ENTER YOUR CAT'S NAME INTO THIS SO...
PLEASE DECIDE ON A NAME FOR YOUR KITTEN AS SOON AS POSSIBLE.
Hospital
Cat Health Notebook
Nakarai ____-chan
URRM... BUT...
TECHNICALLY, HE'S STILL NOT OUR CAT, SO...
HUH ...?
OH, NO...
IT'S NOTHING.
AH, WELL...
HE DID WARM UP TO YOU, PLUM, SO I GUESS...
NYA.
EMPTY
SORRY, PLUM...
I'LL GET YOU DINNER JUST AS SOON AS I'M DONE WITH HIS EYE DROPS.
HRM~
MYAH! MYAH!
IN A MOMENT, ALL RIGHT ...?
I CAN'T GIVE HIM HIS MEDICINE BY MYSELF...
KYAA! HE'S FOAMING AT THE MOUTH!
...
HE'S HAVING A NEGATIVE REACTION TO THE MEDS! BACK TO THE HOSPITAL...!

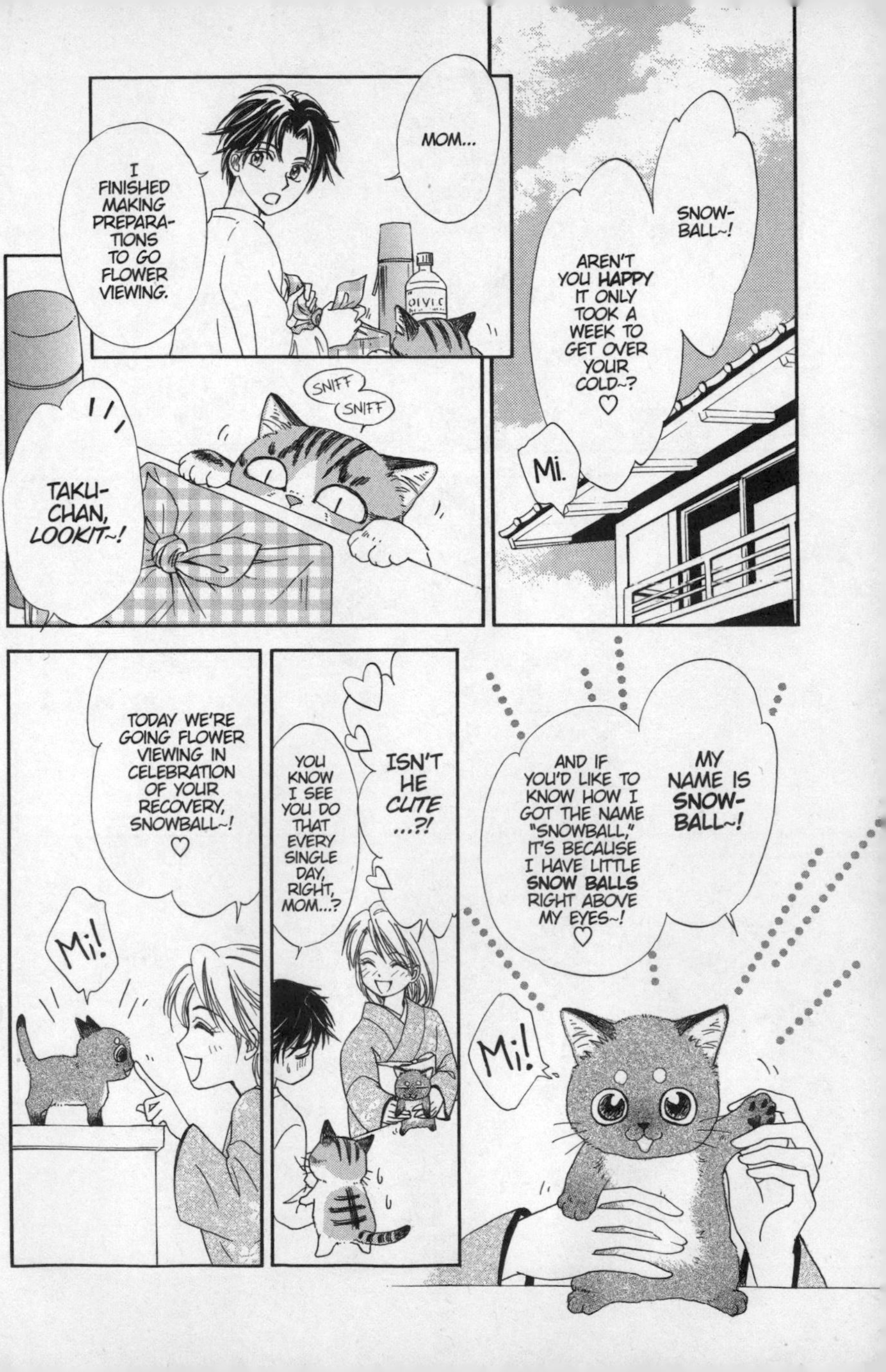
SNOW-BALL~!
AREN'T YOU HAPPY IT ONLY TOOK A WEEK TO GET OVER YOUR COLD~? ♡
Mi.
MOM...
I FINISHED MAKING PREPARATIONS TO GO FLOWER VIEWING.
SNIFF SNIFF
TAKU-CHAN, LOOKIT~!
MY NAME IS SNOW-BALL~!
AND IF YOU'D LIKE TO KNOW HOW I GOT THE NAME "SNOWBALL," IT'S BECAUSE I HAVE LITTLE SNOW BALLS RIGHT ABOVE MY EYES~! ♡
Mi!
ISN'T HE CUTE ...?!
YOU KNOW I SEE YOU DO THAT EVERY SINGLE DAY, RIGHT, MOM...?
TODAY WE'RE GOING FLOWER VIEWING IN CELEBRATION OF YOUR RECOVERY, SNOWBALL~! ♡
Mi!

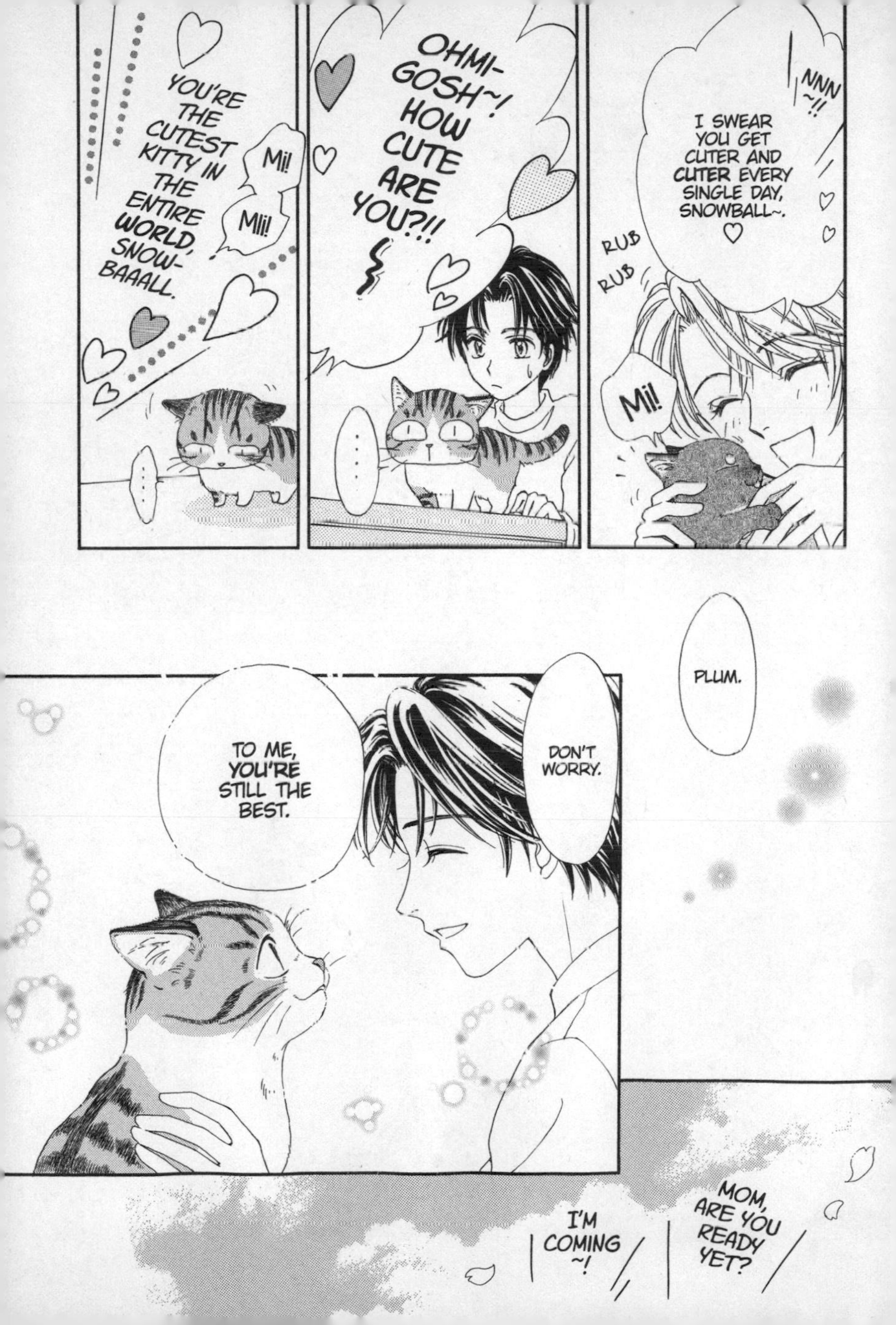
NNN ~!!
I SWEAR YOU GET CUTER AND CUTER EVERY SINGLE DAY, SNOWBALL~.
RUB RUB
Mi!
OHMI-GOSH~! HOW CUTE ARE YOU?!!
...
YOU'RE THE CUTEST KITTY IN THE ENTIRE WORLD, SNOW-BAAALL.
Mi!
Mii!
...
PLUM.
DON'T WORRY.
TO ME, YOU'RE STILL THE BEST.
MOM, ARE YOU READY YET?
I'M COMING ~!

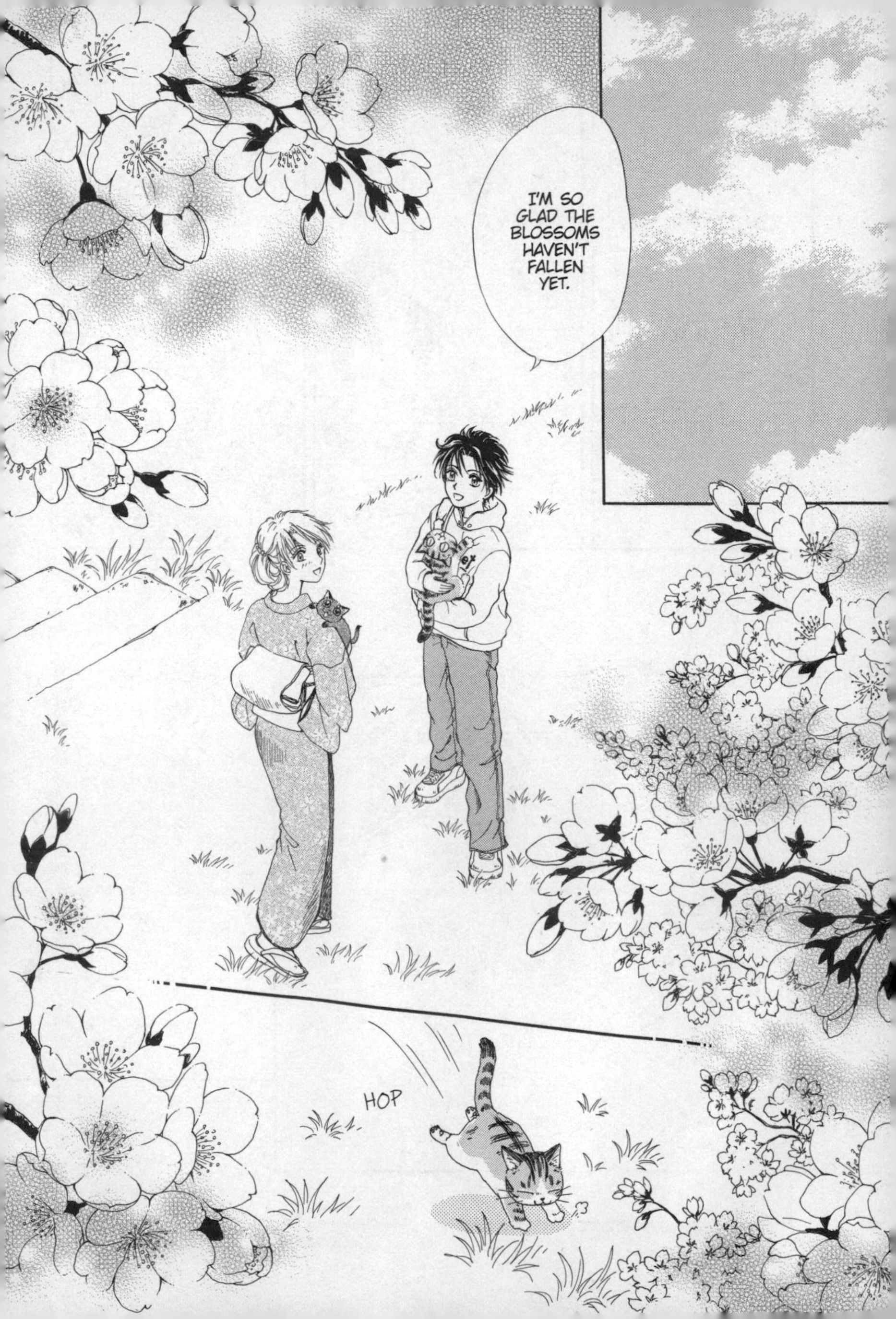
I'M SO GLAD THE BLOSSOMS HAVEN'T FALLEN YET.
HOP

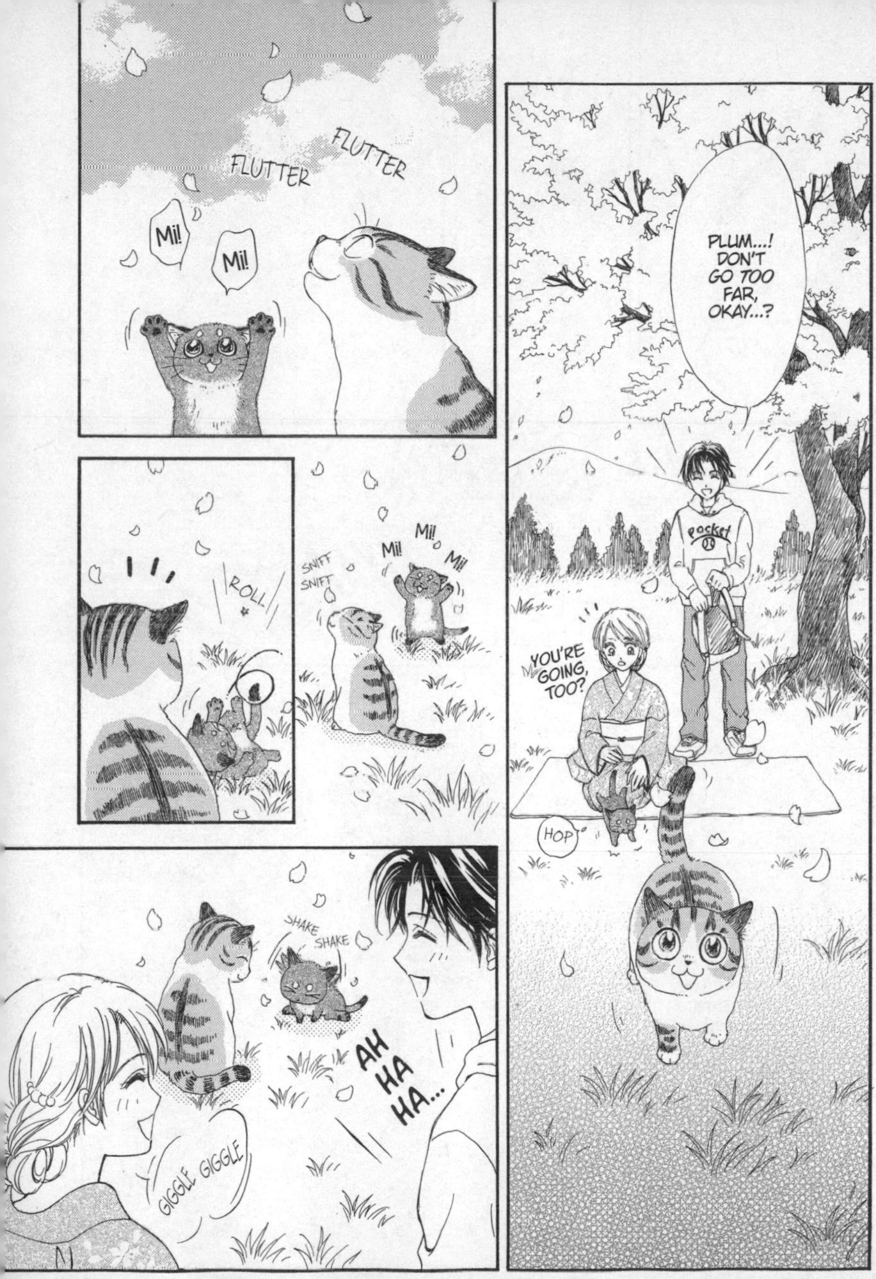
PLUM...! DON'T GO TOO FAR, OKAY...?
YOU'RE GOING, TOO?
HOP
FLUTTER
FLUTTER
Mi!
Mi!
ROLL
SNIFF SNIFF
Mi!
Mi!
Mi!
SHAKE SHAKE
AH HA HA...
GIGGLE GIGGLE

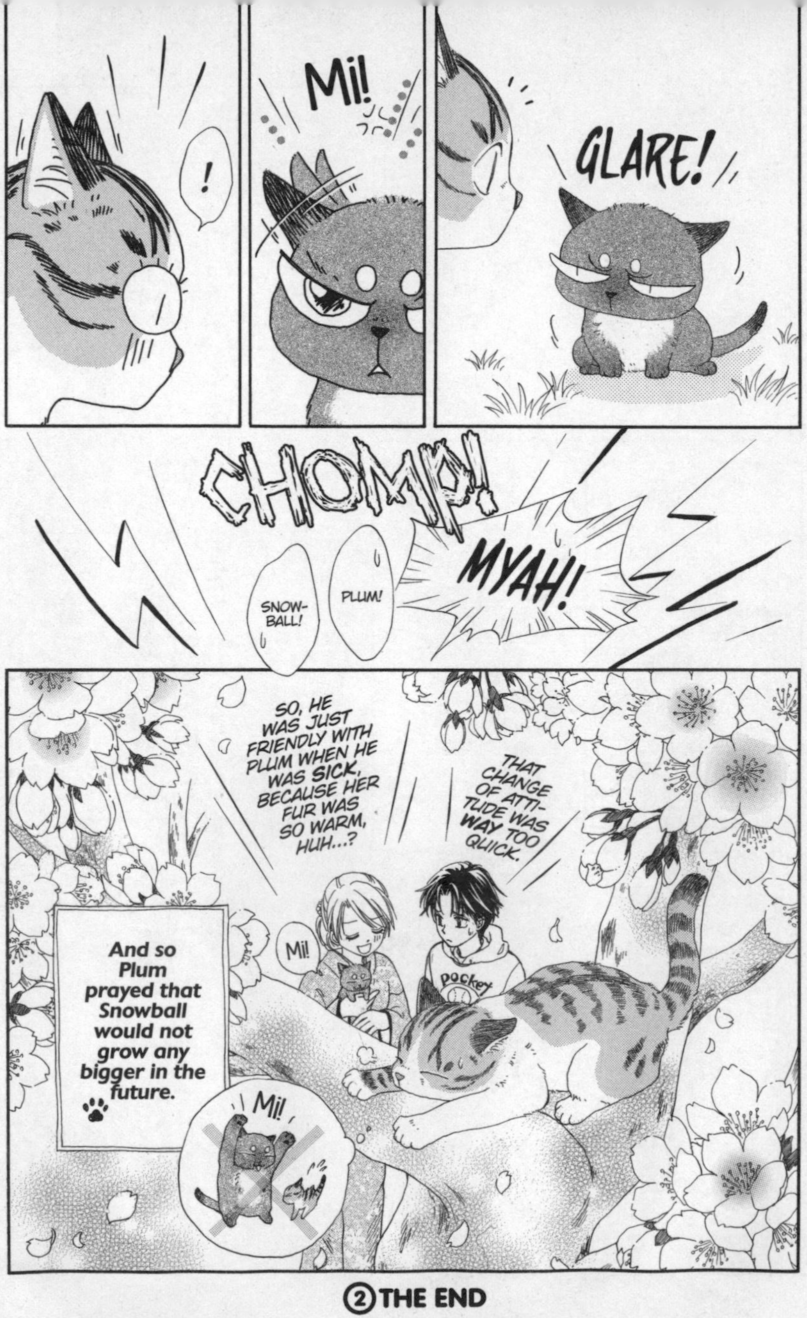
GLARE!
Mi!
!
CHOMP!
MYAH!
PLUM!
SNOW-BALL!
THAT CHANGE OF ATTI-TUDE WAS WAY TOO QUICK.
SO, HE WAS JUST FRIENDLY WITH PLUM WHEN HE WAS SICK, BECAUSE HER FUR WAS SO WARM, HUH...?
Mi!
And so Plum prayed that Snowball would not grow any bigger in the future.
Mi!

② THE END

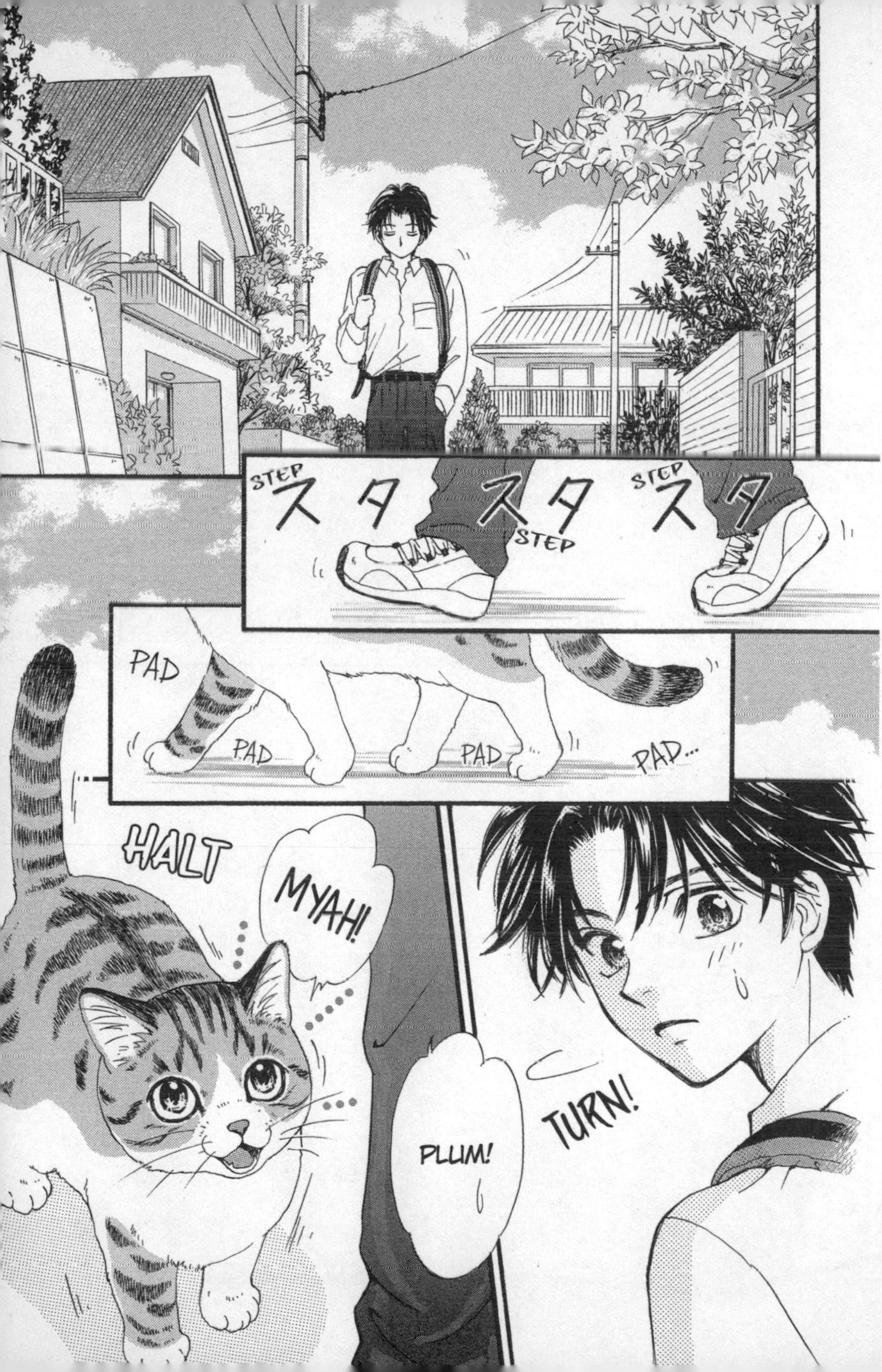
STEP
スタ
STEP
スタ
STEP
スタ
PAD
PAD
PAD
PAD...
TURN!
PLUM!
HALT
MYAH!

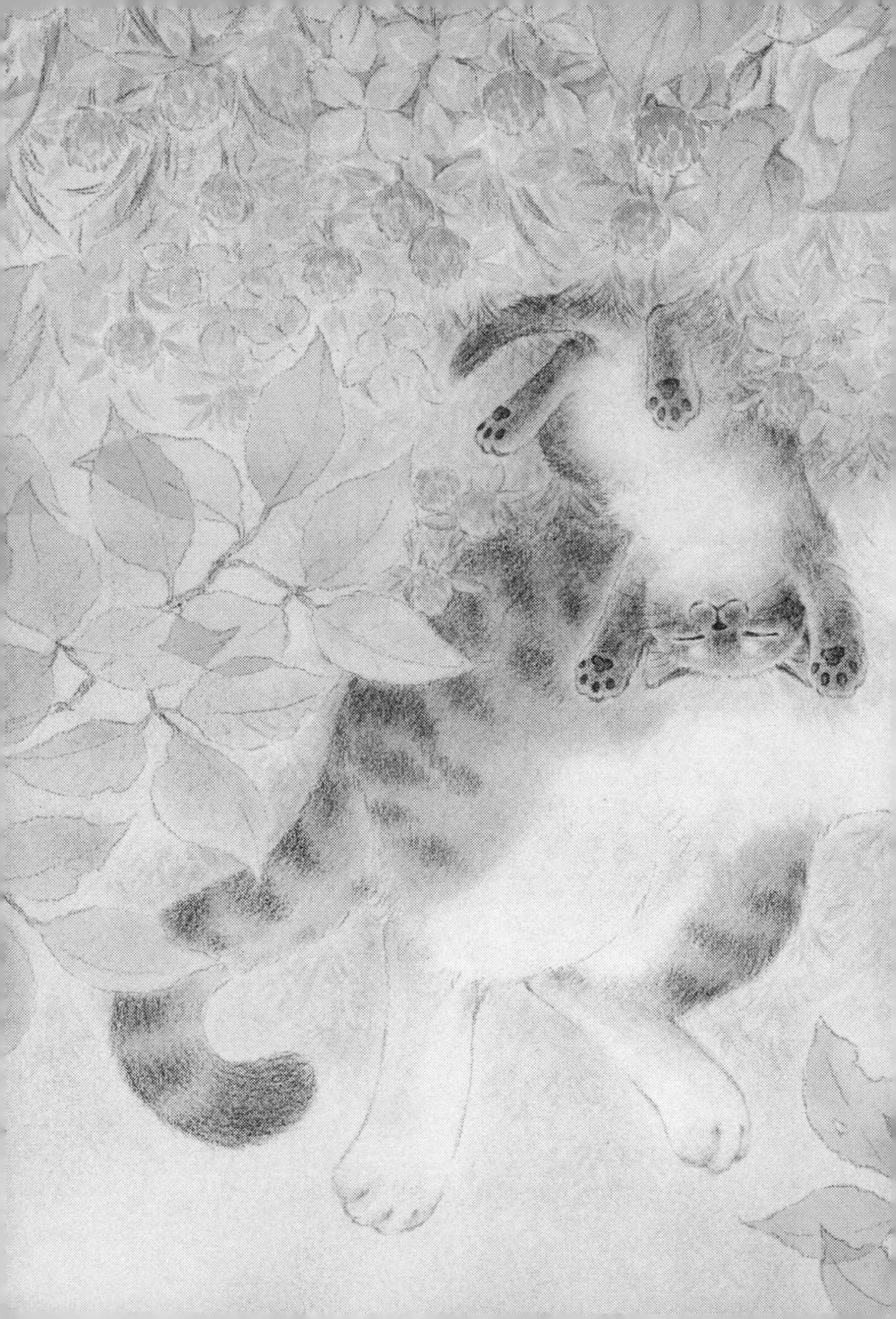

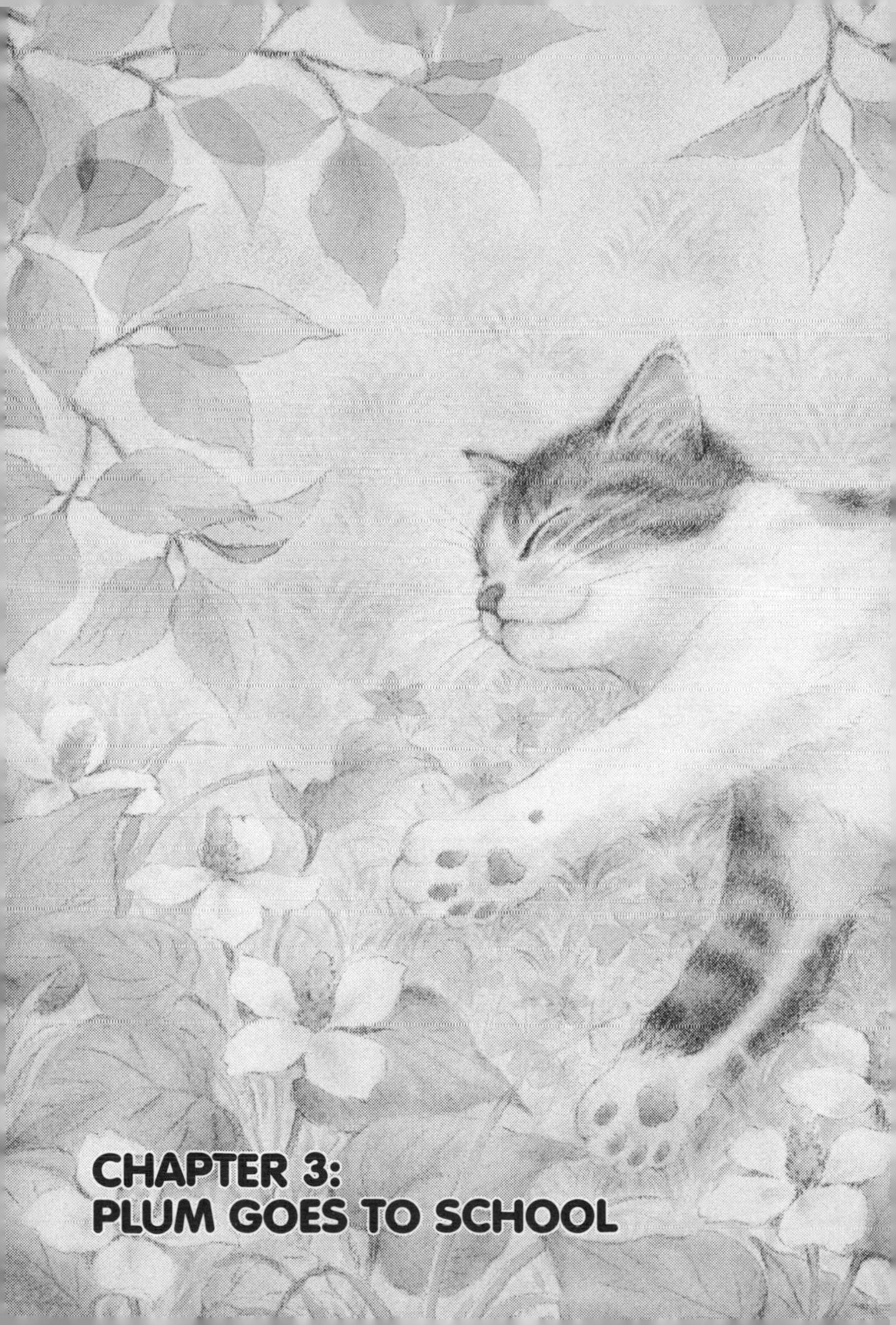

CHAPTER 3: PLUM GOES TO SCHOOL

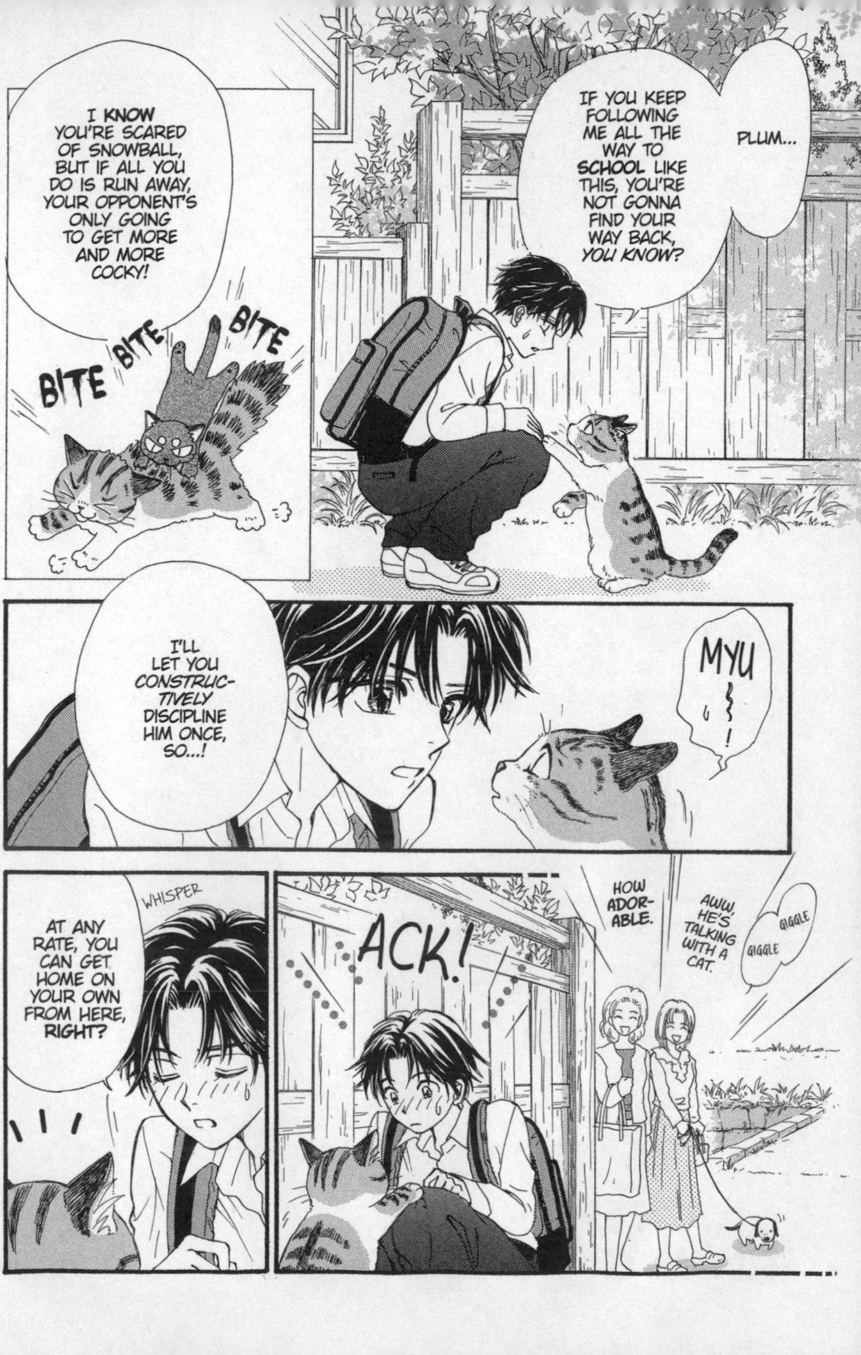
PLUM...
IF YOU KEEP FOLLOWING ME ALL THE WAY TO SCHOOL LIKE THIS, YOU'RE NOT GONNA FIND YOUR WAY BACK, YOU KNOW?
I KNOW YOU'RE SCARED OF SNOWBALL, BUT IF ALL YOU DO IS RUN AWAY, YOUR OPPONENT'S ONLY GOING TO GET MORE AND MORE COCKY!
BITE BITE BITE
MYU...!
I'LL LET YOU CONSTRUCTIVELY DISCIPLINE HIM ONCE, SO...!
GIGGLE
GIGGLE
AWW, HE'S TALKING WITH A CAT.
HOW ADORABLE.
ACK!
WHISPER
AT ANY RATE, YOU CAN GET HOME ON YOUR OWN FROM HERE, RIGHT?

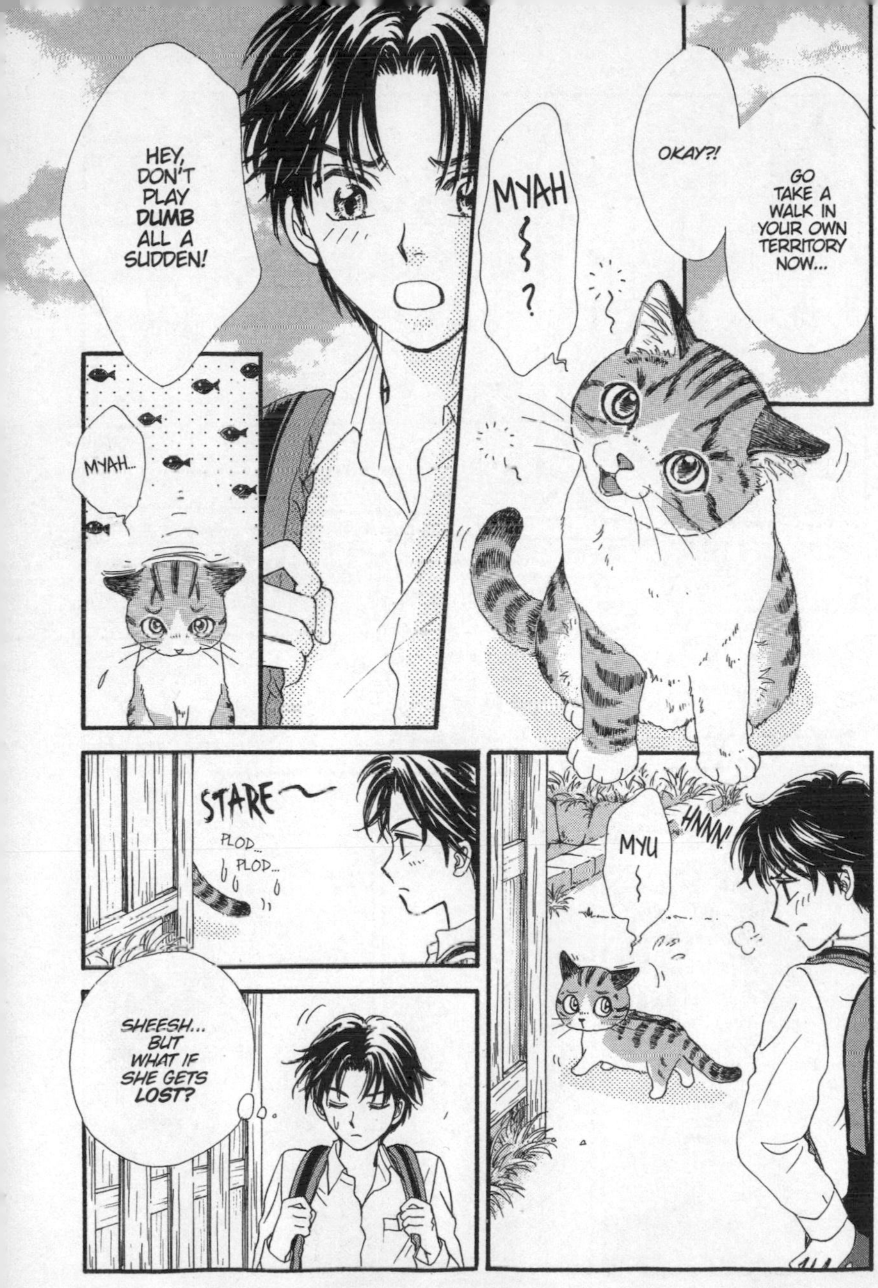
GO TAKE A WALK IN YOUR OWN TERRITORY NOW...
OKAY?!
MYAH ~?
HEY, DON'T PLAY DUMB ALL A SUDDEN!
MYAH...
HNNN!
MYU ~
STARE ~
PLOD... PLOD...
SHEESH... BUT WHAT IF SHE GETS LOST?

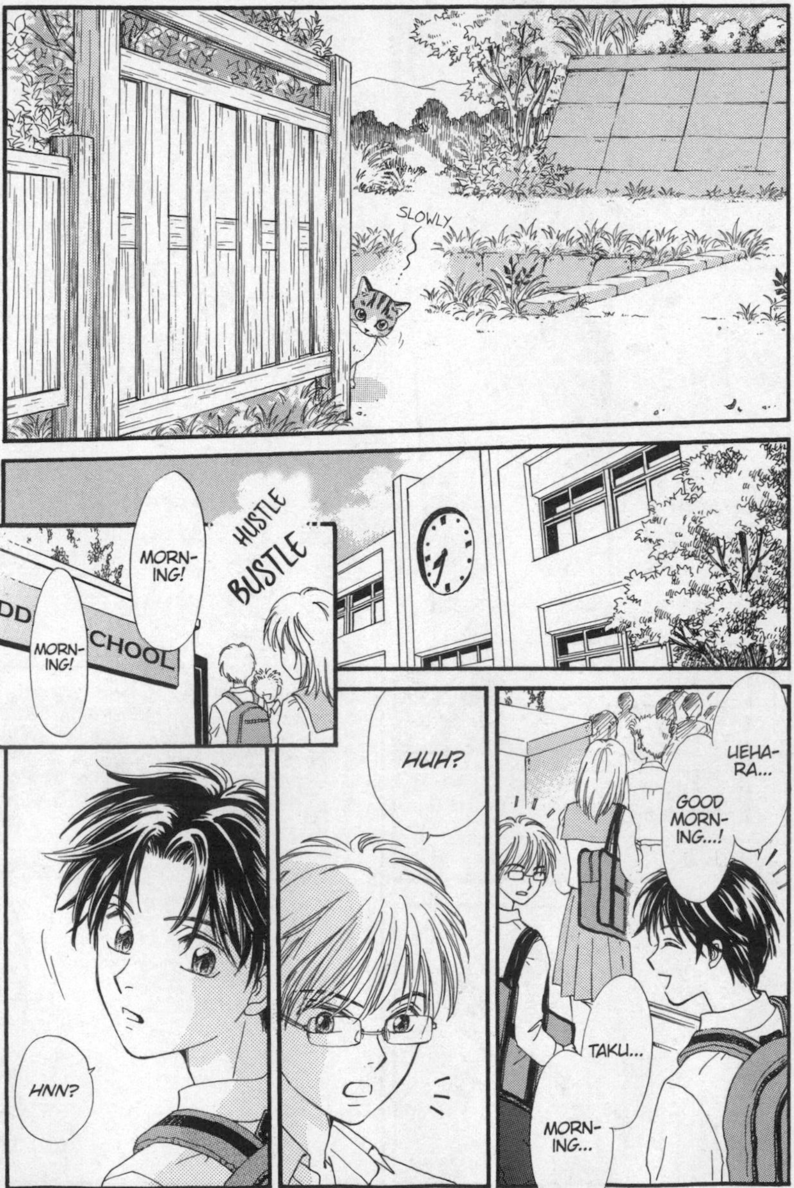
SLOWLY
HUSTLE BUSTLE
MORNING!
MIDD CHOOL
MORNING!
UEHARA...
GOOD MORNING...!
TAKU...
MORNING...
HUH?
HNN?

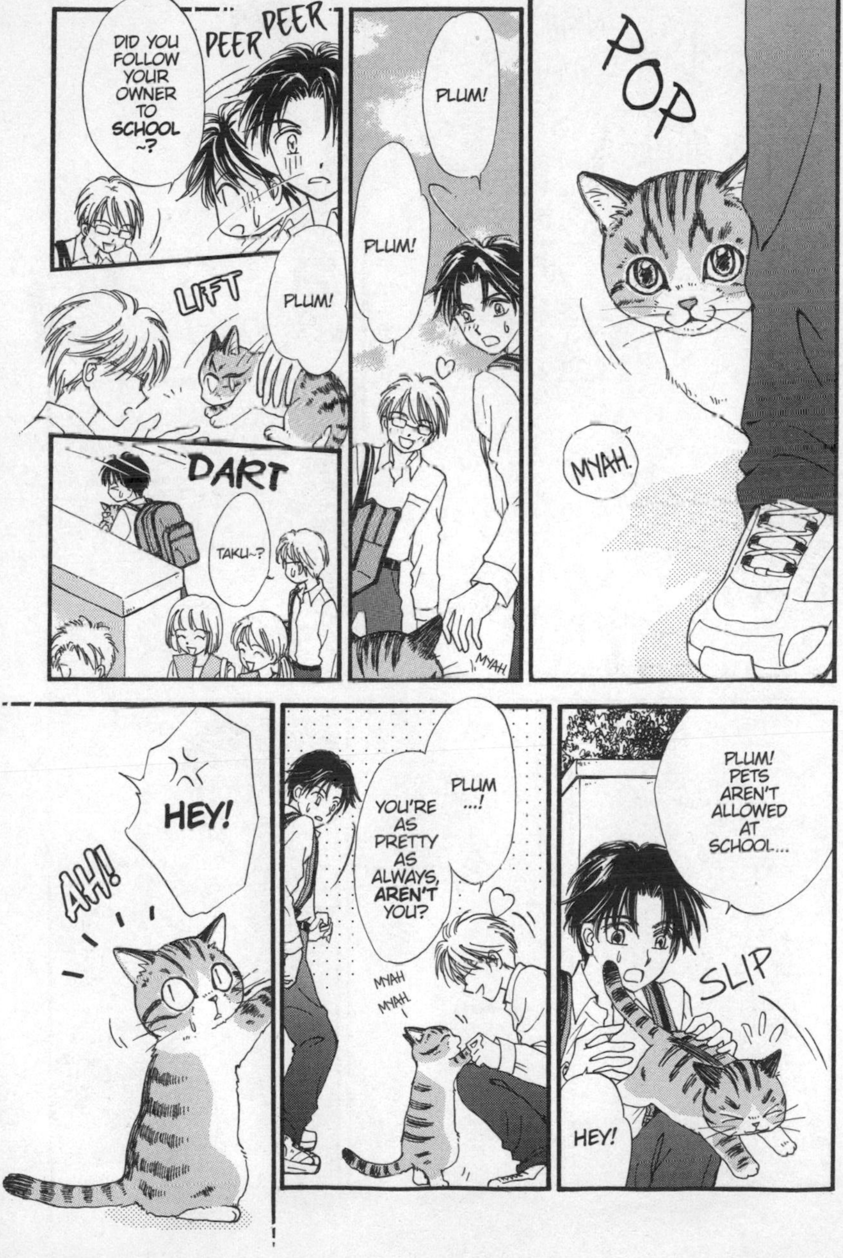
POP
MYAH.
PLUM!
PLUM!
MYAH
PEER PEER
DID YOU FOLLOW YOUR OWNER TO SCHOOL ~?
LIFT
PLUM!
DART
TAKU~?
PLUM! PETS AREN'T ALLOWED AT SCHOOL...
SLIP
HEY!
PLUM ...!
YOU'RE AS PRETTY AS ALWAYS, AREN'T YOU?
MYAH MYAH
HEY!
AH!

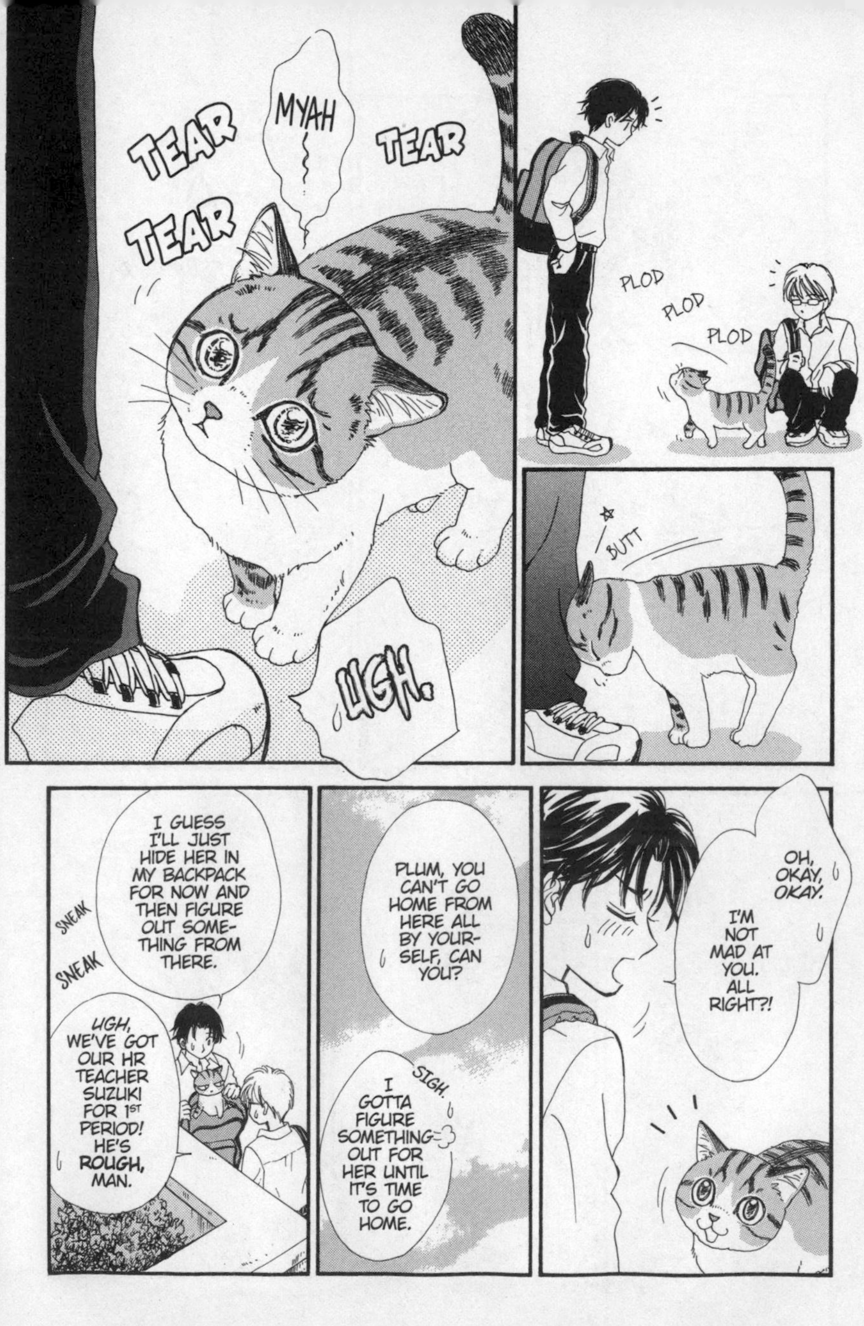
PLOD
PLOD
PLOD
BUTT
TEAR
MYAH
TEAR
TEAR
UGH.
OH, OKAY, OKAY.
I'M NOT MAD AT YOU. ALL RIGHT?!
PLUM, YOU CAN'T GO HOME FROM HERE ALL BY YOURSELF, CAN YOU?
SIGH.
I GOTTA FIGURE SOMETHING OUT FOR HER UNTIL IT'S TIME TO GO HOME.
I GUESS I'LL JUST HIDE HER IN MY BACKPACK FOR NOW AND THEN FIGURE OUT SOMETHING FROM THERE.
SNEAK
SNEAK
UGH, WE'VE GOT OUR HR TEACHER SUZUKI FOR 1ST PERIOD! HE'S ROUGH, MAN.

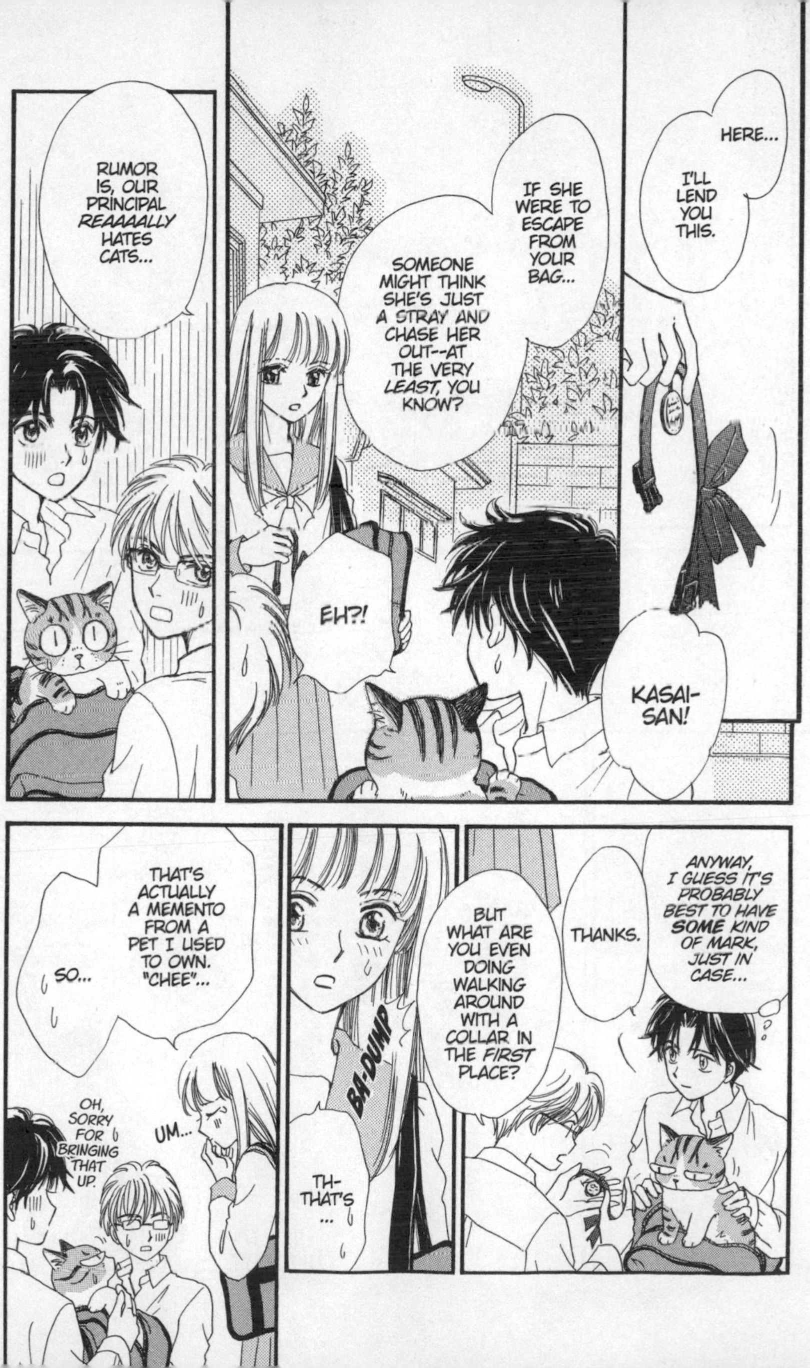
HERE...
I'LL LEND YOU THIS.
KASAI-SAN!
IF SHE WERE TO ESCAPE FROM YOUR BAG...
SOMEONE MIGHT THINK SHE'S JUST A STRAY AND CHASE HER OUT--AT THE VERY *LEAST*, YOU KNOW?
EH?!
RUMOR IS, OUR PRINCIPAL *REAAAALLY* HATES CATS...
ANYWAY, I GUESS IT'S PROBABLY BEST TO HAVE **SOME** KIND OF MARK, JUST IN CASE...
THANKS.
BUT WHAT ARE YOU EVEN DOING WALKING AROUND WITH A COLLAR IN THE *FIRST* PLACE?
BA-DUMP
TH-THAT'S...
THAT'S ACTUALLY A MEMENTO FROM A PET I USED TO OWN. "CHEE"...
SO...
UM...
OH, SORRY FOR BRINGING THAT UP.

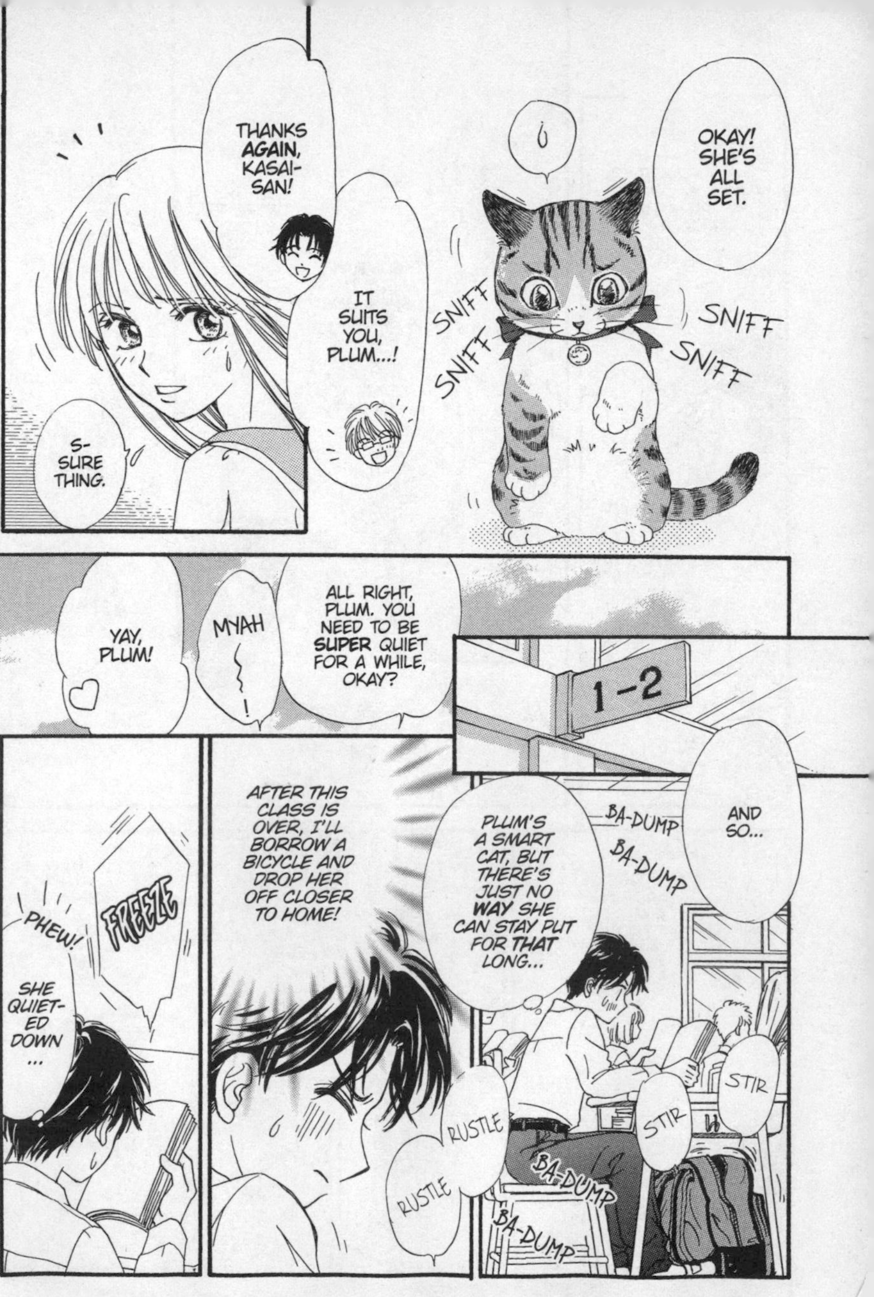
OKAY! SHE'S ALL SET.
SNIFF
SNIFF
SNIFF
SNIFF
THANKS AGAIN, KASAI-SAN!
IT SUITS YOU, PLUM...!
S-SURE THING.
1-2
ALL RIGHT, PLUM. YOU NEED TO BE SUPER QUIET FOR A WHILE, OKAY?
MYAH
!
YAY, PLUM!
AND SO...
BA-DUMP
BA-DUMP
PLUM'S A SMART CAT, BUT THERE'S JUST NO WAY SHE CAN STAY PUT FOR THAT LONG...
STIR
STIR
RUSTLE
RUSTLE
BA-DUMP
BA-DUMP
AFTER THIS CLASS IS OVER, I'LL BORROW A BICYCLE AND DROP HER OFF CLOSER TO HOME!
FREEZE
PHEW!
SHE QUIET-ED DOWN ...

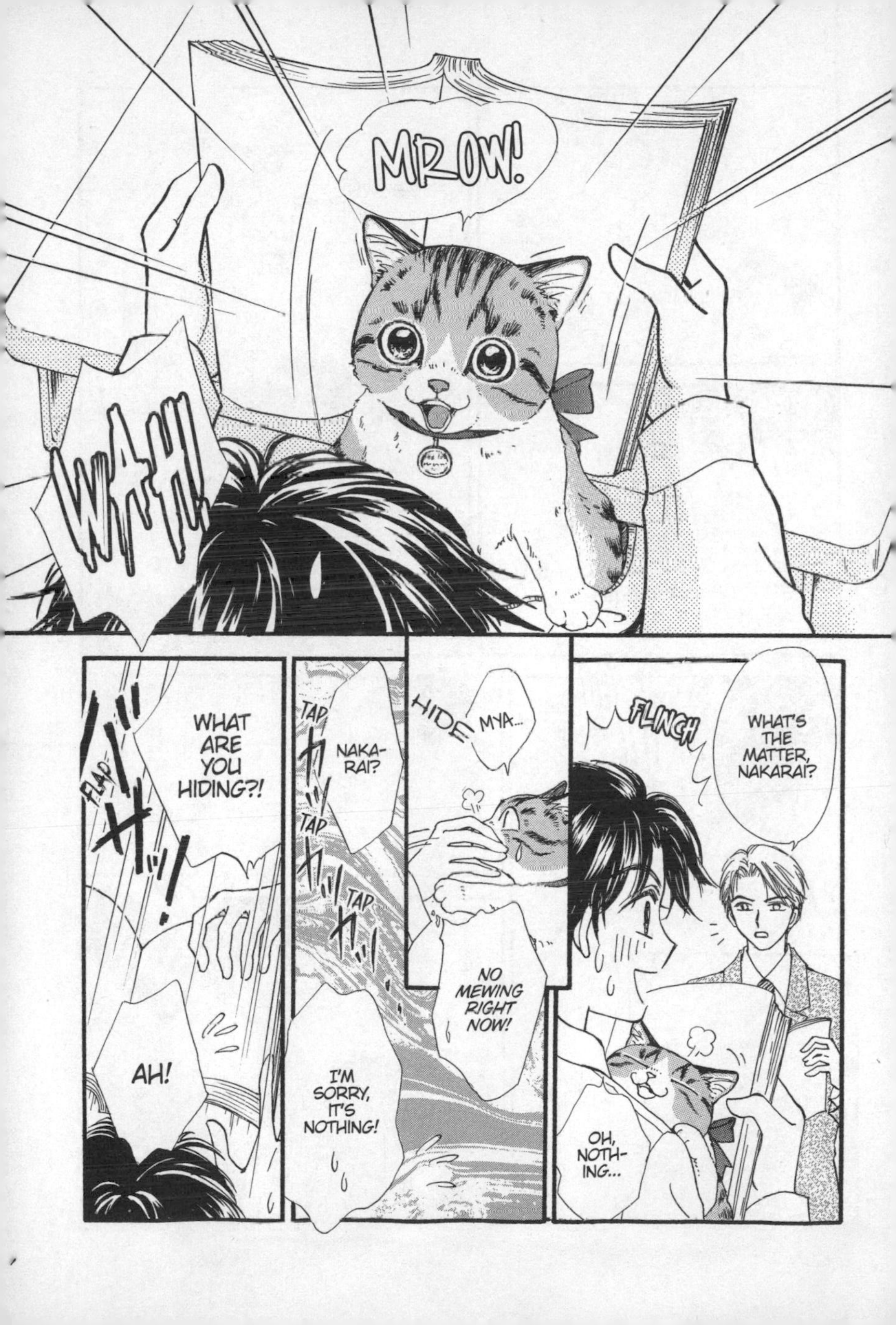
MROW!
WAH!
FLINCH
WHAT'S THE MATTER, NAKARAI?
OH, NOTHING...
HIDE
MYA...
NO MEWING RIGHT NOW!
TAP TAP TAP
NAKA-RAI?
I'M SORRY, IT'S NOTHING!
WHAT ARE YOU HIDING?!
FLAP
AH!

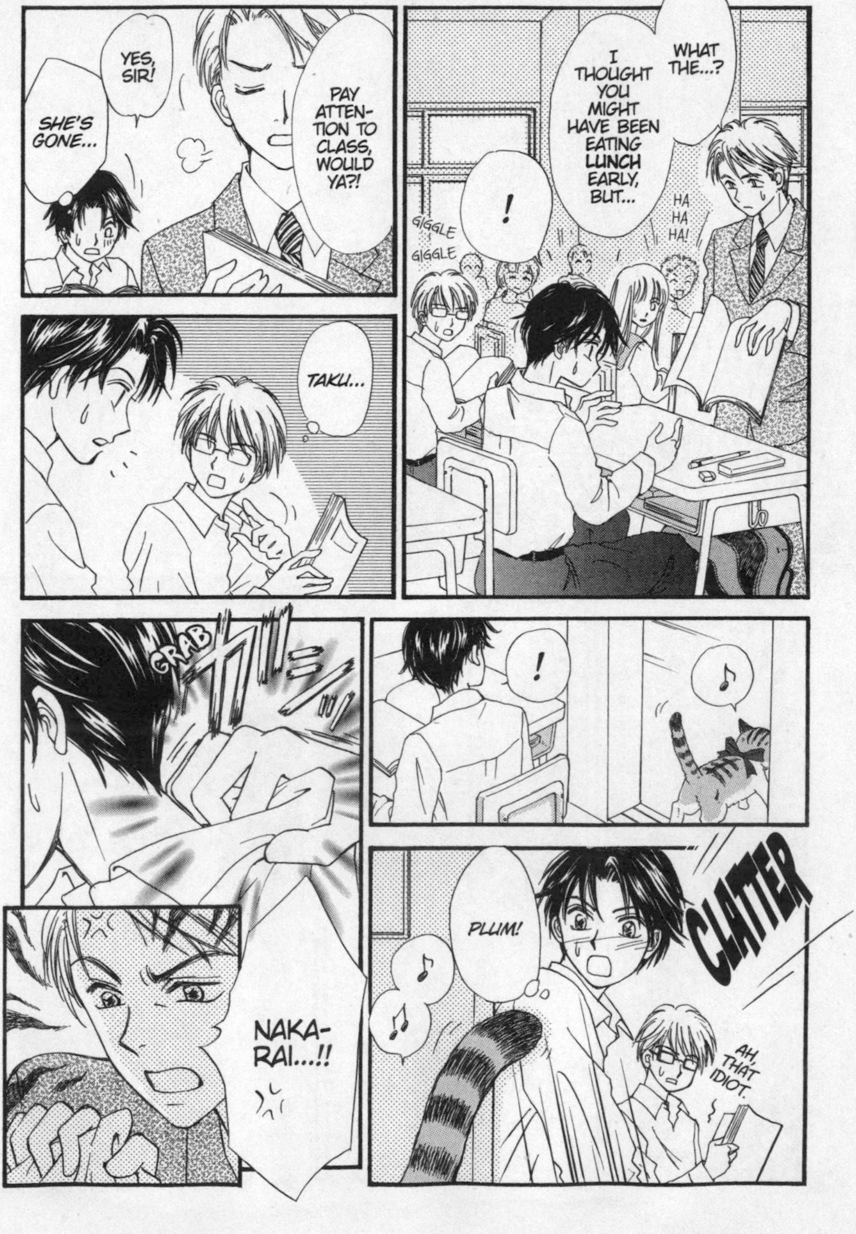
WHAT THE...?
I THOUGHT YOU MIGHT HAVE BEEN EATING LUNCH EARLY, BUT...
HA HA HA!
!
GIGGLE GIGGLE
PAY ATTENTION TO CLASS, WOULD YA?!
YES, SIR!
SHE'S GONE...
TAKU...
!
♪
PLUM!
♪
♪
CLATTER
AH, THAT IDIOT.
GRAB
NAKA-RAI...!!

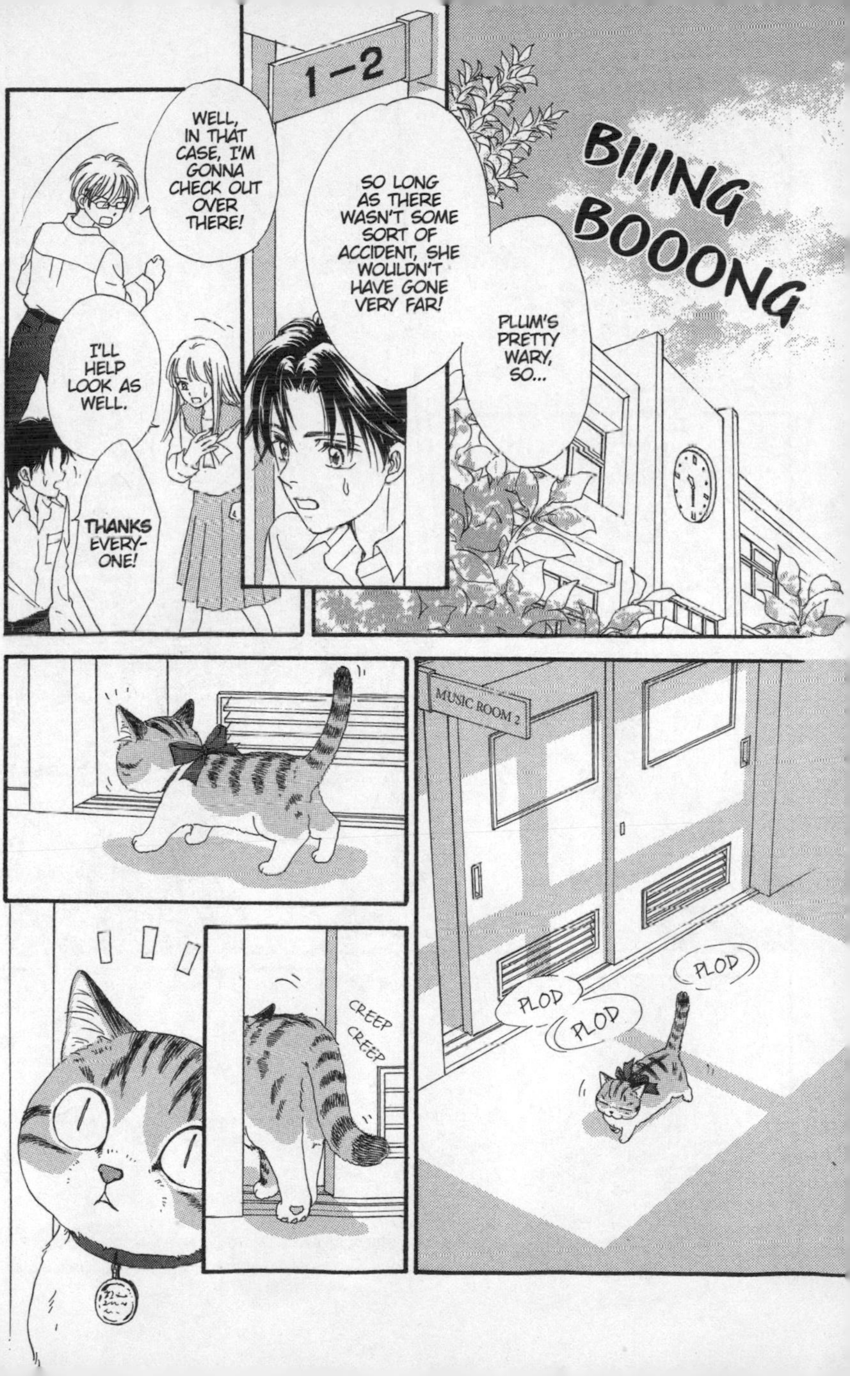
BIIING BOOONG
SO LONG AS THERE WASN'T SOME SORT OF ACCIDENT, SHE WOULDN'T HAVE GONE VERY FAR!
PLUM'S PRETTY WARY, SO...
1-2
WELL, IN THAT CASE, I'M GONNA CHECK OUT OVER THERE!
I'LL HELP LOOK AS WELL.
THANKS EVERY-ONE!
MUSIC ROOM 2
PLOD
PLOD
PLOD
CREEP CREEP

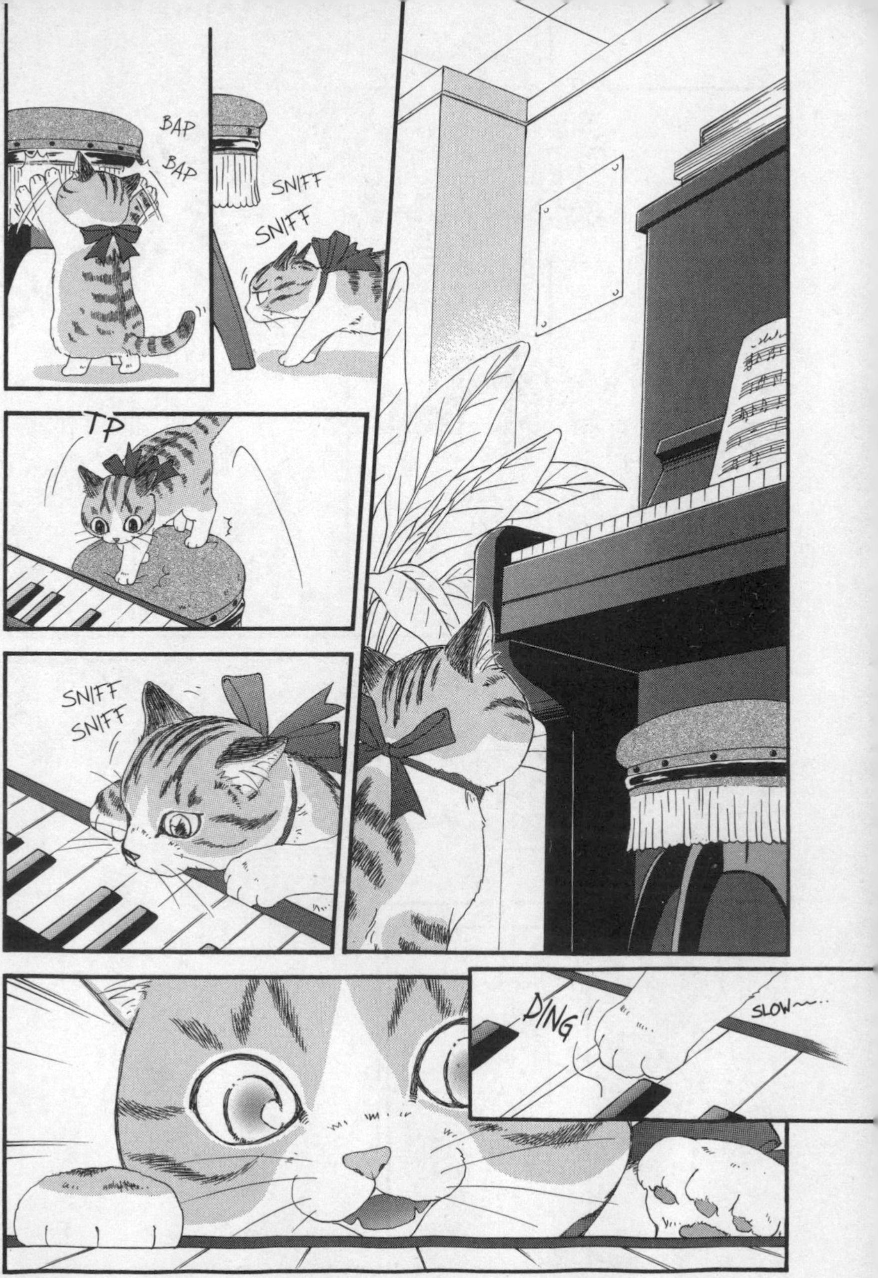
SNIFF
SNIFF
BAP
BAP
TP
SNIFF
SNIFF
SLOW~~...
DING

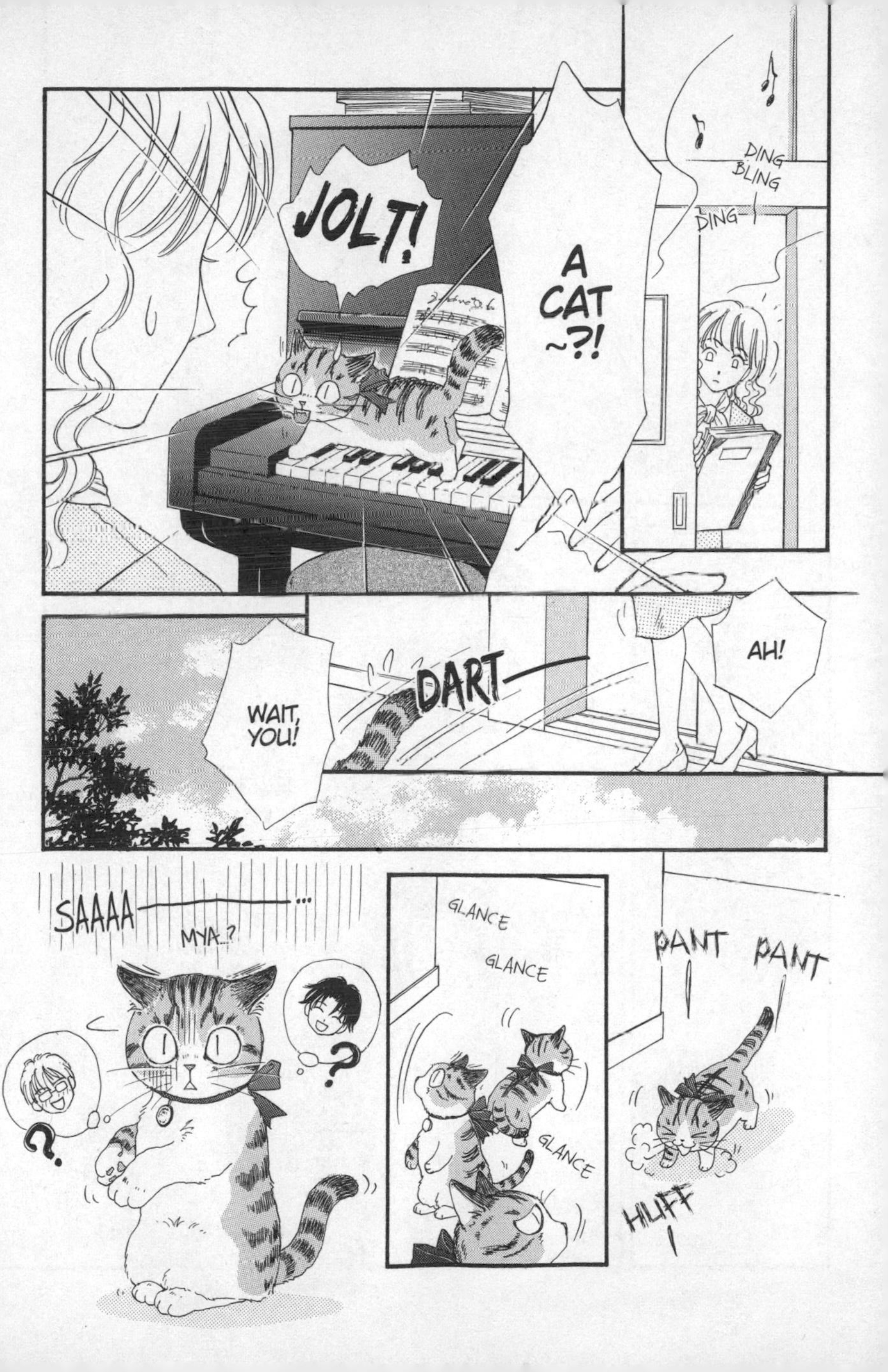
DING BLING
DING
A CAT ~?!
JOLT!
AH!
DART
WAIT, YOU!
PANT PANT
HUFF
GLANCE
GLANCE
GLANCE
SAAAA…
MYA..?
?
?

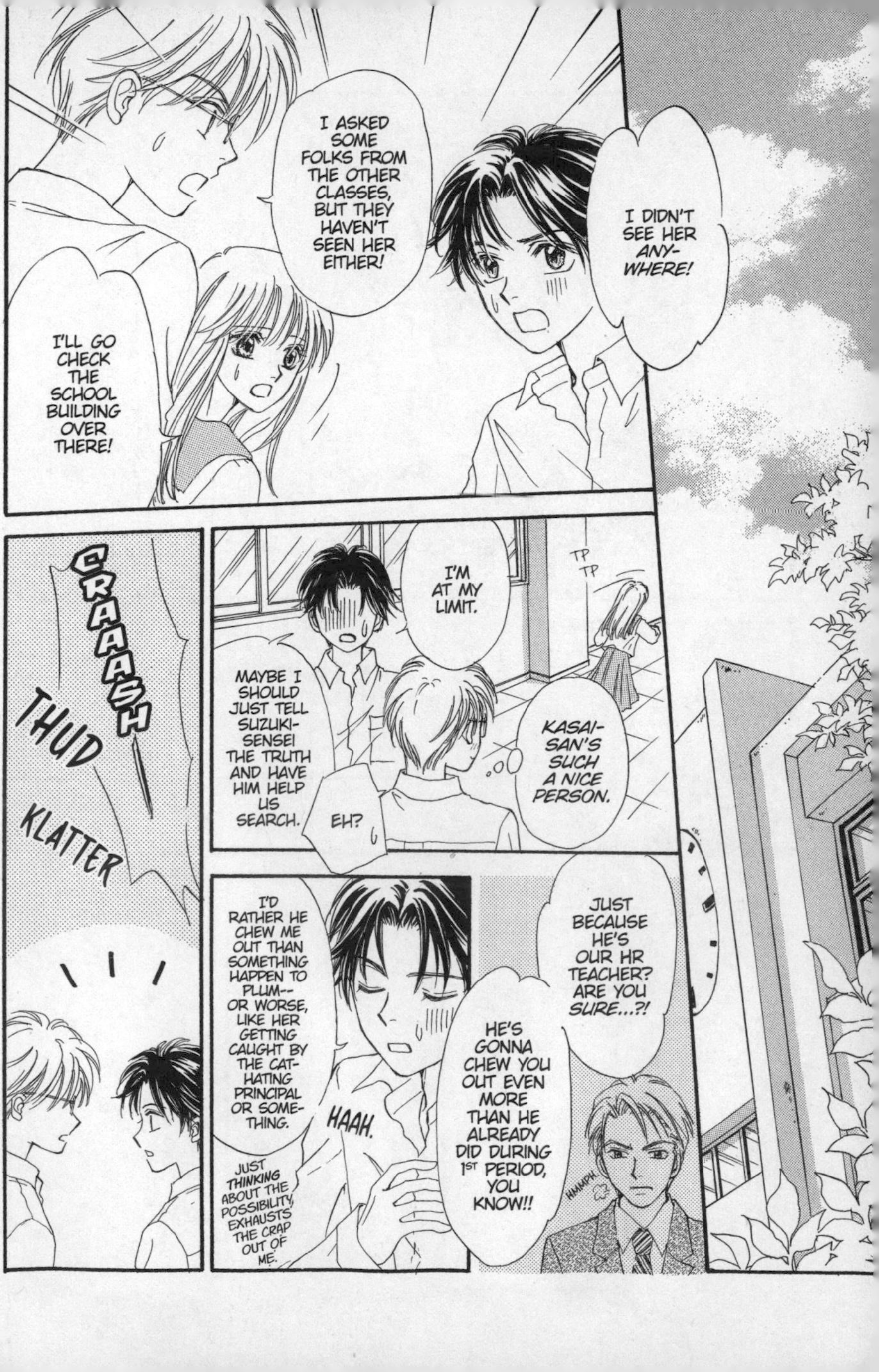
I DIDN'T SEE HER ANY-WHERE!
I ASKED SOME FOLKS FROM THE OTHER CLASSES, BUT THEY HAVEN'T SEEN HER EITHER!
I'LL GO CHECK THE SCHOOL BUILDING OVER THERE!
TP TP
I'M AT MY LIMIT.
KASAI-SAN'S SUCH A NICE PERSON.
MAYBE I SHOULD JUST TELL SUZUKI-SENSEI THE TRUTH AND HAVE HIM HELP US SEARCH.
EH?
JUST BECAUSE HE'S OUR HR TEACHER? ARE YOU SURE...?!
HE'S GONNA CHEW YOU OUT EVEN MORE THAN HE ALREADY DID DURING 1ST PERIOD, YOU KNOW!!
HMMPH.
I'D RATHER HE CHEW ME OUT THAN SOMETHING HAPPEN TO PLUM-- OR WORSE, LIKE HER GETTING CAUGHT BY THE CAT-HATING PRINCIPAL OR SOME-THING.
HAAH.
JUST THINKING ABOUT THE POSSIBILITY EXHAUSTS THE CRAP OUT OF ME.
CRAAASH
THUD
KLATTER

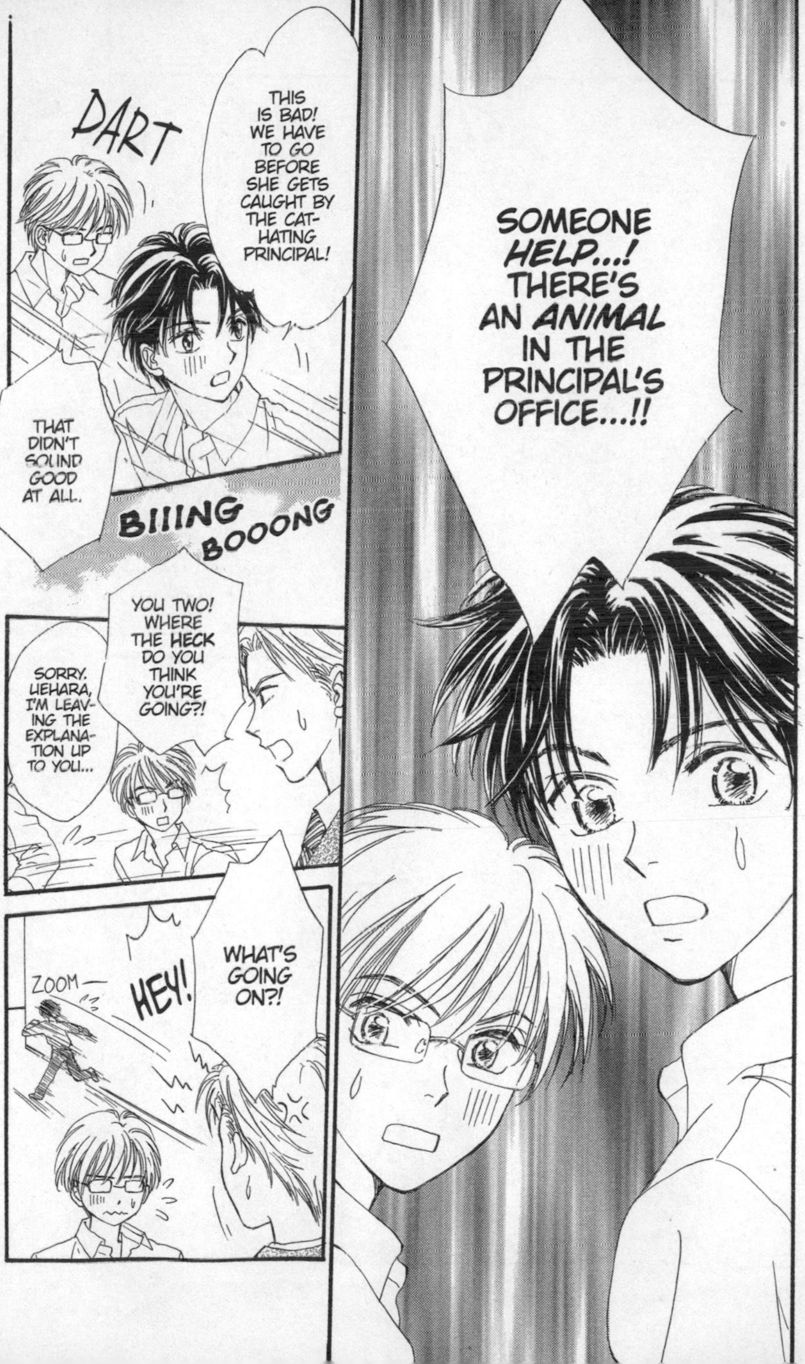
SOMEONE *HELP*...! THERE'S AN *ANIMAL* IN THE PRINCIPAL'S OFFICE...!!
THIS IS BAD! WE HAVE TO GO BEFORE SHE GETS CAUGHT BY THE CAT-HATING PRINCIPAL!
DART
THAT DIDN'T SOUND GOOD AT ALL.
BIIING BOOONG
YOU TWO! WHERE THE HECK DO YOU THINK YOU'RE GOING?!
SORRY. UEHARA, I'M LEAVING THE EXPLANATION UP TO YOU...
HEY!
WHAT'S GOING ON?!
ZOOM

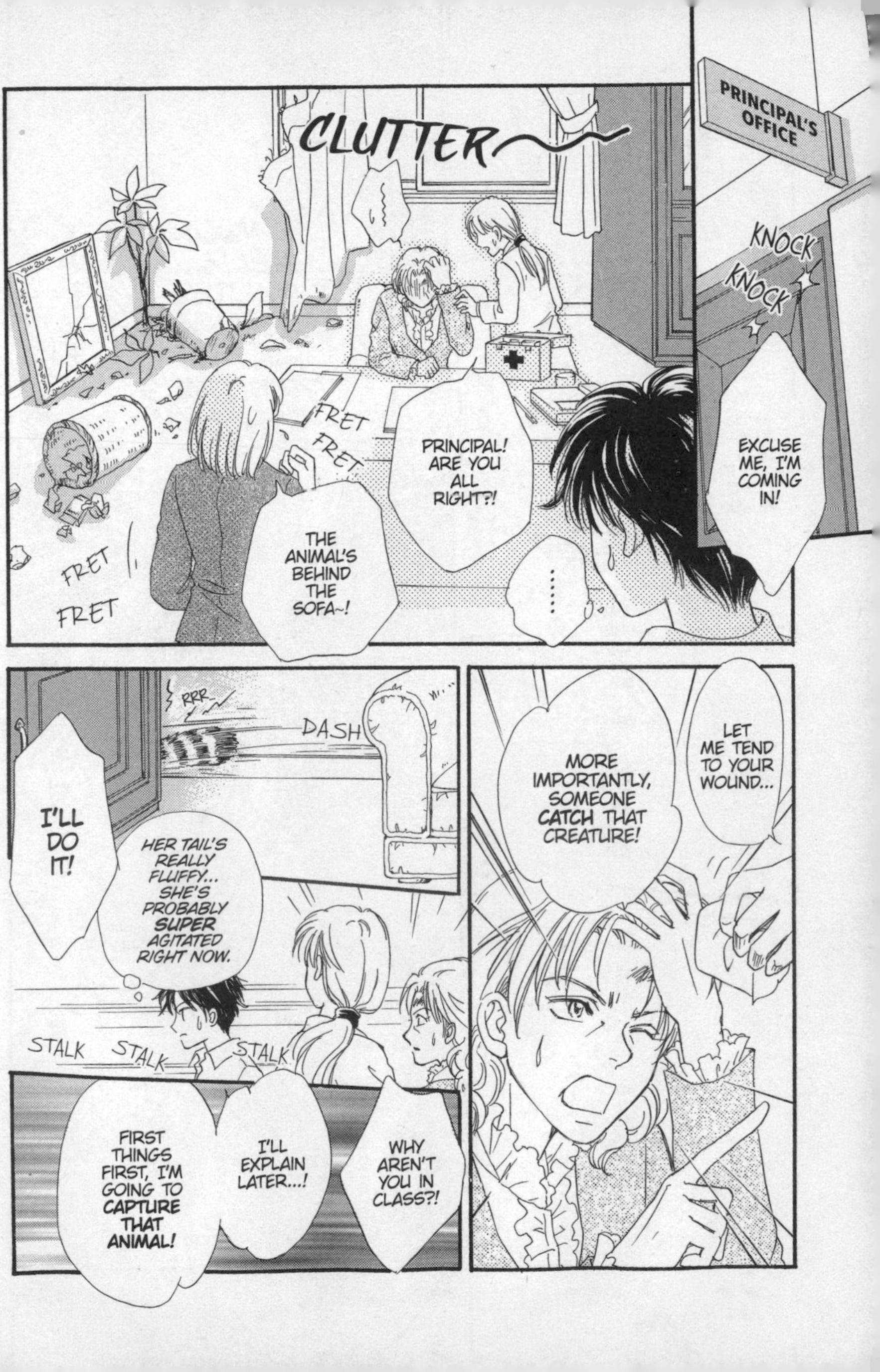
PRINCIPAL'S OFFICE
KNOCK KNOCK
EXCUSE ME, I'M COMING IN!
CLUTTER
PRINCIPAL! ARE YOU ALL RIGHT?!
......
THE ANIMAL'S BEHIND THE SOFA~!
FRET FRET
FRET FRET
LET ME TEND TO YOUR WOUND...
MORE IMPORTANTLY, SOMEONE CATCH THAT CREATURE!
RRR
DASH
I'LL DO IT!
HER TAIL'S REALLY FLUFFY... SHE'S PROBABLY SUPER AGITATED RIGHT NOW.
STALK STALK STALK
WHY AREN'T YOU IN CLASS?!
I'LL EXPLAIN LATER...!
FIRST THINGS FIRST, I'M GOING TO CAPTURE THAT ANIMAL!

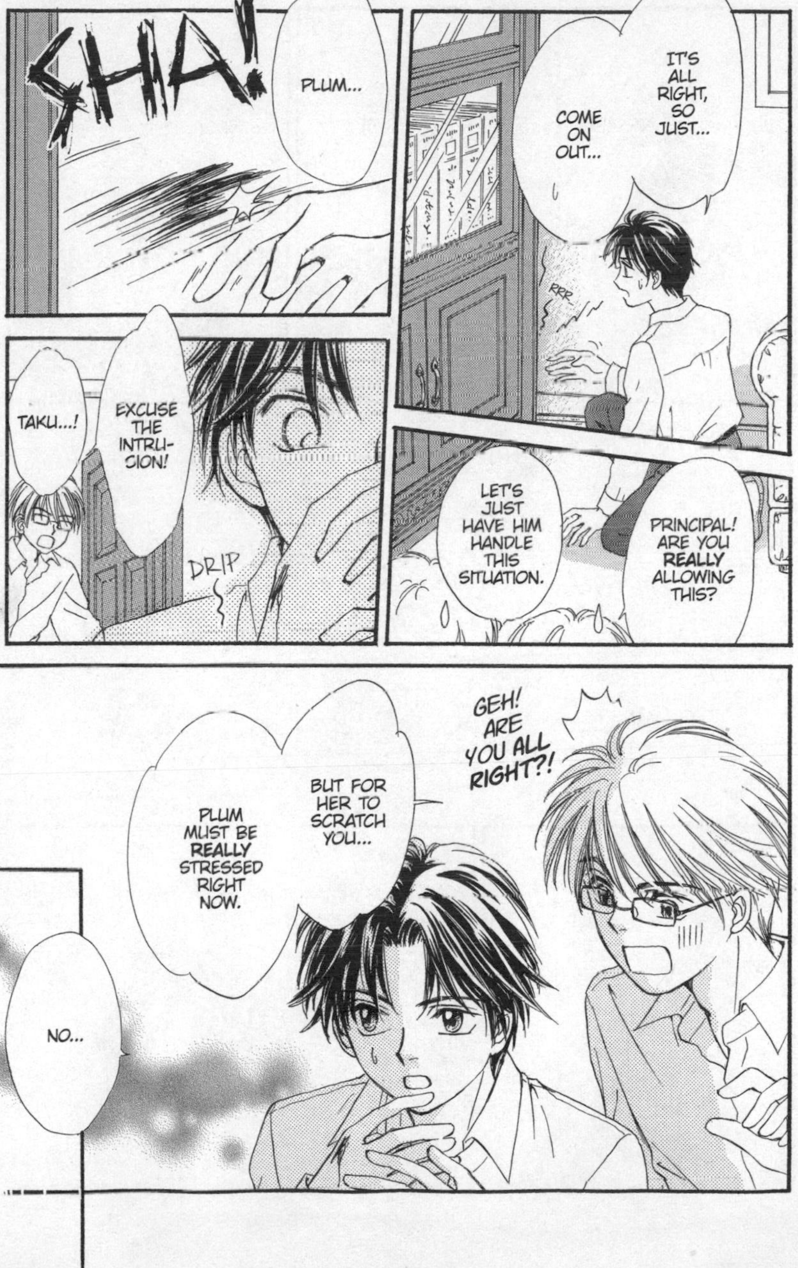
IT'S ALL RIGHT, SO JUST...
COME ON OUT...
SHA!
PLUM...
RRR
PRINCIPAL! ARE YOU REALLY ALLOWING THIS?
LET'S JUST HAVE HIM HANDLE THIS SITUATION.
EXCUSE THE INTRU-SION!
TAKU...!
DRIP
GEH! ARE YOU ALL RIGHT?!
BUT FOR HER TO SCRATCH YOU...
PLUM MUST BE REALLY STRESSED RIGHT NOW.
NO...

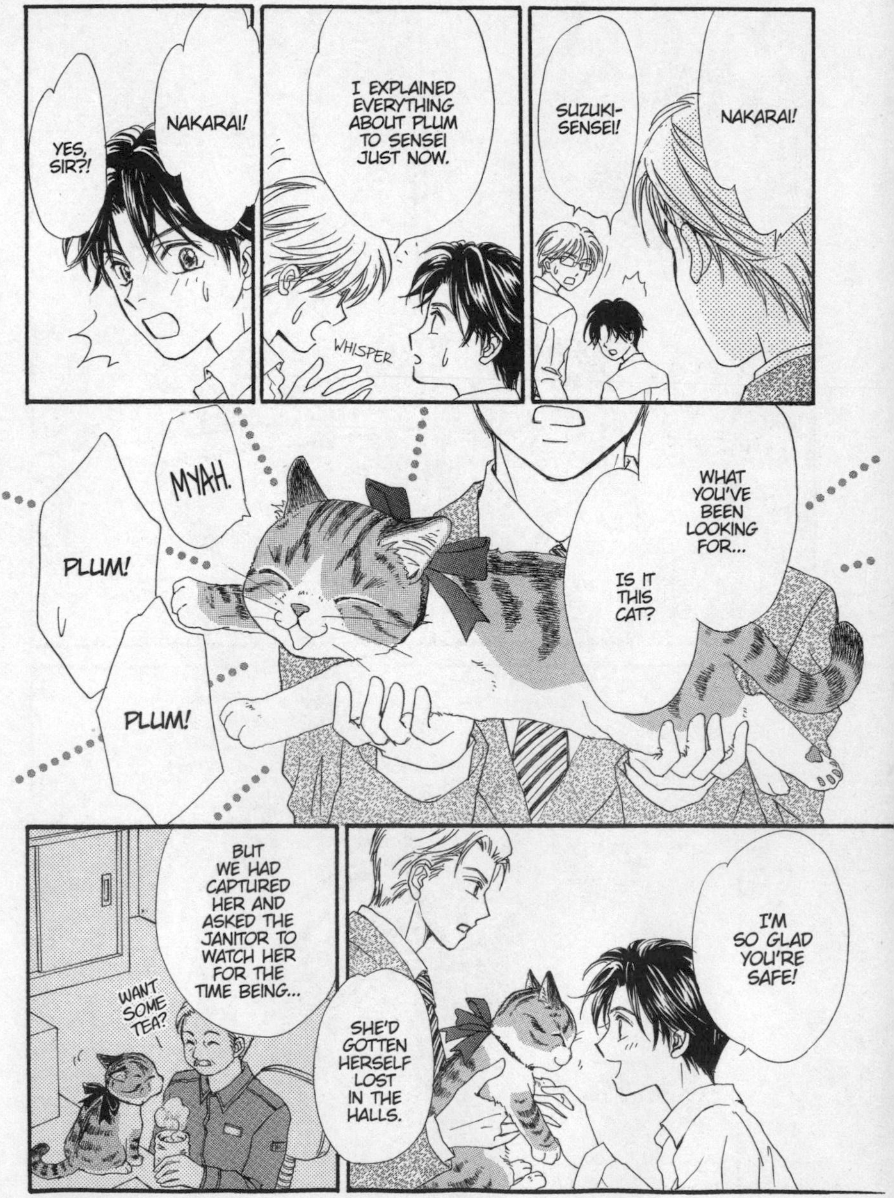
NAKARAI!
SUZUKI-SENSEI!
I EXPLAINED EVERYTHING ABOUT PLUM TO SENSEI JUST NOW.
WHISPER
NAKARAI!
YES, SIR?!
WHAT YOU'VE BEEN LOOKING FOR...
IS IT THIS CAT?
MYAH.
PLUM!
PLUM!
I'M SO GLAD YOU'RE SAFE!
SHE'D GOTTEN HERSELF LOST IN THE HALLS.
BUT WE HAD CAPTURED HER AND ASKED THE JANITOR TO WATCH HER FOR THE TIME BEING...
WANT SOME TEA?

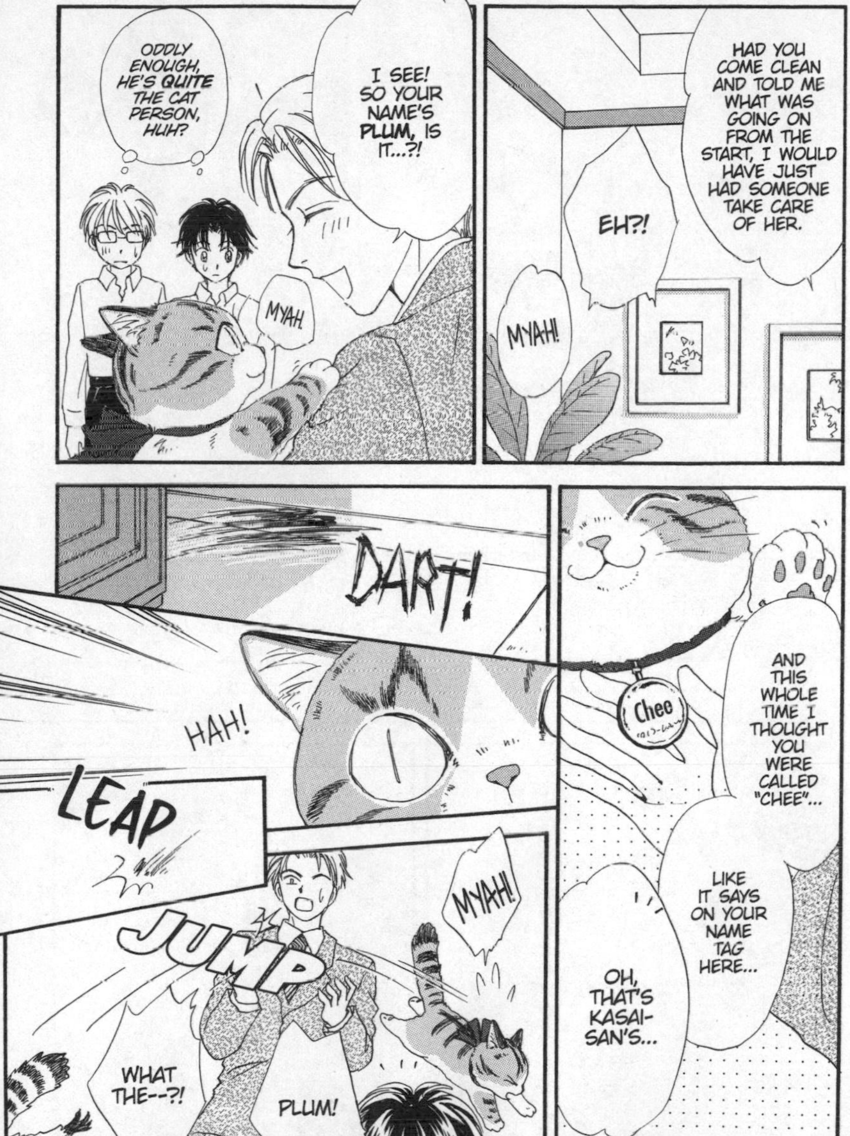
HAD YOU COME CLEAN AND TOLD ME WHAT WAS GOING ON FROM THE START, I WOULD HAVE JUST HAD SOMEONE TAKE CARE OF HER.
EH?!
MYAH!
I SEE! SO YOUR NAME'S PLUM, IS IT...?!
ODDLY ENOUGH, HE'S QUITE THE CAT PERSON, HUH?
MYAH.
AND THIS WHOLE TIME I THOUGHT YOU WERE CALLED "CHEE"...
Chee
LIKE IT SAYS ON YOUR NAME TAG HERE...
OH, THAT'S KASAI-SAN'S...
DART!
HAH!
LEAP
MYAH!
JUMP
PLUM!
WHAT THE--?!

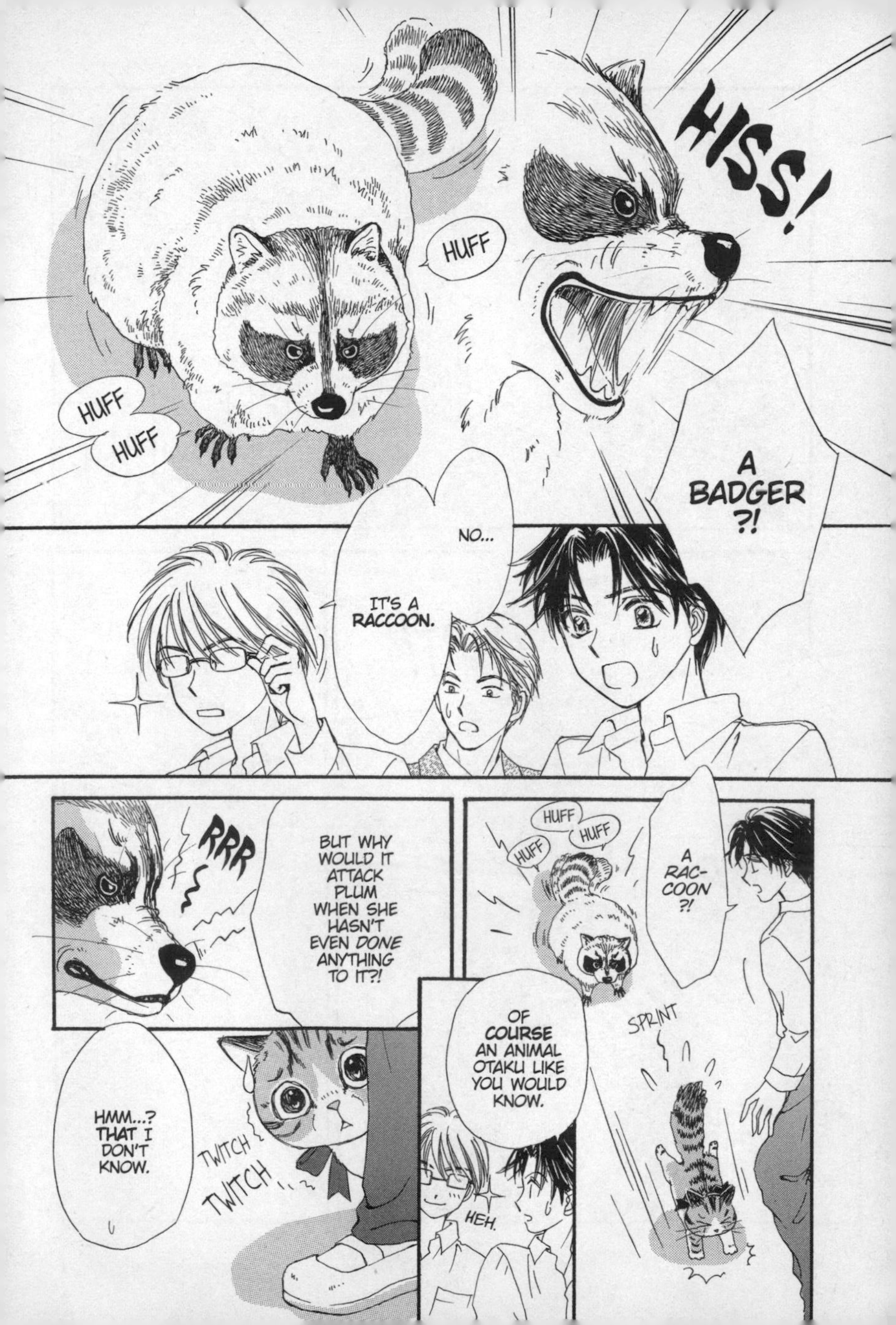
HISS!
HUFF
HUFF
HUFF
A BADGER ?!
NO...
IT'S A RACCOON.
A RAC-COON ?!
HUFF
HUFF
HUFF
SPRINT
RRR
BUT WHY WOULD IT ATTACK PLUM WHEN SHE HASN'T EVEN *DONE* ANYTHING TO IT?!
OF COURSE AN ANIMAL OTAKU LIKE YOU WOULD KNOW.
HEH.
TWITCH
TWITCH
HMM...? THAT I DON'T KNOW.

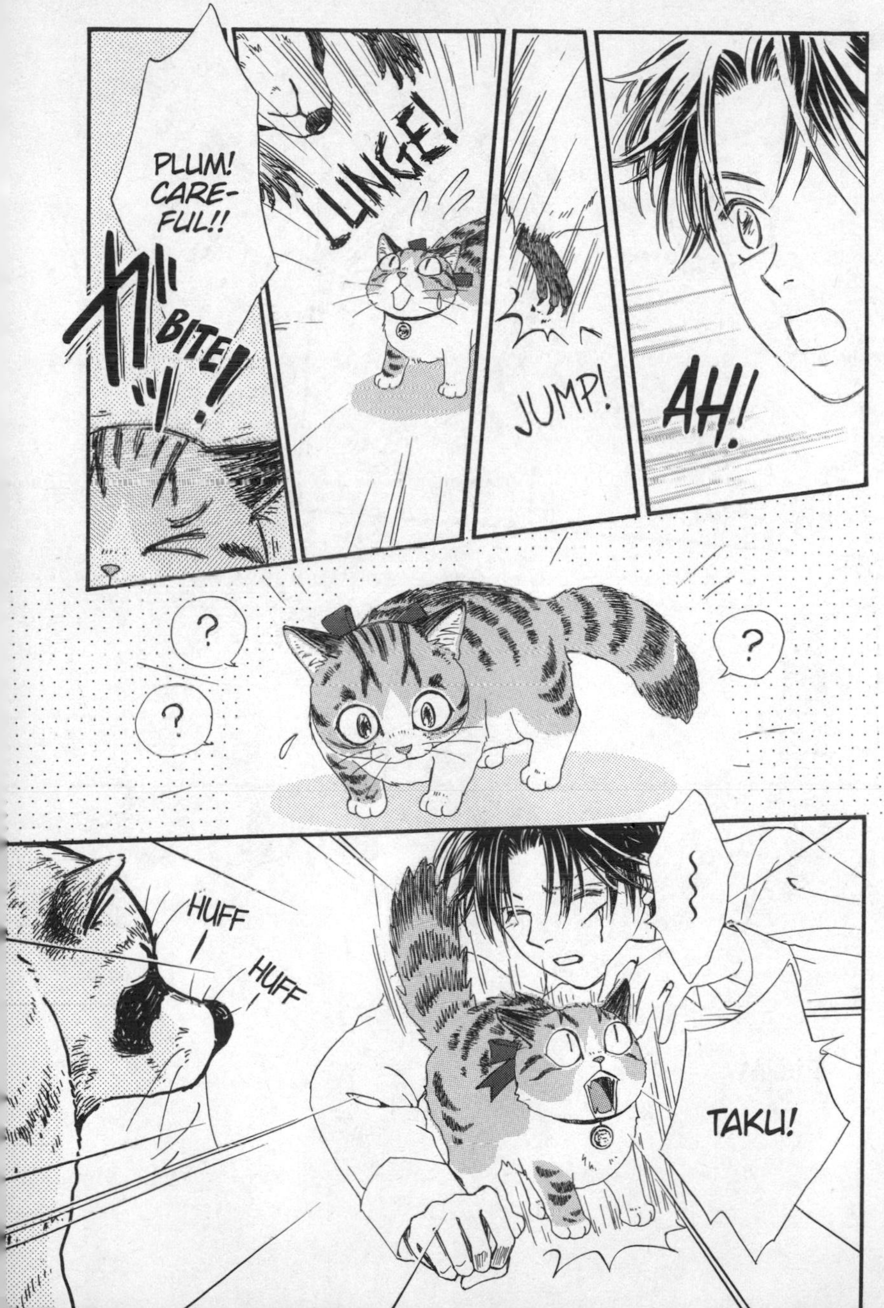
AH!
JUMP!
LUNGE!
PLUM! CARE-FUL!!
BITE!
?
?
?
TAKU!
HUFF HUFF

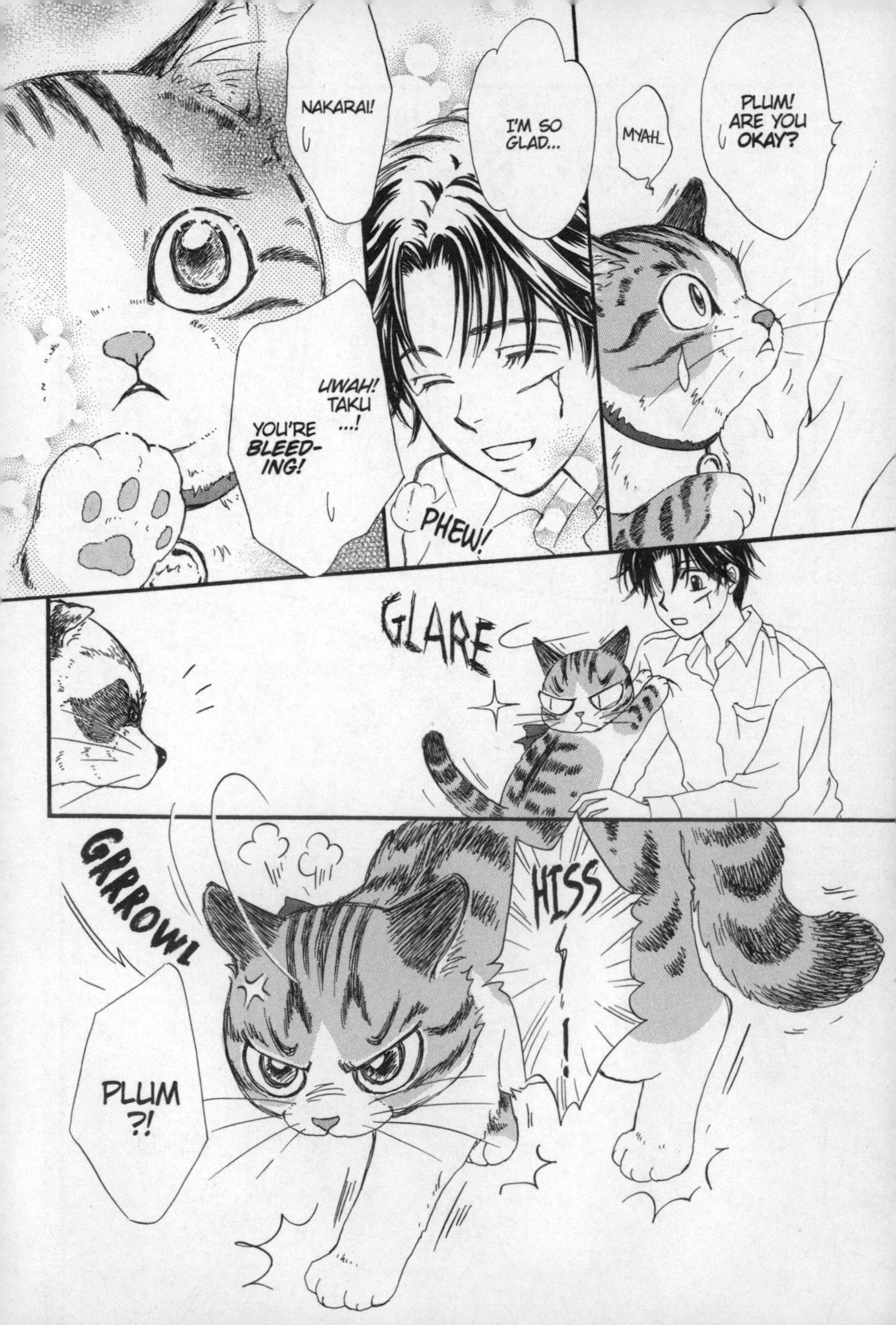
PLUM! ARE YOU OKAY?
MYAH.
I'M SO GLAD...
PHEW!
NAKARAI!
UWAH! TAKU ...!
YOU'RE BLEED-ING!
GLARE
HISS
GRRROWL
PLUM ?!

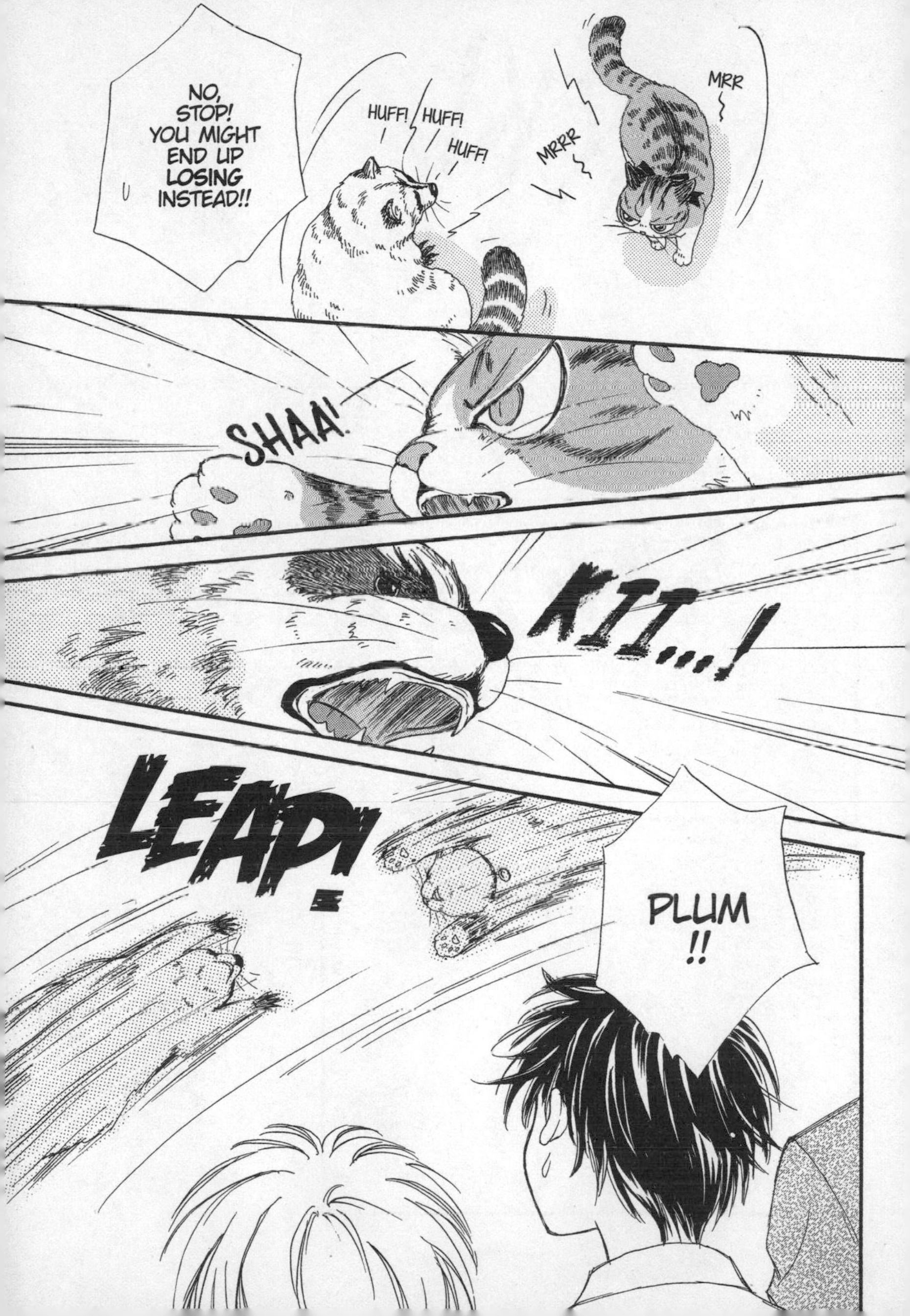
MRR
MRRR
HUFF! HUFF!
HUFF!
NO, STOP! YOU MIGHT END UP LOSING INSTEAD!!
SHAA!
KII...!
LEAP!
PLUM !!

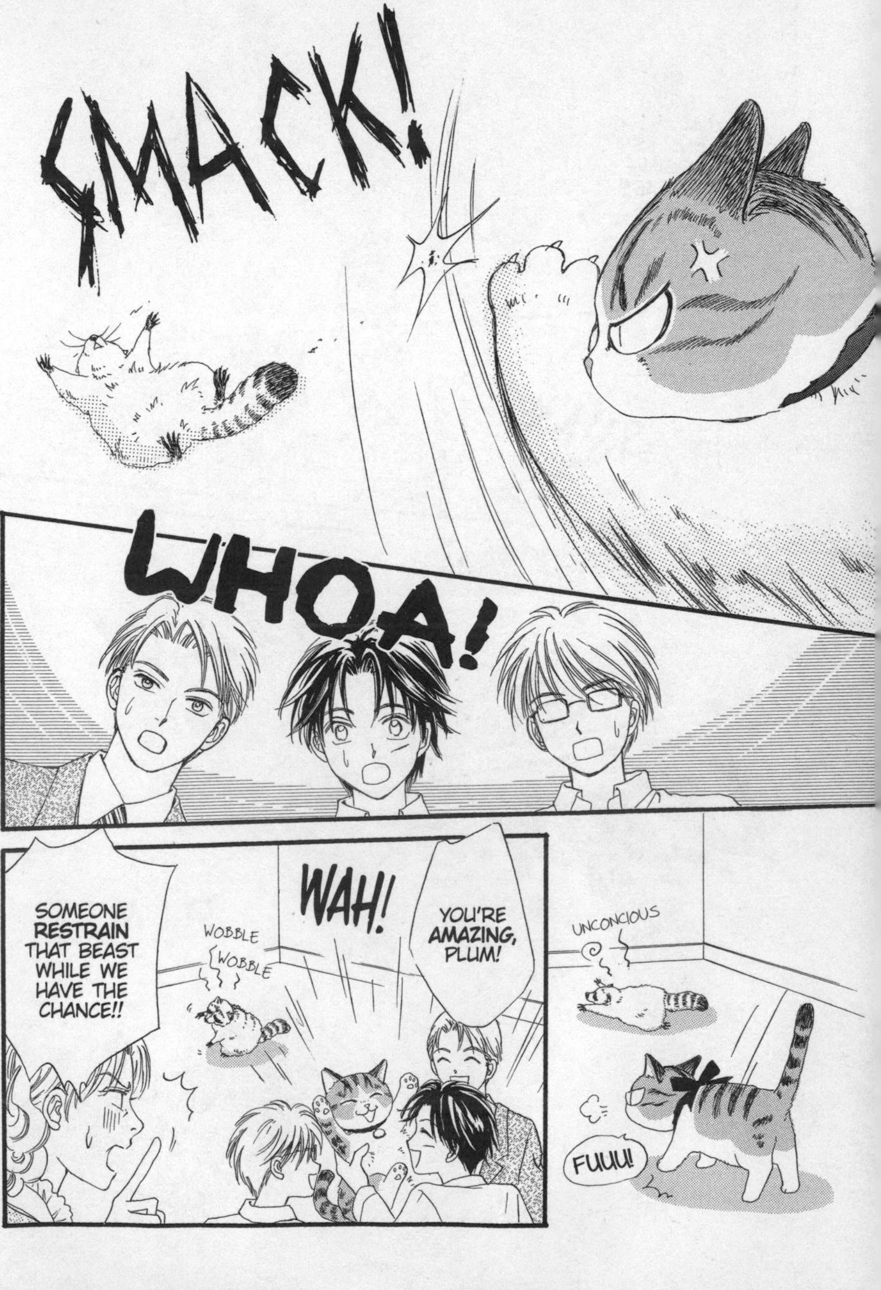
SMACK!
WHOA!
UNCONCIOUS
FUUU!
YOU'RE AMAZING, PLUM!
WAH!
WOBBLE WOBBLE
SOMEONE RESTRAIN THAT BEAST WHILE WE HAVE THE CHANCE!!

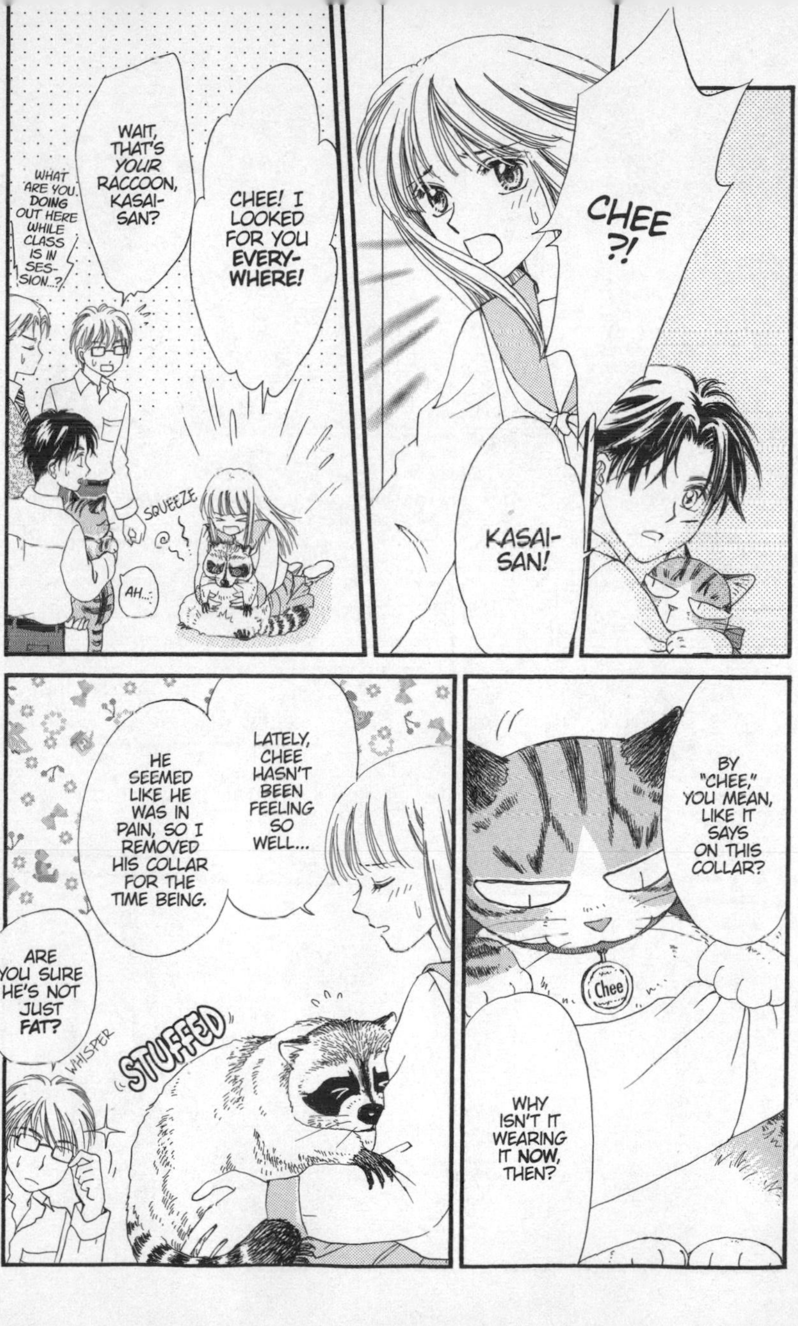
KASAI-SAN!
CHEE ?!
CHEE! I LOOKED FOR YOU EVERY-WHERE!
WAIT, THAT'S YOUR RACCOON, KASAI-SAN?
WHAT ARE YOU DOING OUT HERE WHILE CLASS IS IN SES-SION...?
SQUEEZE
AH...
BY "CHEE," YOU MEAN, LIKE IT SAYS ON THIS COLLAR?
Chee
WHY ISN'T IT WEARING IT NOW, THEN?
LATELY, CHEE HASN'T BEEN FEELING SO WELL...
HE SEEMED LIKE HE WAS IN PAIN, SO I REMOVED HIS COLLAR FOR THE TIME BEING.
STUFFED
ARE YOU SURE HE'S NOT JUST FAT?
WHISPER

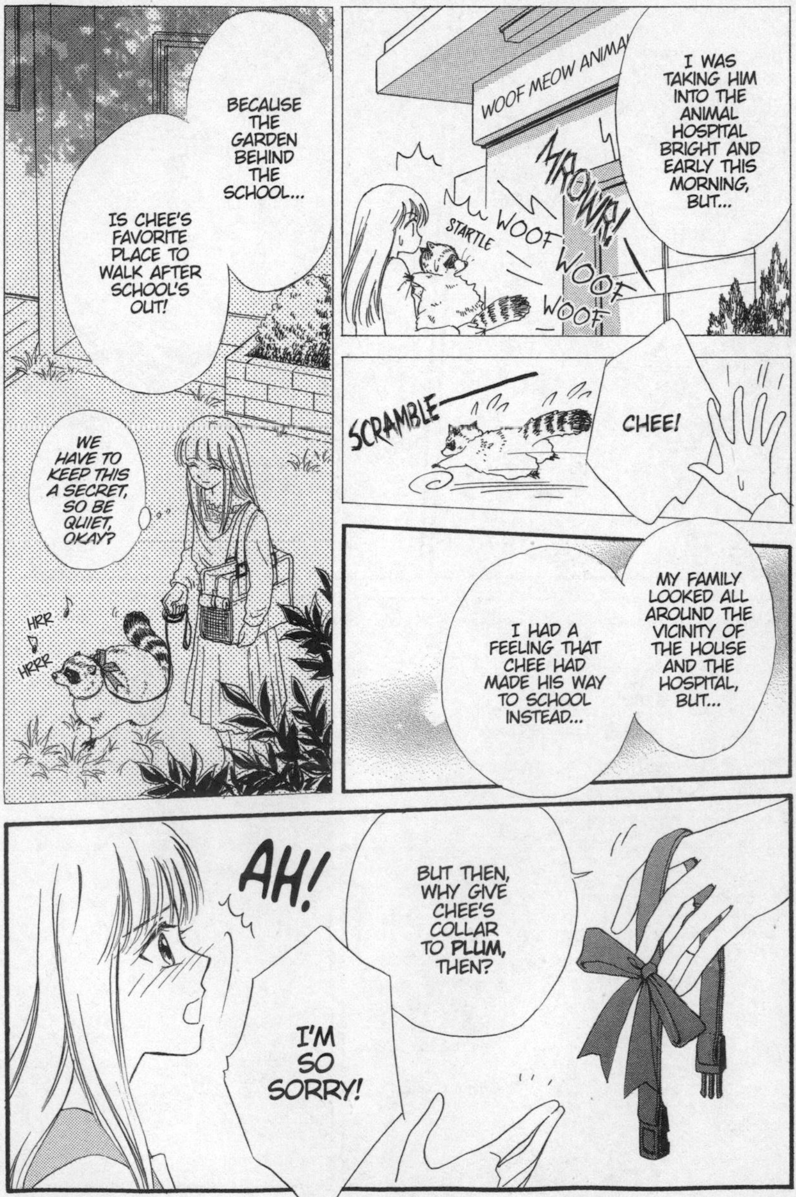
WOOF MEOW ANIMAL
I WAS TAKING HIM INTO THE ANIMAL HOSPITAL BRIGHT AND EARLY THIS MORNING, BUT...
MROWR!
WOOF WOOF WOOF WOOF
STARTLE
CHEE!
SCRAMBLE
MY FAMILY LOOKED ALL AROUND THE VICINITY OF THE HOUSE AND THE HOSPITAL, BUT...
I HAD A FEELING THAT CHEE HAD MADE HIS WAY TO SCHOOL INSTEAD...
BECAUSE THE GARDEN BEHIND THE SCHOOL...
IS CHEE'S FAVORITE PLACE TO WALK AFTER SCHOOL'S OUT!
WE HAVE TO KEEP THIS A SECRET, SO BE QUIET, OKAY?
HRR
HRRR
BUT THEN, WHY GIVE CHEE'S COLLAR TO PLUM, THEN?
AH!
I'M SO SORRY!

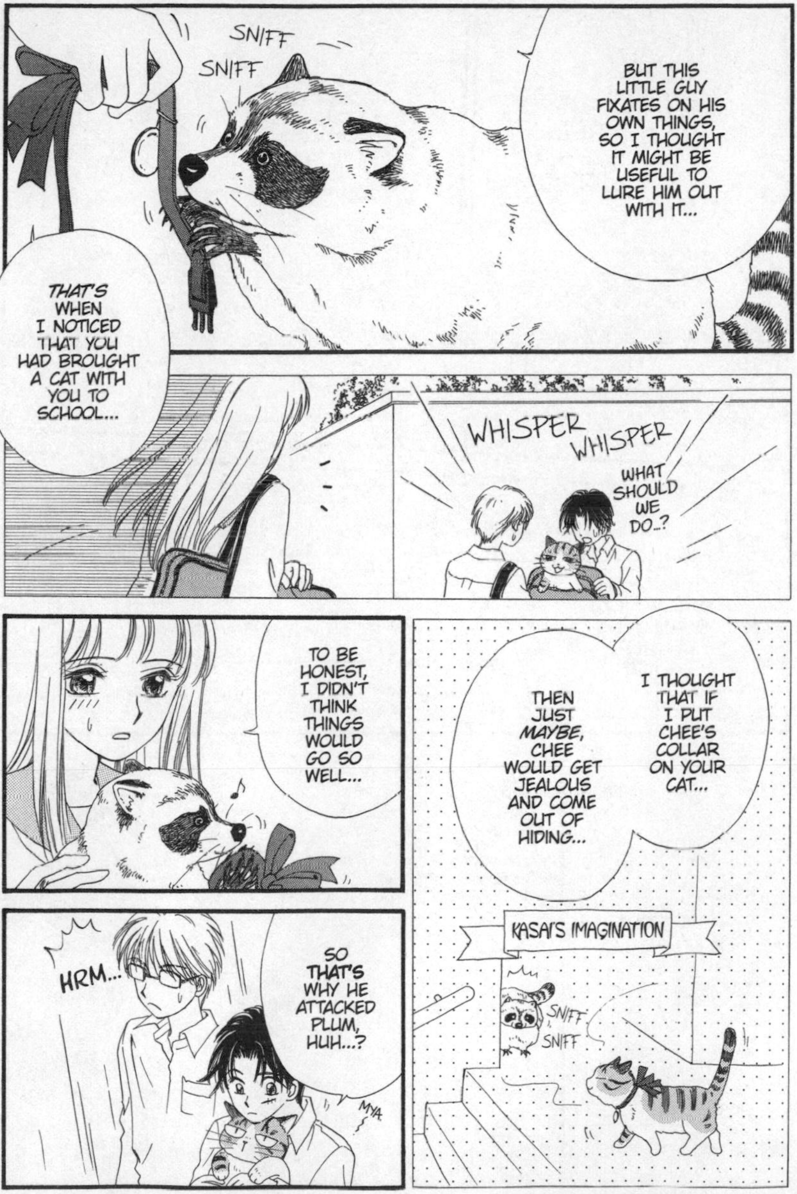
BUT THIS LITTLE GUY FIXATES ON HIS OWN THINGS, SO I THOUGHT IT MIGHT BE USEFUL TO LURE HIM OUT WITH IT...
SNIFF
SNIFF
THAT'S WHEN I NOTICED THAT YOU HAD BROUGHT A CAT WITH YOU TO SCHOOL...
WHISPER
WHISPER
WHAT SHOULD WE DO..?
I THOUGHT THAT IF I PUT CHEE'S COLLAR ON YOUR CAT...
THEN JUST *MAYBE*, CHEE WOULD GET JEALOUS AND COME OUT OF HIDING...
KASAI'S IMAGINATION
SNIFF
SNIFF
TO BE HONEST, I DIDN'T THINK THINGS WOULD GO SO WELL...
HRM...
SO THAT'S WHY HE ATTACKED PLUM, HUH...?
MYA

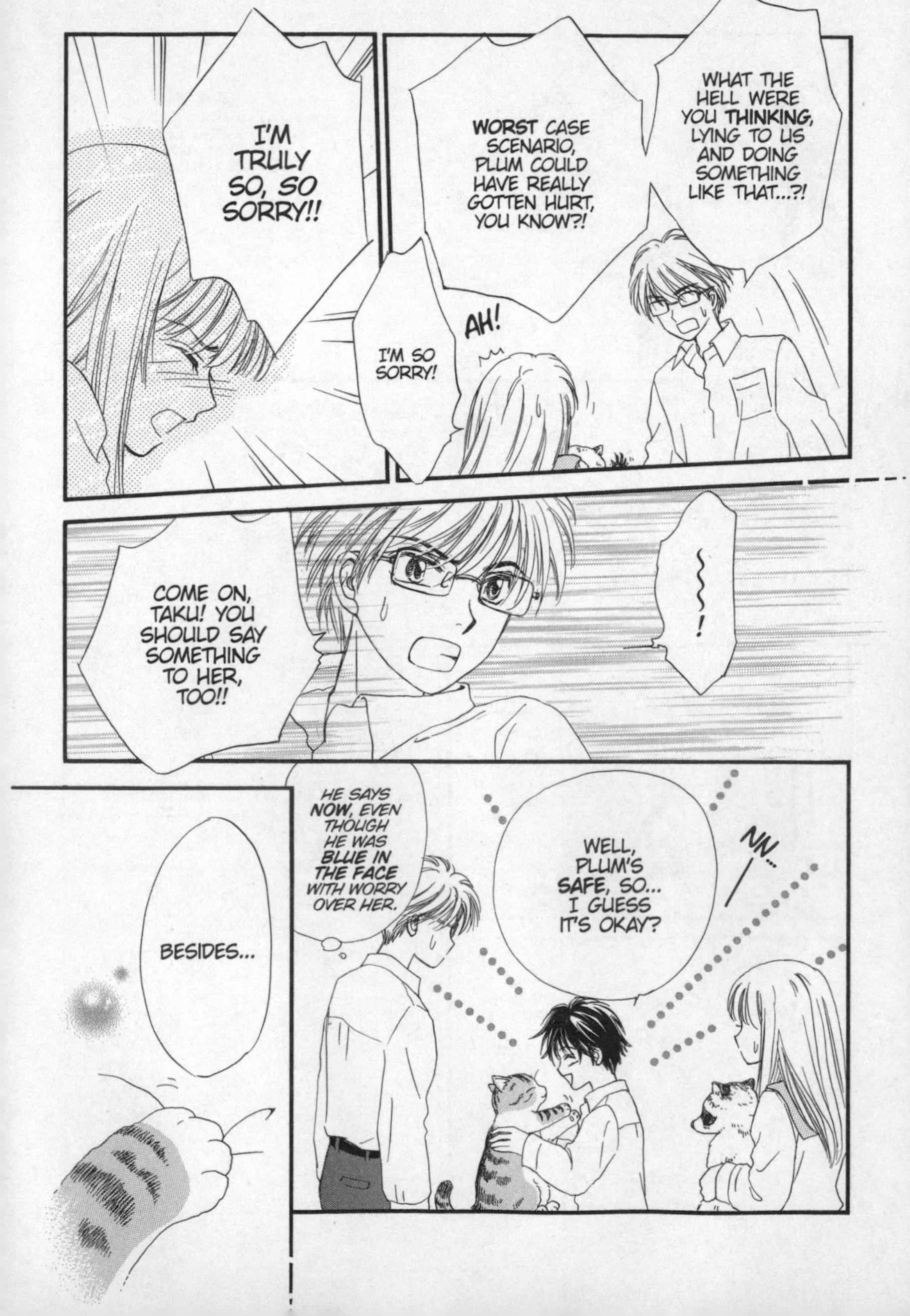
WHAT THE HELL WERE YOU THINKING, LYING TO US AND DOING SOMETHING LIKE THAT...?!
WORST CASE SCENARIO, PLUM COULD HAVE REALLY GOTTEN HURT, YOU KNOW?!
AH!
I'M SO SORRY!
I'M TRULY SO, SO SORRY!!
...!
COME ON, TAKU! YOU SHOULD SAY SOMETHING TO HER, TOO!!
NN...
WELL, PLUM'S SAFE, SO... I GUESS IT'S OKAY?
HE SAYS NOW, EVEN THOUGH HE WAS BLUE IN THE FACE WITH WORRY OVER HER.
BESIDES...

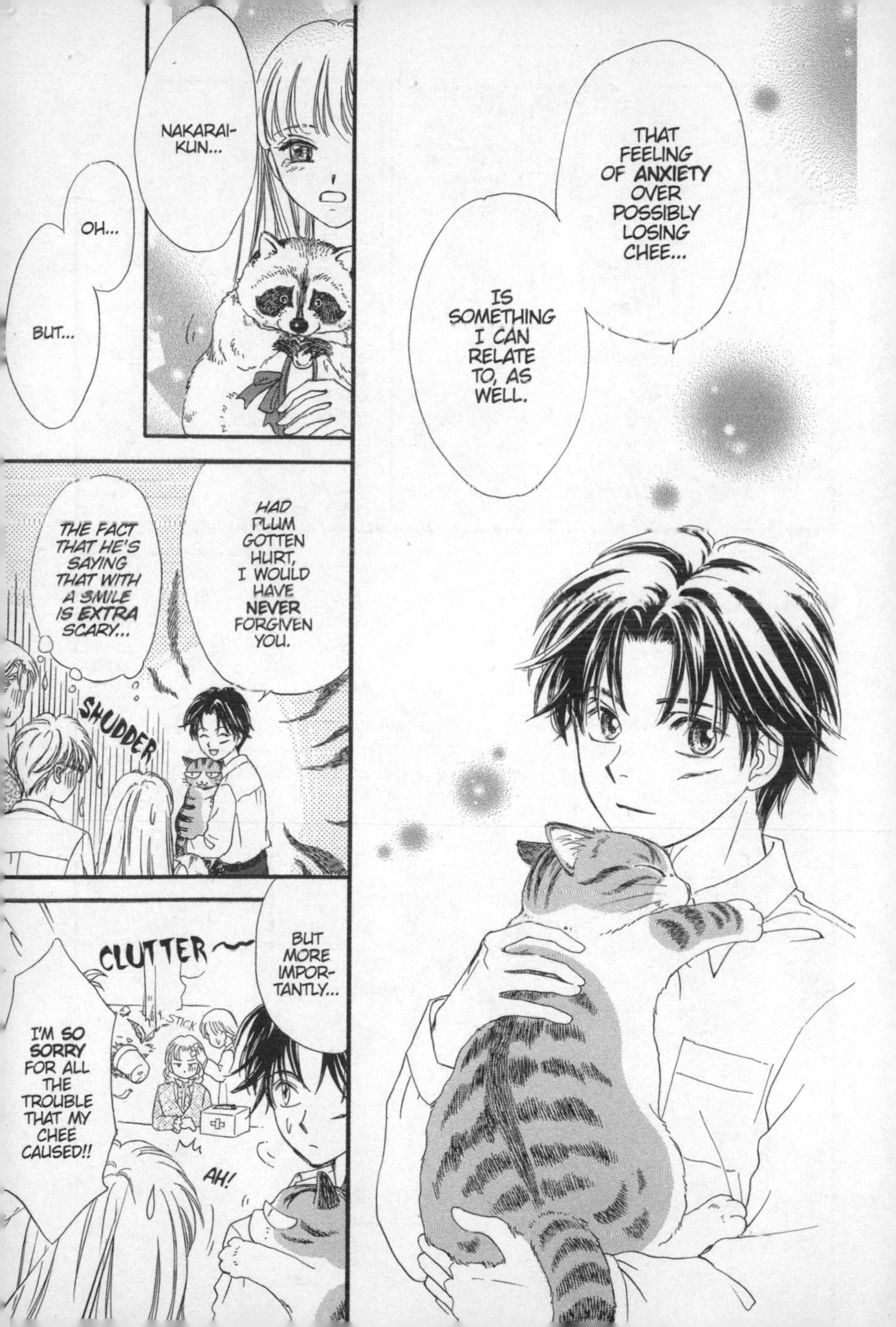
THAT FEELING OF ANXIETY OVER POSSIBLY LOSING CHEE...
IS SOMETHING I CAN RELATE TO, AS WELL.
NAKARAI-KUN...
OH...
BUT...
HAD PLUM GOTTEN HURT, I WOULD HAVE NEVER FORGIVEN YOU.
THE FACT THAT HE'S SAYING THAT WITH A SMILE IS EXTRA SCARY...
SHUDDER
BUT MORE IMPORTANTLY...
CLUTTER~
STICK
I'M SO SORRY FOR ALL THE TROUBLE THAT MY CHEE CAUSED!!
AH!

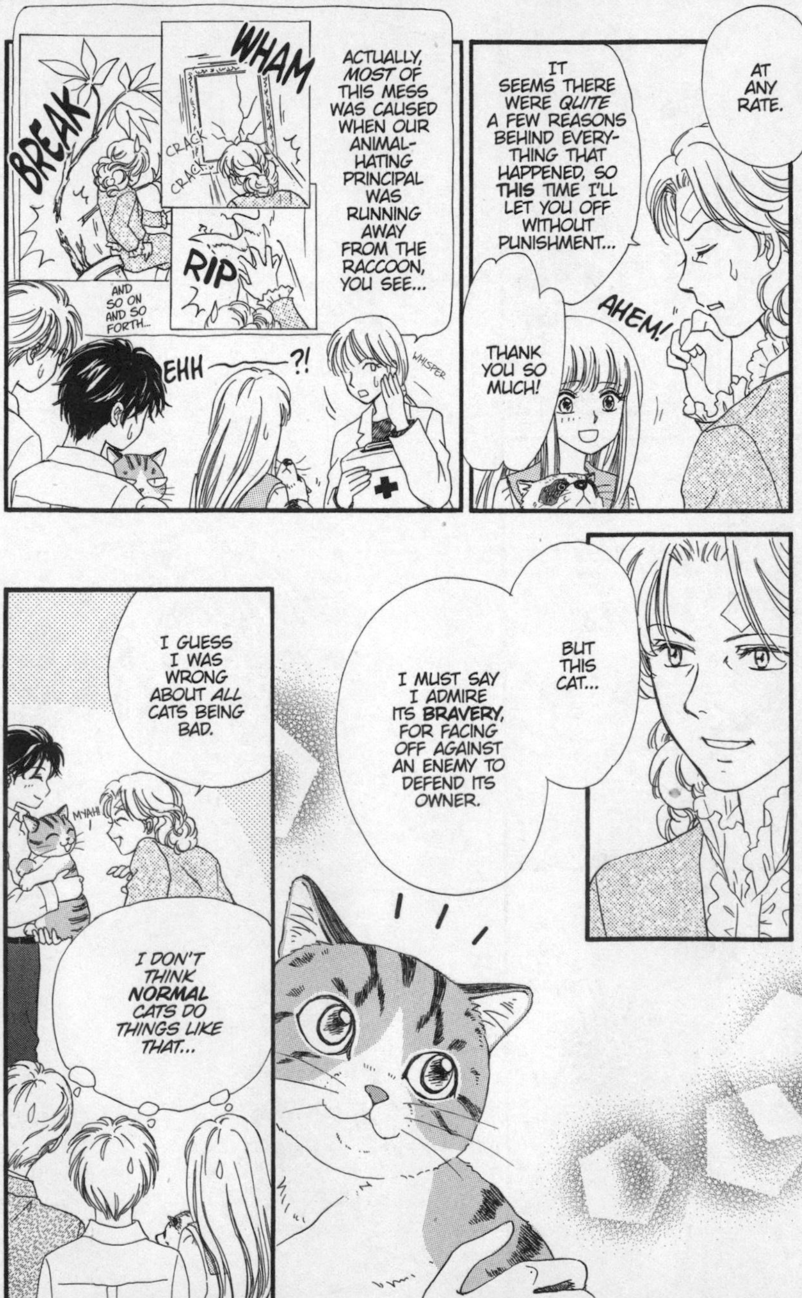
AT ANY RATE.
IT SEEMS THERE WERE QUITE A FEW REASONS BEHIND EVERYTHING THAT HAPPENED, SO THIS TIME I'LL LET YOU OFF WITHOUT PUNISHMENT...
AHEM!
THANK YOU SO MUCH!
ACTUALLY, MOST OF THIS MESS WAS CAUSED WHEN OUR ANIMAL-HATING PRINCIPAL WAS RUNNING AWAY FROM THE RACCOON, YOU SEE...
WHAM
BREAK
CRACK
CRACK
RIP
AND SO ON AND SO FORTH...
WHISPER
EHH—?!
BUT THIS CAT...
I MUST SAY I ADMIRE ITS BRAVERY, FOR FACING OFF AGAINST AN ENEMY TO DEFEND ITS OWNER.
I GUESS I WAS WRONG ABOUT ALL CATS BEING BAD.
MYAH!
I DON'T THINK NORMAL CATS DO THINGS LIKE THAT...

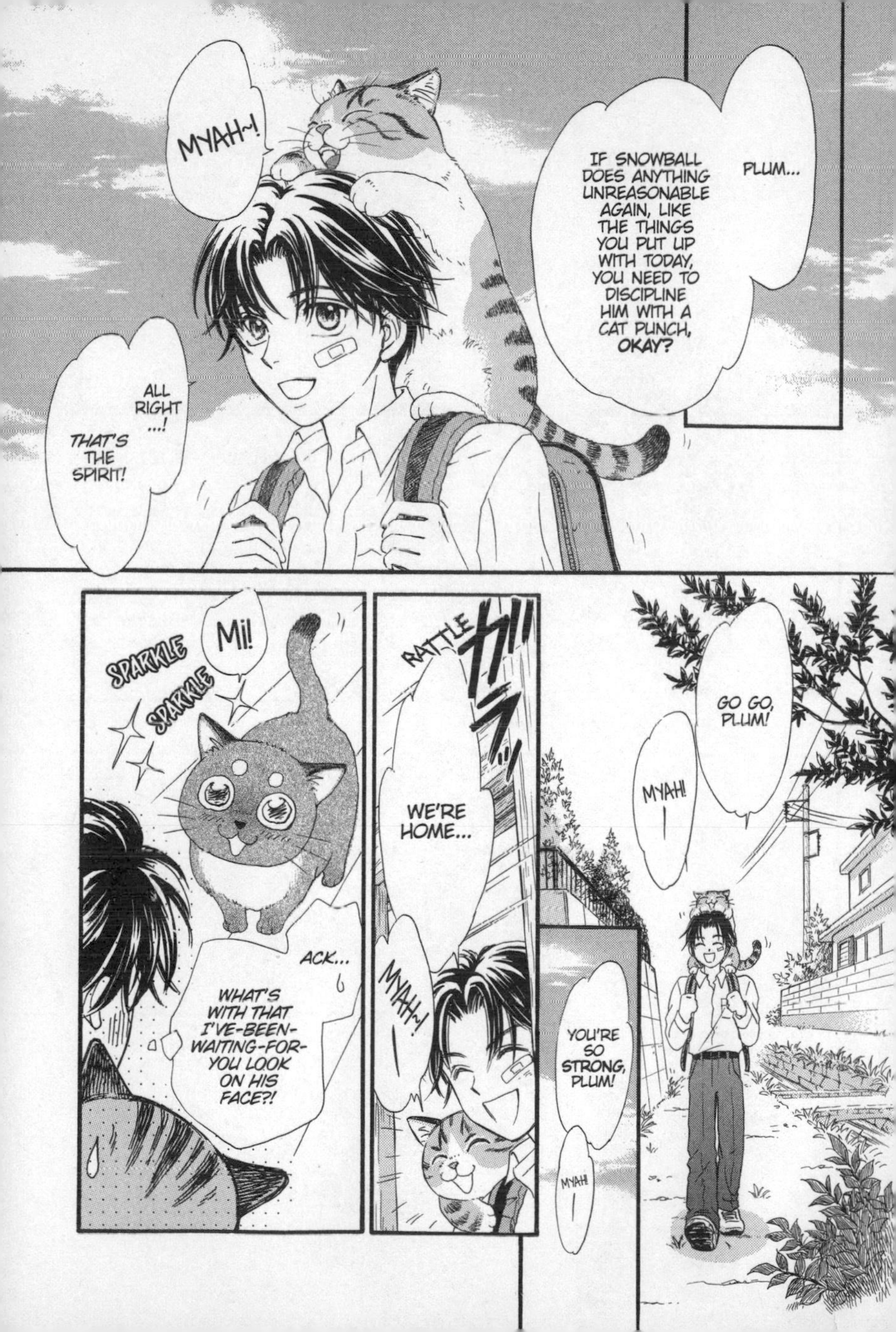
PLUM...
IF SNOWBALL DOES ANYTHING UNREASONABLE AGAIN, LIKE THE THINGS YOU PUT UP WITH TODAY, YOU NEED TO DISCIPLINE HIM WITH A CAT PUNCH, OKAY?
MYAH~!
ALL RIGHT ...!
THAT'S THE SPIRIT!
GO GO, PLUM!
MYAH! !
YOU'RE SO STRONG, PLUM!
MYAH! !
RATTLE
WE'RE HOME...
MYAH~!
Mi!
SPARKLE SPARKLE
ACK...
WHAT'S WITH THAT I'VE-BEEN-WAITING-FOR-YOU LOOK ON HIS FACE?!

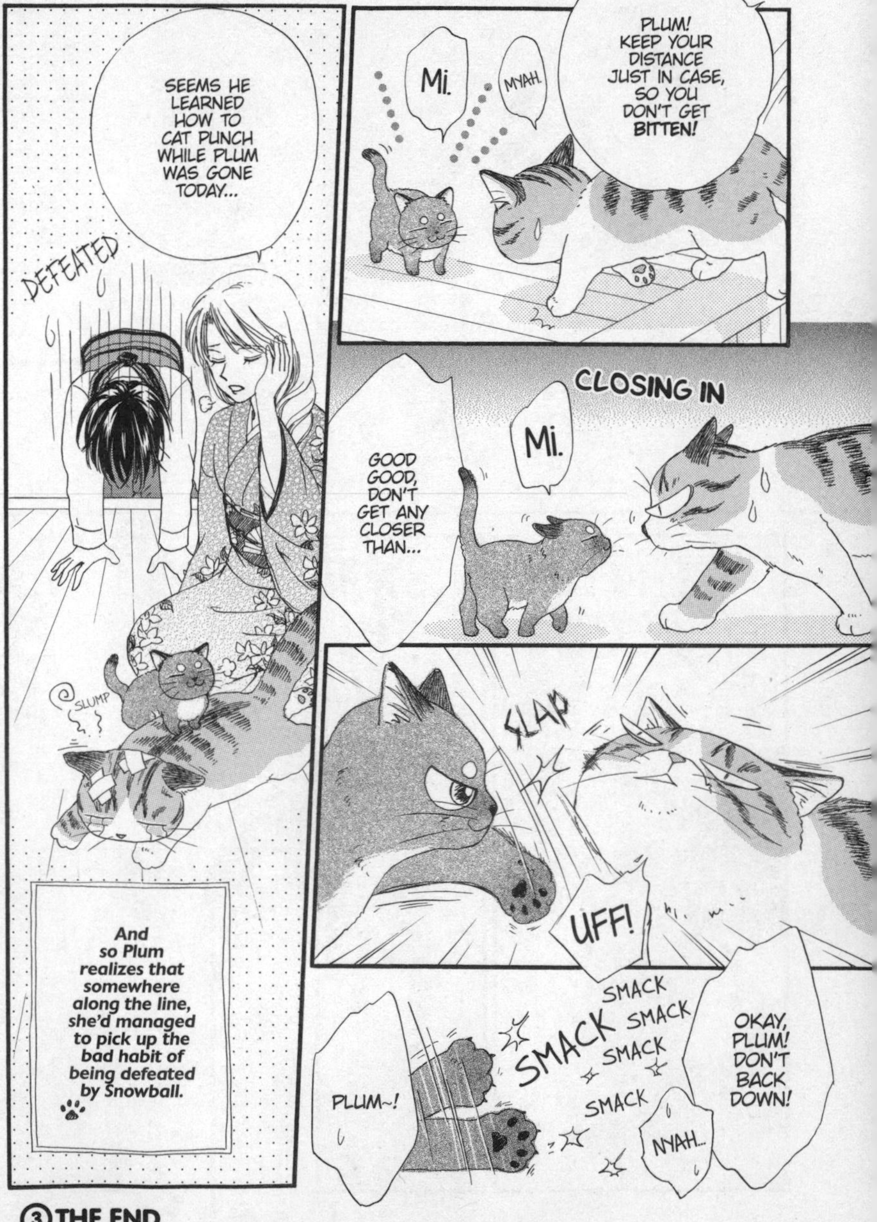
PLUM! KEEP YOUR DISTANCE JUST IN CASE, SO YOU DON'T GET BITTEN!
MYAH.
Mi.
CLOSING IN
Mi.
GOOD GOOD, DON'T GET ANY CLOSER THAN...
SLAP
UFF!
OKAY, PLUM! DON'T BACK DOWN!
SMACK SMACK SMACK SMACK SMACK
NYAH...
PLUM~!
SEEMS HE LEARNED HOW TO CAT PUNCH WHILE PLUM WAS GONE TODAY...
DEFEATED
SLUMP
And so Plum realizes that somewhere along the line, she'd managed to pick up the bad habit of being defeated by Snowball.

③ THE END

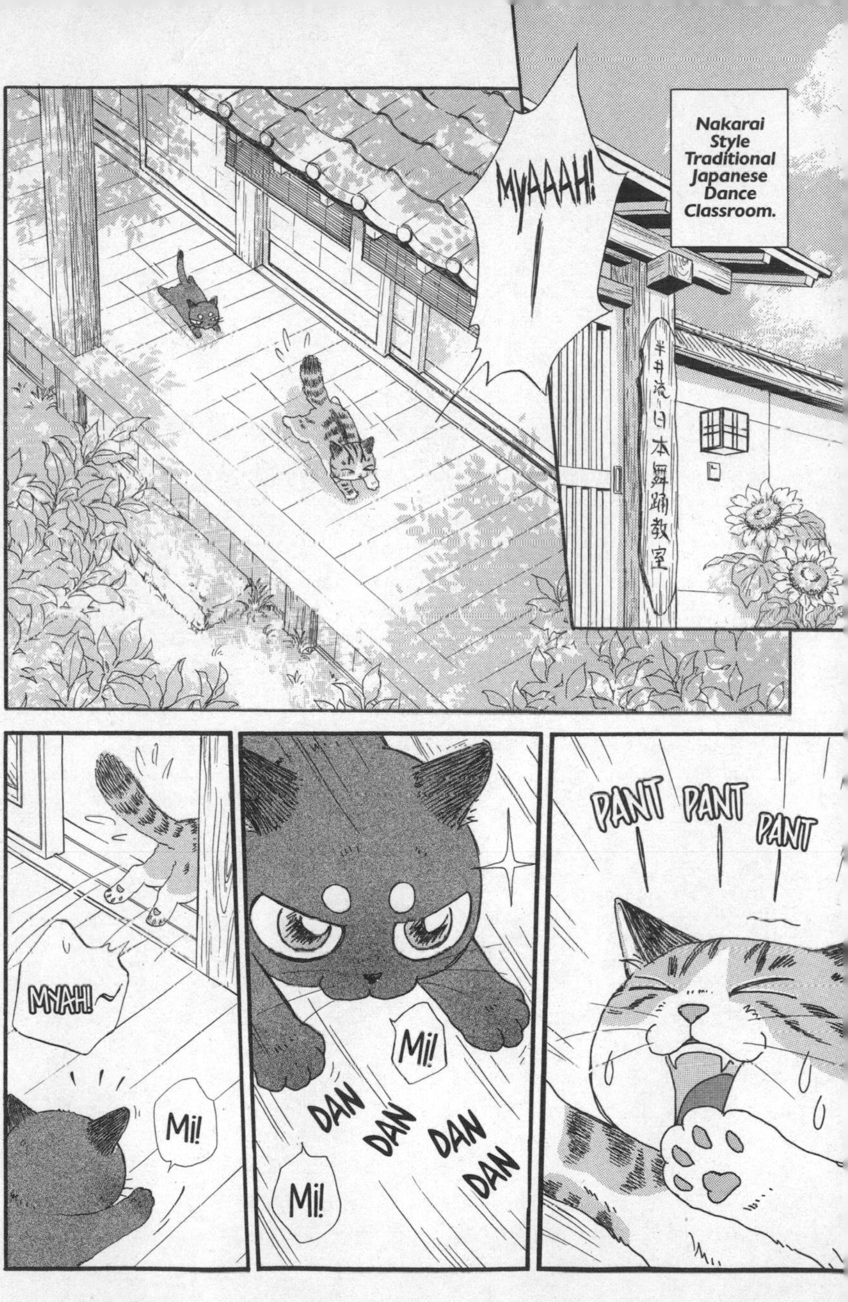
Nakarai Style Traditional Japanese Dance Classroom.
半井流日本舞踊教室
MYAAAH!
PANT PANT PANT
Mi!
DAN DAN DAN DAN
Mi!
MYAH!~
Mi!

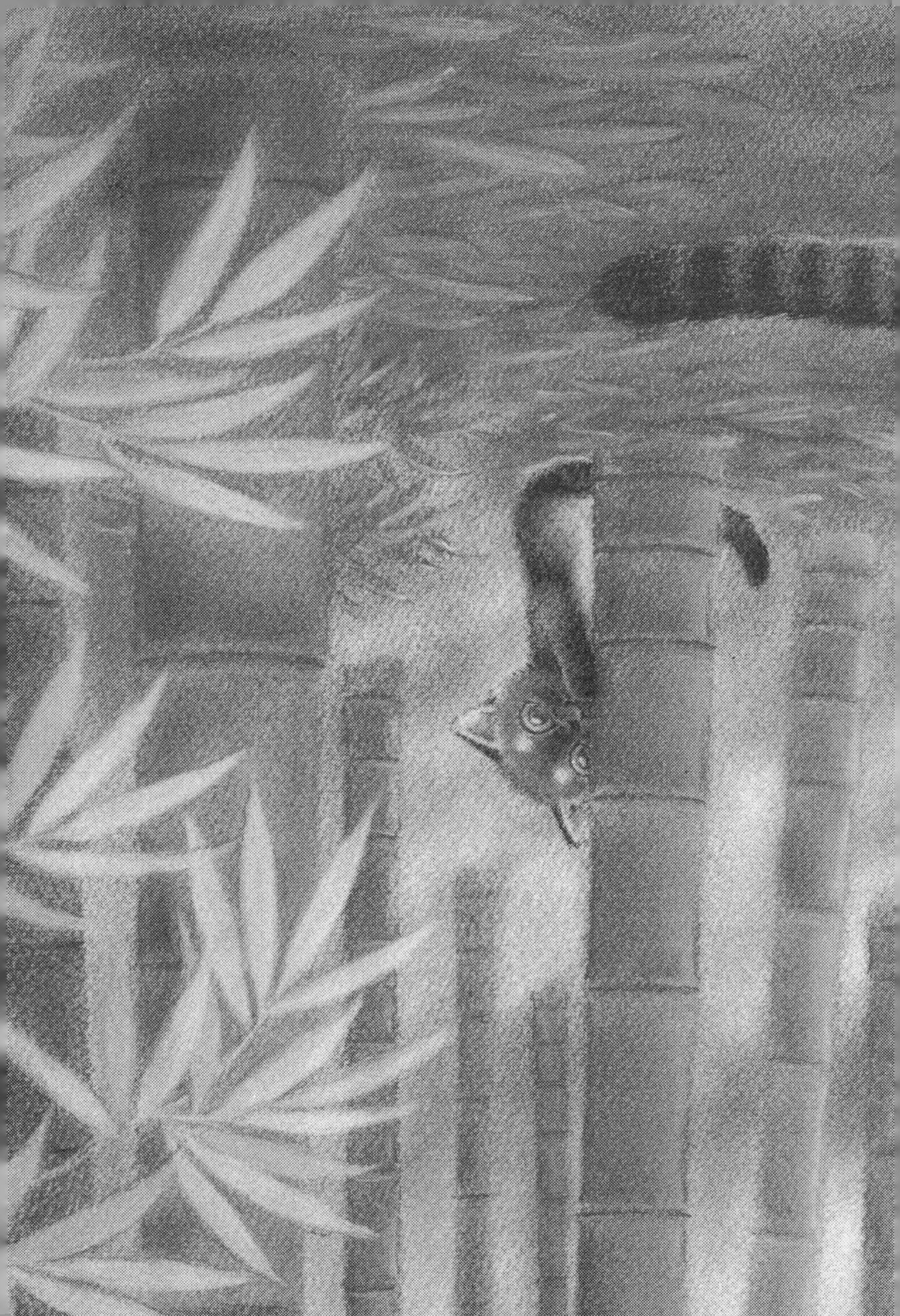

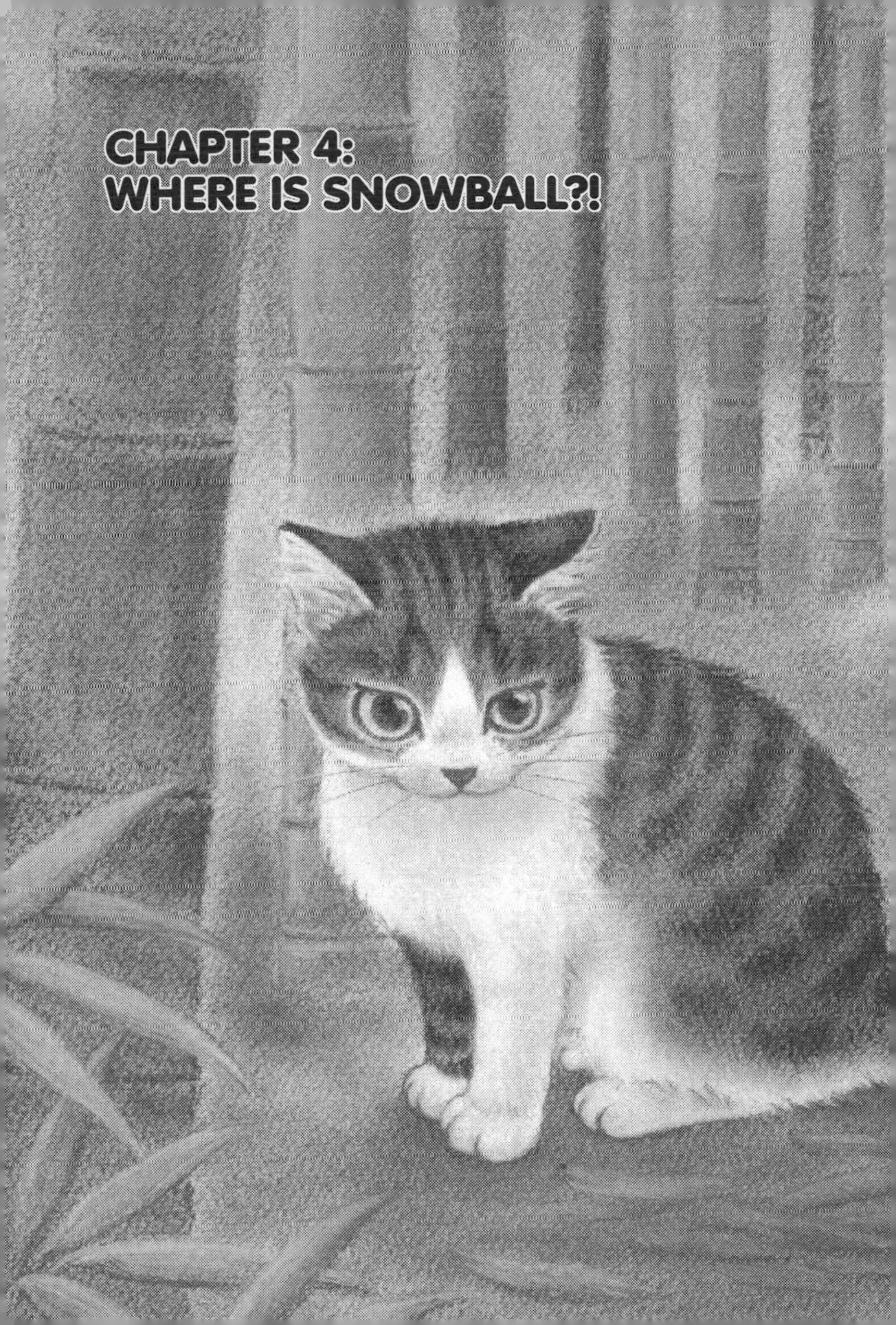
CHAPTER 4:
WHERE IS SNOWBALL?!

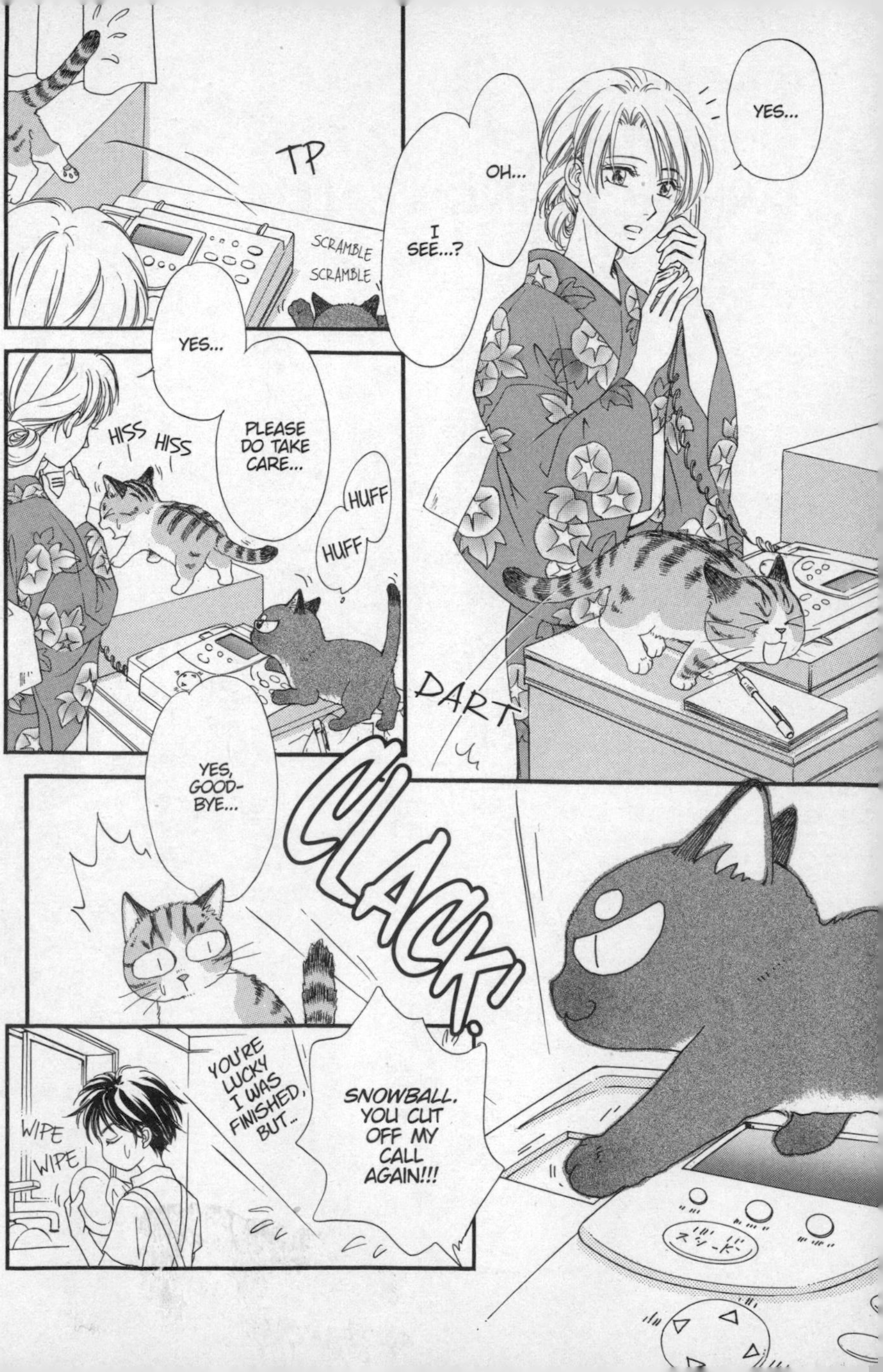
YES...
OH...
I SEE...?
DART
TP
SCRAMBLE
SCRAMBLE
YES...
PLEASE DO TAKE CARE...
HISS
HISS
HUFF
HUFF
YES, GOOD-BYE...
CLACK.
SNOWBALL. YOU CUT OFF MY CALL AGAIN!!!
YOU'RE LUCKY I WAS FINISHED, BUT...
WIPE
WIPE

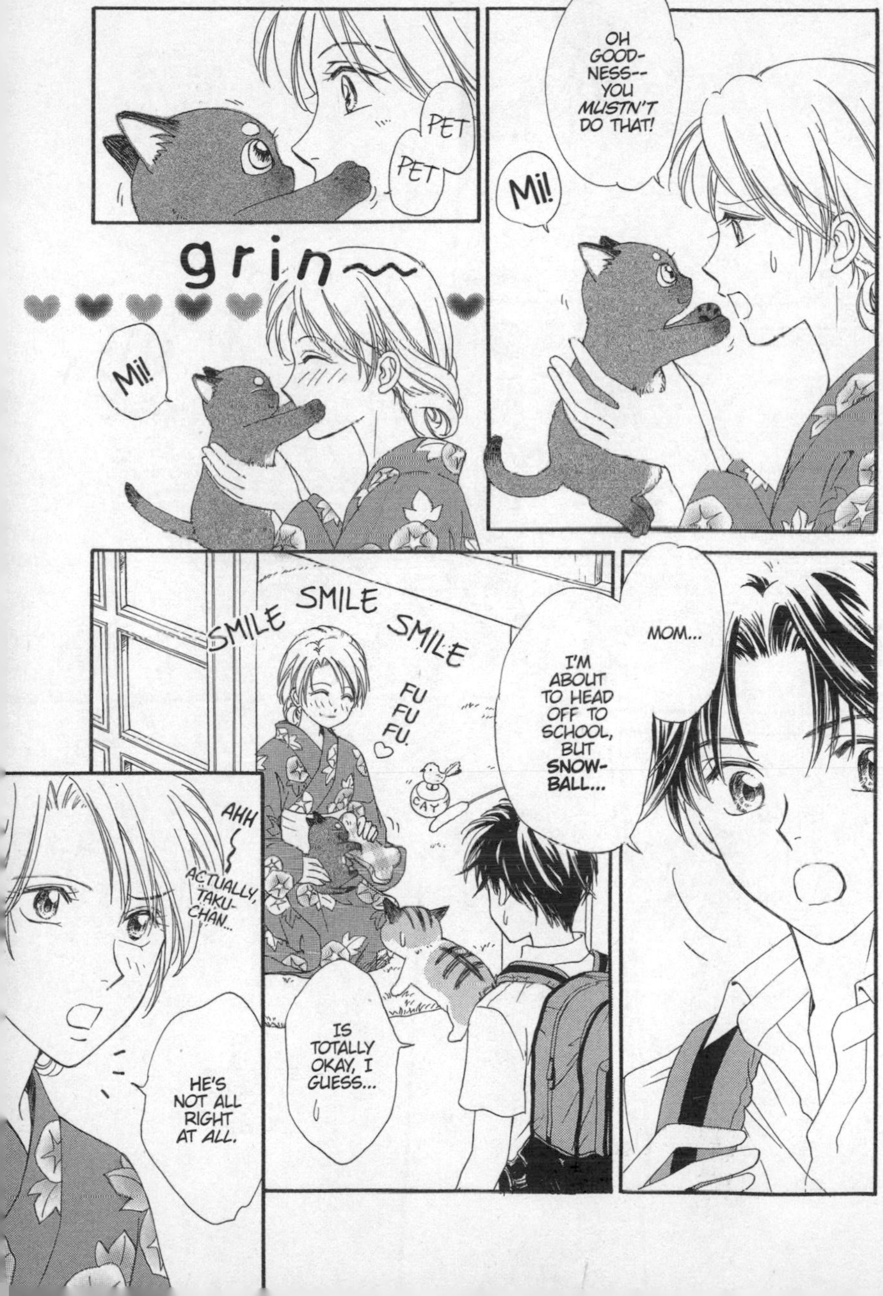
OH GOODNESS--YOU MUSTN'T DO THAT!
Mi!
PET PET
grin~~
Mi!
MOM...
I'M ABOUT TO HEAD OFF TO SCHOOL, BUT SNOWBALL...
SMILE SMILE SMILE
FU FU FU.
CAT
IS TOTALLY OKAY, I GUESS...
AHH
ACTUALLY, TAKU-CHAN...
HE'S NOT ALL RIGHT AT ALL.

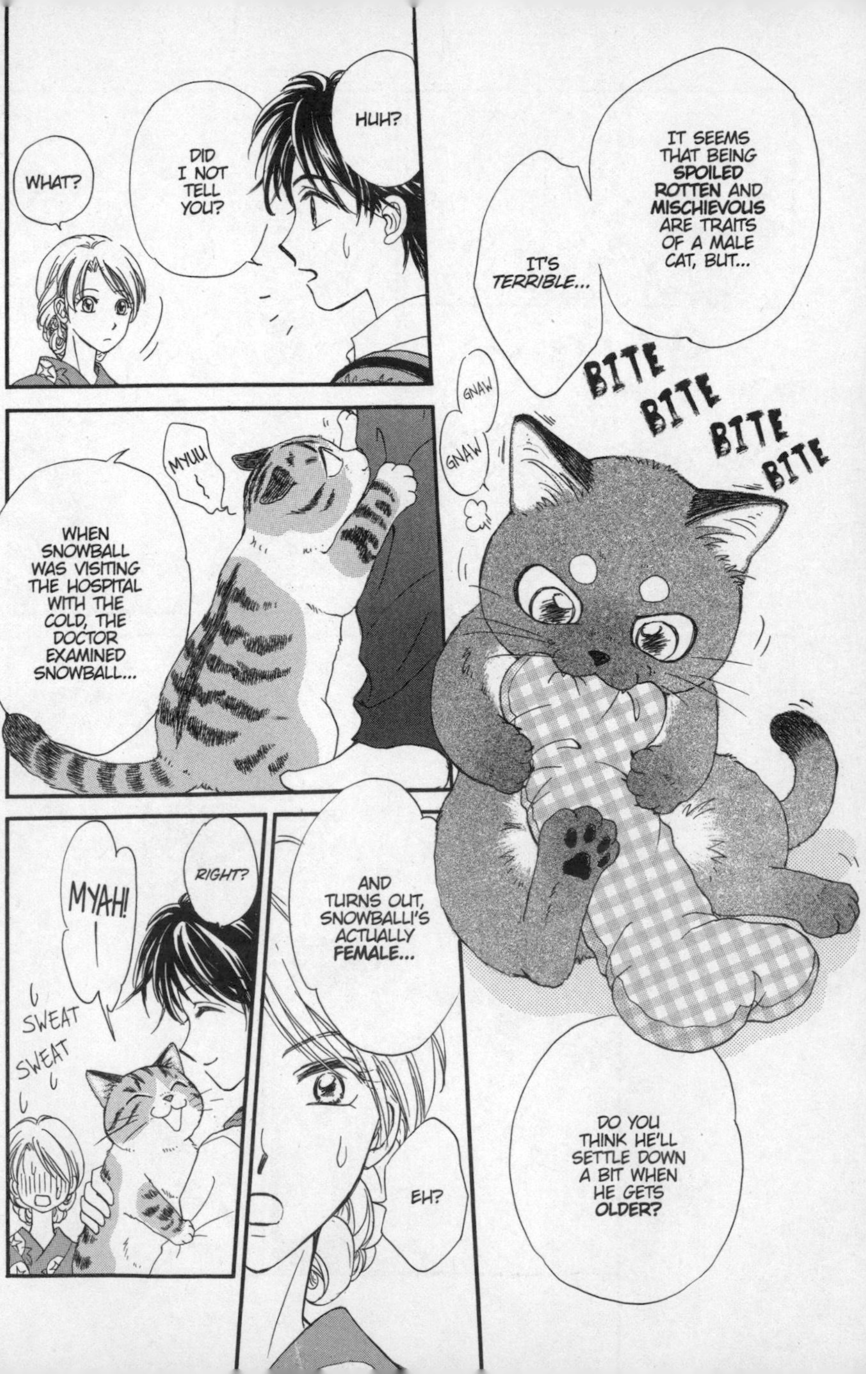
IT SEEMS THAT BEING SPOILED ROTTEN AND MISCHIEVOUS ARE TRAITS OF A MALE CAT, BUT...
IT'S TERRIBLE...
BITE BITE BITE BITE
GNAW
GNAW
DO YOU THINK HE'LL SETTLE DOWN A BIT WHEN HE GETS OLDER?
HUH?
DID I NOT TELL YOU?
WHAT?
WHEN SNOWBALL WAS VISITING THE HOSPITAL WITH THE COLD, THE DOCTOR EXAMINED SNOWBALL...
MYUU
AND TURNS OUT, SNOWBALLI'S ACTUALLY FEMALE...
EH?
RIGHT?
MYAH!
SWEAT
SWEAT

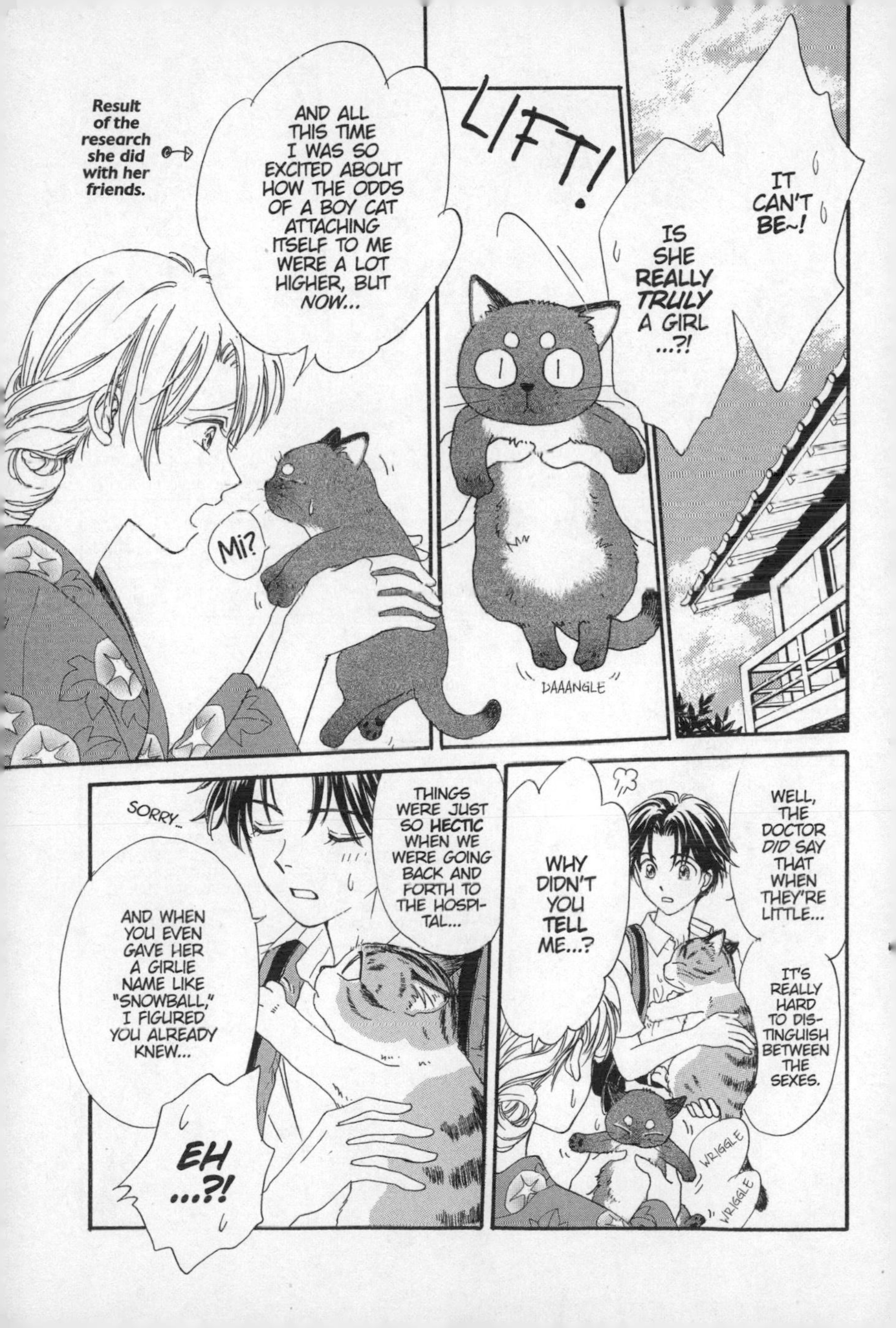
IT CAN'T BE~!
IS SHE REALLY TRULY A GIRL ...?!
LIFT!
DAAANGLE
AND ALL THIS TIME I WAS SO EXCITED ABOUT HOW THE ODDS OF A BOY CAT ATTACHING ITSELF TO ME WERE A LOT HIGHER, BUT NOW...
Result of the research she did with her friends.
Mi?
WELL, THE DOCTOR DID SAY THAT WHEN THEY'RE LITTLE...
IT'S REALLY HARD TO DIS-TINGUISH BETWEEN THE SEXES.
WRIGGLE
WRIGGLE
WHY DIDN'T YOU TELL ME...?
THINGS WERE JUST SO HECTIC WHEN WE WERE GOING BACK AND FORTH TO THE HOSPI-TAL...
SORRY...
AND WHEN YOU EVEN GAVE HER A GIRLIE NAME LIKE "SNOWBALL," I FIGURED YOU ALREADY KNEW...
EH ...?!

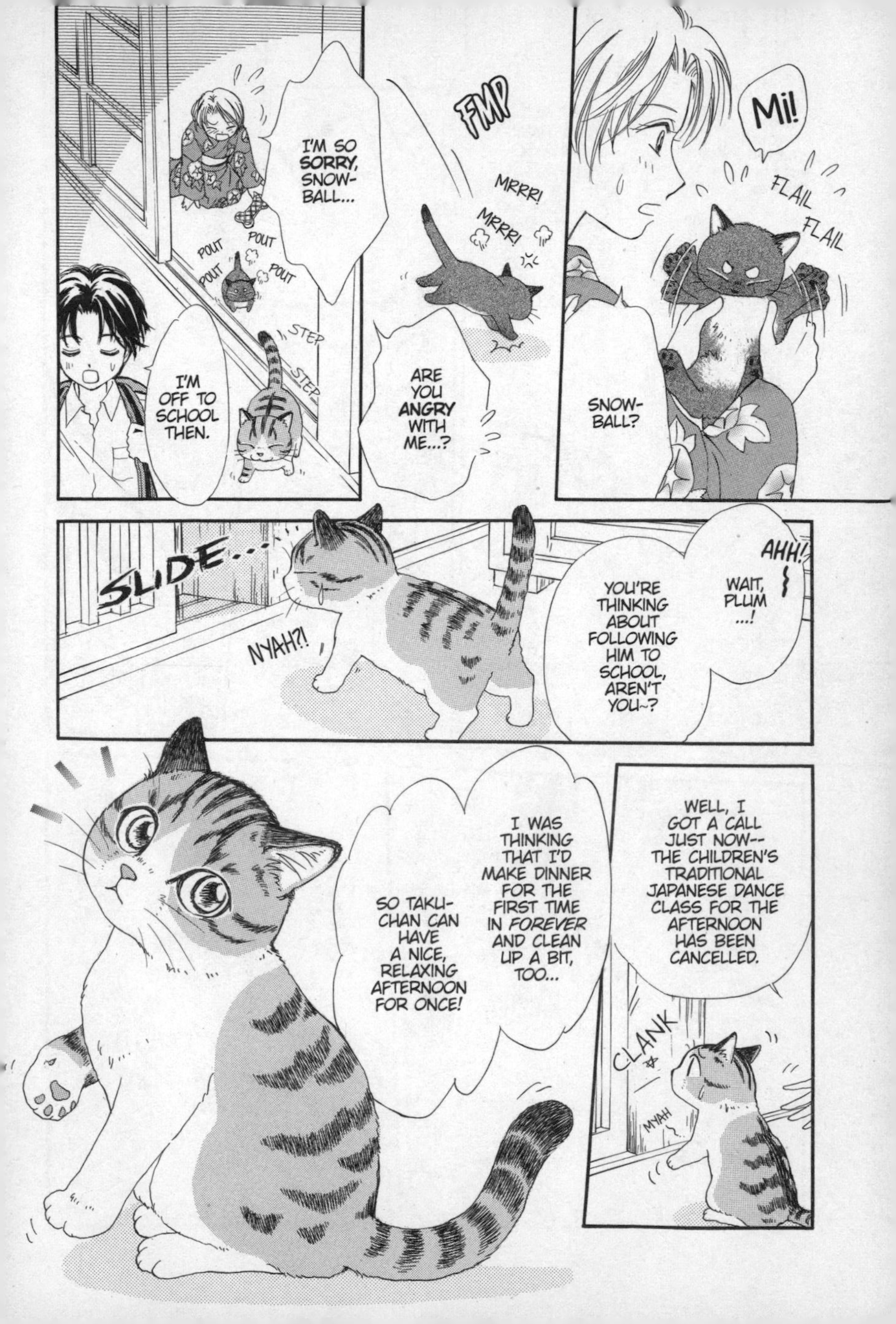
Mi!
FLAIL
FLAIL
SNOW-BALL?
FMP
MRRR!
MRRR!
ARE YOU ANGRY WITH ME...?
I'M SO SORRY, SNOW-BALL...
POUT
POUT
POUT
POUT
STEP
STEP
I'M OFF TO SCHOOL THEN.
AHH!
WAIT, PLUM ...!
YOU'RE THINKING ABOUT FOLLOWING HIM TO SCHOOL, AREN'T YOU~?
NYAH?!
SLIDE...
WELL, I GOT A CALL JUST NOW-- THE CHILDREN'S TRADITIONAL JAPANESE DANCE CLASS FOR THE AFTERNOON HAS BEEN CANCELLED.
CLANK
MYAH
I WAS THINKING THAT I'D MAKE DINNER FOR THE FIRST TIME IN FOREVER AND CLEAN UP A BIT, TOO...
SO TAKU-CHAN CAN HAVE A NICE, RELAXING AFTERNOON FOR ONCE!

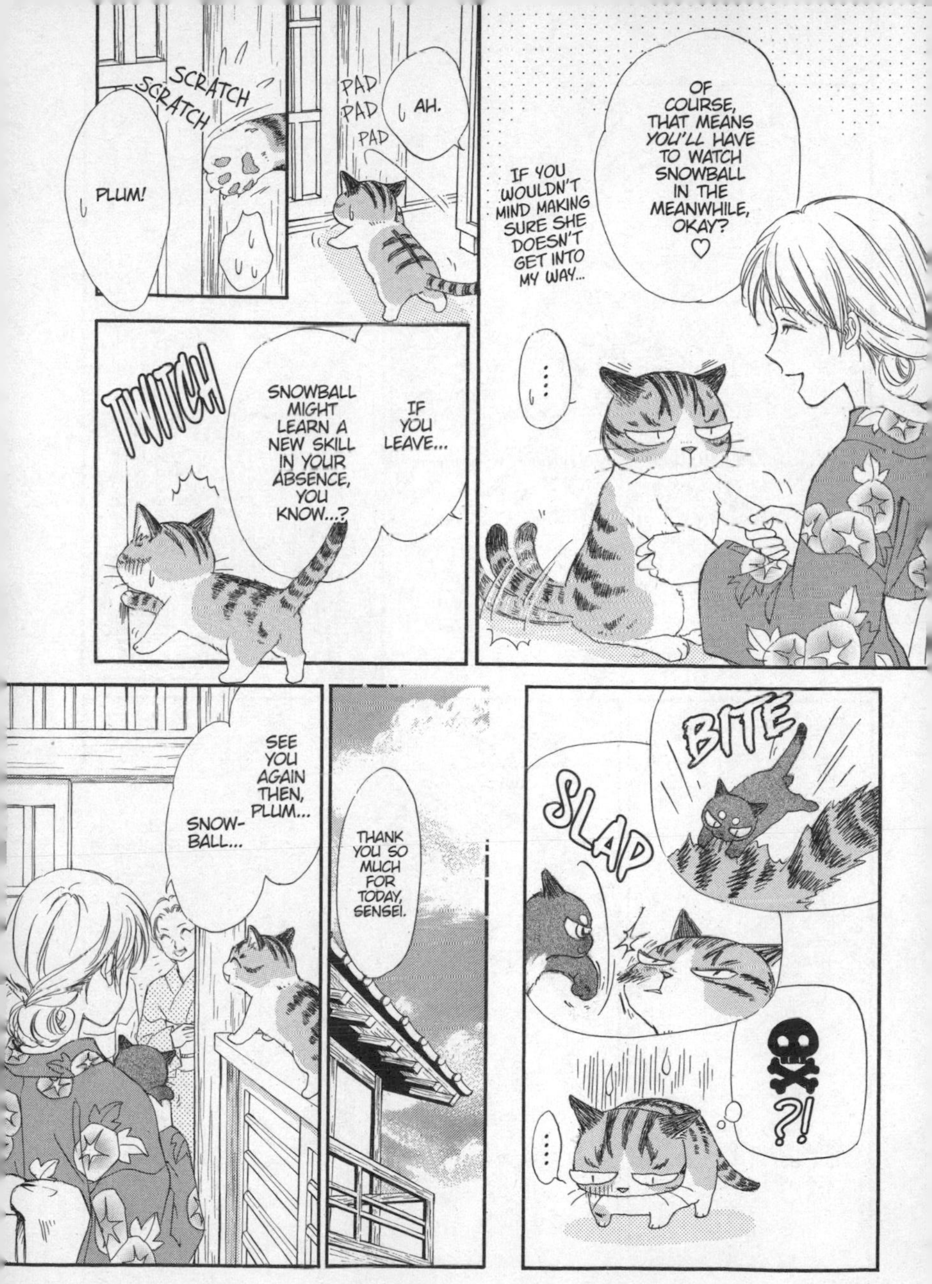
IF YOU WOULDN'T MIND MAKING SURE SHE DOESN'T GET INTO MY WAY...
OF COURSE, THAT MEANS YOU'LL HAVE TO WATCH SNOWBALL IN THE MEANWHILE, OKAY? ♡
.....
SCRATCH SCRATCH
PLUM!
PAD PAD PAD
AH.
IF YOU LEAVE...
SNOWBALL MIGHT LEARN A NEW SKILL IN YOUR ABSENCE, YOU KNOW...?
TWITCH
BITE
SLAP
?!
.....
THANK YOU SO MUCH FOR TODAY, SENSEI.
SEE YOU AGAIN THEN, PLUM...
SNOW-BALL...

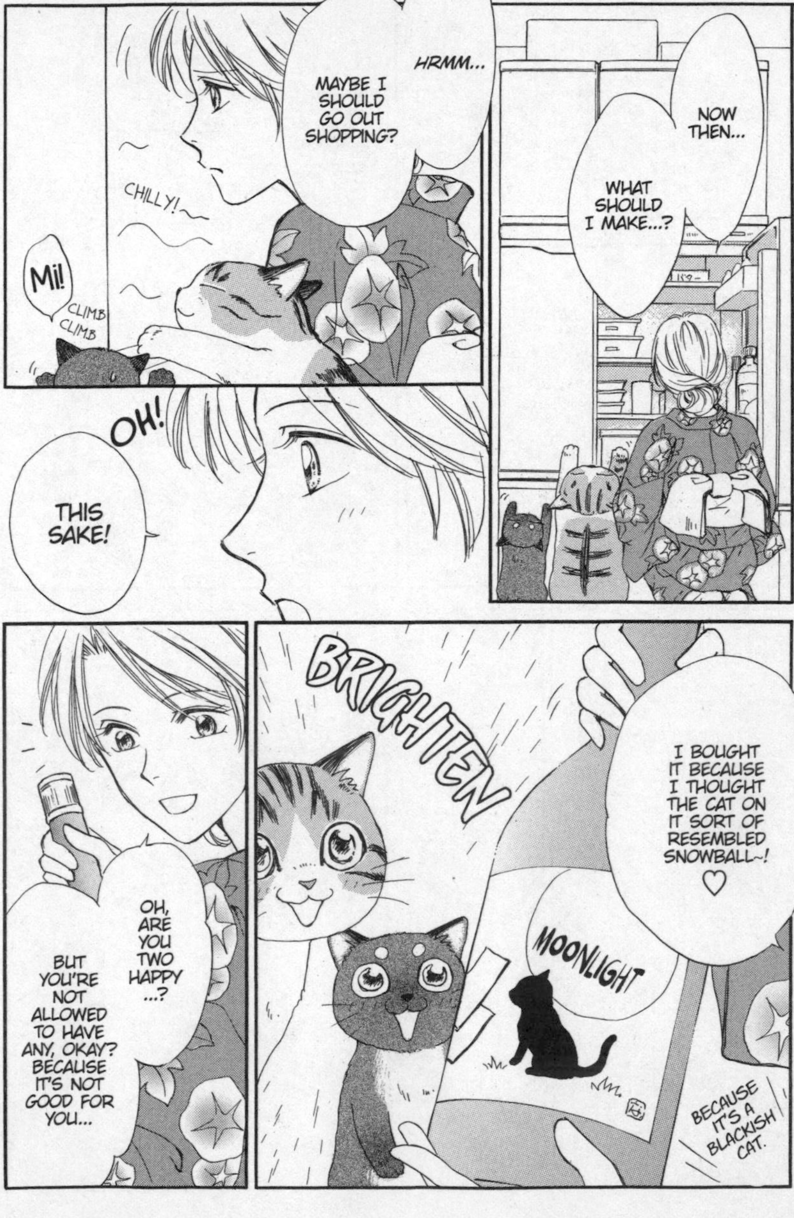
NOW THEN...
WHAT SHOULD I MAKE...?
HRMM...
MAYBE I SHOULD GO OUT SHOPPING?
CHILLY!~
Mi!
CLIMB CLIMB
OH!
THIS SAKE!
I BOUGHT IT BECAUSE I THOUGHT THE CAT ON IT SORT OF RESEMBLED SNOWBALL~! ♡
BRIGHTEN
MOONLIGHT
BECAUSE IT'S A BLACKISH CAT.
OH, ARE YOU TWO HAPPY...?
BUT YOU'RE NOT ALLOWED TO HAVE ANY, OKAY? BECAUSE IT'S NOT GOOD FOR YOU...

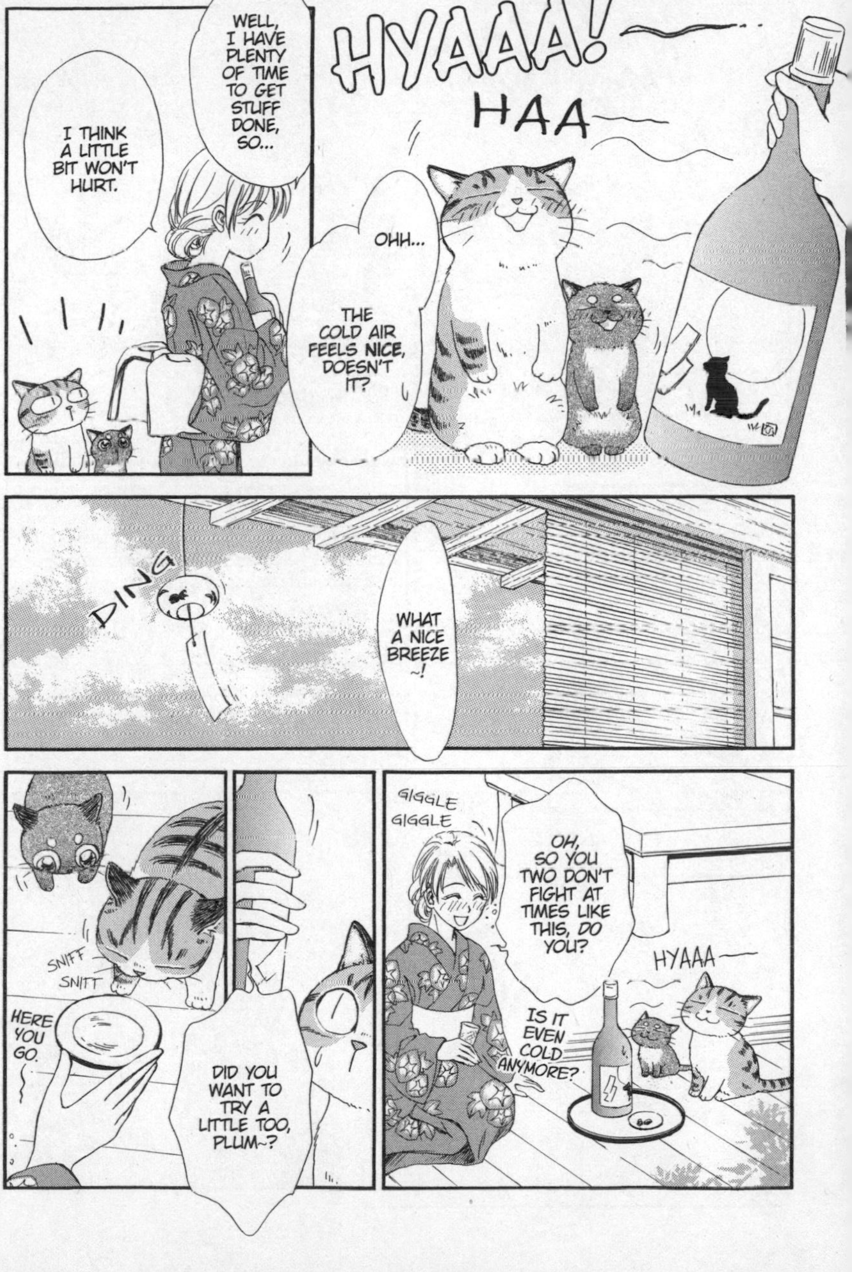
HYAAA!
HAA
OHH...
THE COLD AIR FEELS NICE, DOESN'T IT?
WELL, I HAVE PLENTY OF TIME TO GET STUFF DONE, SO...
I THINK A LITTLE BIT WON'T HURT.
DING
WHAT A NICE BREEZE ~!
GIGGLE GIGGLE
OH, SO YOU TWO DON'T FIGHT AT TIMES LIKE THIS, DO YOU?
HYAAA—
IS IT EVEN COLD ANYMORE?
DID YOU WANT TO TRY A LITTLE TOO, PLUM~?
SNIFF
SNIFF
HERE YOU GO.

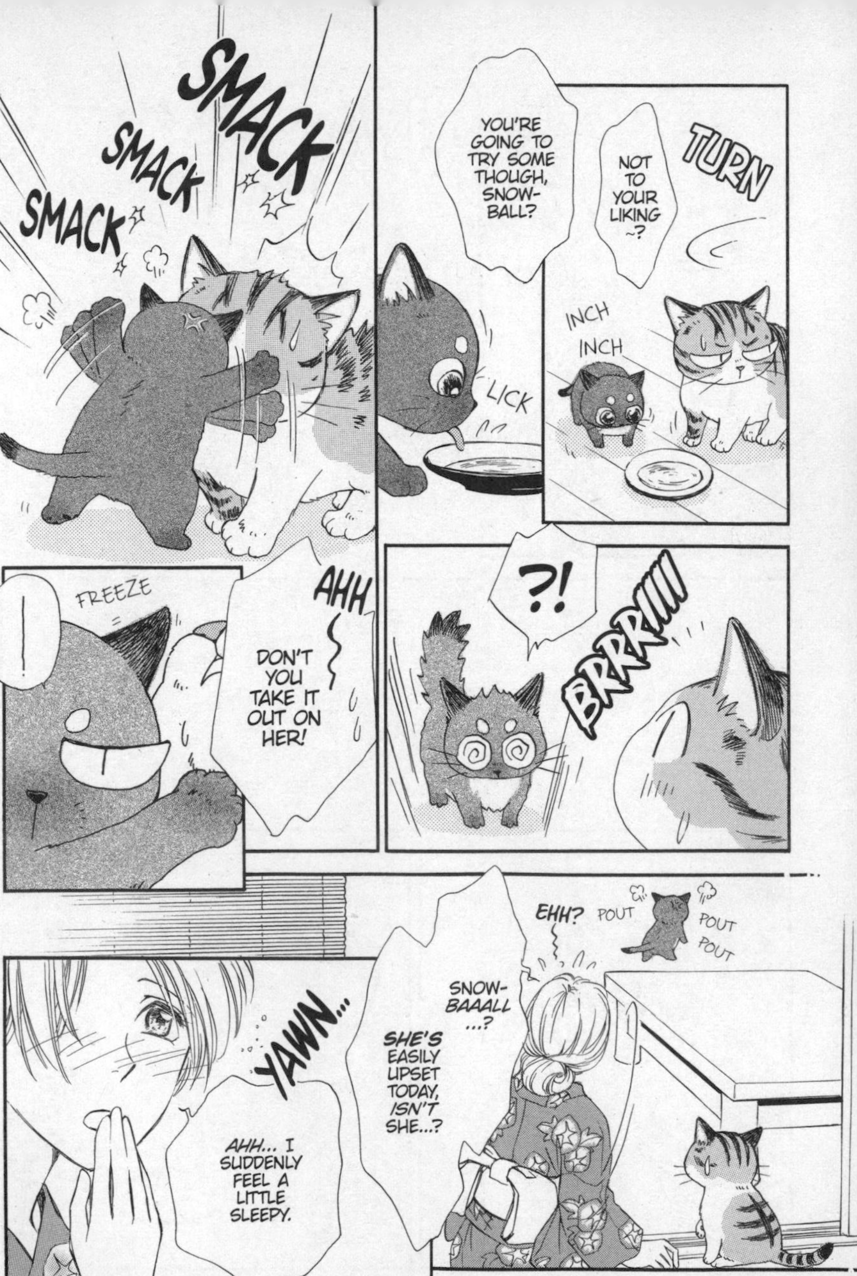
TURN
NOT TO YOUR LIKING ~?
YOU'RE GOING TO TRY SOME THOUGH, SNOW-BALL?
INCH INCH
LICK
SMACK
SMACK
SMACK
?!
BRRRIII
AHH
DON'T YOU TAKE IT OUT ON HER!
FREEZE
!
EHH? POUT
POUT POUT
SNOW-BAAALL ...?
SHE'S EASILY UPSET TODAY, ISN'T SHE...?
YAWN...
AHH... I SUDDENLY FEEL A LITTLE SLEEPY.

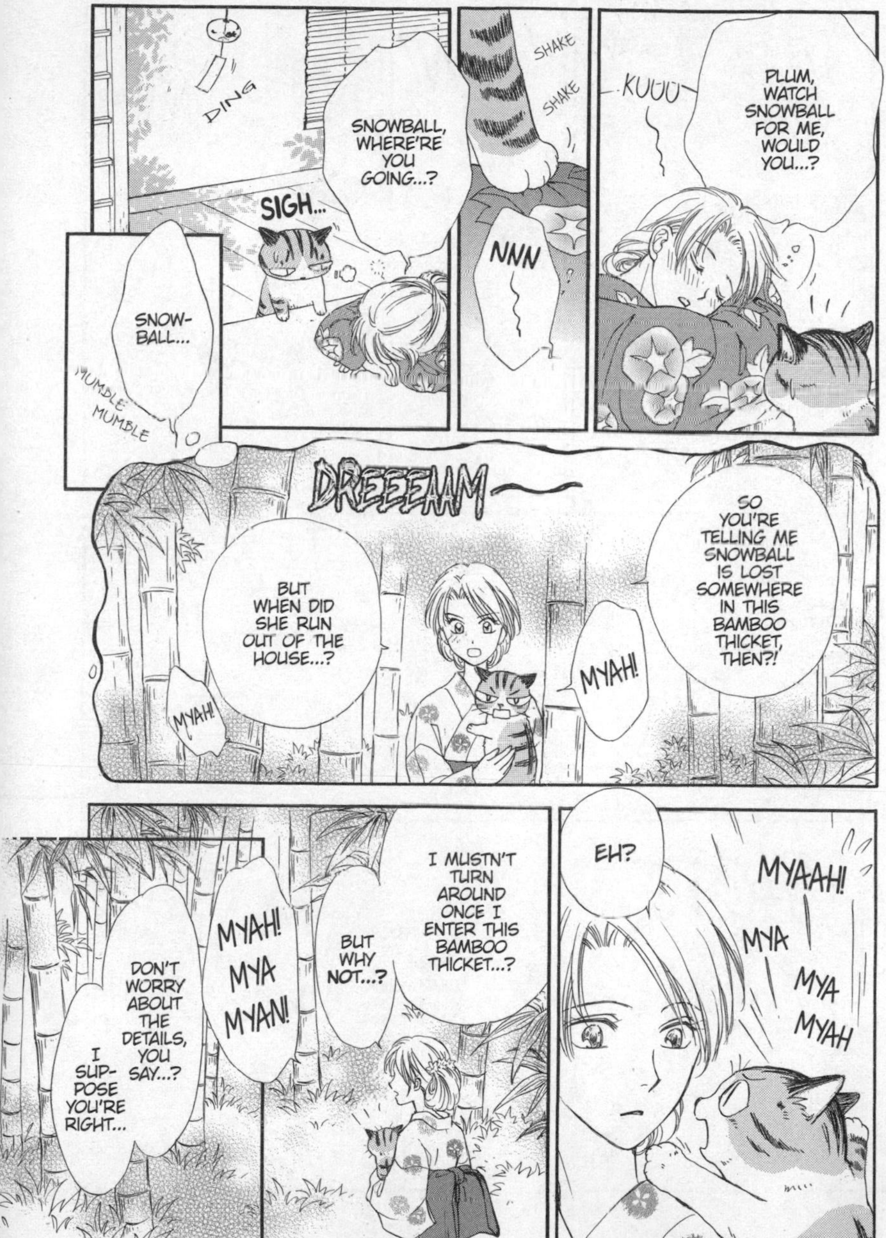
PLUM, WATCH SNOWBALL FOR ME, WOULD YOU...?
KUUU
SHAKE
SHAKE
NNN
SNOWBALL, WHERE'RE YOU GOING...?
DING
SIGH...
SNOW-BALL...
MUMBLE MUMBLE
DREEEAAM—
SO YOU'RE TELLING ME SNOWBALL IS LOST SOMEWHERE IN THIS BAMBOO THICKET, THEN?!
MYAH!
BUT WHEN DID SHE RUN OUT OF THE HOUSE...?
MYAH!
MYAAH!
MYA
MYA
MYAH
EH?
I MUSTN'T TURN AROUND ONCE I ENTER THIS BAMBOO THICKET...?
BUT WHY NOT...?
MYAH! MYA MYAN!
DON'T WORRY ABOUT THE DETAILS, YOU SAY...?
I SUP-POSE YOU'RE RIGHT...

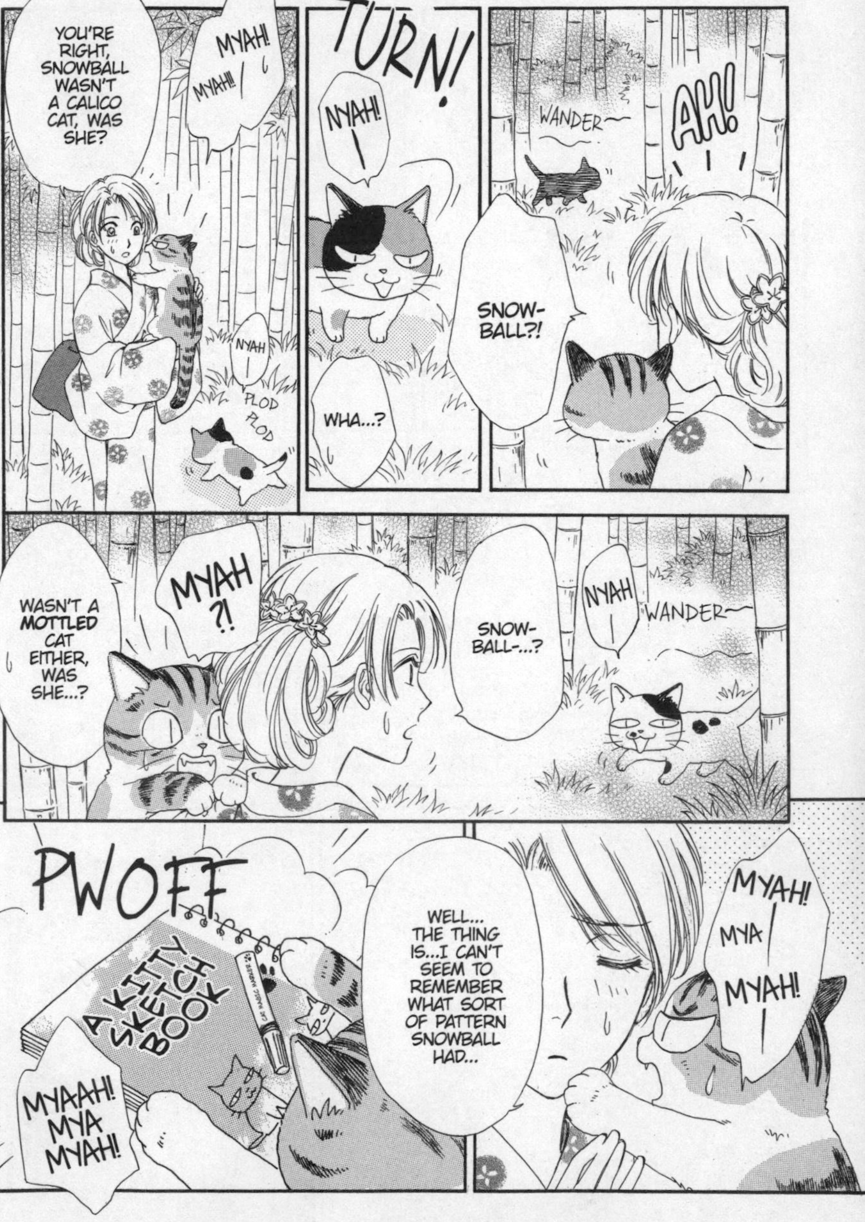
AH!
WANDER~
SNOW-BALL?!
TURN!
NYAH!
WHA...?
MYAH!
MYAH!!
YOU'RE RIGHT, SNOWBALL WASN'T A CALICO CAT, WAS SHE?
NYAH
PLOD PLOD
WANDER~
NYAH
SNOW-BALL-...?
MYAH ?!
WASN'T A MOTTLED CAT EITHER, WAS SHE...?
MYAH! MYA MYAH!
WELL... THE THING IS...I CAN'T SEEM TO REMEMBER WHAT SORT OF PATTERN SNOWBALL HAD...
PWOFF
A KITTY SKETCH BOOK
MYAAH! MYA MYAH!

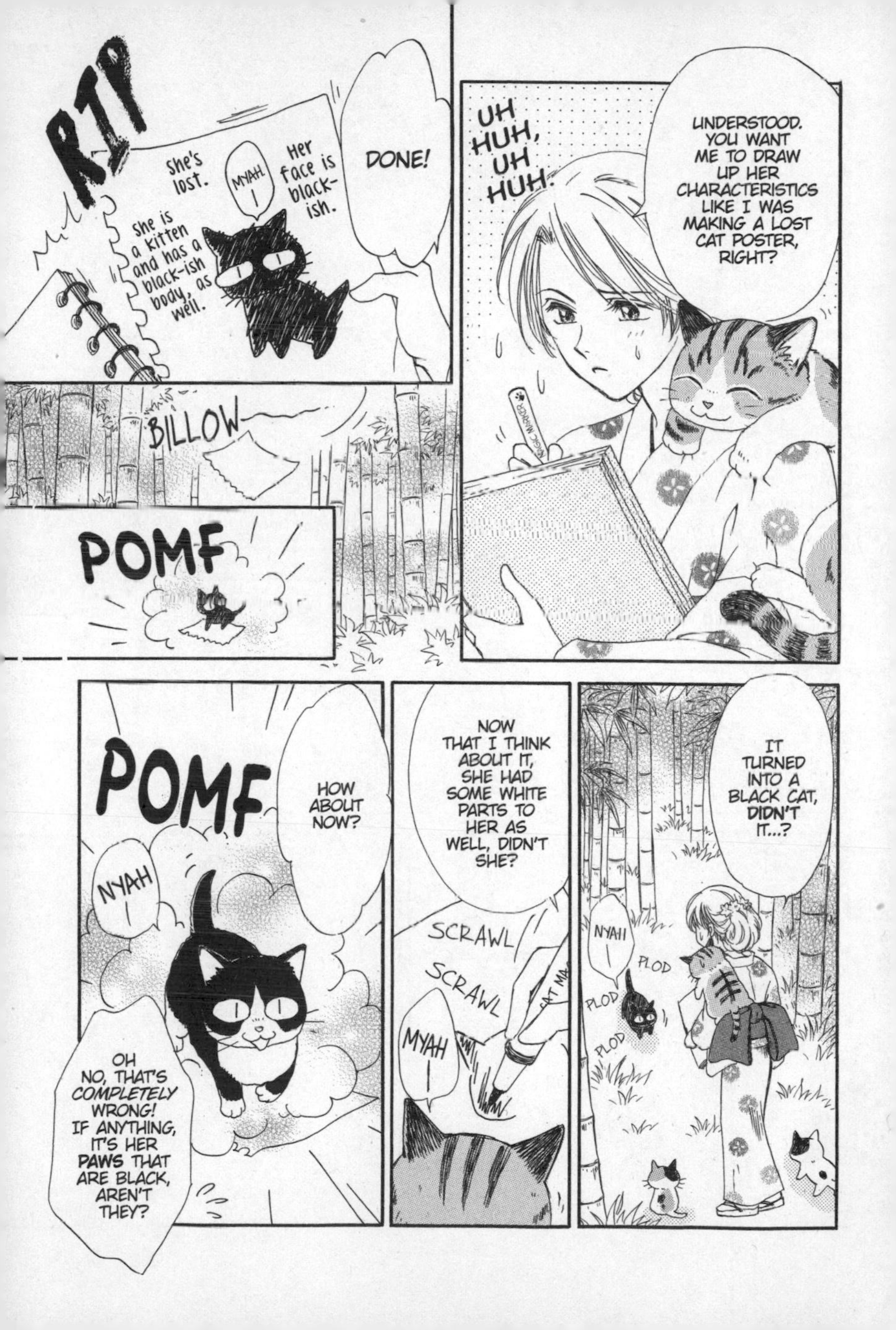
UNDERSTOOD. YOU WANT ME TO DRAW UP HER CHARACTERISTICS LIKE I WAS MAKING A LOST CAT POSTER, RIGHT?
UH HUH, UH HUH.
MAGIC MARKER
DONE!
RIP
She's lost.
Her face is black-ish.
MYAH
She is a kitten and has a black-ish body, as well.
BILLOW
POMF
IT TURNED INTO A BLACK CAT, DIDN'T IT...?
NYAH
PLOD
PLOD
PLOD
NOW THAT I THINK ABOUT IT, SHE HAD SOME WHITE PARTS TO HER AS WELL, DIDN'T SHE?
SCRAWL
SCRAWL
MYAH
POMF
HOW ABOUT NOW?
NYAH
OH NO, THAT'S COMPLETELY WRONG! IF ANYTHING, IT'S HER PAWS THAT ARE BLACK, AREN'T THEY?

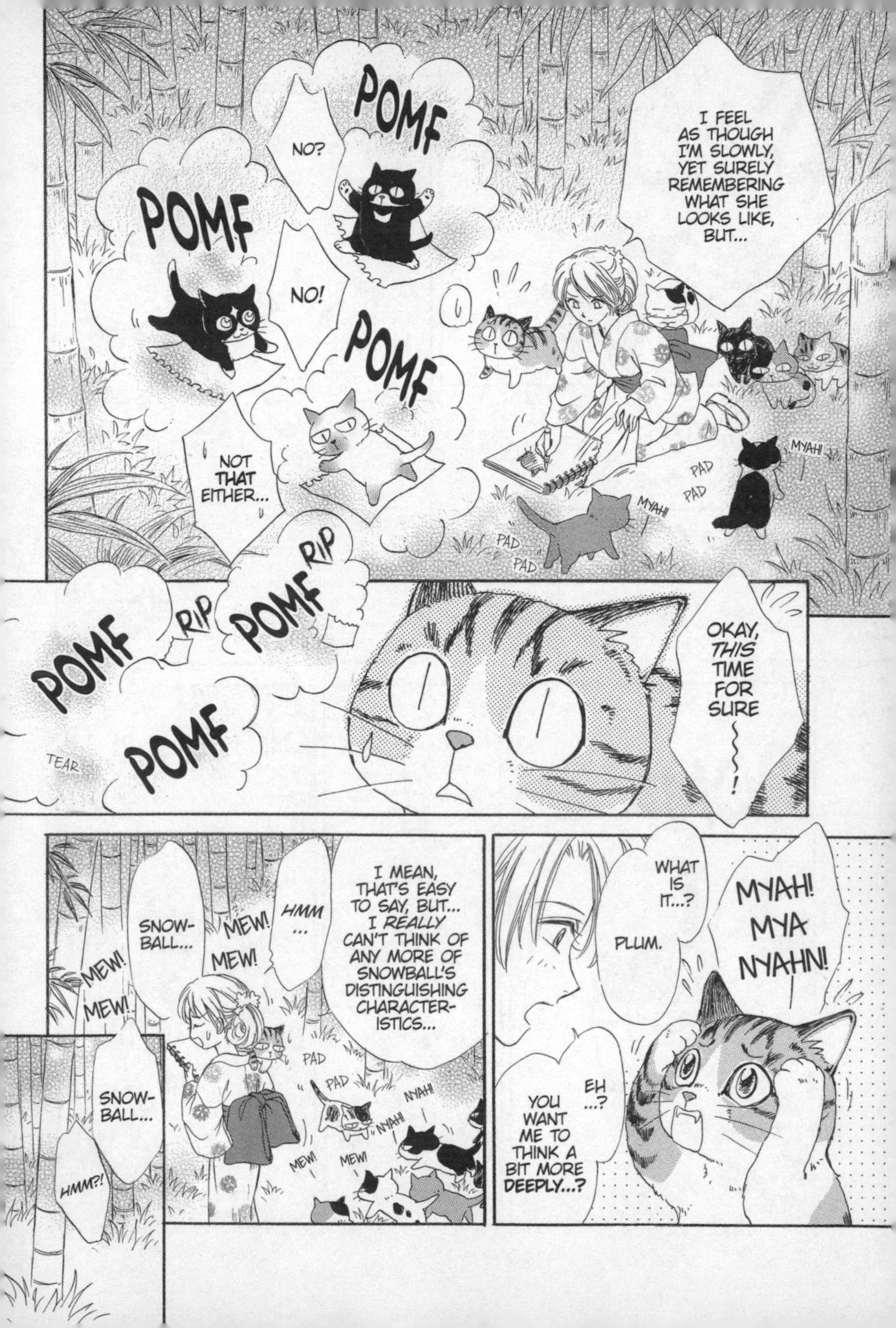
I FEEL AS THOUGH I'M SLOWLY, YET SURELY REMEMBERING WHAT SHE LOOKS LIKE, BUT...
POMF
NO?
POMF
NO!
POMF
NOT THAT EITHER...
MYAH!
PAD
PAD
MYAH!
PAD
PAD
OKAY, THIS TIME FOR SURE~~~!
RIP
POMF
RIP
POMF
POMF
TEAR
MYAH! MYA NYAHN!
WHAT IS IT...?
PLUM.
EH...?
YOU WANT ME TO THINK A BIT MORE DEEPLY...?
I MEAN, THAT'S EASY TO SAY, BUT... I REALLY CAN'T THINK OF ANY MORE OF SNOWBALL'S DISTINGUISHING CHARACTER-ISTICS...
HMM...
MEW!
MEW!
SNOW-BALL...
MEW!
MEW!
PAD
PAD
NYAH!
NYAH!
MEW!
MEW!
SNOW-BALL...
HMM?!

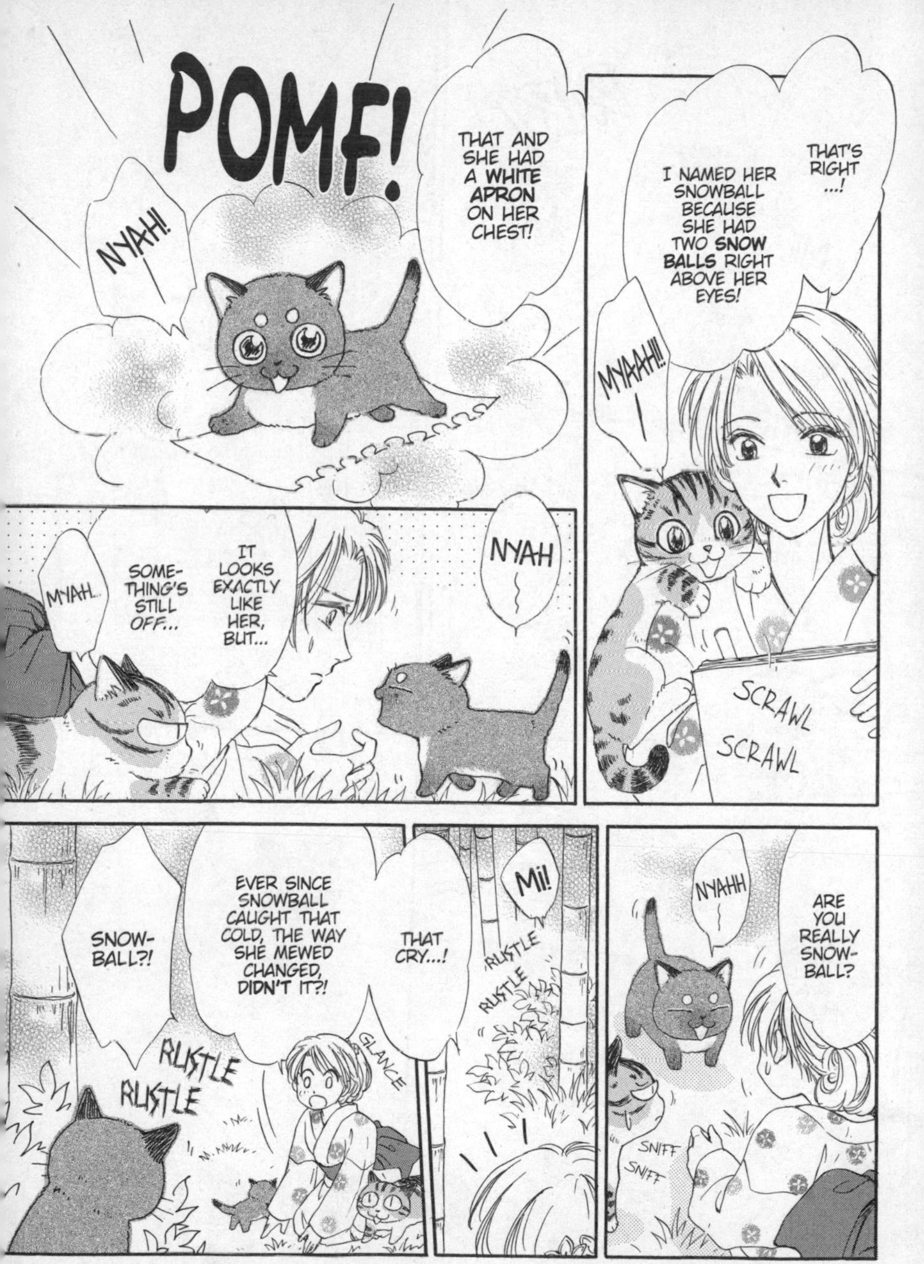
THAT'S RIGHT ...!
I NAMED HER SNOWBALL BECAUSE SHE HAD TWO **SNOW BALLS** RIGHT ABOVE HER EYES!
MYAAH!!
SCRAWL
SCRAWL
THAT AND SHE HAD A **WHITE APRON** ON HER CHEST!
POMF!
NYAH!
NYAH
IT LOOKS EXACTLY LIKE HER, BUT...
SOME-THING'S STILL OFF...
MYAH...
ARE YOU REALLY SNOW-BALL?
NYAHH
SNIFF
SNIFF
Mi!
RUSTLE
RUSTLE
THAT CRY...!
EVER SINCE SNOWBALL CAUGHT THAT COLD, THE WAY SHE MEWED CHANGED, **DIDN'T IT?!**
GLANCE
SNOW-BALL?!
RUSTLE
RUSTLE

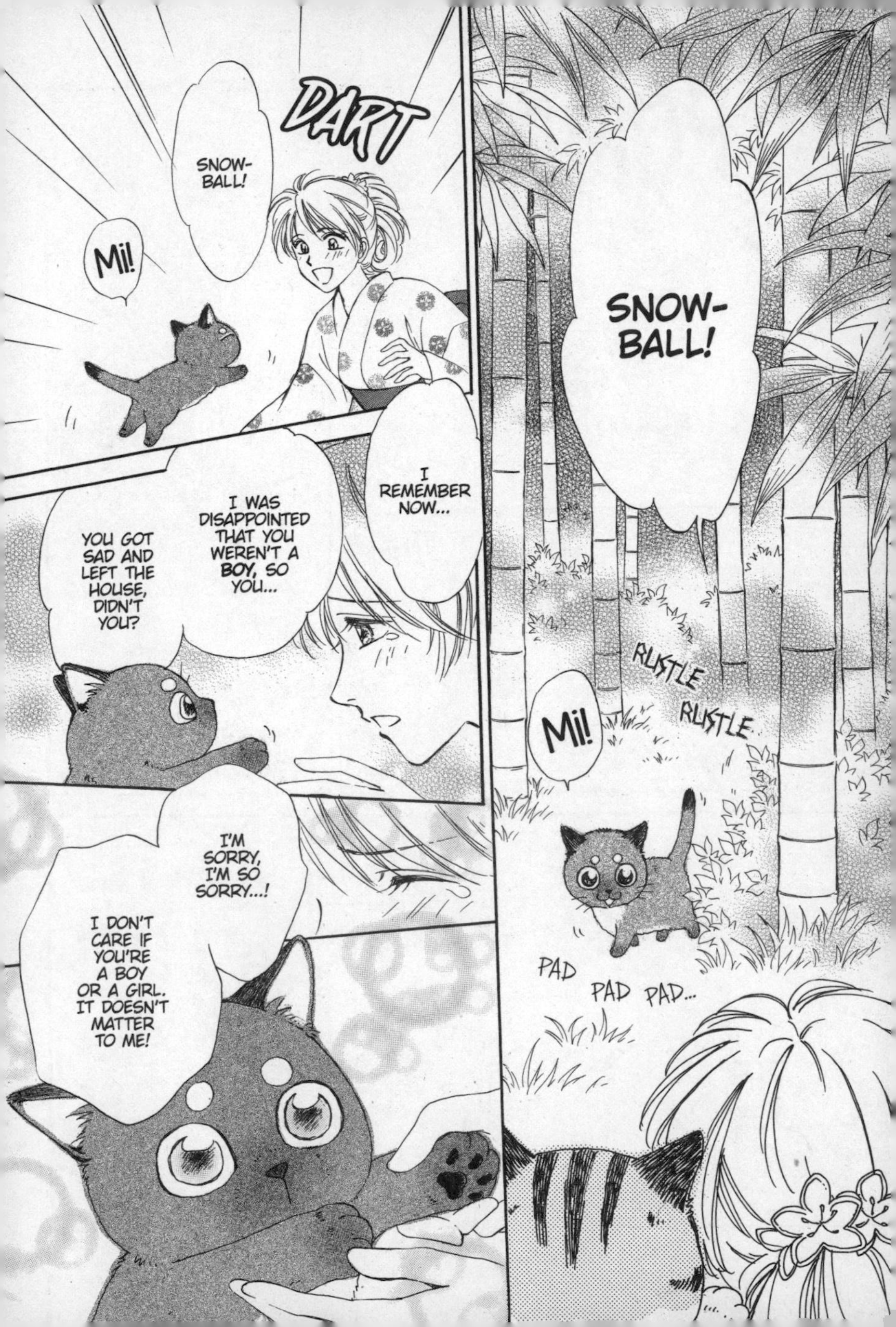
SNOW-BALL!
RUSTLE
RUSTLE
Mi!
PAD
PAD PAD...
DART
SNOW-BALL!
Mi!
I REMEMBER NOW...
I WAS DISAPPOINTED THAT YOU WEREN'T A BOY, SO YOU...
YOU GOT SAD AND LEFT THE HOUSE, DIDN'T YOU?
I'M SORRY, I'M SO SORRY...!
I DON'T CARE IF YOU'RE A BOY OR A GIRL. IT DOESN'T MATTER TO ME!

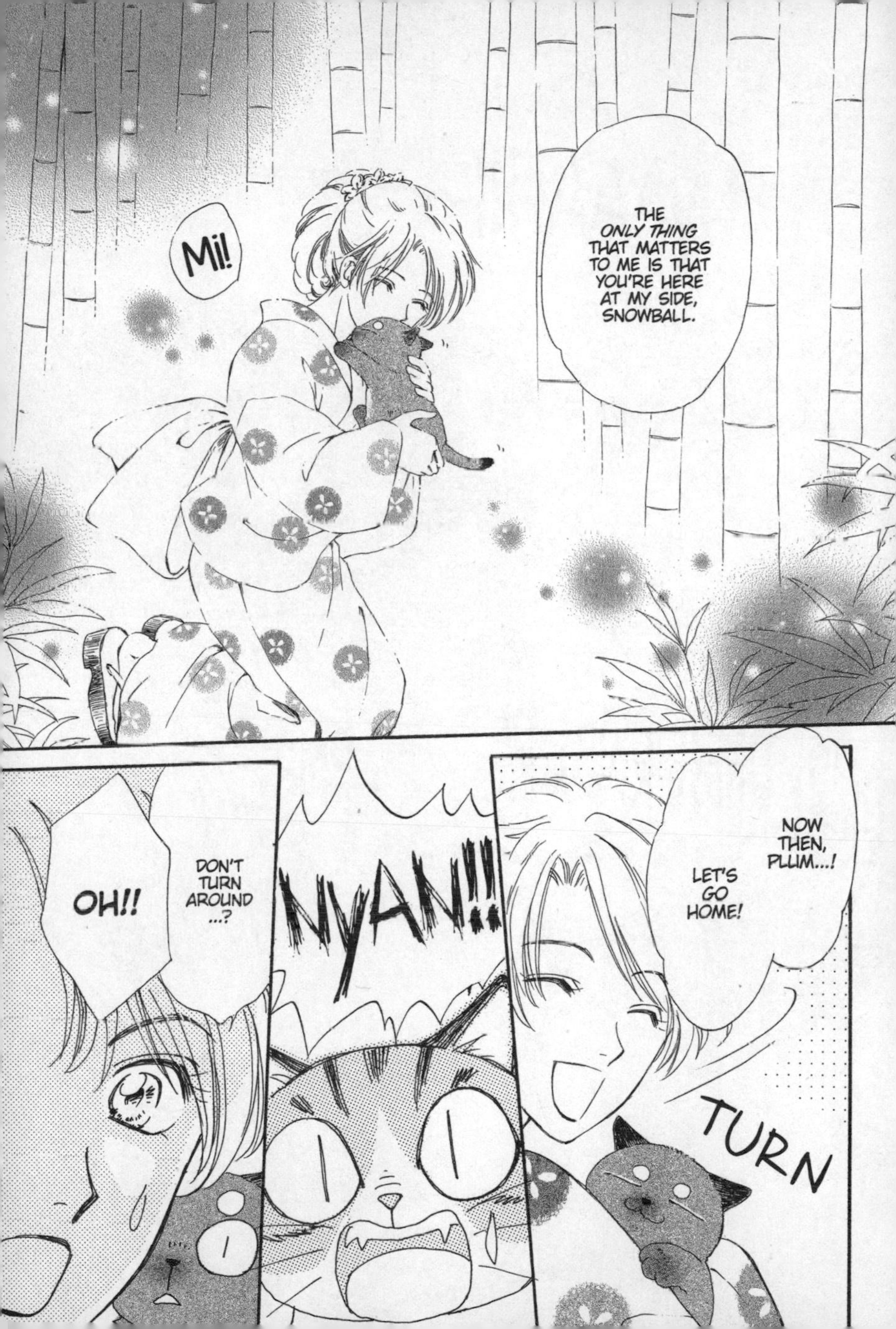
THE ONLY THING THAT MATTERS TO ME IS THAT YOU'RE HERE AT MY SIDE, SNOWBALL.
Mi!
NOW THEN, PLUM...!
LET'S GO HOME!
TURN
NYAN!!
DON'T TURN AROUND ...?
OH!!

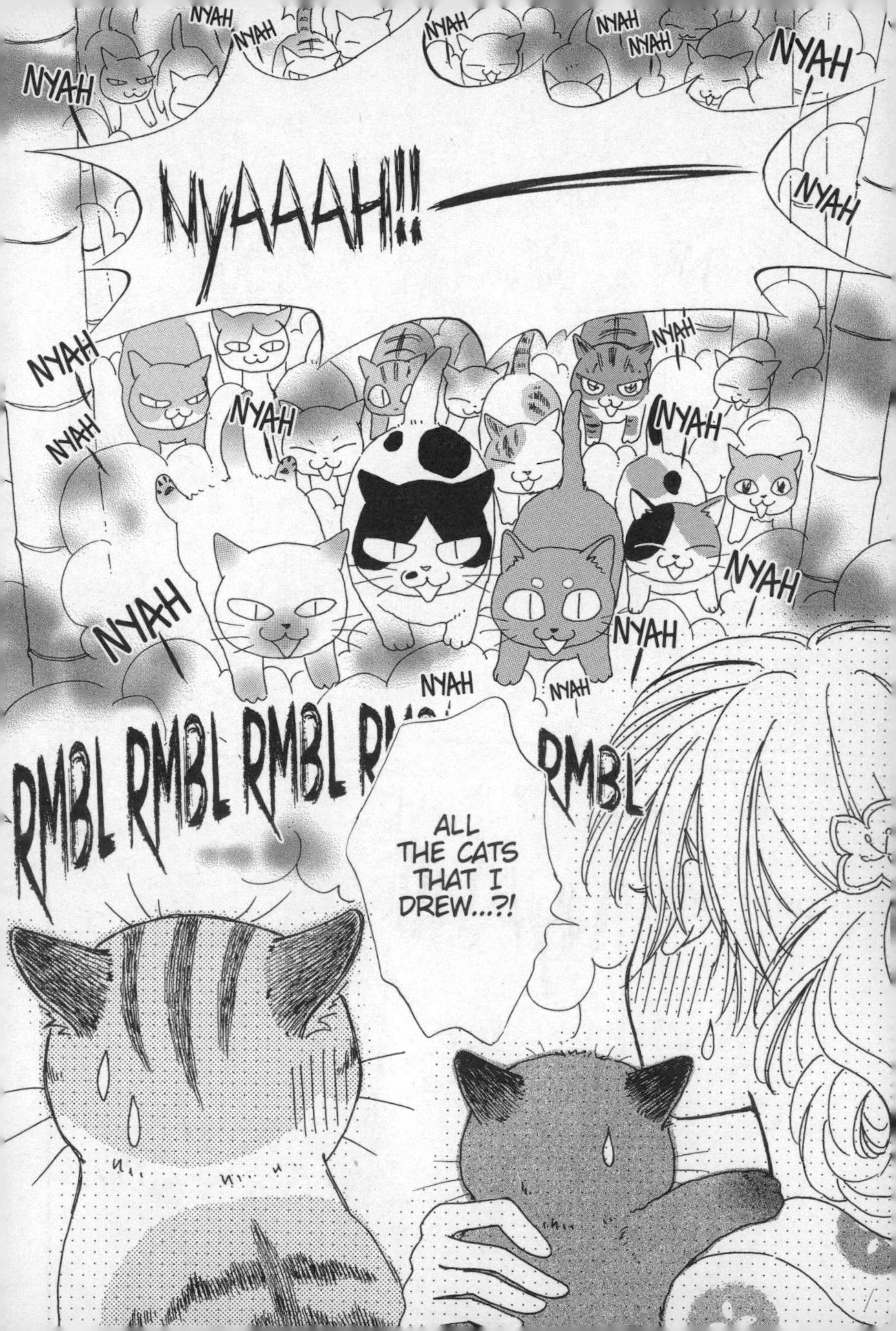
NYAH
NYAH
NYAH
NYAH
NYAH
NYAH
NYAAAH!!
NYAH
NYAH
NYAH
NYAH
NYAH
NYAH
NYAH
NYAH
NYAH
NYAH
RMBL RMBL RMBL RMBL
ALL THE CATS THAT I DREW...?!
"..."
"..."

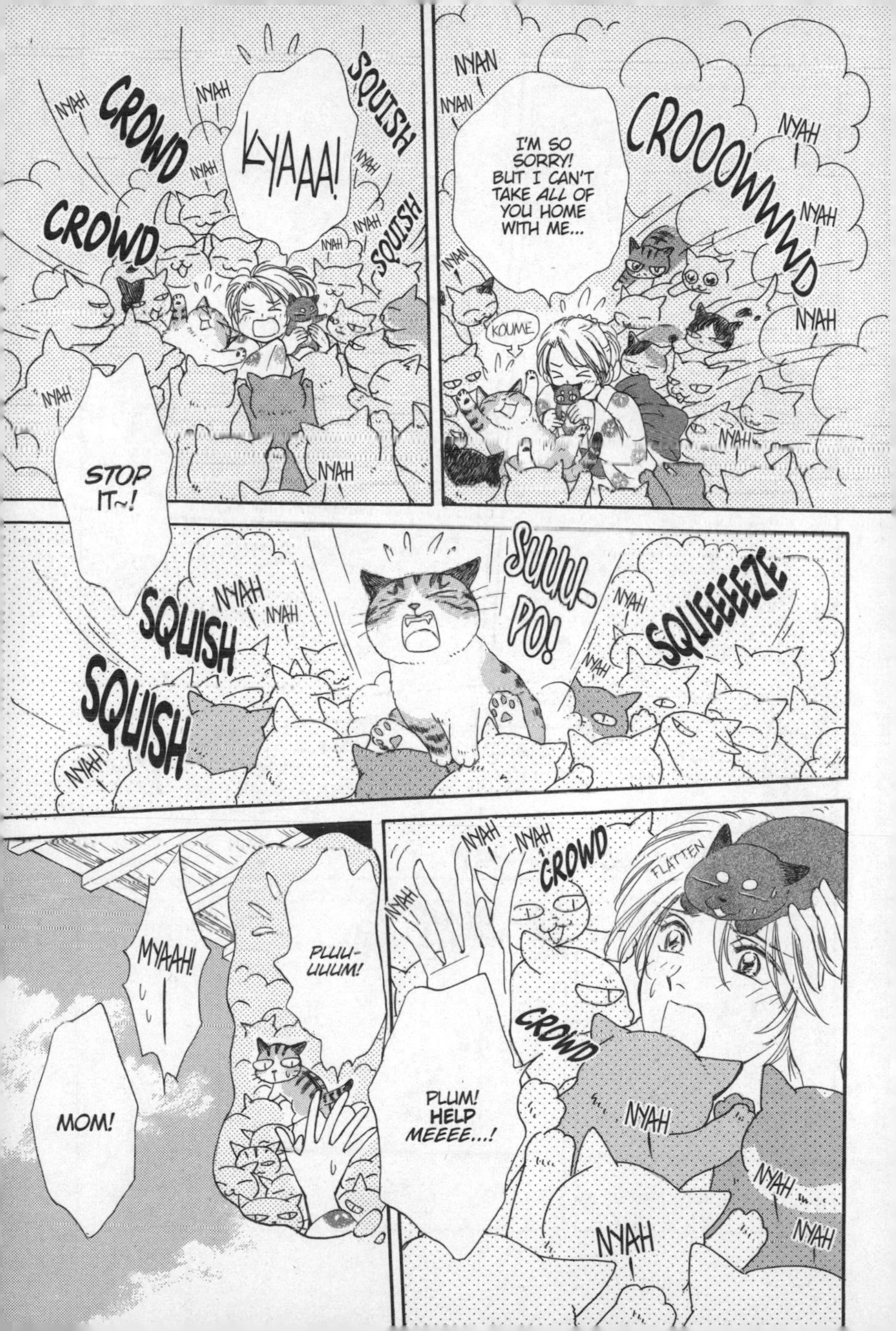
NYAN
NYAN
I'M SO SORRY! BUT I CAN'T TAKE ALL OF YOU HOME WITH ME...
CROOOWWWD
NYAH
NYAH
NYAH
NYAN
KOUME
NYAH
NYAH
CROWD
NYAH
KYAAA!
SQUISH
NYAH
NYAH
SQUISH
CROWD
NYAH
STOP IT~!
NYAH
SUUU-PO!
SQUEEEEZE
NYAH
NYAH
NYAH
NYAH
SQUISH
SQUISH
NYAH
NYAH
NYAH
CROWD
FLATTEN
NYAH
CROWD
PLUM! HELP MEEEE...!
NYAH
NYAH
NYAH
NYAH
PLUU-UUUM!
MYAAH!
MOM!

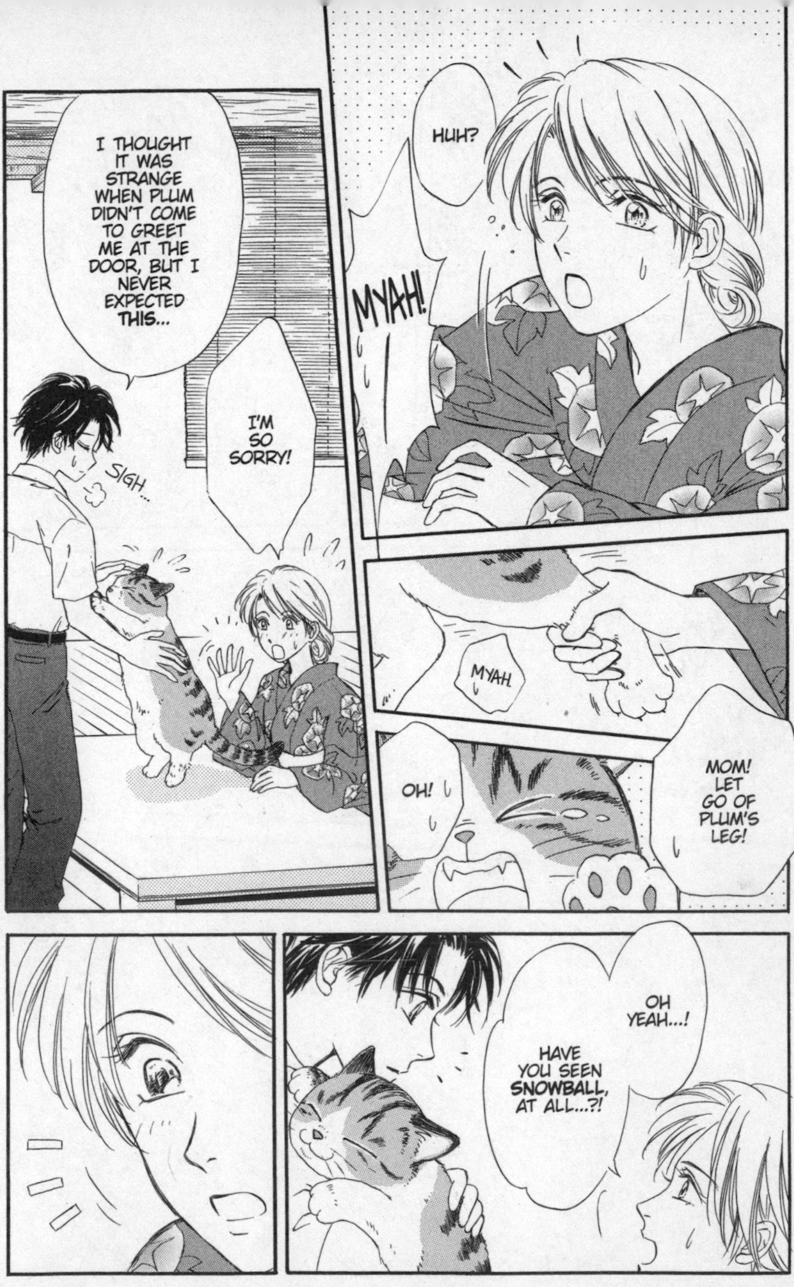
HUH?
MYAH!
MYAH.
MOM! LET GO OF PLUM'S LEG!
OH!
I THOUGHT IT WAS STRANGE WHEN PLUM DIDN'T COME TO GREET ME AT THE DOOR, BUT I NEVER EXPECTED THIS...
I'M SO SORRY!
SIGH...
OH YEAH...!
HAVE YOU SEEN SNOWBALL, AT ALL...?!

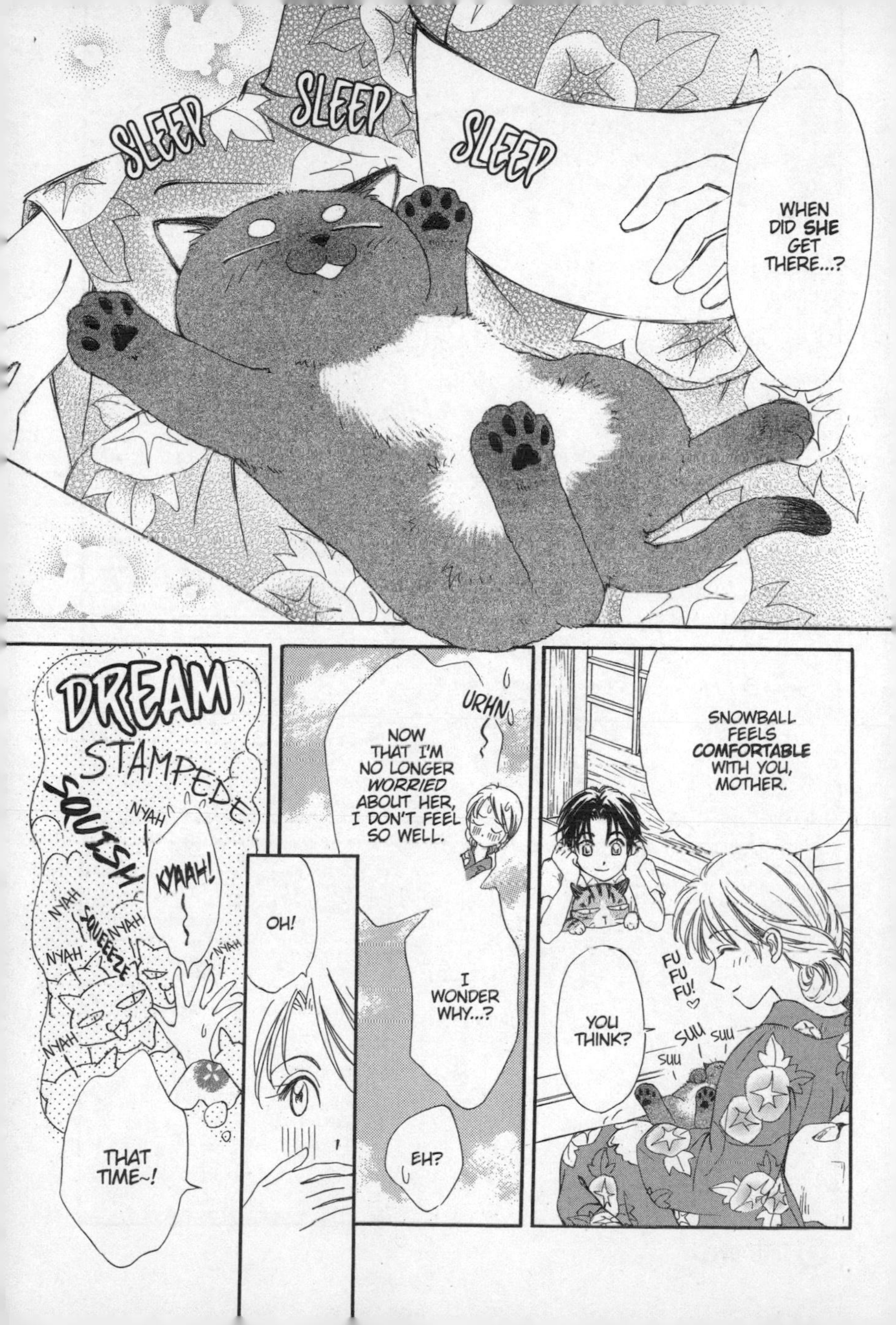
WHEN DID SHE GET THERE...?
SLEEP
SLEEP
SLEEP
SNOWBALL FEELS COMFORTABLE WITH YOU, MOTHER.
FU FU FU!
YOU THINK?
SUU
SUU
SUU
URHN
NOW THAT I'M NO LONGER WORRIED ABOUT HER, I DON'T FEEL SO WELL.
I WONDER WHY...?
EH?
OH!
DREAM
STAMPEDE
SQUISH
KYAAH!
NYAH
NYAH
NYAH
SQUEEEZE
NYAH
NYAH
NYAH
THAT TIME~!

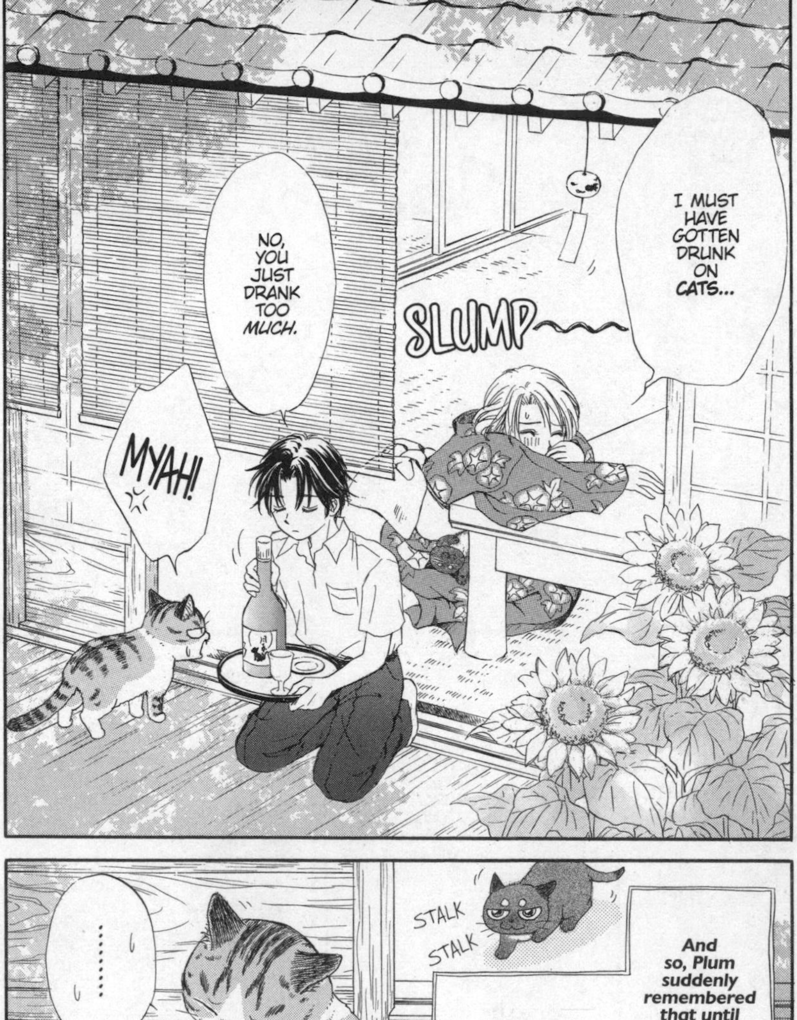
I MUST HAVE GOTTEN DRUNK ON CATS...
SLUMP
NO, YOU JUST DRANK TOO MUCH.
MYAH!

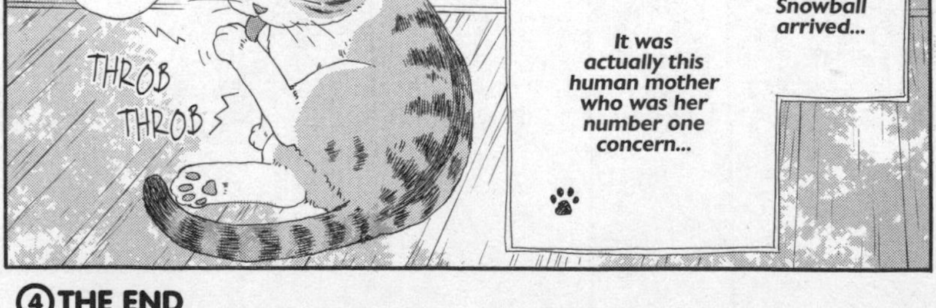
And so, Plum suddenly remembered that until Snowball arrived...
It was actually this human mother who was her number one concern...
STALK STALK
......
THROB THROB

④ THE END

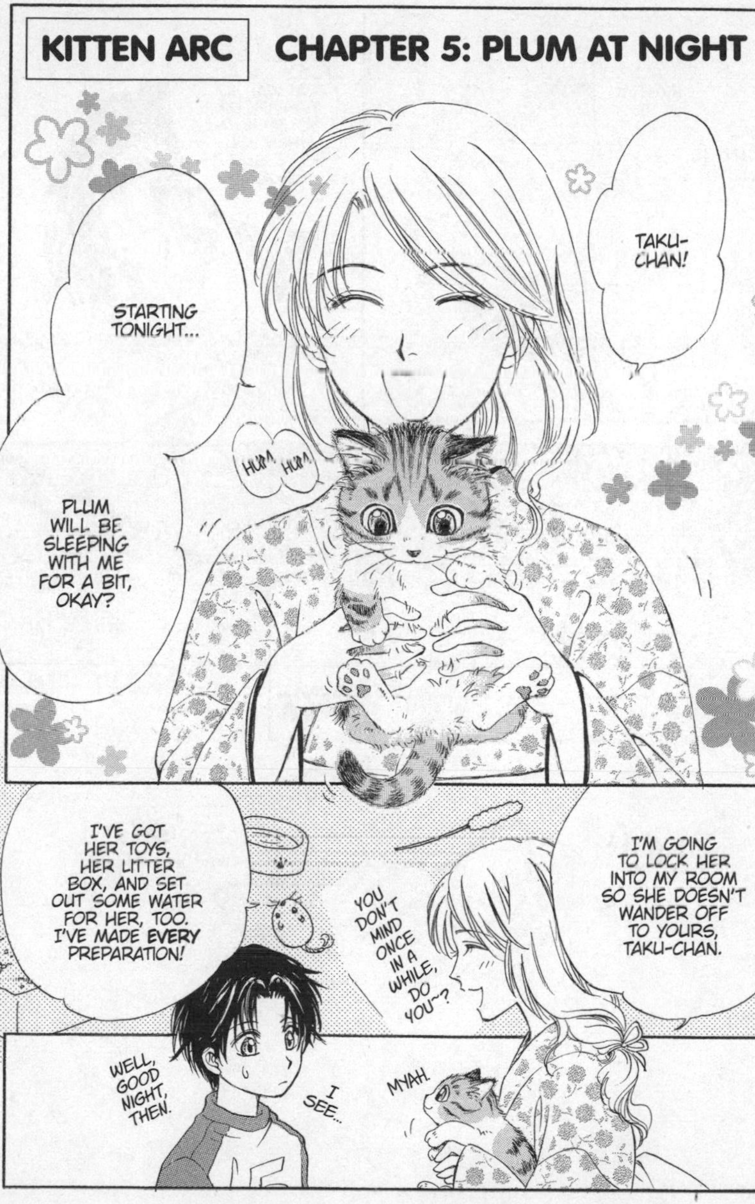
KITTEN ARC CHAPTER 5: PLUM AT NIGHT
TAKU-CHAN!
STARTING TONIGHT...
HUPA, HUPA
PLUM WILL BE SLEEPING WITH ME FOR A BIT, OKAY?
I'M GOING TO LOCK HER INTO MY ROOM SO SHE DOESN'T WANDER OFF TO YOURS, TAKU-CHAN.
YOU DON'T MIND ONCE IN A WHILE, DO YOU~?
I'VE GOT HER TOYS, HER LITTER BOX, AND SET OUT SOME WATER FOR HER, TOO. I'VE MADE EVERY PREPARATION!
MYAH.
I SEE...
WELL, GOOD NIGHT, THEN.

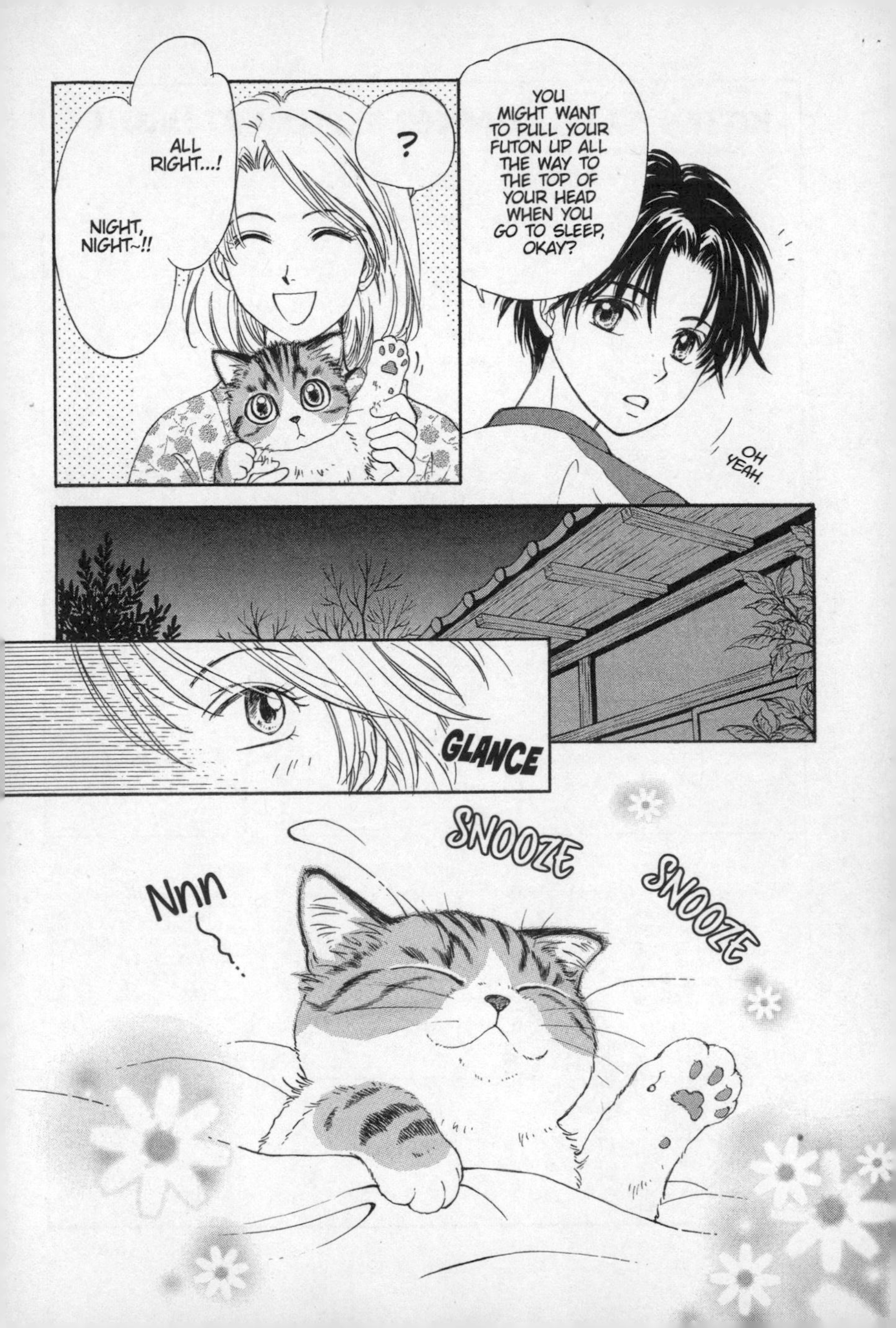
YOU MIGHT WANT TO PULL YOUR FUTON UP ALL THE WAY TO THE TOP OF YOUR HEAD WHEN YOU GO TO SLEEP, OKAY?
OH YEAH.
?
ALL RIGHT...!
NIGHT, NIGHT~!!
GLANCE
SNOOZE
SNOOZE
Nnn ~...

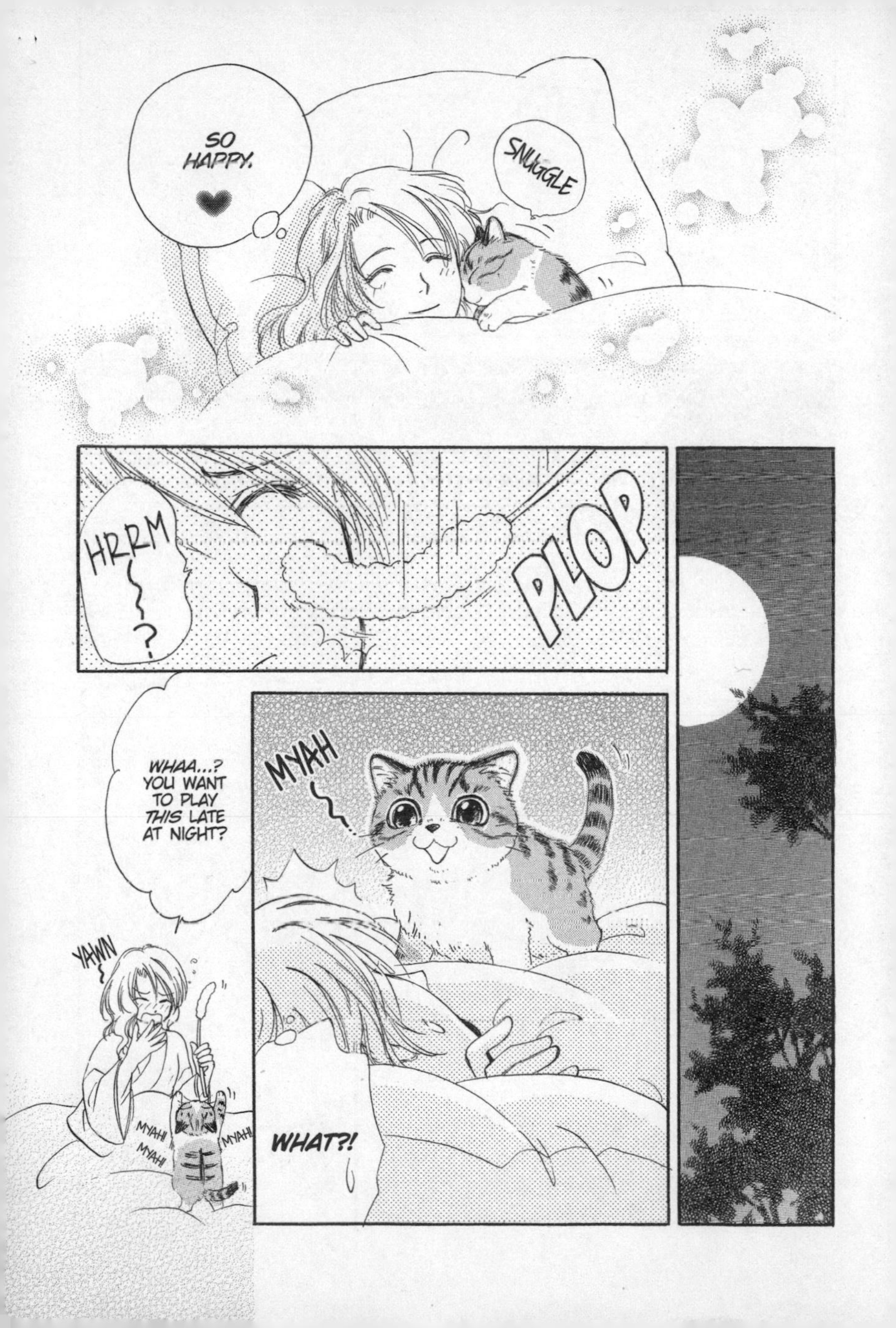
SNUGGLE
SO HAPPY.
PLOP
HRRM~~?
MYAH~~
WHAT?!
WHAA...? YOU WANT TO PLAY THIS LATE AT NIGHT?
YAWN
MYAH! MYAH! MYAH!

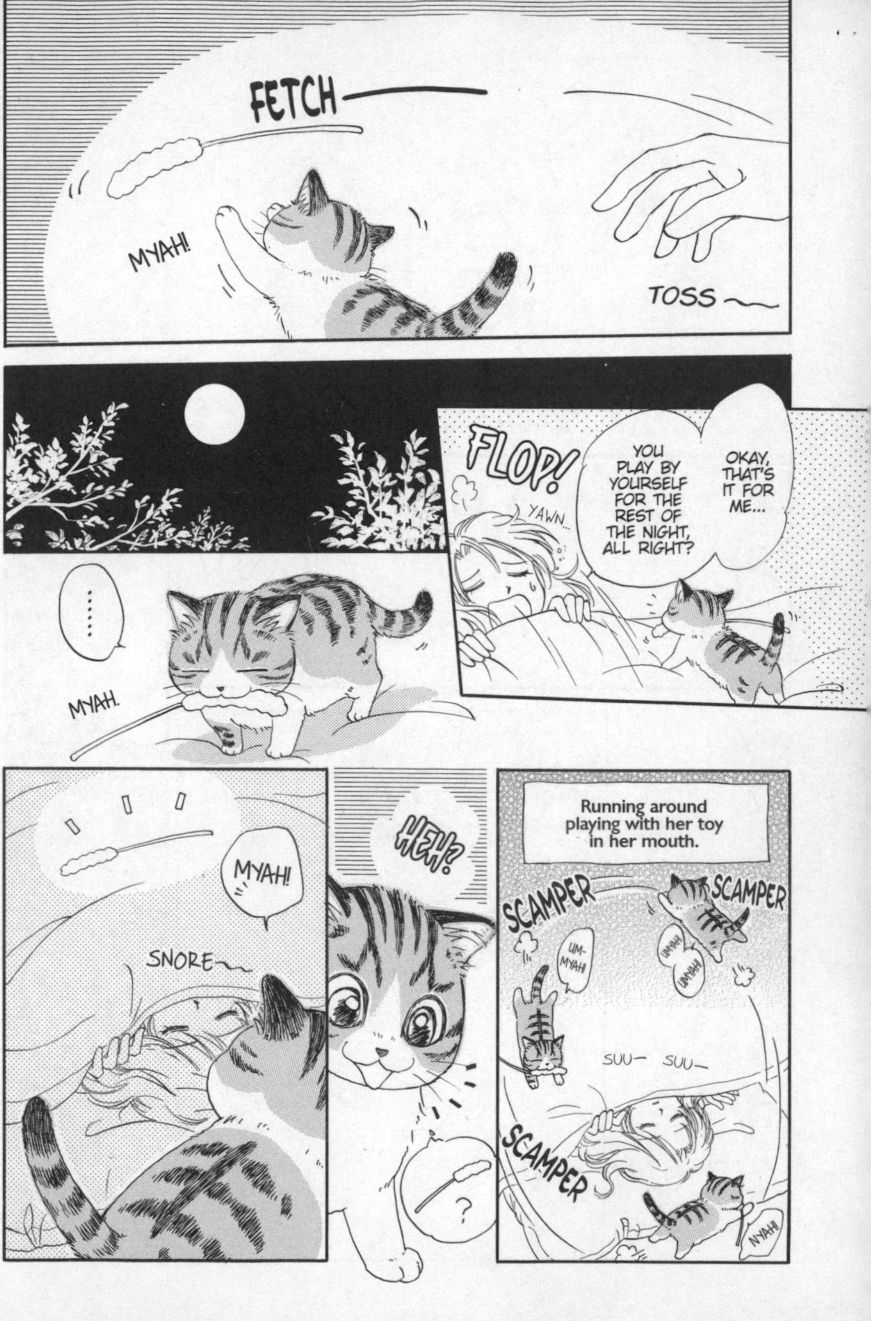
TOSS~
FETCH—
MYAH!
OKAY, THAT'S IT FOR ME...
YOU PLAY BY YOURSELF FOR THE REST OF THE NIGHT, ALL RIGHT?
FLOP!
YAWN...
......
MYAH.
Running around playing with her toy in her mouth.
SCAMPER
SCAMPER
UMYAH!
UMYAH!
UM-MYAH!
SUU— SUU—
SCAMPER
NYAH!
HEH?
?
MYAH!
SNORE~

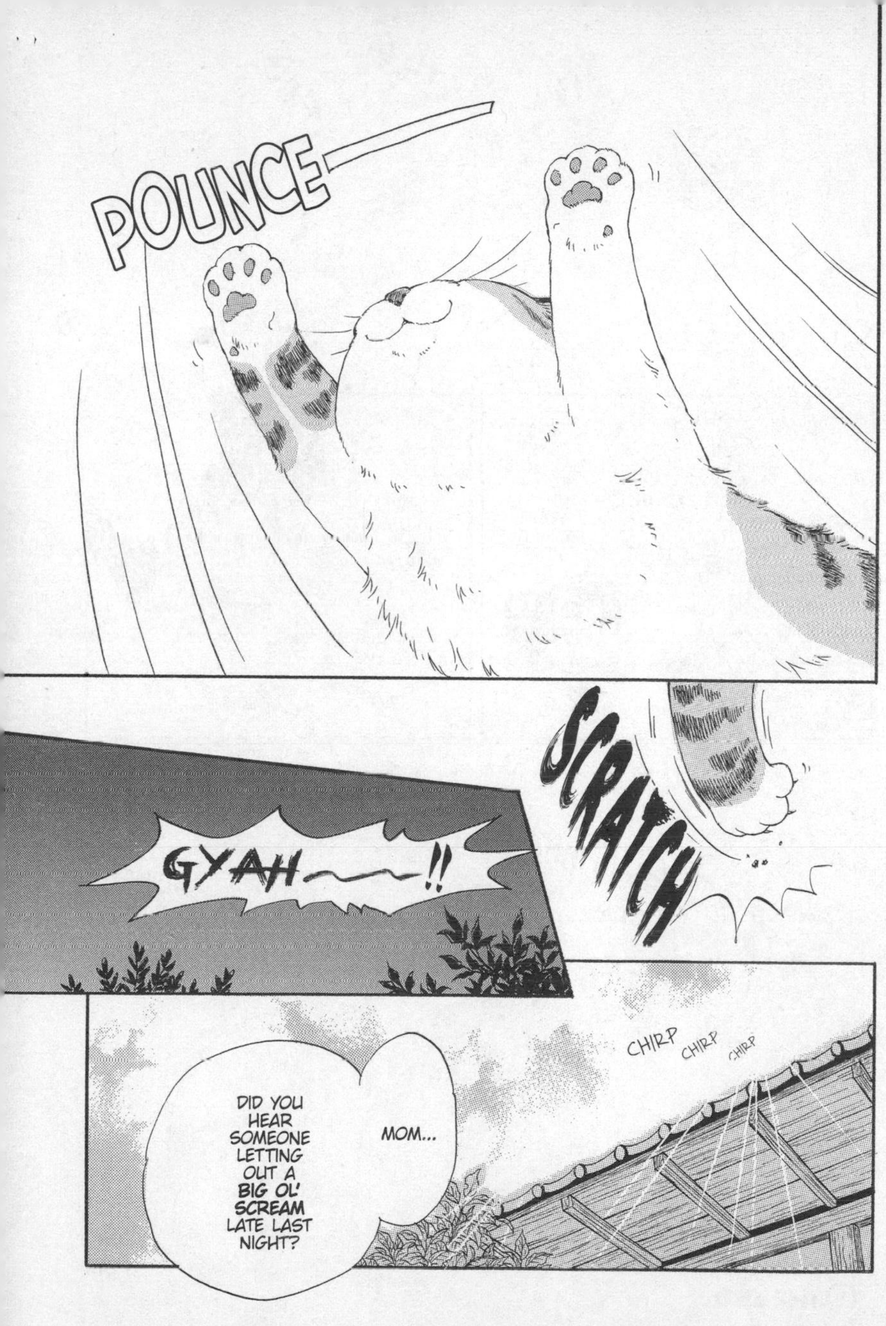
POUNCE
SCRATCH
GYAH——!!
CHIRP CHIRP CHIRP
MOM...
DID YOU HEAR SOMEONE LETTING OUT A **BIG OL' SCREAM** LATE LAST NIGHT?

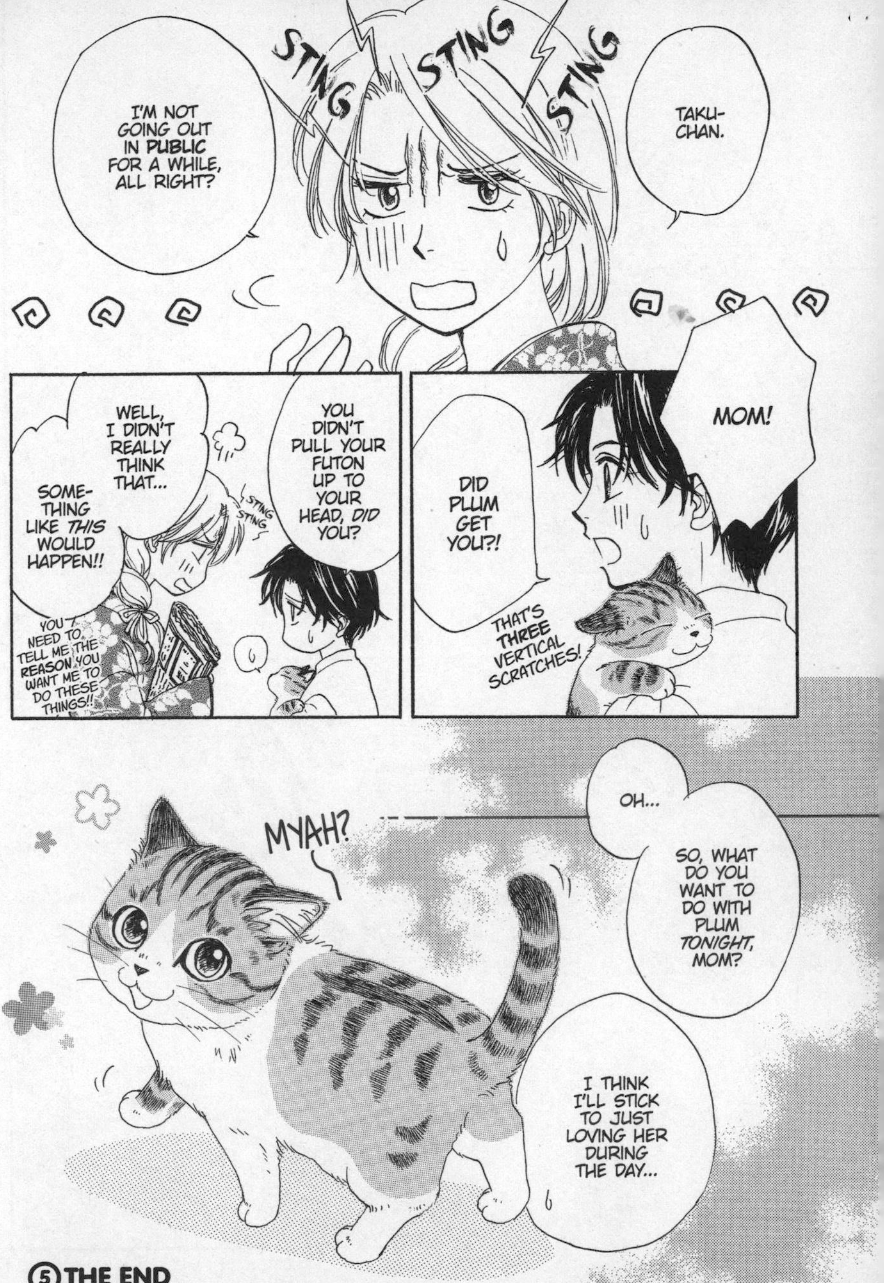
TAKU-CHAN.
STING STING STING
I'M NOT GOING OUT IN PUBLIC FOR A WHILE, ALL RIGHT?
MOM!
DID PLUM GET YOU?!
THAT'S THREE VERTICAL SCRATCHES!
YOU DIDN'T PULL YOUR FUTON UP TO YOUR HEAD, DID YOU?
STING STING
WELL, I DIDN'T REALLY THINK THAT...
SOME-THING LIKE THIS WOULD HAPPEN!!
YOU NEED TO TELL ME THE REASON YOU WANT ME TO DO THESE THINGS!!
OH...
SO, WHAT DO YOU WANT TO DO WITH PLUM TONIGHT, MOM?
I THINK I'LL STICK TO JUST LOVING HER DURING THE DAY...
MYAH?

5 THE END

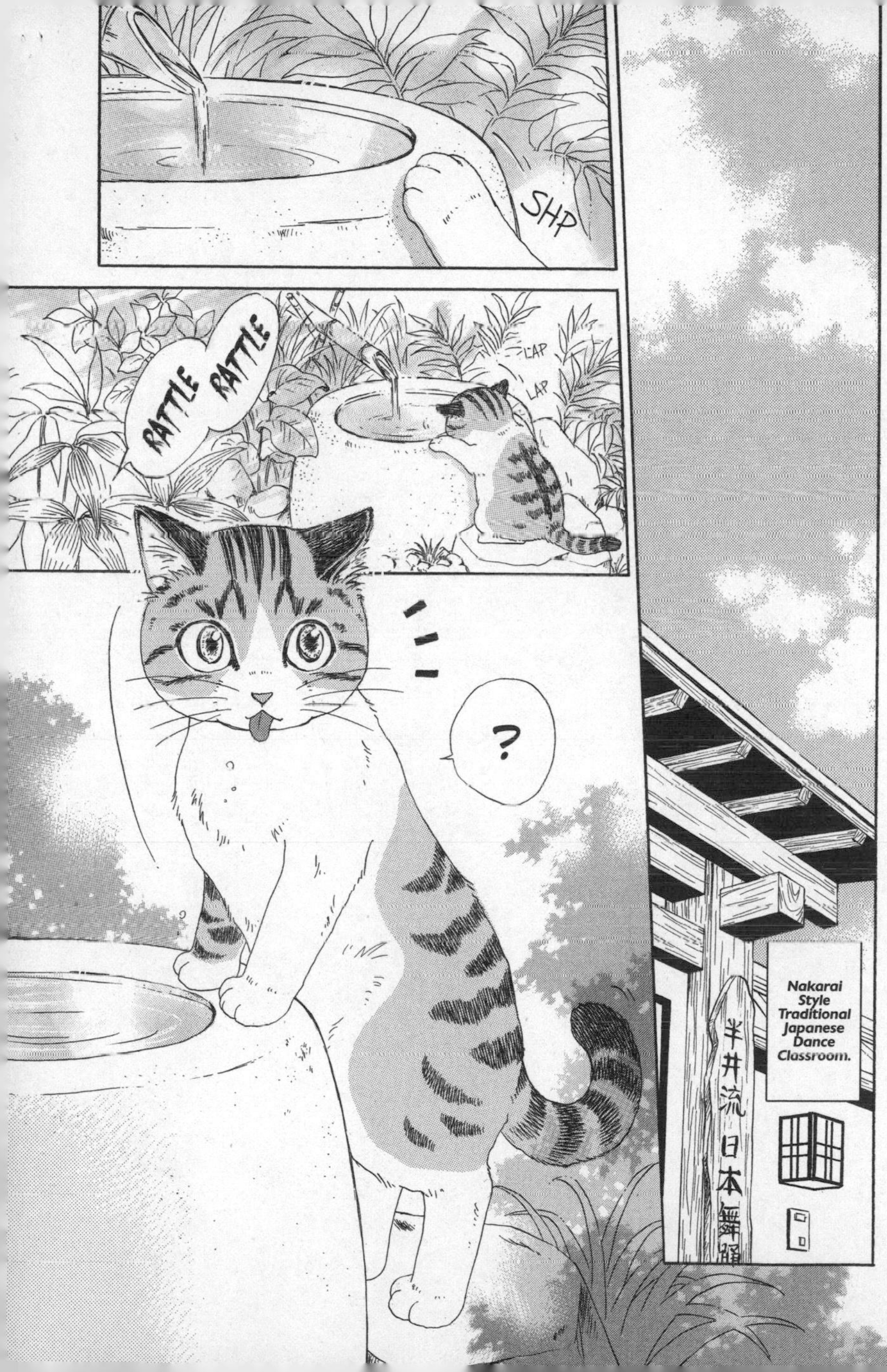
Nakarai Style Traditional Japanese Dance Classroom.
半井流日本舞踊
SHP
RATTLE RATTLE
LAP
LAP
?

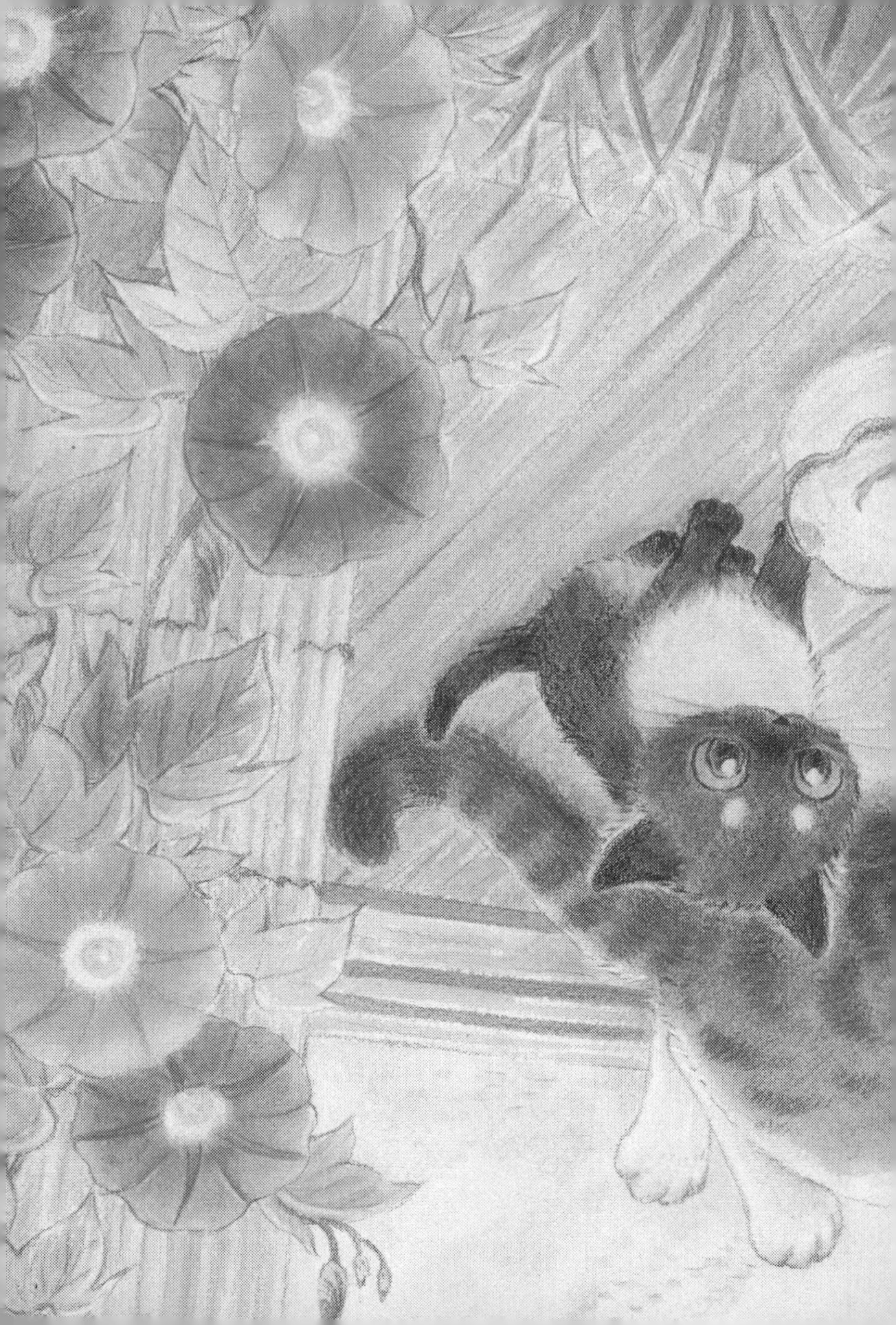

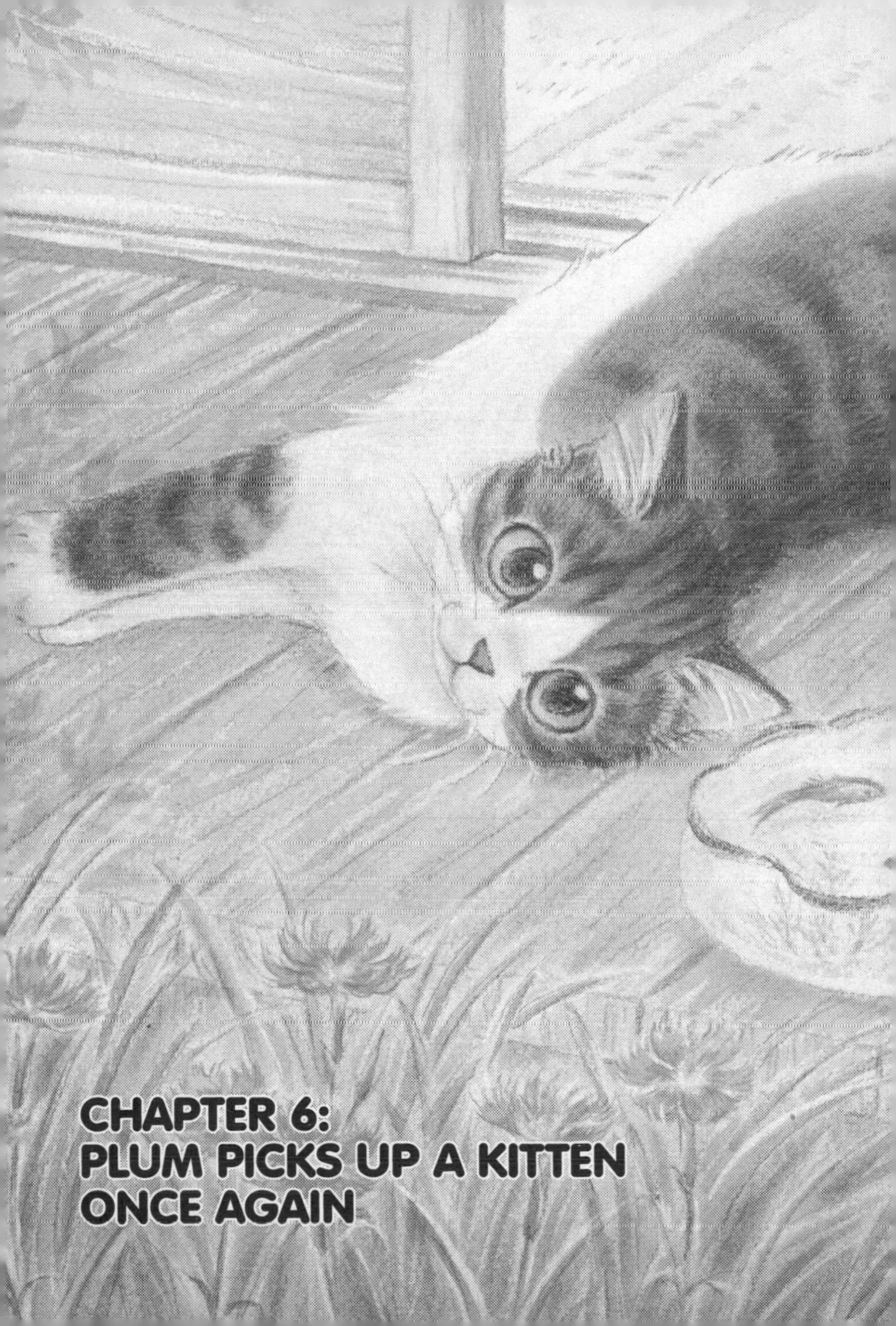
CHAPTER 6:
PLUM PICKS UP A KITTEN
ONCE AGAIN

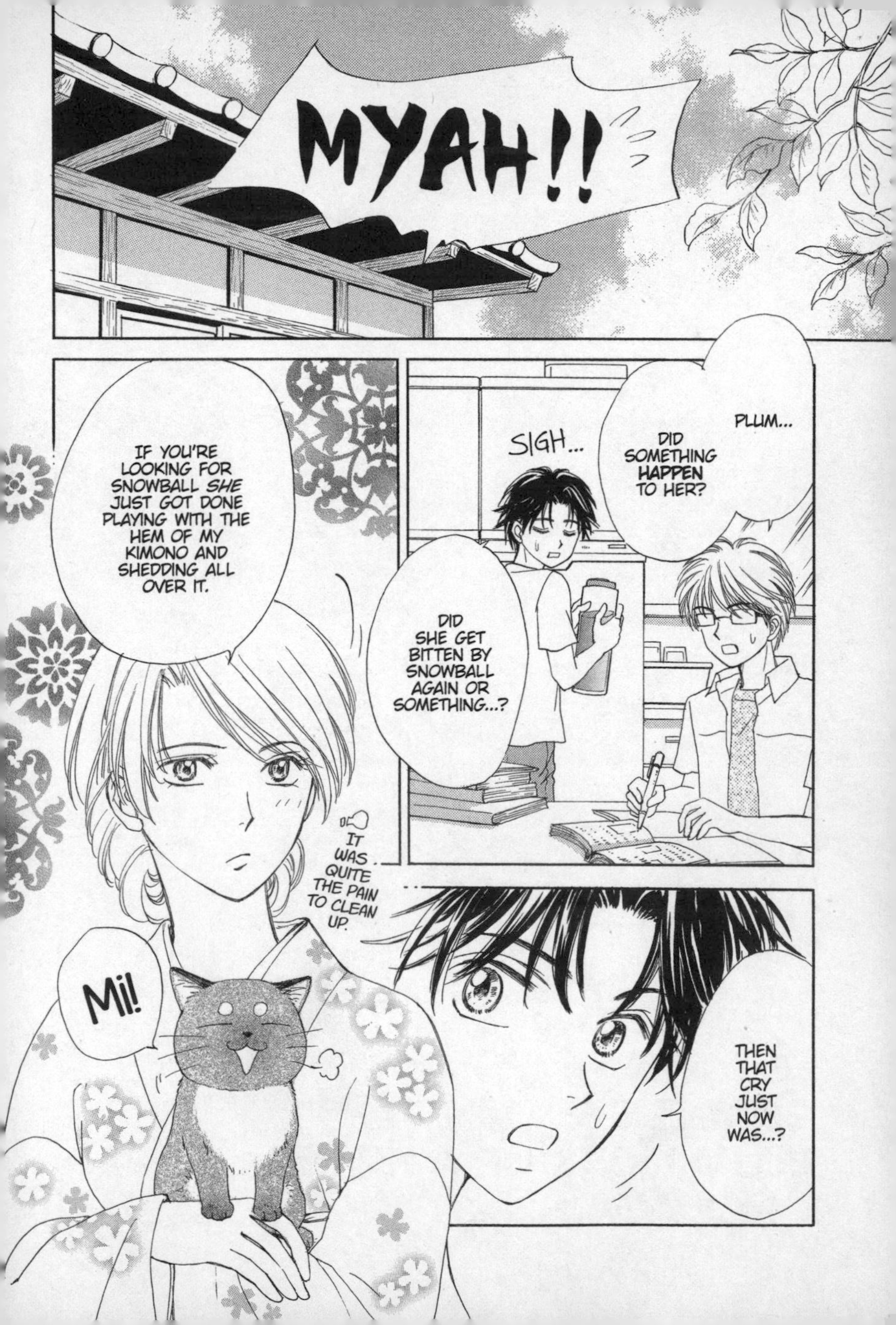
MYAH!!
PLUM... DID SOMETHING HAPPEN TO HER?
SIGH...
DID SHE GET BITTEN BY SNOWBALL AGAIN OR SOMETHING...?
IF YOU'RE LOOKING FOR SNOWBALL SHE JUST GOT DONE PLAYING WITH THE HEM OF MY KIMONO AND SHEDDING ALL OVER IT.
IT WAS... QUITE THE PAIN TO CLEAN UP.
THEN THAT CRY JUST NOW WAS...?
Mi!

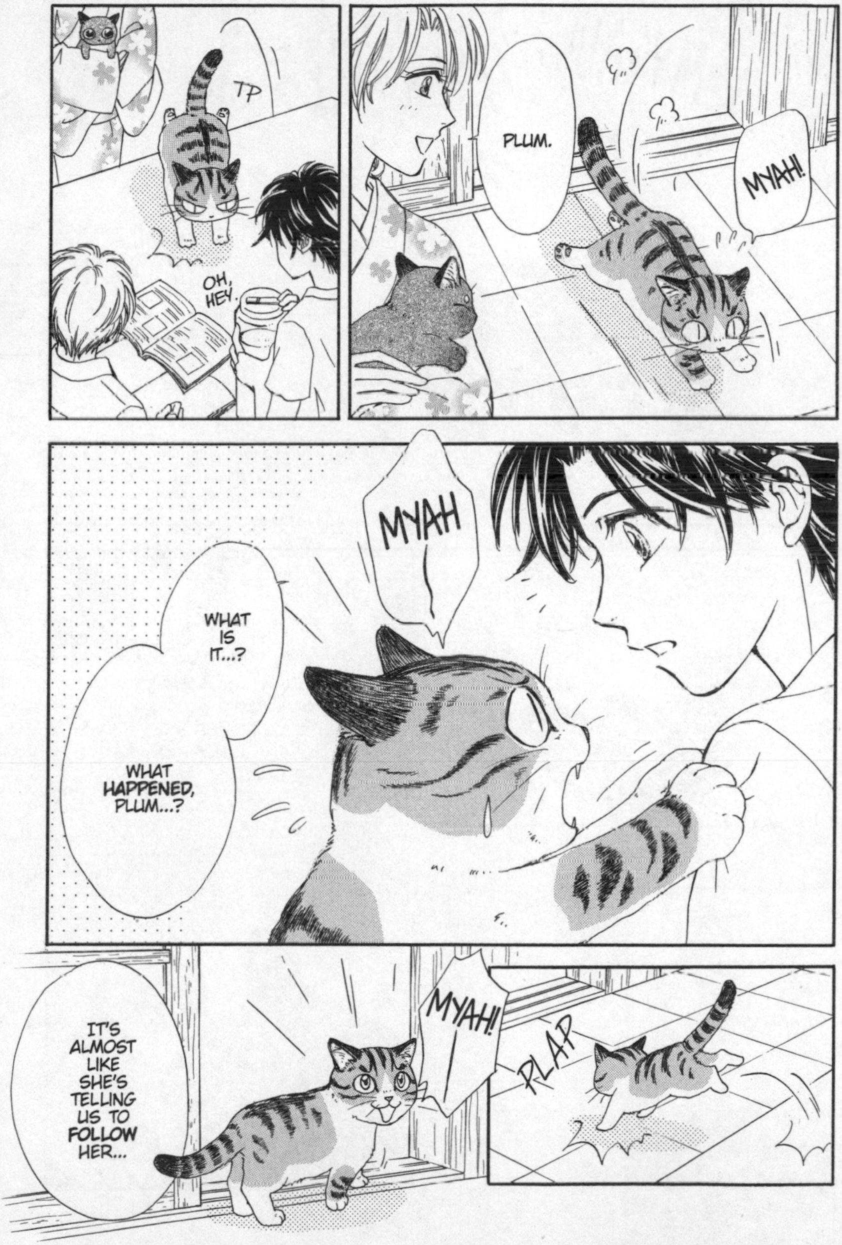
MYAH!
PLUM.
TP
OH, HEY.
MYAH
WHAT IS IT...?
WHAT HAPPENED, PLUM...?
RLAP
MYAH!
IT'S ALMOST LIKE SHE'S TELLING US TO FOLLOW HER...

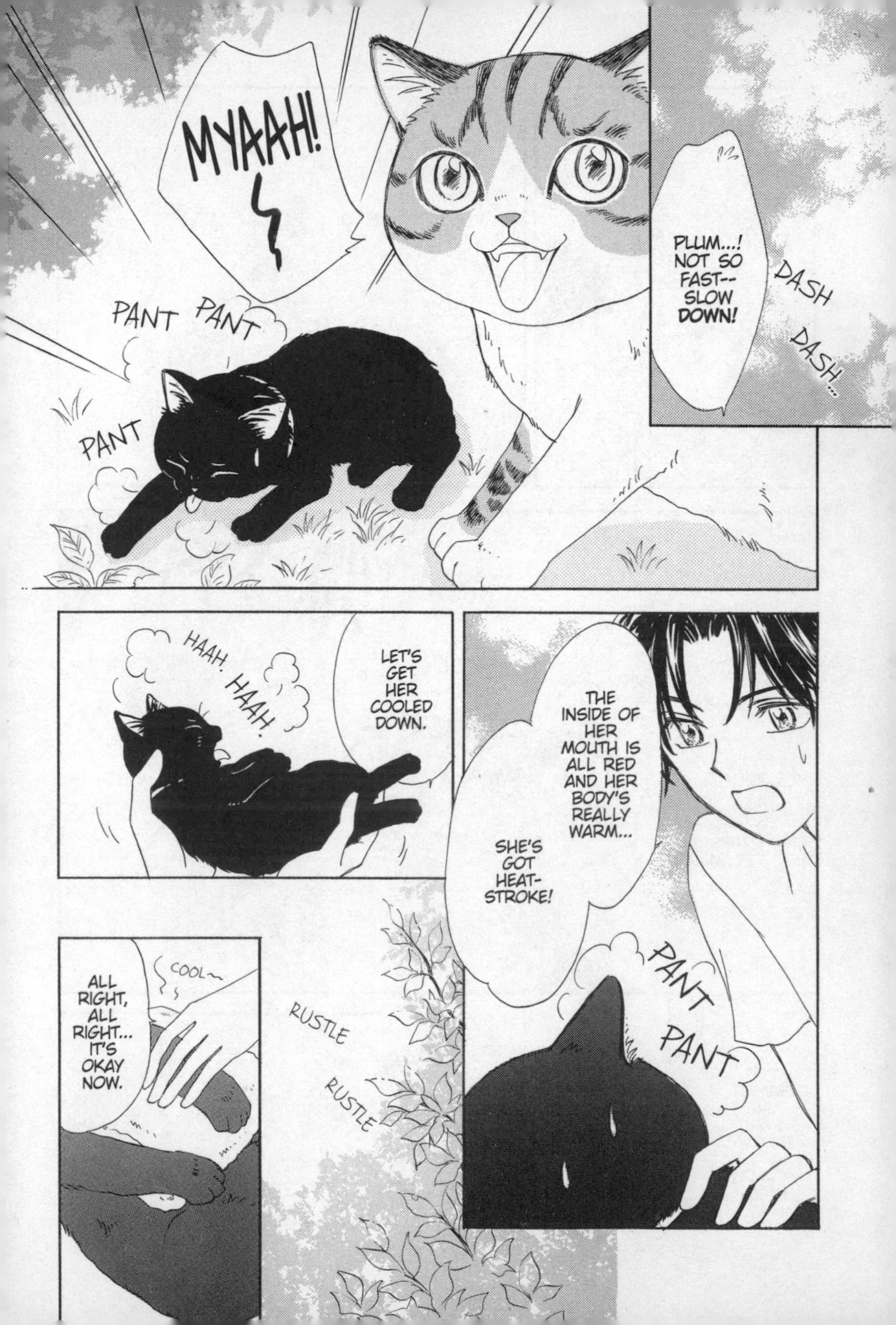
PLUM...! NOT SO FAST-- SLOW DOWN!
DASH DASH...
MYAAH!
PANT PANT
PANT
THE INSIDE OF HER MOUTH IS ALL RED AND HER BODY'S REALLY WARM...
SHE'S GOT HEAT-STROKE!
PANT PANT
LET'S GET HER COOLED DOWN.
HAAH. HAAH.
RUSTLE
RUSTLE
COOL~
ALL RIGHT, ALL RIGHT... IT'S OKAY NOW.

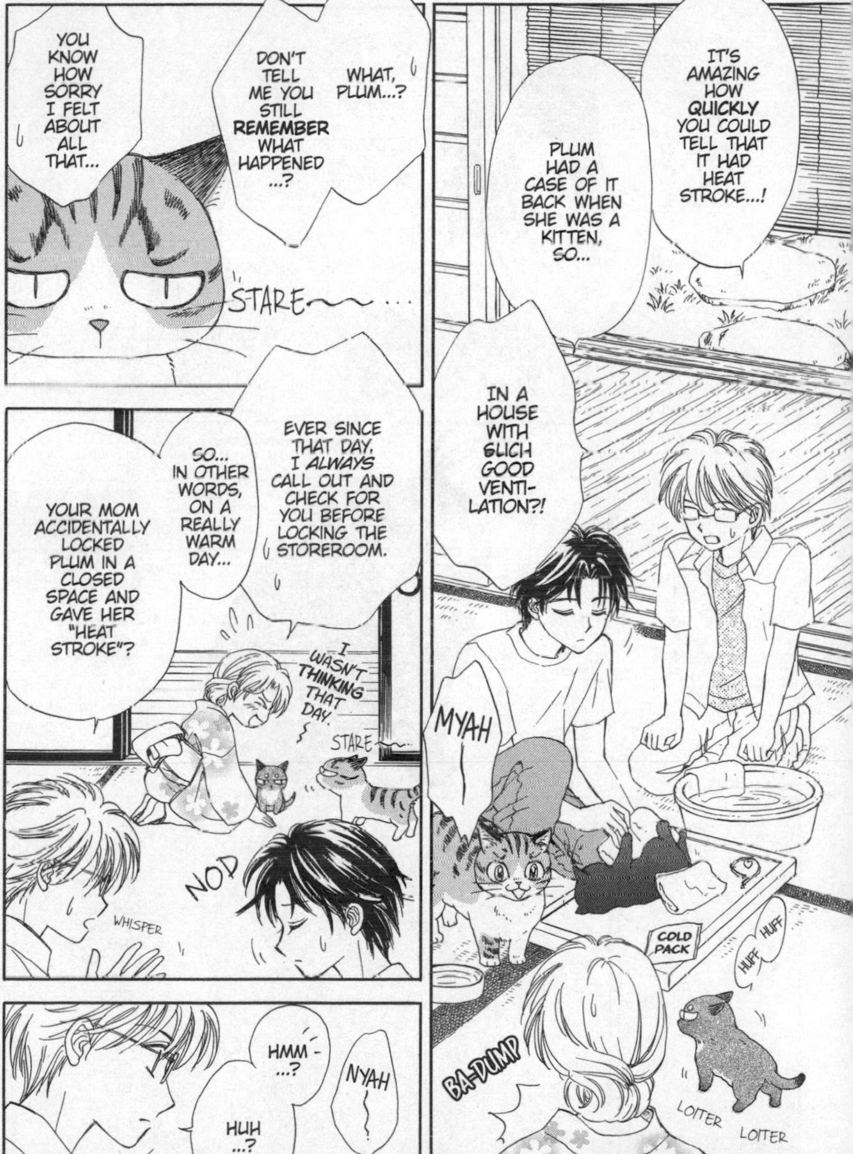
IT'S AMAZING HOW QUICKLY YOU COULD TELL THAT IT HAD HEAT STROKE...!
PLUM HAD A CASE OF IT BACK WHEN SHE WAS A KITTEN, SO...
IN A HOUSE WITH SUCH GOOD VENTI-LATION?!
MYAH
COLD PACK
HUFF HUFF
BA-DUMP
LOITER LOITER
WHAT, PLUM...?
DON'T TELL ME YOU STILL REMEMBER WHAT HAPPENED ...?
YOU KNOW HOW SORRY I FELT ABOUT ALL THAT...
STARE~~~...
EVER SINCE THAT DAY, I ALWAYS CALL OUT AND CHECK FOR YOU BEFORE LOCKING THE STOREROOM.
SO... IN OTHER WORDS, ON A REALLY WARM DAY...
YOUR MOM ACCIDENTALLY LOCKED PLUM IN A CLOSED SPACE AND GAVE HER "HEAT STROKE"?
I WASN'T THINKING THAT DAY.
STARE~~
NOD
WHISPER
HMM - ...?
NYAH
HUH ...?

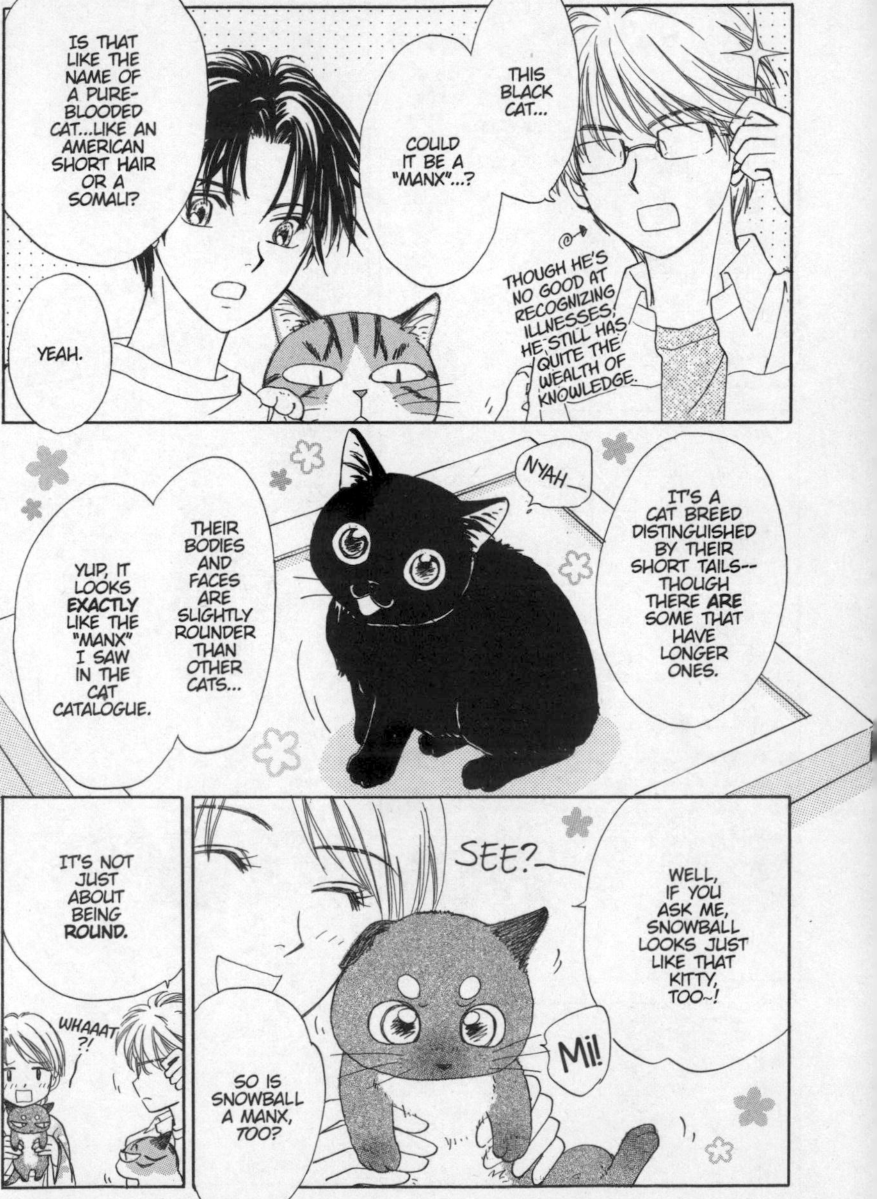
THIS BLACK CAT...
COULD IT BE A "MANX"...?
THOUGH HE'S NO GOOD AT RECOGNIZING ILLNESSES, HE STILL HAS QUITE THE WEALTH OF KNOWLEDGE.
IS THAT LIKE THE NAME OF A PURE-BLOODED CAT...LIKE AN AMERICAN SHORT HAIR OR A SOMALI?
YEAH.
NYAH
IT'S A CAT BREED DISTINGUISHED BY THEIR SHORT TAILS--THOUGH THERE ARE SOME THAT HAVE LONGER ONES.
THEIR BODIES AND FACES ARE SLIGHTLY ROUNDER THAN OTHER CATS...
YUP, IT LOOKS EXACTLY LIKE THE "MANX" I SAW IN THE CAT CATALOGUE.
SEE?
WELL, IF YOU ASK ME, SNOWBALL LOOKS JUST LIKE THAT KITTY, TOO~!
Mi!
SO IS SNOWBALL A MANX, TOO?
IT'S NOT JUST ABOUT BEING ROUND.
WHAAAT ?!

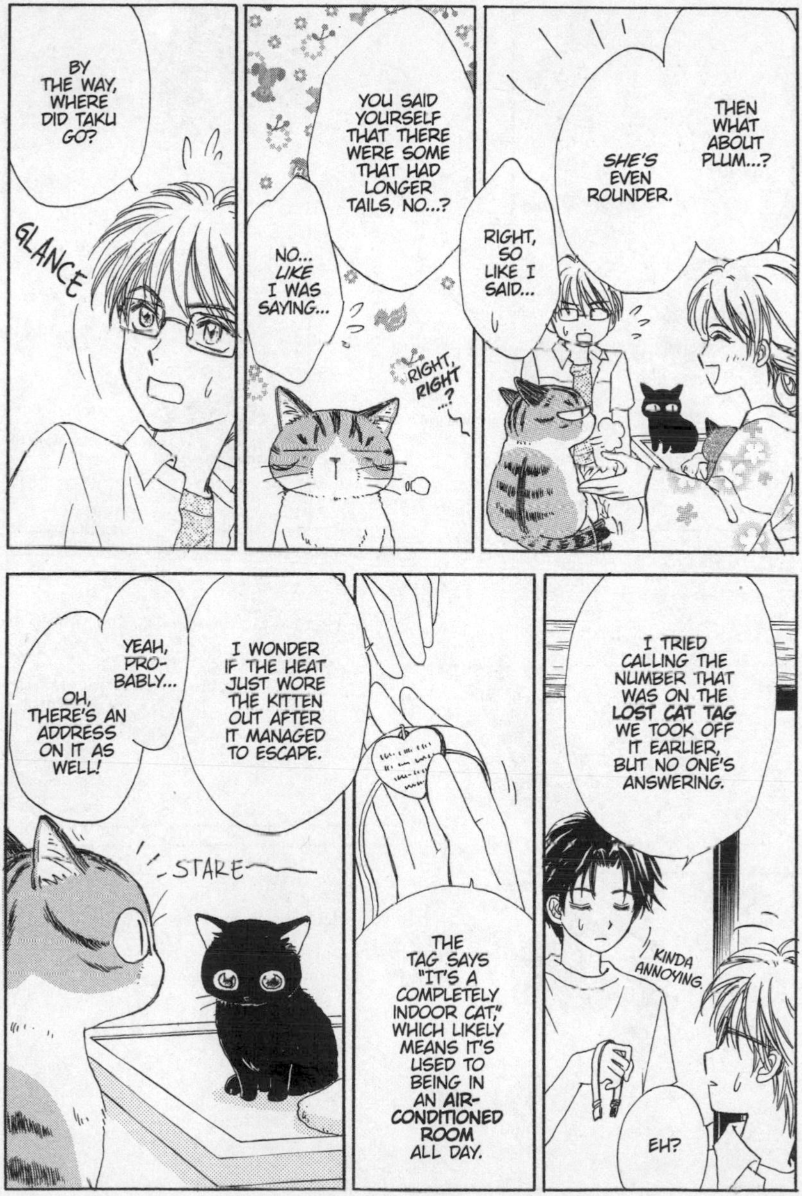
THEN WHAT ABOUT PLUM...?
SHE'S EVEN ROUNDER.
RIGHT, SO LIKE I SAID...
YOU SAID YOURSELF THAT THERE WERE SOME THAT HAD LONGER TAILS, NO...?
NO... LIKE I WAS SAYING...
RIGHT, RIGHT ...?
BY THE WAY, WHERE DID TAKU GO?
GLANCE
I TRIED CALLING THE NUMBER THAT WAS ON THE LOST CAT TAG WE TOOK OFF IT EARLIER, BUT NO ONE'S ANSWERING.
KINDA ANNOYING.
EH?
THE TAG SAYS "IT'S A COMPLETELY INDOOR CAT," WHICH LIKELY MEANS IT'S USED TO BEING IN AN AIR-CONDITIONED ROOM ALL DAY.
I WONDER IF THE HEAT JUST WORE THE KITTEN OUT AFTER IT MANAGED TO ESCAPE.
YEAH, PRO-BABLY...
OH, THERE'S AN ADDRESS ON IT AS WELL!
STARE

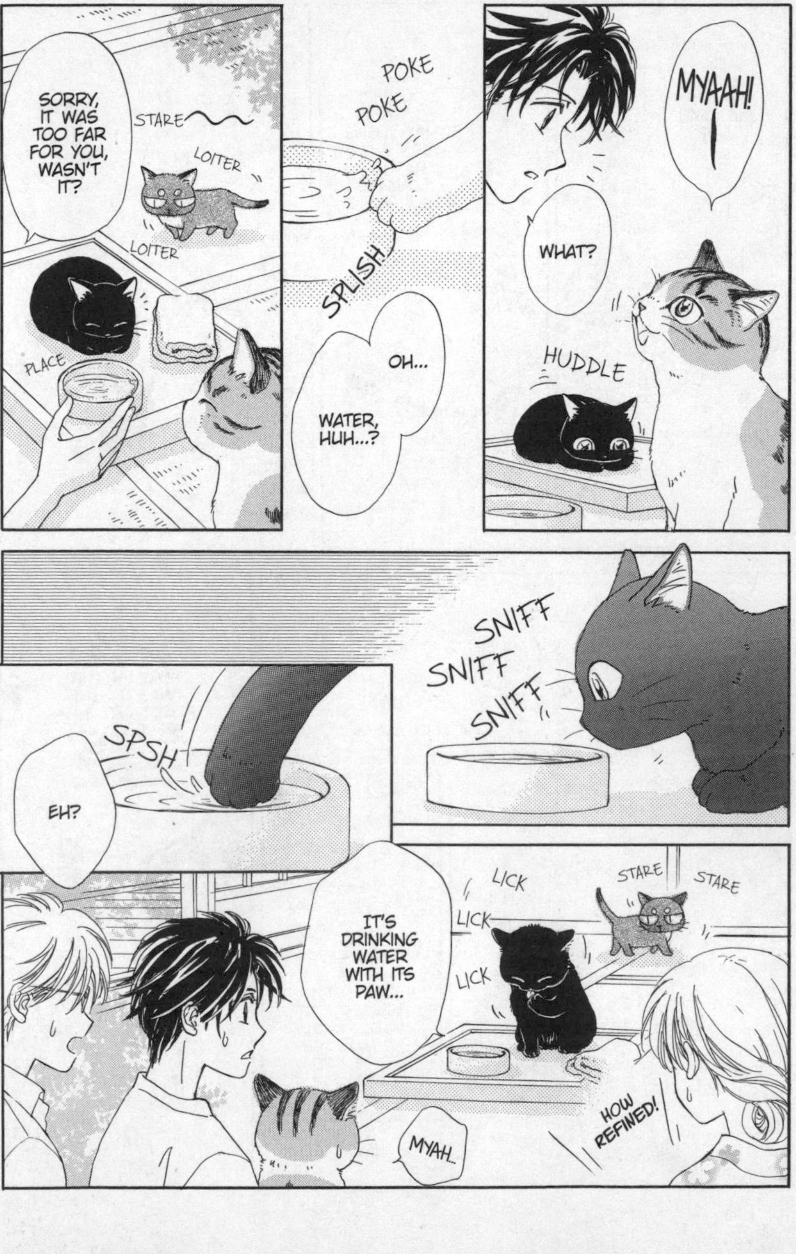
MYAAH!
WHAT?
HUDDLE
POKE
POKE
SPLISH
OH...
WATER, HUH...?
SORRY, IT WAS TOO FAR FOR YOU, WASN'T IT?
STARE
LOITER
LOITER
PLACE
SNIFF
SNIFF
SNIFF
SPSH
EH?
STARE
STARE
LICK
LICK
LICK
IT'S DRINKING WATER WITH ITS PAW...
HOW REFINED!
MYAH.

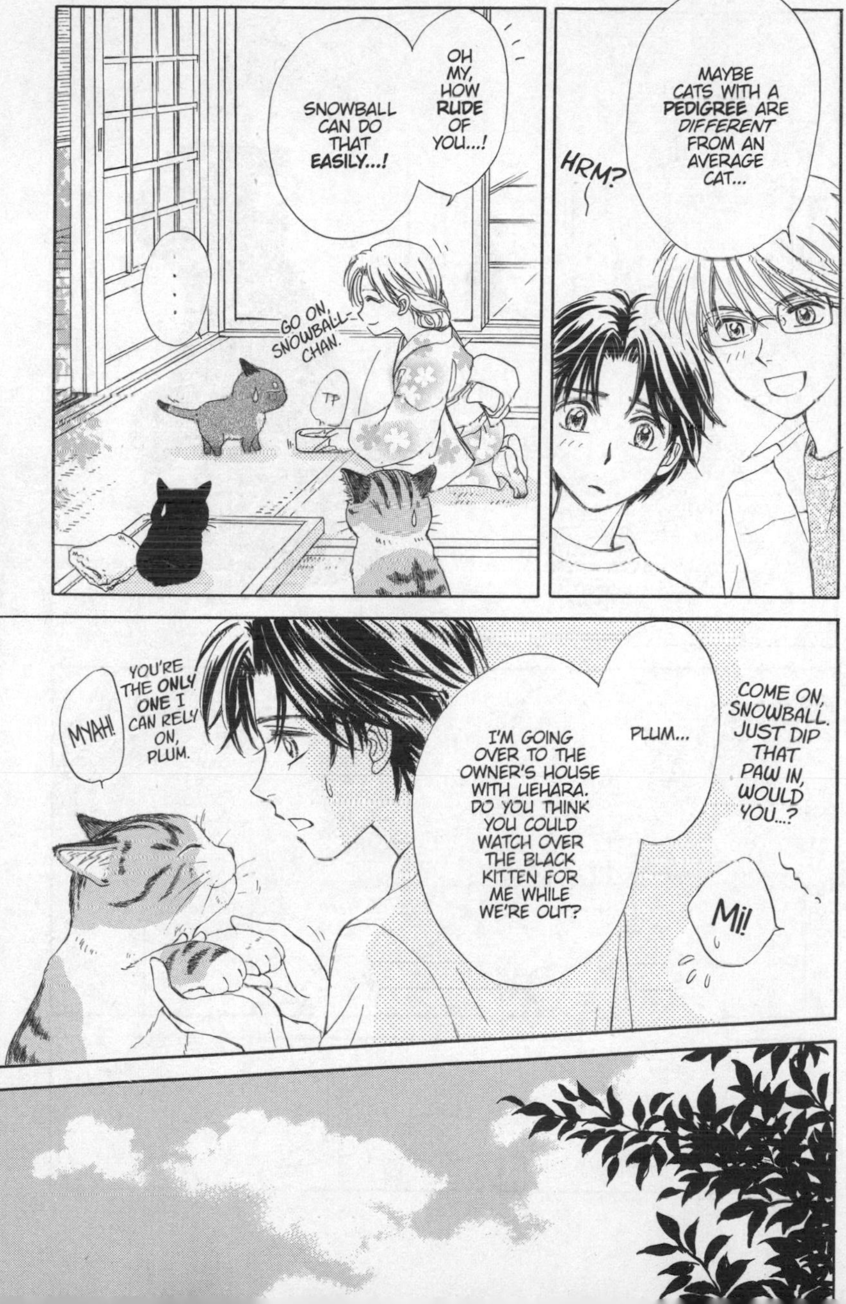
MAYBE CATS WITH A PEDIGREE ARE DIFFERENT FROM AN AVERAGE CAT...
HRM?
OH MY, HOW RUDE OF YOU...!
SNOWBALL CAN DO THAT EASILY...!
...
GO ON, SNOWBALL-CHAN.
TP
COME ON, SNOWBALL. JUST DIP THAT PAW IN, WOULD YOU...?
Mi!
PLUM...
I'M GOING OVER TO THE OWNER'S HOUSE WITH UEHARA. DO YOU THINK YOU COULD WATCH OVER THE BLACK KITTEN FOR ME WHILE WE'RE OUT?
YOU'RE THE ONLY ONE I CAN RELY ON, PLUM.
MYAH!

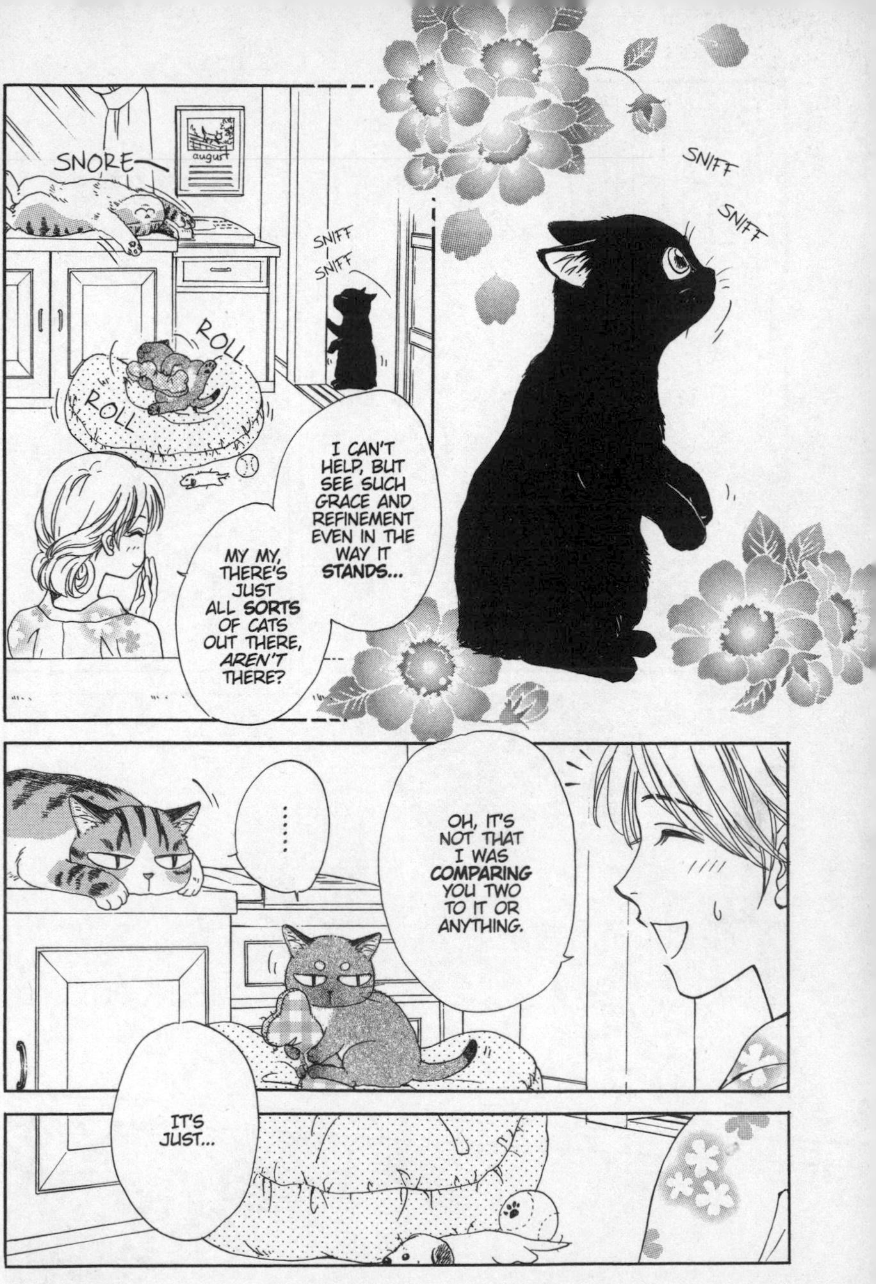
SNIFF
SNIFF
SNIFF
SNIFF
SNORE
ROLL
ROLL
I CAN'T HELP, BUT SEE SUCH GRACE AND REFINEMENT EVEN IN THE WAY IT STANDS...
MY MY, THERE'S JUST ALL SORTS OF CATS OUT THERE, AREN'T THERE?
OH, IT'S NOT THAT I WAS COMPARING YOU TWO TO IT OR ANYTHING.
......
IT'S JUST...

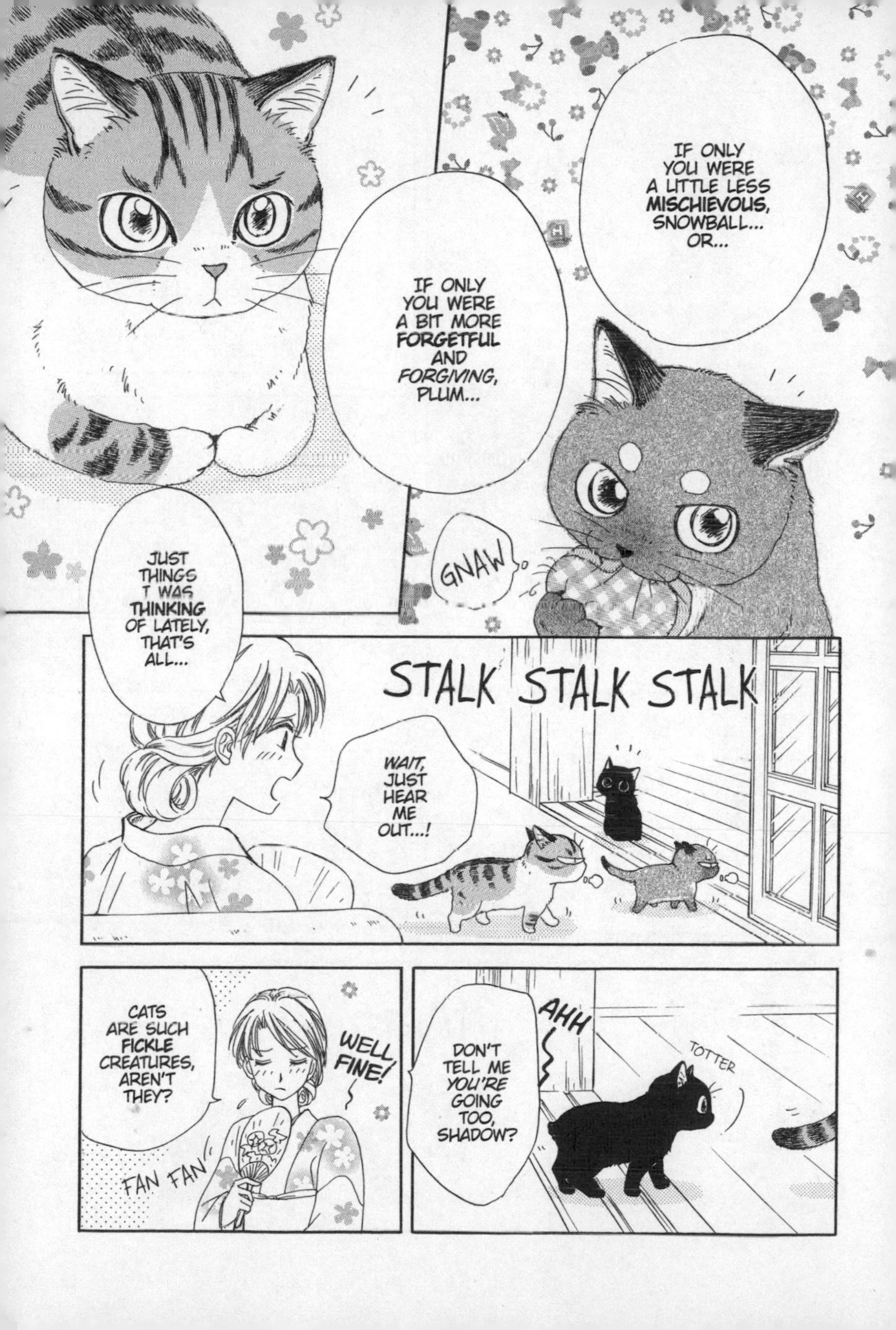
IF ONLY YOU WERE A LITTLE LESS MISCHIEVOUS, SNOWBALL... OR...
IF ONLY YOU WERE A BIT MORE FORGETFUL AND FORGIVING, PLUM...
GNAW
JUST THINGS I WAS THINKING OF LATELY, THAT'S ALL...
STALK STALK STALK
WAIT, JUST HEAR ME OUT...!
CATS ARE SUCH FICKLE CREATURES, AREN'T THEY?
WELL FINE!
FAN FAN
AHH
DON'T TELL ME YOU'RE GOING TOO, SHADOW?
TOTTER

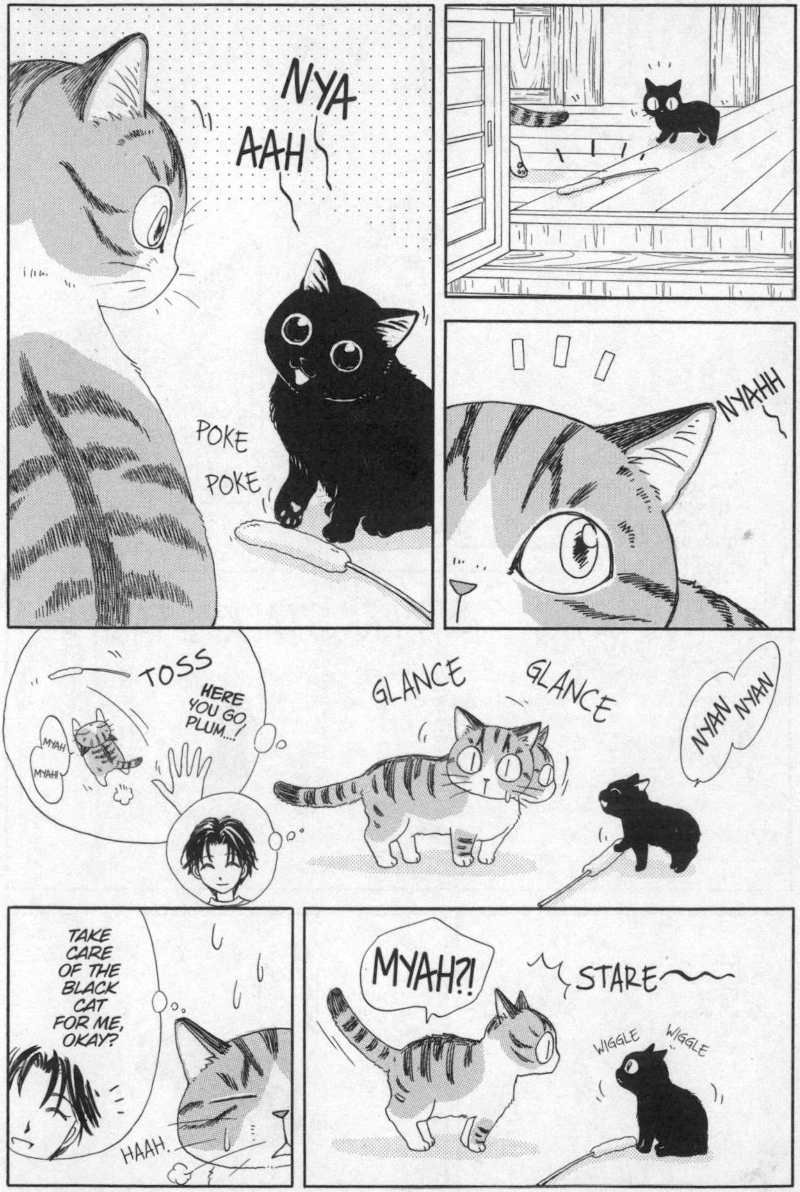
NYAHH
NYA AAH
POKE POKE
NYAN NYAN
GLANCE GLANCE
TOSS
HERE YOU GO, PLUM...!
MYAH
MYAH!
MYAH?!
STARE
WIGGLE WIGGLE
TAKE CARE OF THE BLACK CAT FOR ME, OKAY?
HAAH.

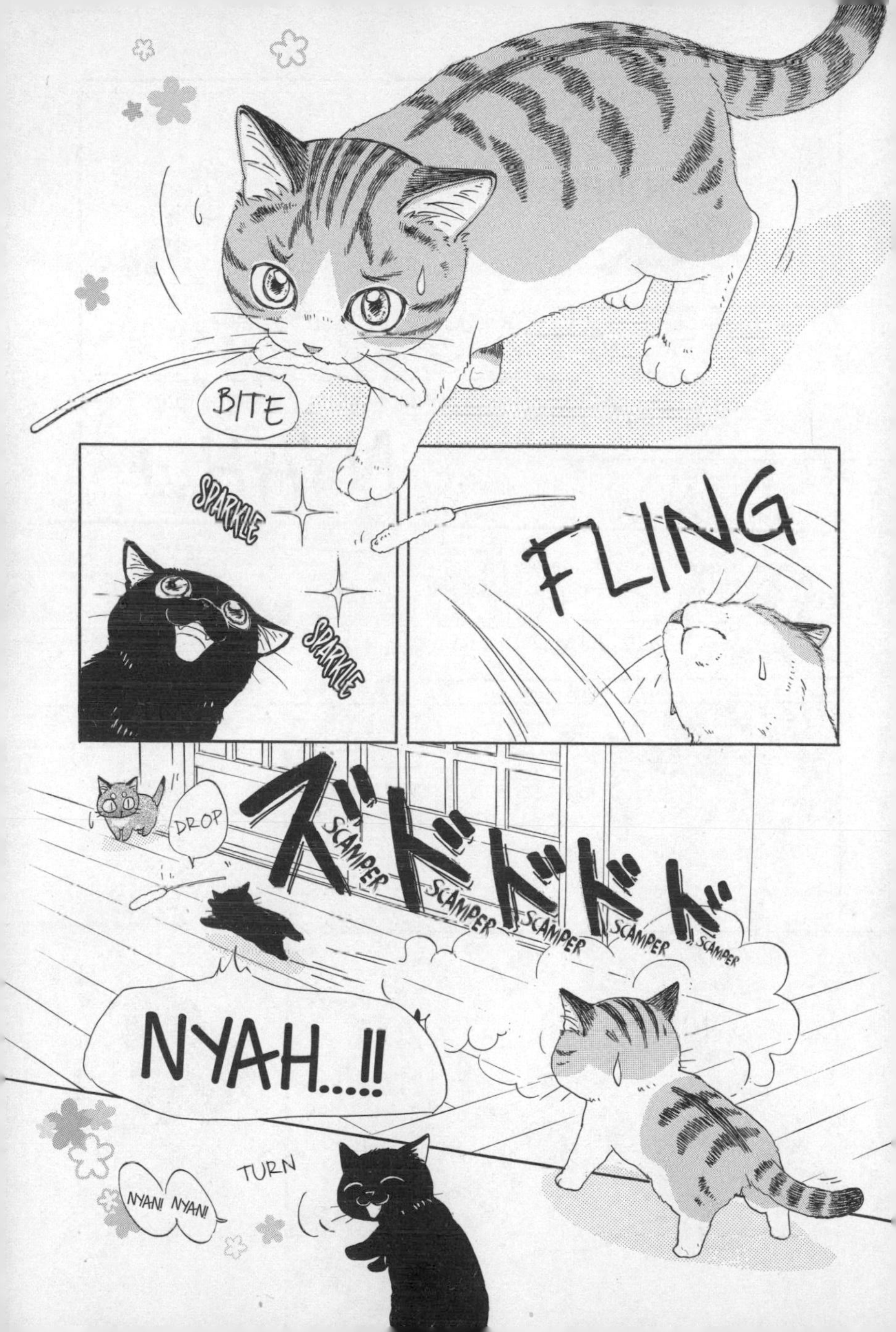
BITE
FLING
SPARKLE
SPARKLE
ズドドドド
SCAMPER SCAMPER SCAMPER SCAMPER SCAMPER
DROP
NYAH...!!
TURN
NYAN! NYAN!

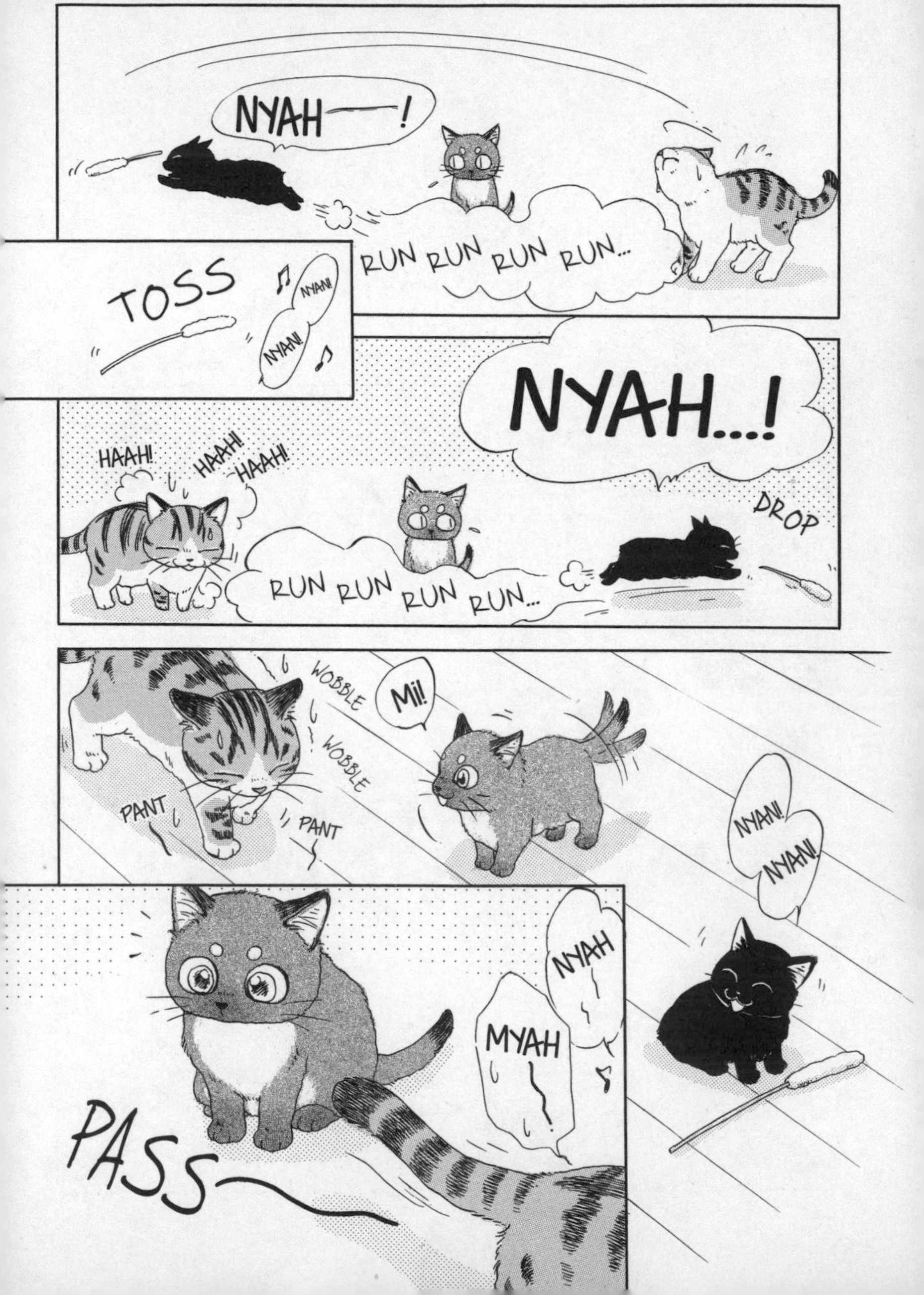
NYAH——!
RUN RUN RUN RUN...
TOSS
NYAN!
NYAN!
NYAH...!
DROP
RUN RUN RUN RUN...
HAAH!
HAAH!
HAAH!
NYAN!
NYAN!
Mi!
WOBBLE
WOBBLE
PANT
PANT
NYAH
MYAH
PASS

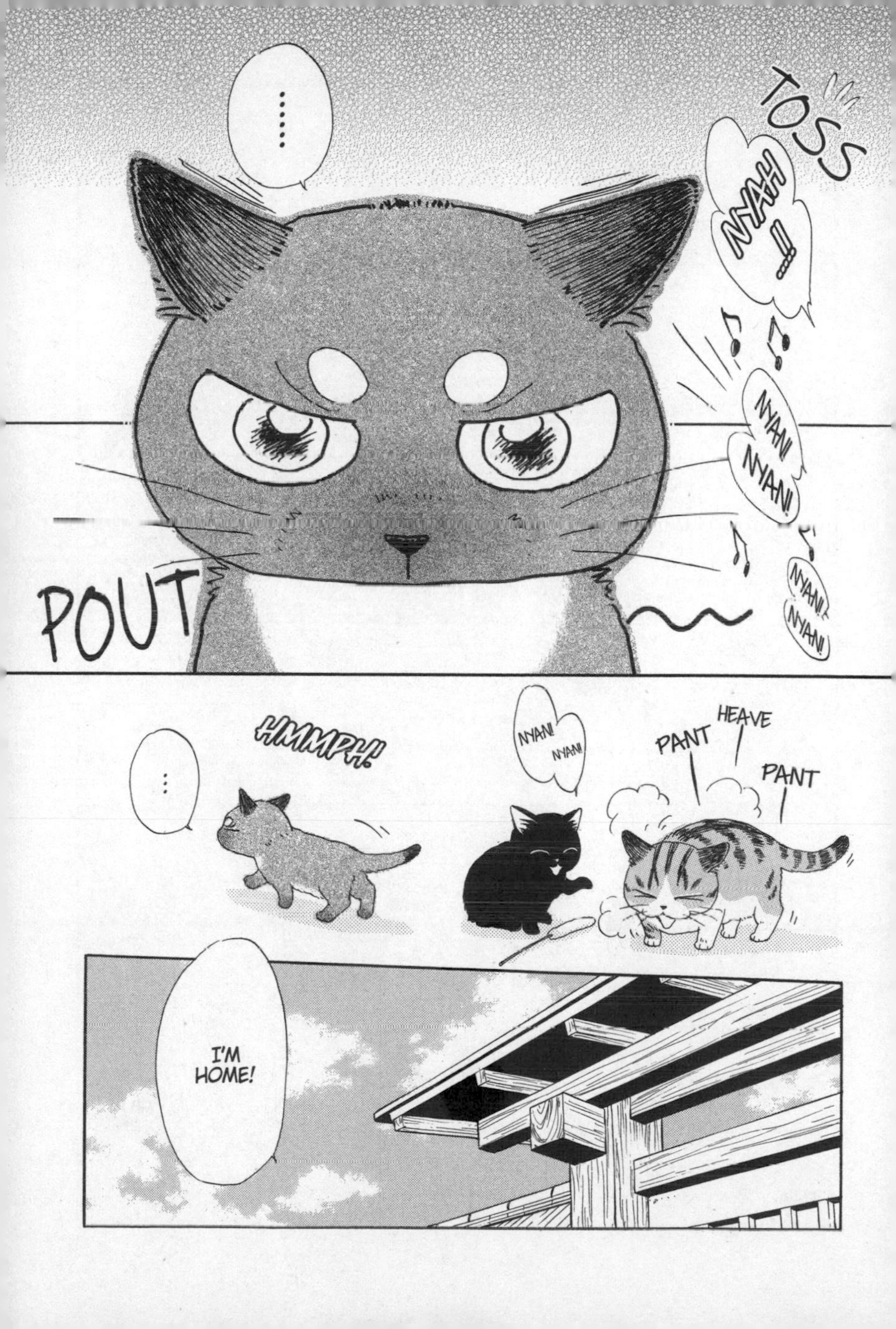
TOSS
NYAH!!
NYAN! NYAN!
NYAN! NYAN!
......
POUT
PANT
HEAVE
PANT
NYAN! NYAN!
HMMPH!
...
I'M HOME!

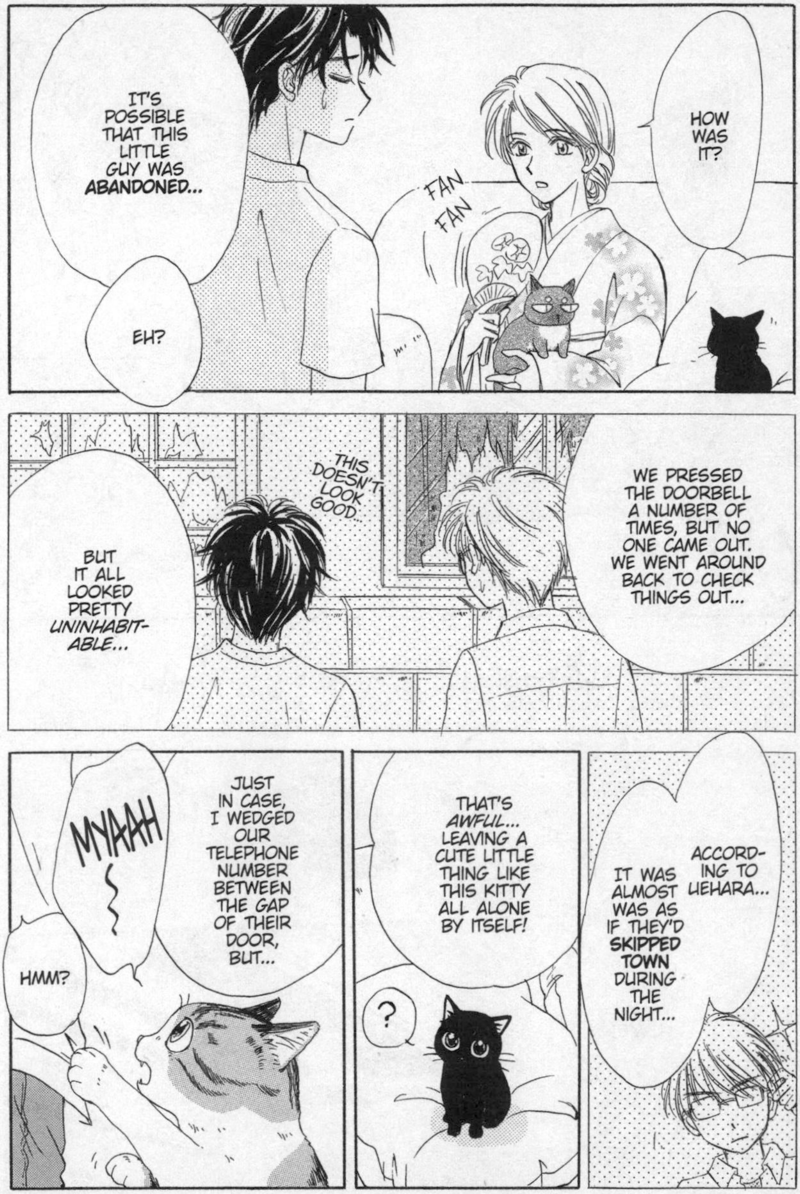
HOW WAS IT?
FAN FAN
IT'S POSSIBLE THAT THIS LITTLE GUY WAS ABANDONED...
EH?
WE PRESSED THE DOORBELL A NUMBER OF TIMES, BUT NO ONE CAME OUT. WE WENT AROUND BACK TO CHECK THINGS OUT...
THIS DOESN'T LOOK GOOD...
BUT IT ALL LOOKED PRETTY UNINHABIT-ABLE...
ACCORD-ING TO UEHARA...
IT WAS ALMOST WAS AS IF THEY'D SKIPPED TOWN DURING THE NIGHT...
THAT'S AWFUL... LEAVING A CUTE LITTLE THING LIKE THIS KITTY ALL ALONE BY ITSELF!
?
JUST IN CASE, I WEDGED OUR TELEPHONE NUMBER BETWEEN THE GAP OF THEIR DOOR, BUT...
MYAAH
HMM?

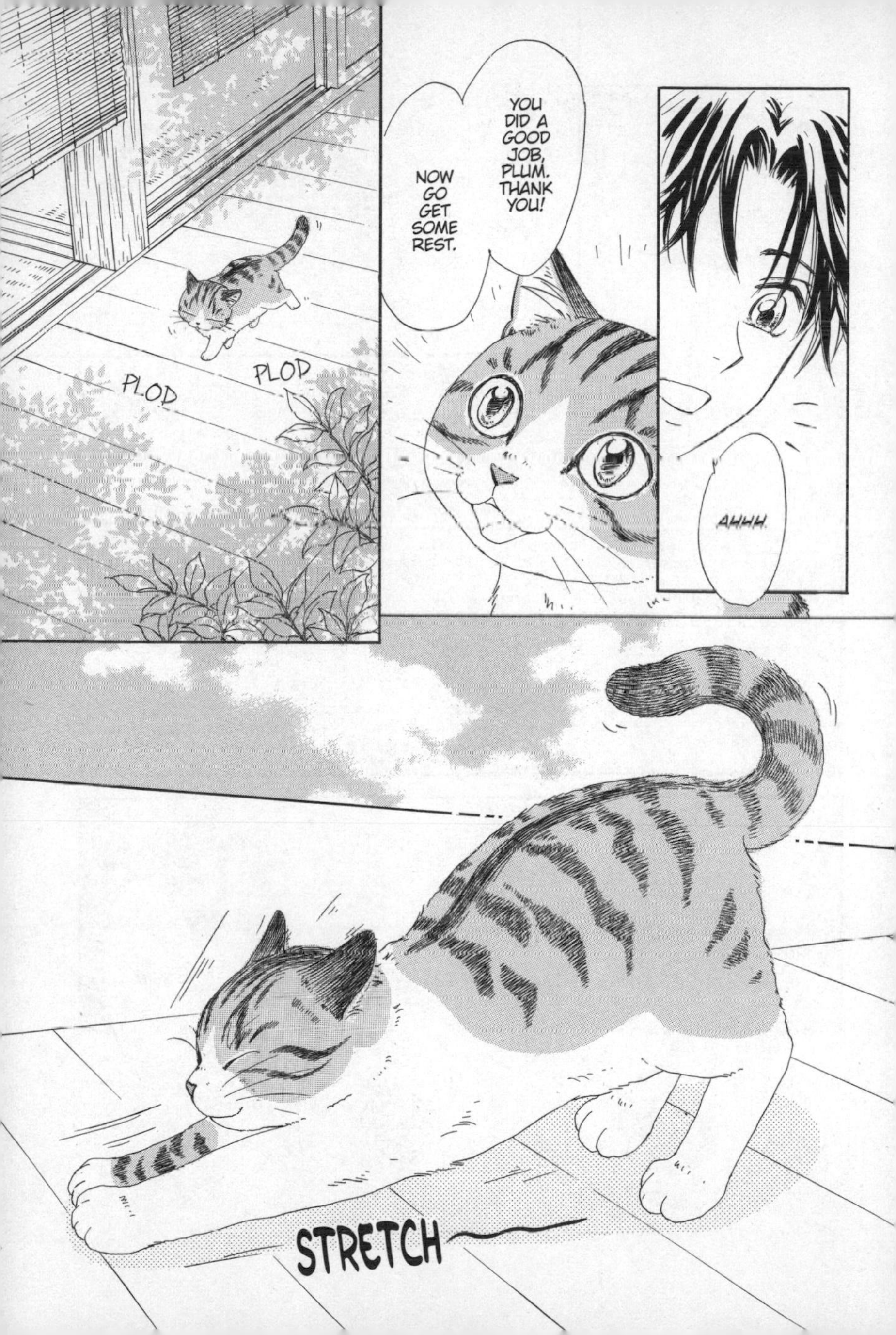
AHHH.
YOU DID A GOOD JOB, PLUM. THANK YOU!
NOW GO GET SOME REST.
PLOD
PLOD
STRETCH

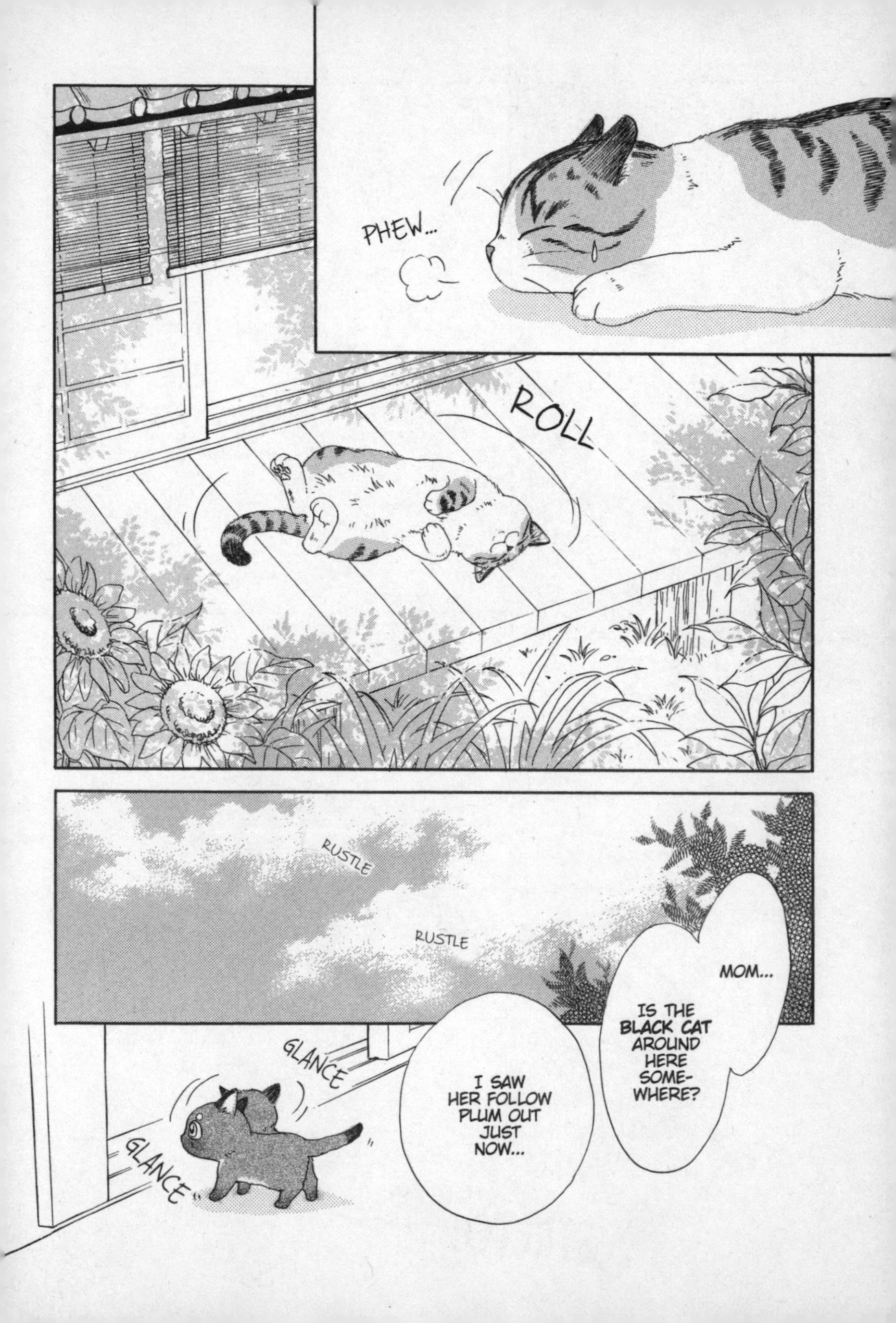
PHEW...
ROLL
RUSTLE
RUSTLE
MOM...
IS THE BLACK CAT AROUND HERE SOME-WHERE?
I SAW HER FOLLOW PLUM OUT JUST NOW...
GLANCE
GLANCE

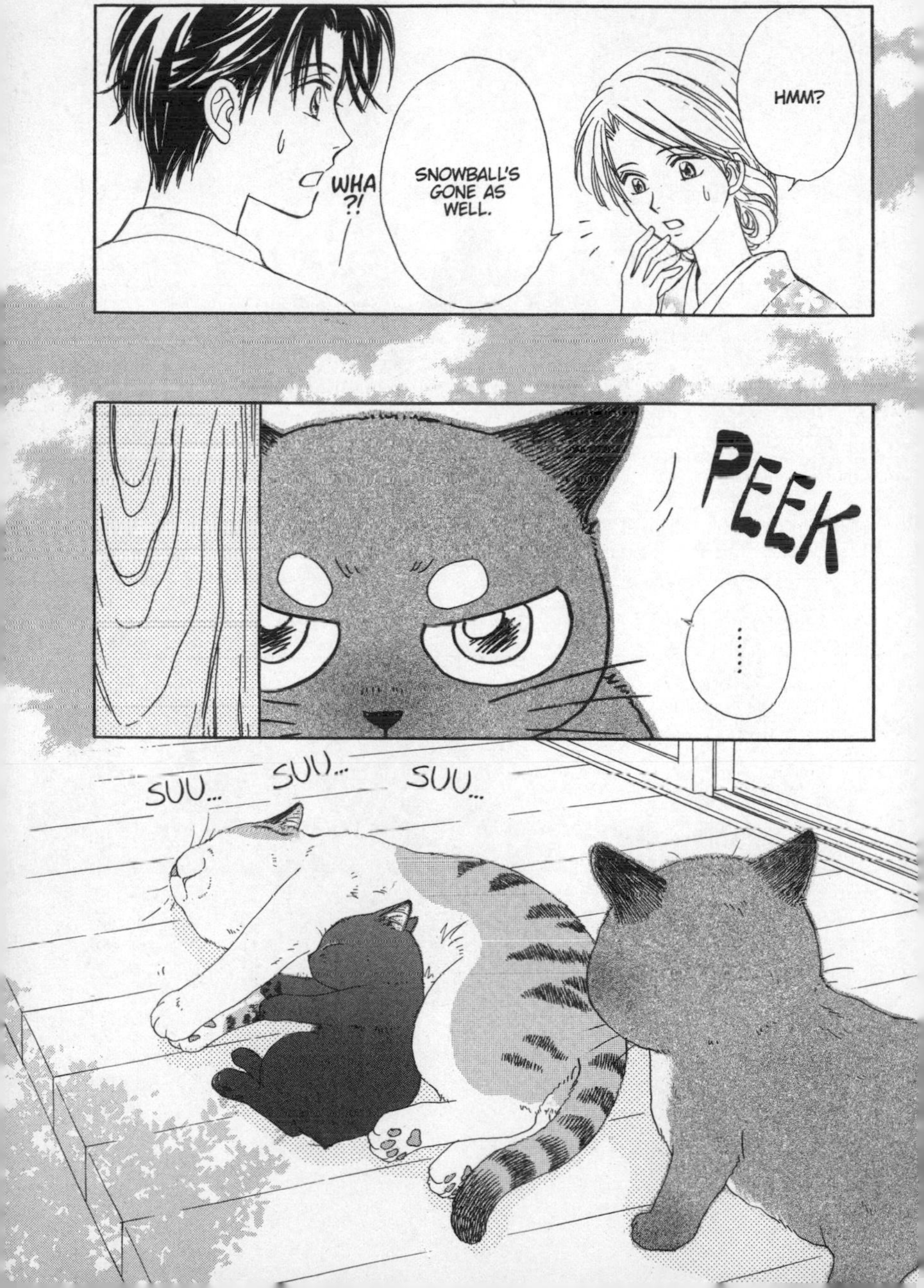
HMM?
SNOWBALL'S GONE AS WELL.
WHA ?!
PEEK
......
SUU...
SUU...
SUU...

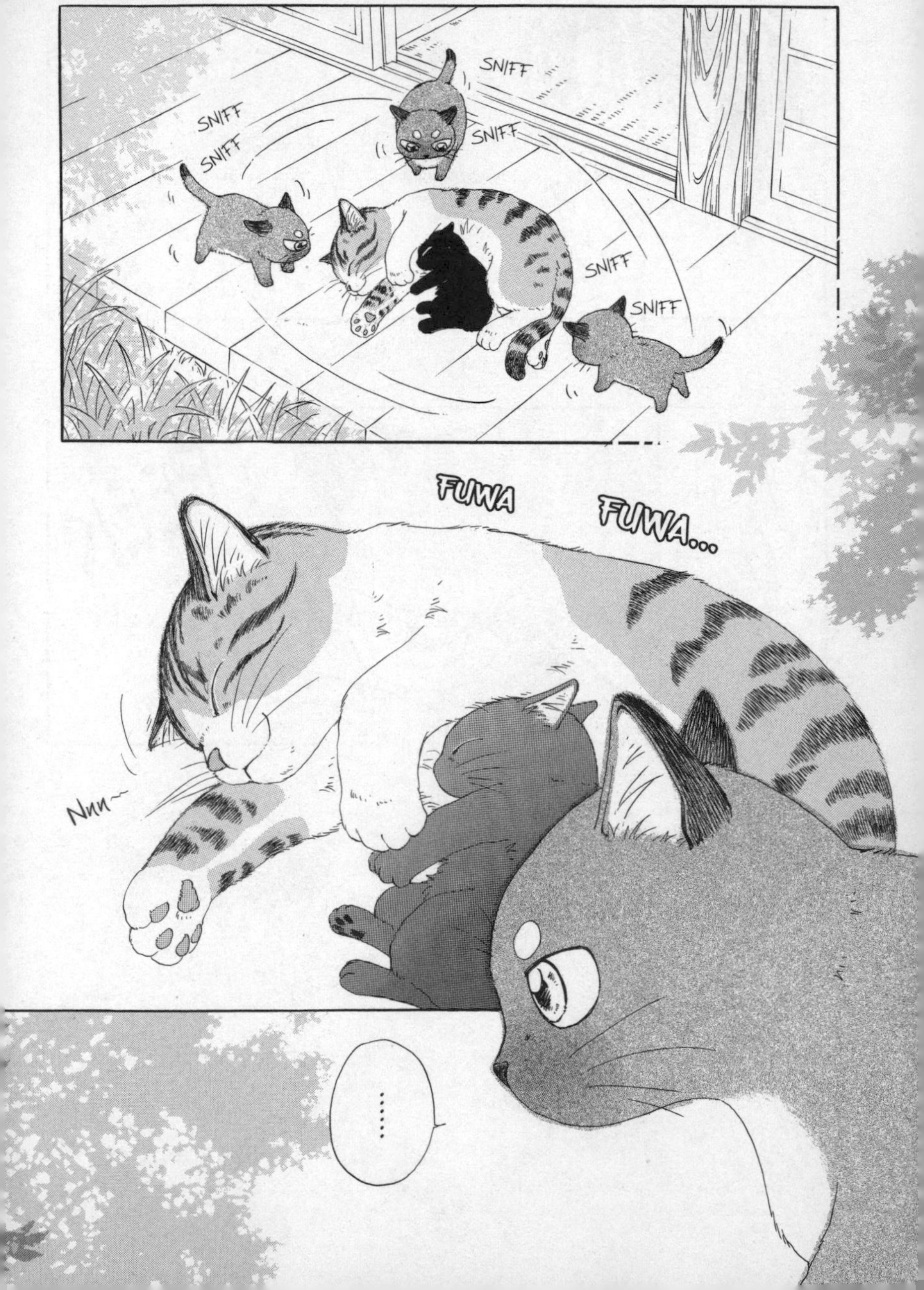
SNIFF
SNIFF
SNIFF
SNIFF
SNIFF
SNIFF
FUWA
FUWA...
Nnn~
......

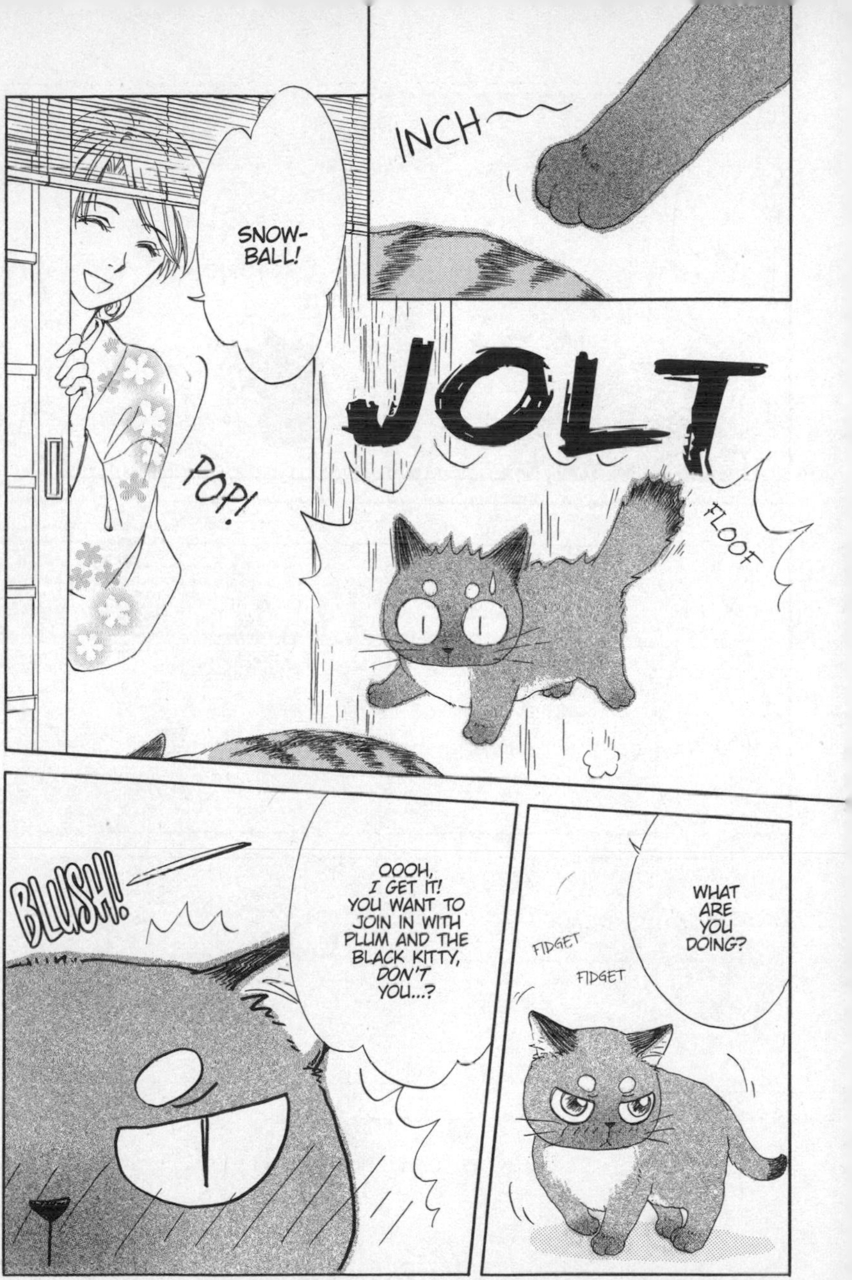
INCH
SNOW-BALL!
JOLT
POP!
FLOOF
WHAT ARE YOU DOING?
FIDGET
FIDGET
OOOH, I GET IT! YOU WANT TO JOIN IN WITH PLUM AND THE BLACK KITTY, DON'T YOU...?
BLUSH!

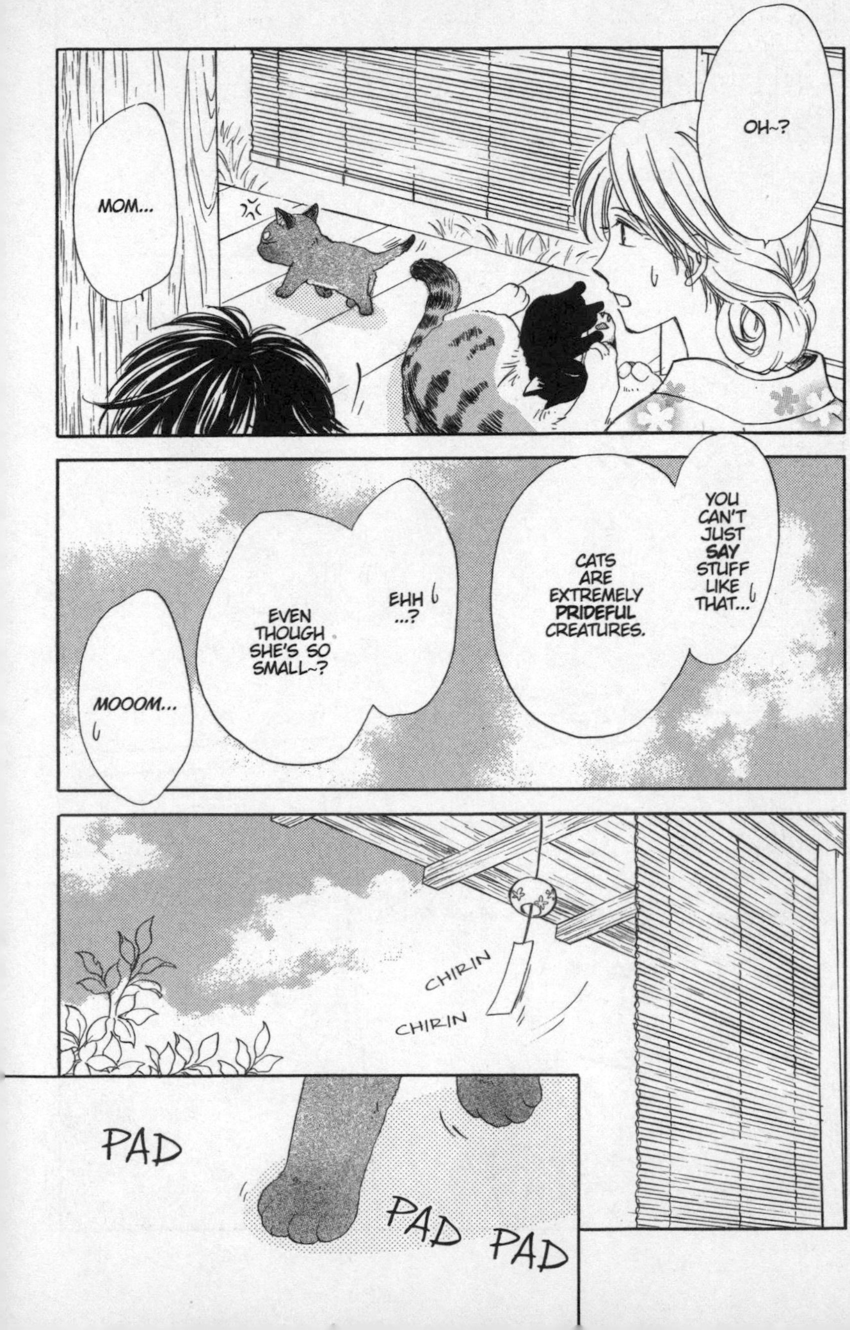
OH~?
MOM...
YOU CAN'T JUST SAY STUFF LIKE THAT...
CATS ARE EXTREMELY PRIDEFUL CREATURES.
EHH ...?
EVEN THOUGH SHE'S SO SMALL~?
MOOOM...
CHIRIN
CHIRIN
PAD
PAD PAD

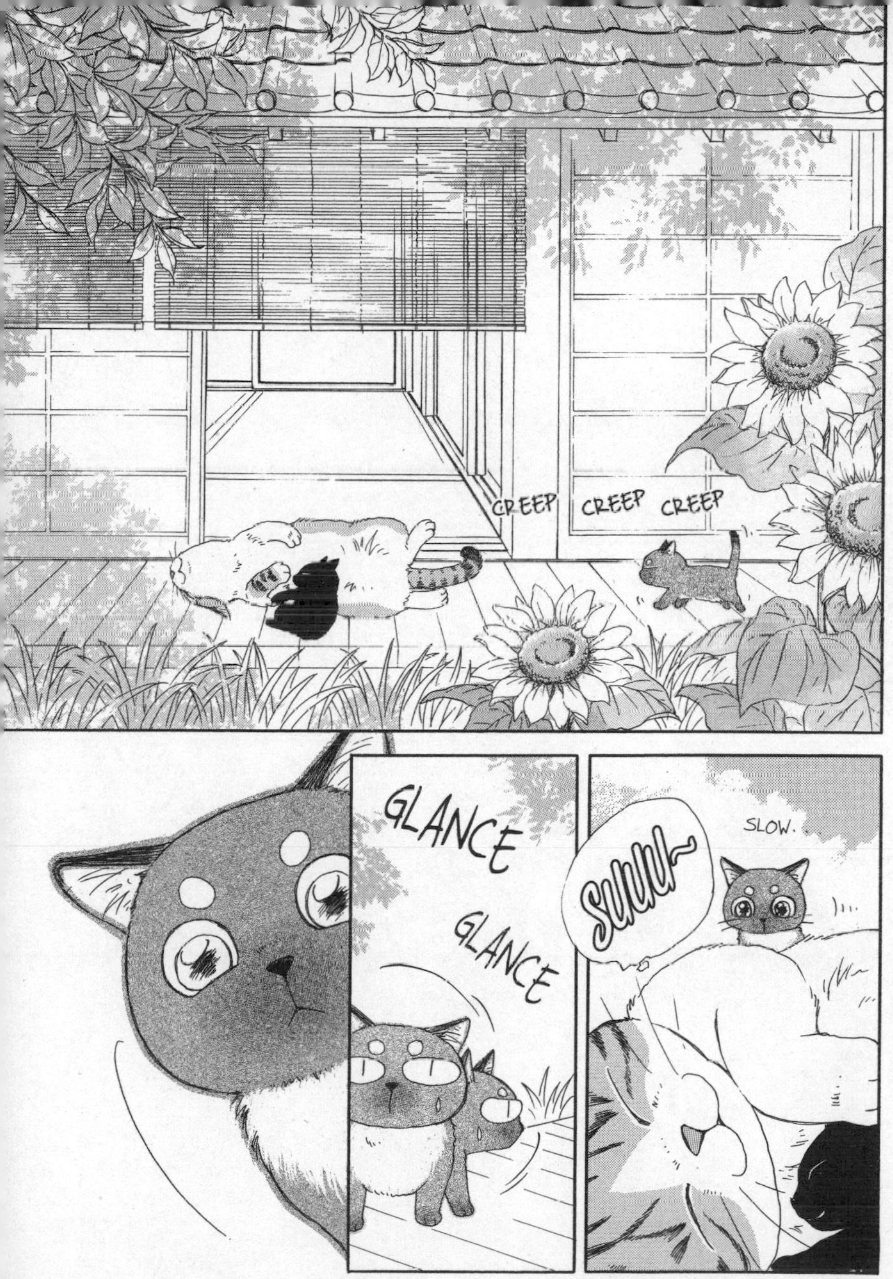
CREEP
CREEP
CREEP
SUUU~
SLOW.
GLANCE
GLANCE

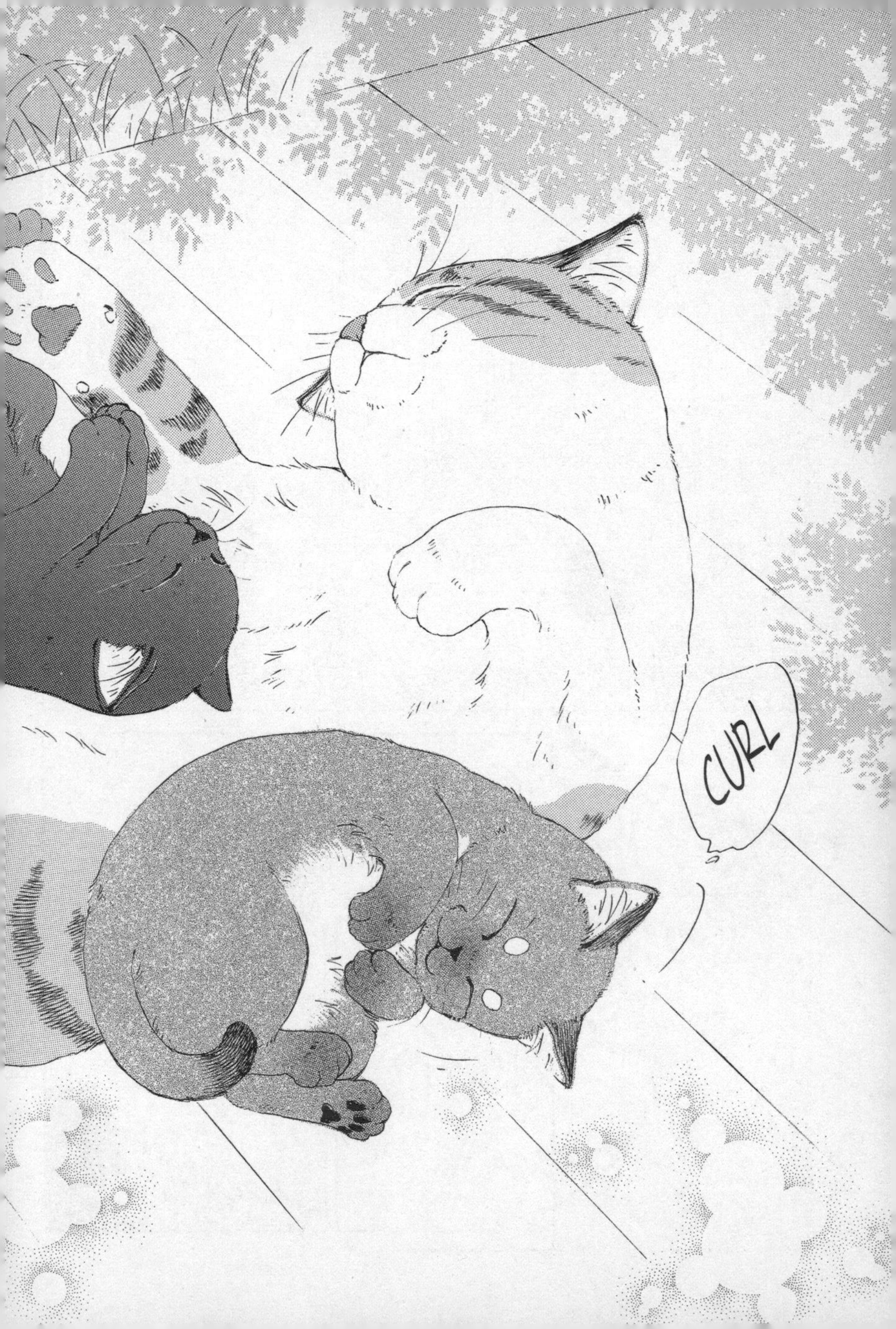
CURL

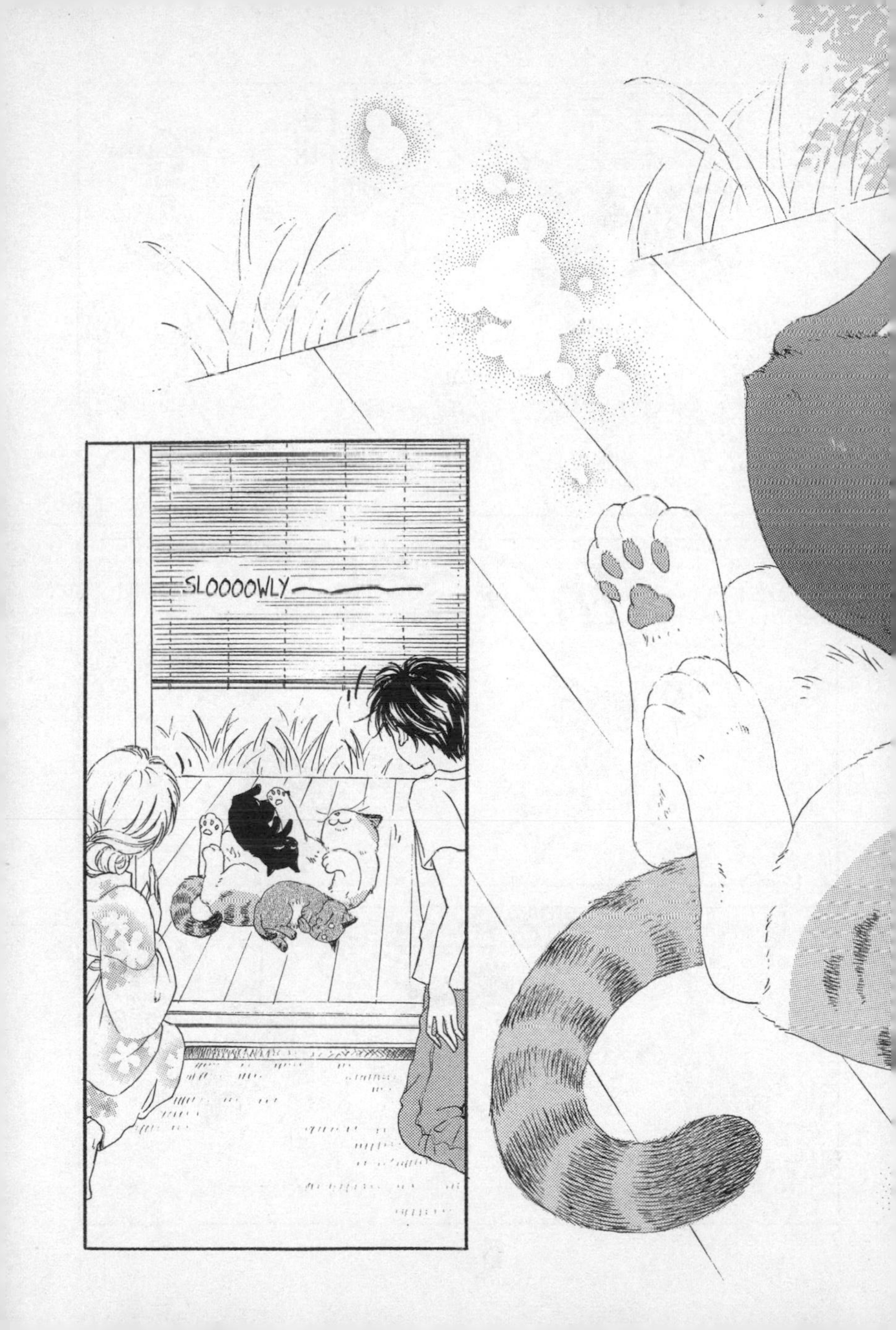
SLOOOOWLY

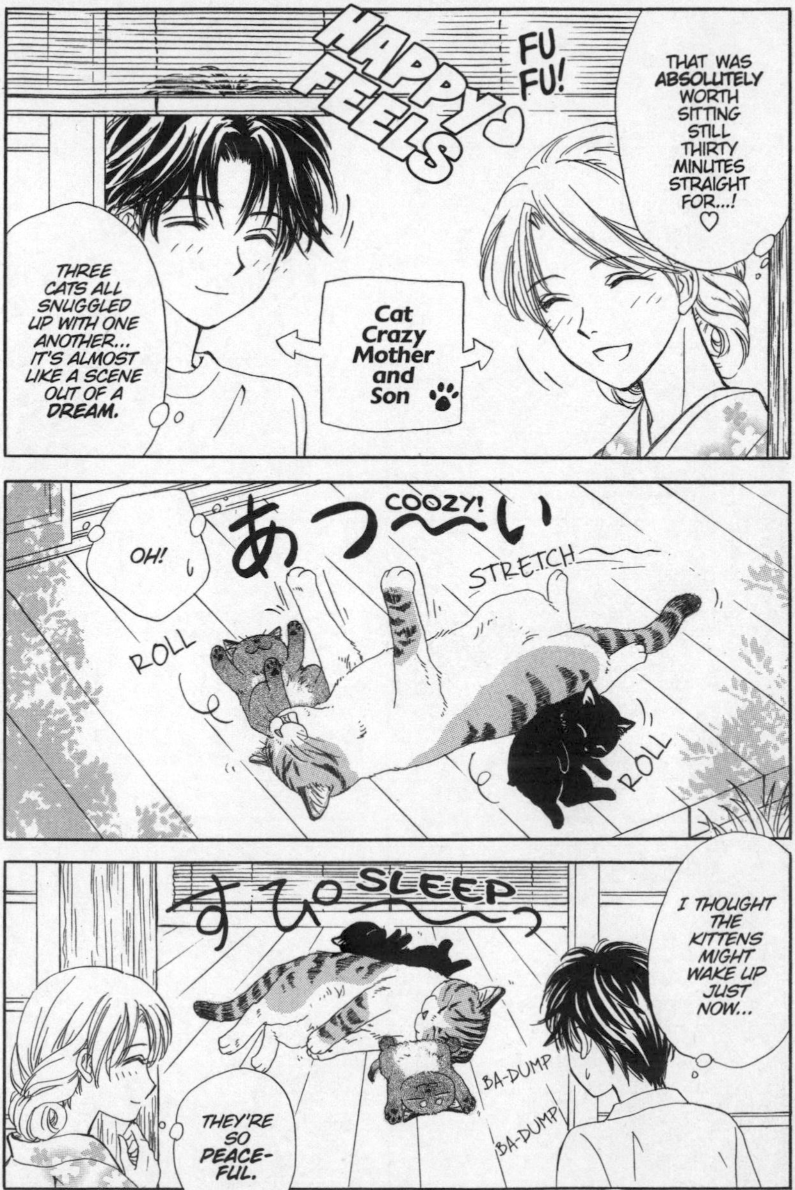
THAT WAS ABSOLUTELY WORTH SITTING STILL THIRTY MINUTES STRAIGHT FOR...! ♡
FU FU!
HAPPY FEELS ♡
THREE CATS ALL SNUGGLED UP WITH ONE ANOTHER... IT'S ALMOST LIKE A SCENE OUT OF A DREAM.
Cat Crazy Mother and Son
あつ〜〜い
COOZY!
OH!
STRETCH
ROLL
ROLL
I THOUGHT THE KITTENS MIGHT WAKE UP JUST NOW...
すぴ〜〜っ
SLEEP
BA-DUMP
BA-DUMP
THEY'RE SO PEACE-FUL.

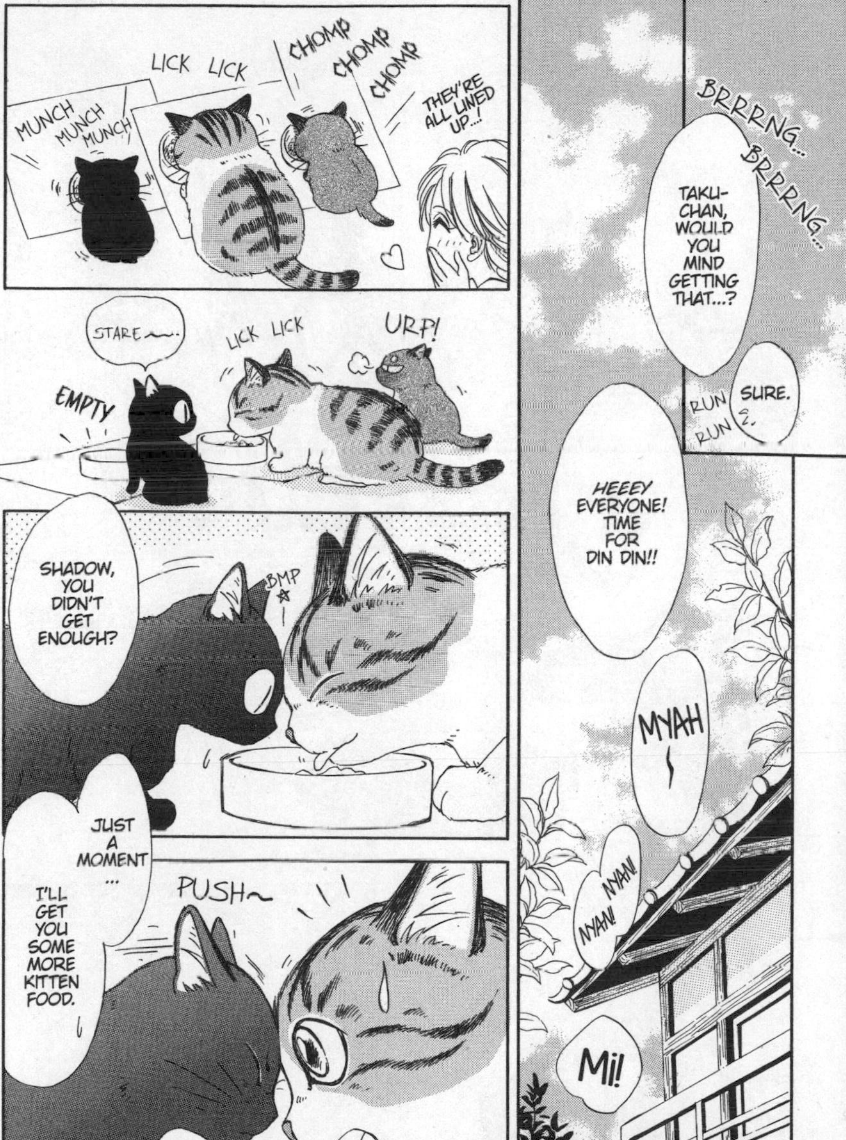
BRRRNG... BRRRNG...
TAKU-CHAN, WOULD YOU MIND GETTING THAT...?
SURE.
RUN RUN
HEEEY EVERYONE! TIME FOR DIN DIN!!
MYAH~
NYAN! NYAN!
Mi!
CHOMP CHOMP CHOMP
THEY'RE ALL LINED UP...!
LICK LICK
MUNCH MUNCH MUNCH
URP!
LICK LICK
STARE~~...
EMPTY
SHADOW, YOU DIDN'T GET ENOUGH?
BMP
JUST A MOMENT...
I'LL GET YOU SOME MORE KITTEN FOOD.
PUSH~

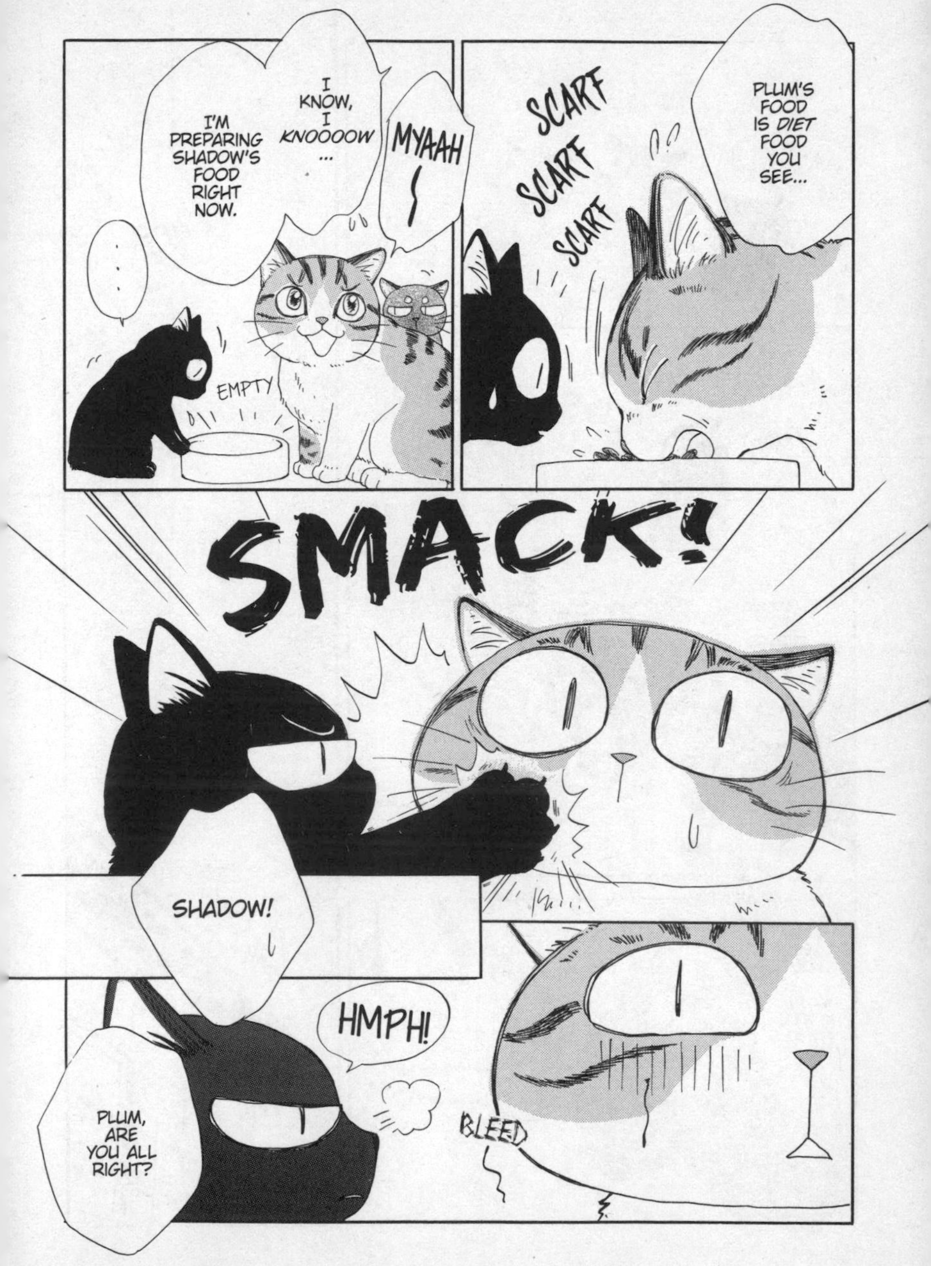
PLUM'S FOOD IS *DIET* FOOD YOU SEE...
SCARF
SCARF
SCARF
I'M PREPARING SHADOW'S FOOD RIGHT NOW.
I KNOW, I *KNOOOOW* ...
MYAAH
...
EMPTY
SMACK!
SHADOW!
BLEED
HMPH!
PLUM, ARE YOU ALL RIGHT?

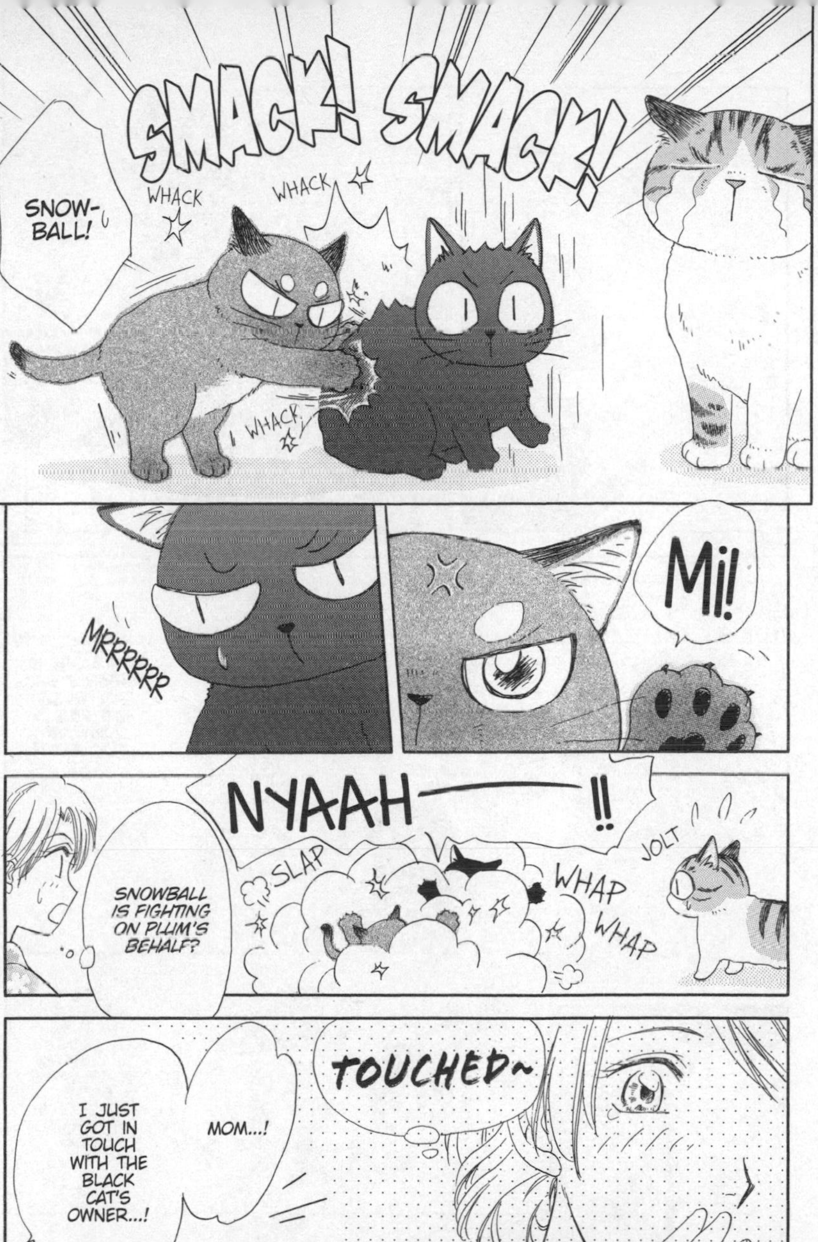
SMACK! SMACK!
WHACK
WHACK
SNOW-BALL!
WHACK
Mi!
MRRRRRR
NYAAH——!!
JOLT
WHAP
WHAP
SLAP
SNOWBALL IS FIGHTING ON PLUM'S BEHALF?
TOUCHED~
MOM...!
I JUST GOT IN TOUCH WITH THE BLACK CAT'S OWNER...!

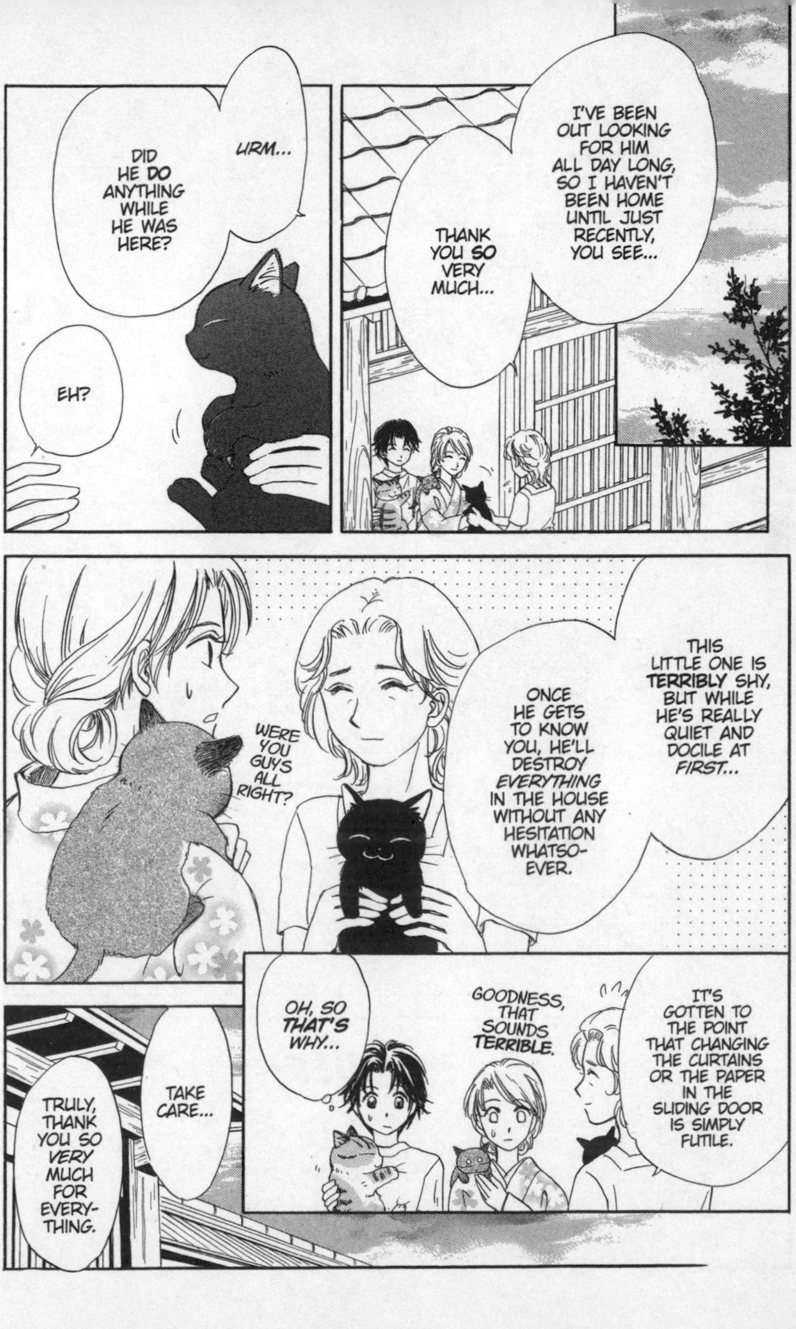
I'VE BEEN OUT LOOKING FOR HIM ALL DAY LONG, SO I HAVEN'T BEEN HOME UNTIL JUST RECENTLY, YOU SEE...
THANK YOU SO VERY MUCH...
URM...
DID HE DO ANYTHING WHILE HE WAS HERE?
EH?
THIS LITTLE ONE IS TERRIBLY SHY, BUT WHILE HE'S REALLY QUIET AND DOCILE AT FIRST...
ONCE HE GETS TO KNOW YOU, HE'LL DESTROY EVERYTHING IN THE HOUSE WITHOUT ANY HESITATION WHATSO-EVER.
WERE YOU GUYS ALL RIGHT?
IT'S GOTTEN TO THE POINT THAT CHANGING THE CURTAINS OR THE PAPER IN THE SLIDING DOOR IS SIMPLY FUTILE.
GOODNESS, THAT SOUNDS TERRIBLE.
OH, SO THAT'S WHY...
TAKE CARE...
TRULY, THANK YOU SO VERY MUCH FOR EVERY-THING.

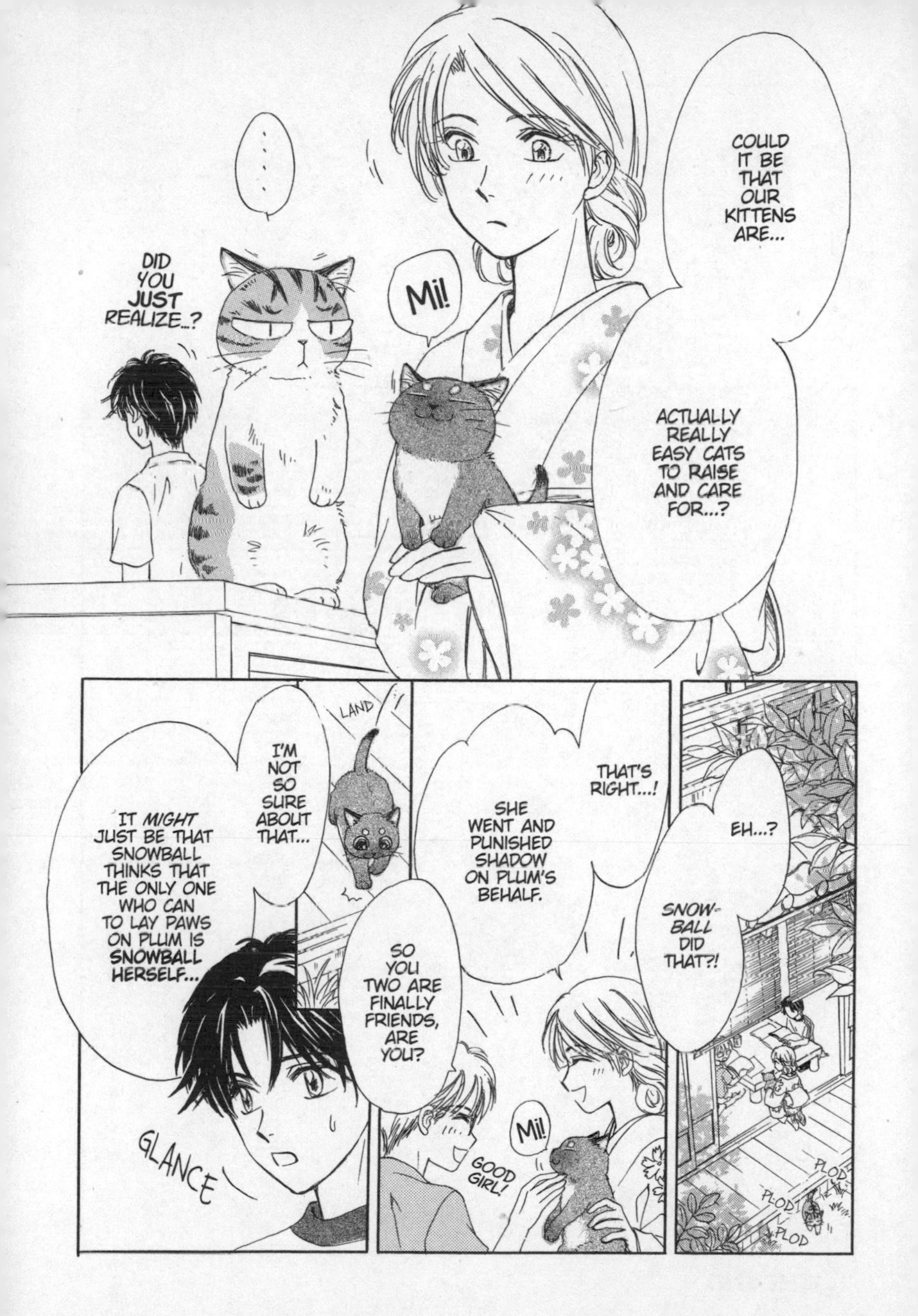
COULD IT BE THAT OUR KITTENS ARE...
ACTUALLY REALLY EASY CATS TO RAISE AND CARE FOR...?
Mi!
...
DID YOU JUST REALIZE...?
EH...?
SNOW-BALL DID THAT?!
PLOD PLOD PLOD
THAT'S RIGHT...!
SHE WENT AND PUNISHED SHADOW ON PLUM'S BEHALF.
SO YOU TWO ARE FINALLY FRIENDS, ARE YOU?
Mi!
GOOD GIRL!
LAND
I'M NOT SO SURE ABOUT THAT...
IT MIGHT JUST BE THAT SNOWBALL THINKS THAT THE ONLY ONE WHO CAN TO LAY PAWS ON PLUM IS SNOWBALL HERSELF...
GLANCE

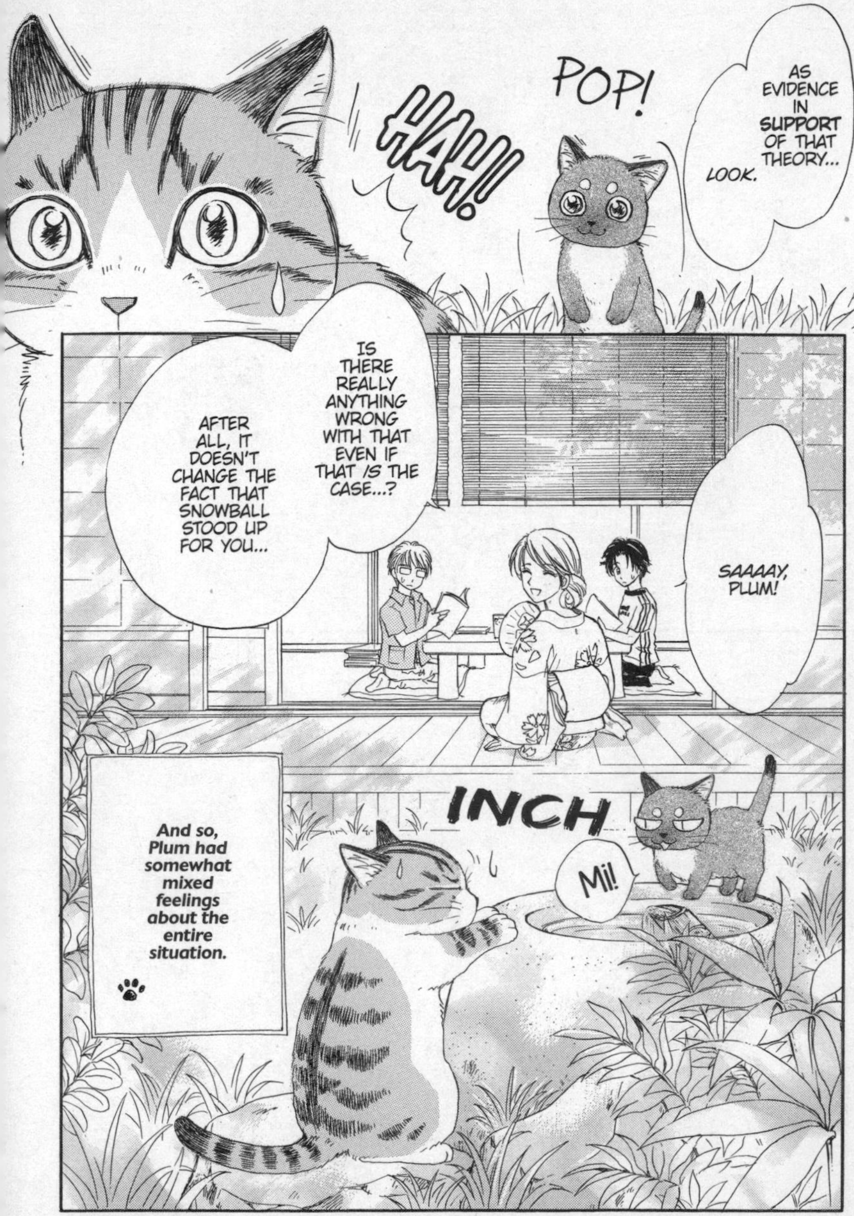
AS EVIDENCE IN SUPPORT OF THAT THEORY...
LOOK.
POP!
HAH!!
IS THERE REALLY ANYTHING WRONG WITH THAT EVEN IF THAT IS THE CASE...?
AFTER ALL, IT DOESN'T CHANGE THE FACT THAT SNOWBALL STOOD UP FOR YOU...
SAAAAY, PLUM!
INCH
Mi!
And so, Plum had somewhat mixed feelings about the entire situation.

⑥ THE END

CHAPTER 7: CHRISTMAS DAY

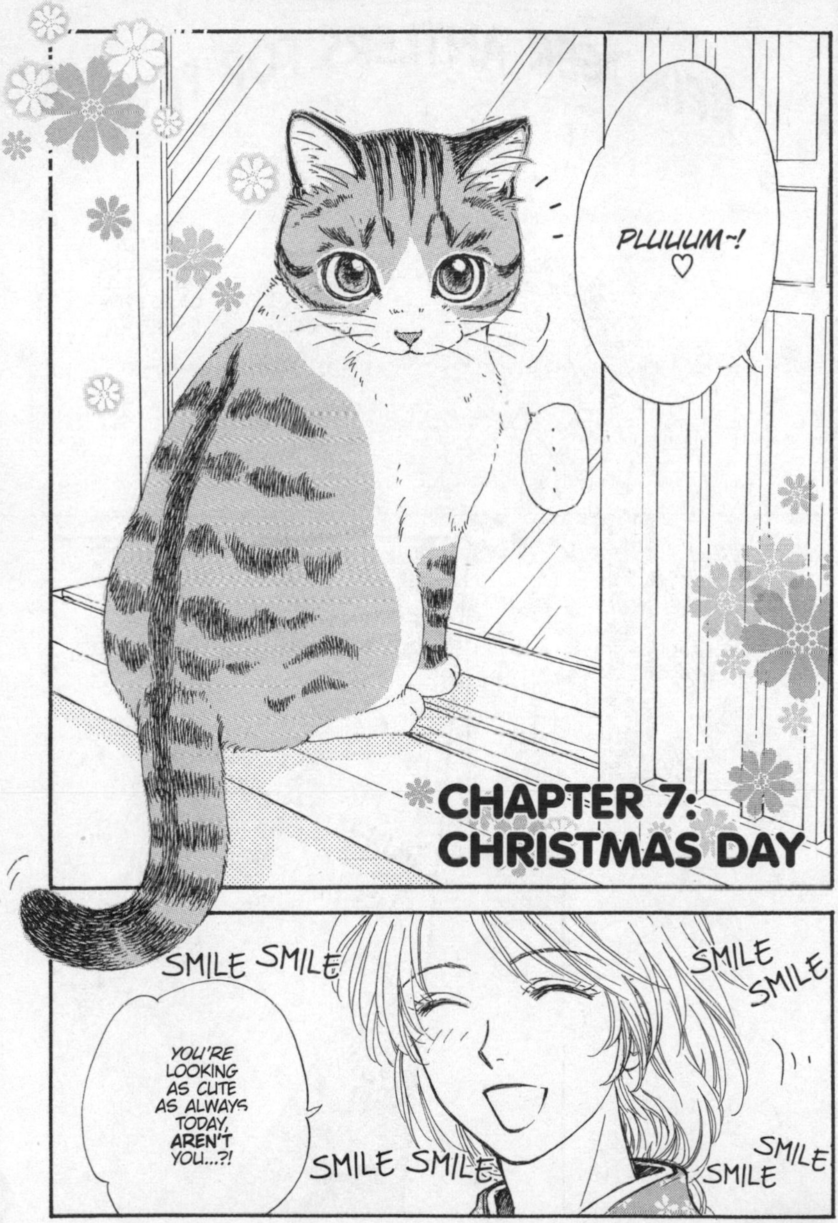
PLUUUM~! ♡
SMILE SMILE
SMILE SMILE
SMILE SMILE
YOU'RE LOOKING AS CUTE AS ALWAYS TODAY, AREN'T YOU...?!
SMILE SMILE

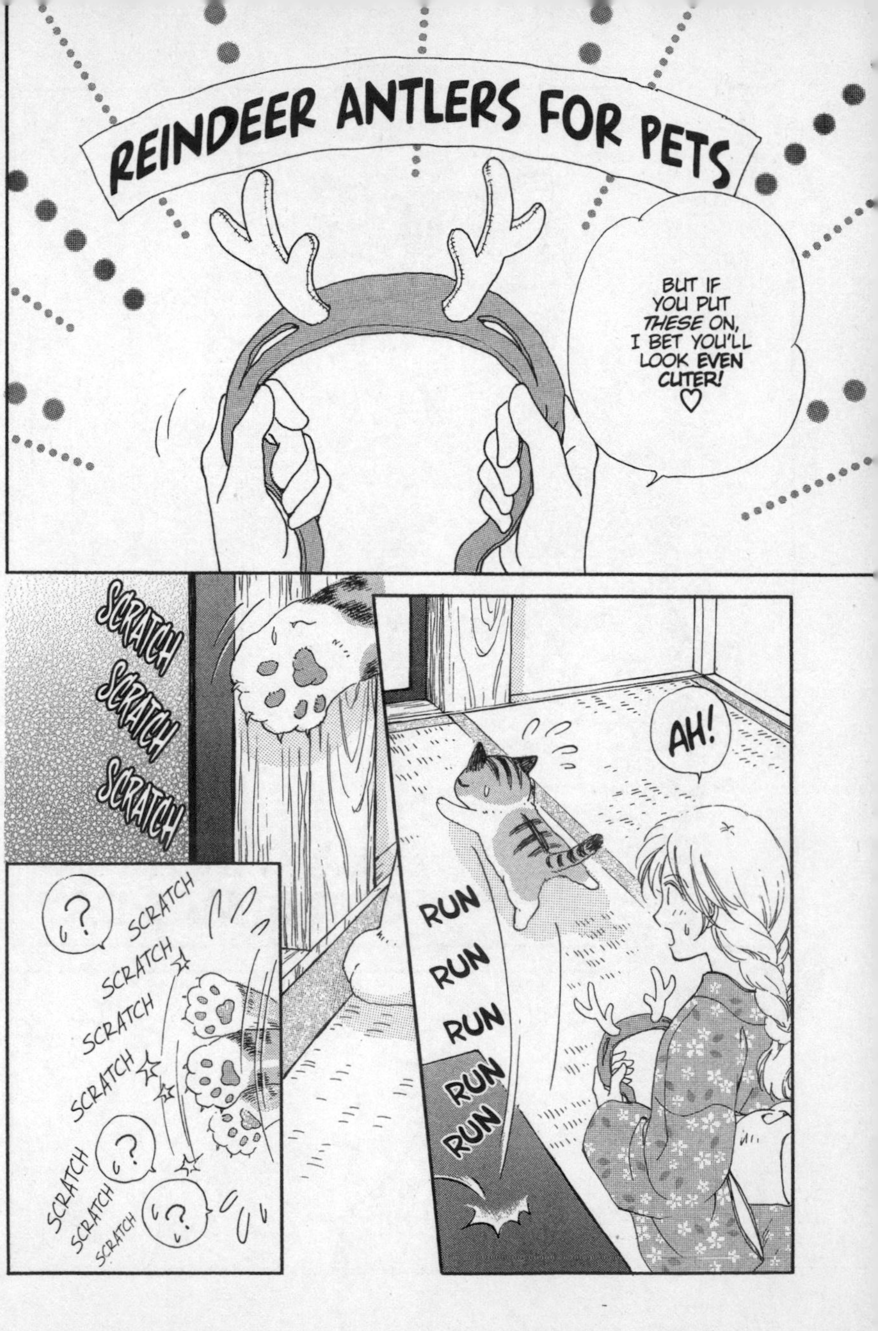
REINDEER ANTLERS FOR PETS
BUT IF YOU PUT *THESE* ON, I BET YOU'LL LOOK EVEN CUTER! ♡
AH!
RUN RUN RUN RUN RUN
SCRATCH SCRATCH SCRATCH
?
SCRATCH SCRATCH SCRATCH SCRATCH
?
SCRATCH SCRATCH SCRATCH
?

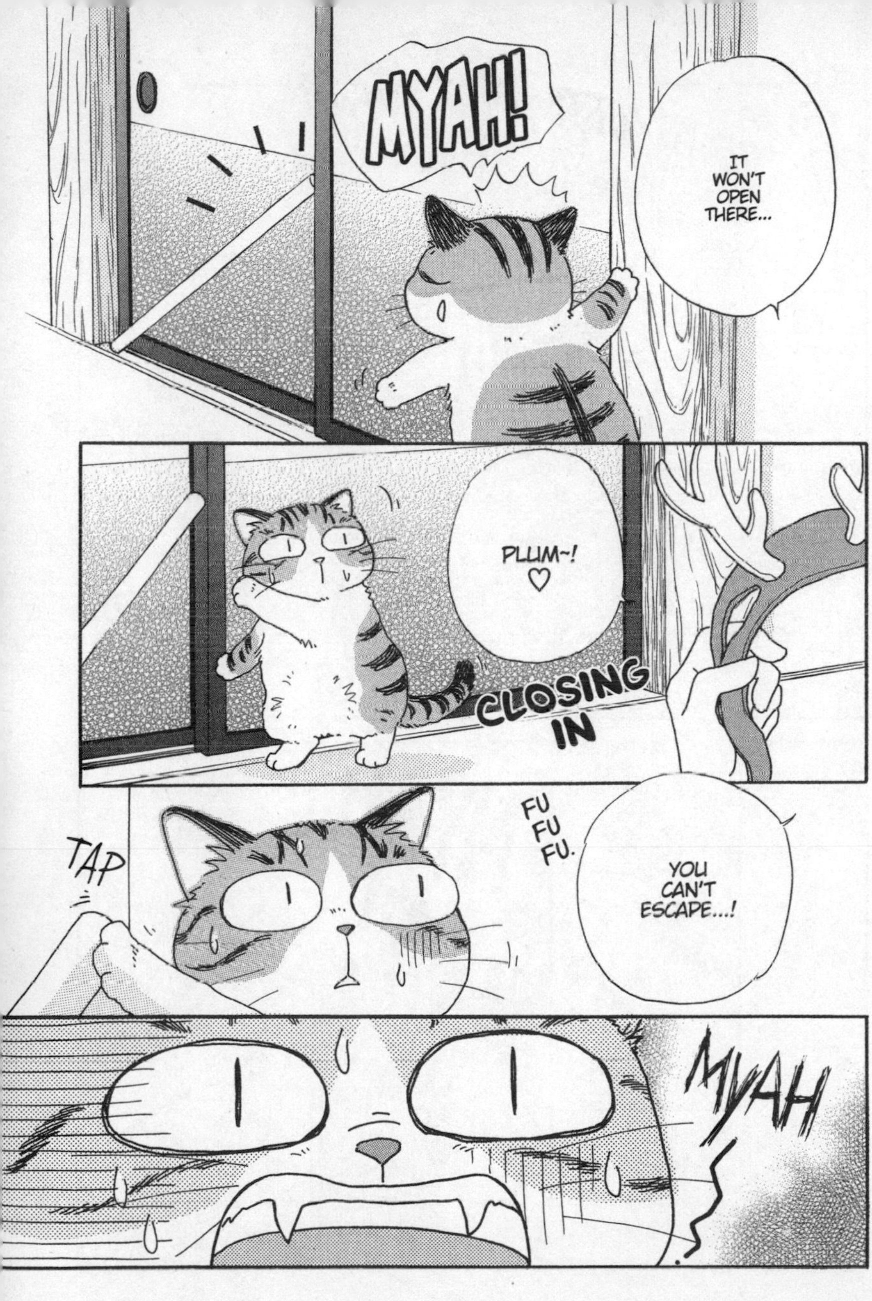
IT WON'T OPEN THERE...
MYAH!
PLUM~! ♡
CLOSING IN
FU FU FU.
YOU CAN'T ESCAPE...!
TAP
MYAH

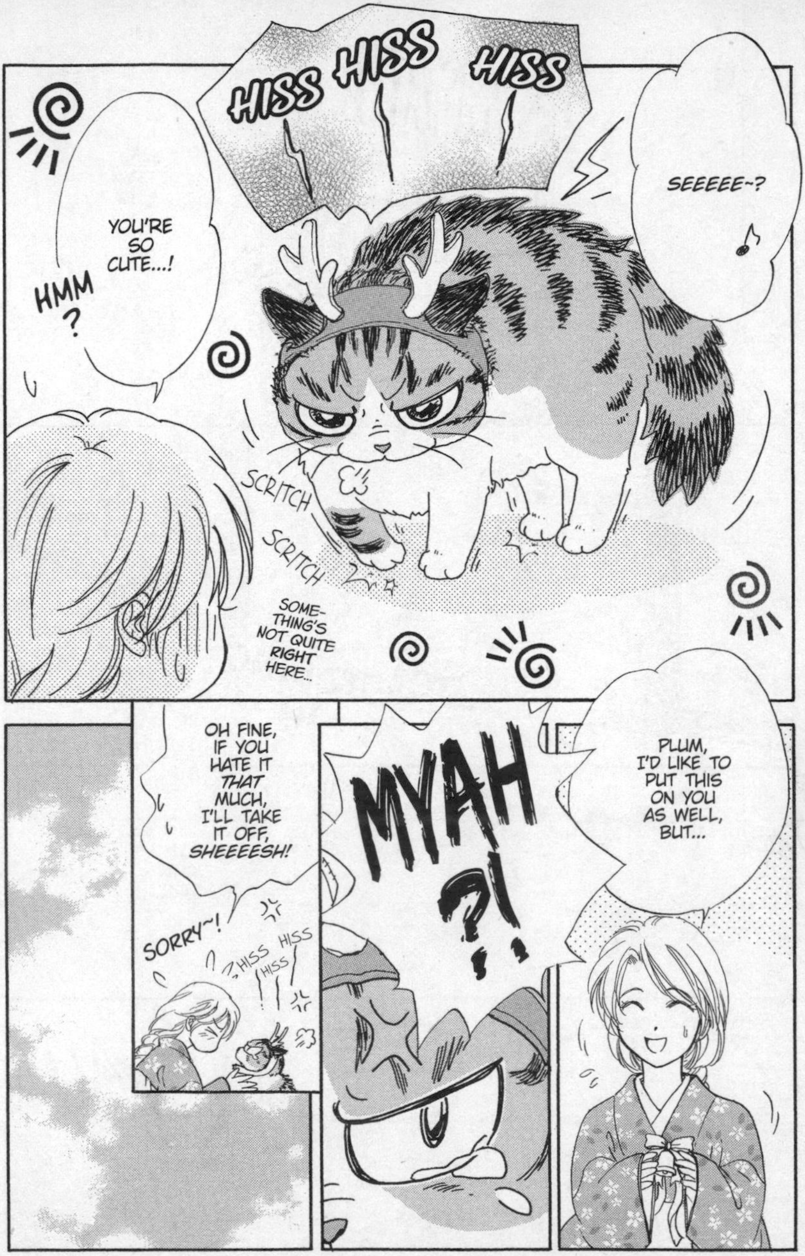
SEEEEE~?
HISS HISS HISS
YOU'RE SO CUTE...!
HMM?
SCRITCH SCRITCH
SOMETHING'S NOT QUITE RIGHT HERE...
PLUM, I'D LIKE TO PUT THIS ON YOU AS WELL, BUT...
MYAH ?!
OH FINE, IF YOU HATE IT *THAT* MUCH, I'LL TAKE IT OFF, *SHEEEESH!*
SORRY~!
HISS HISS HISS

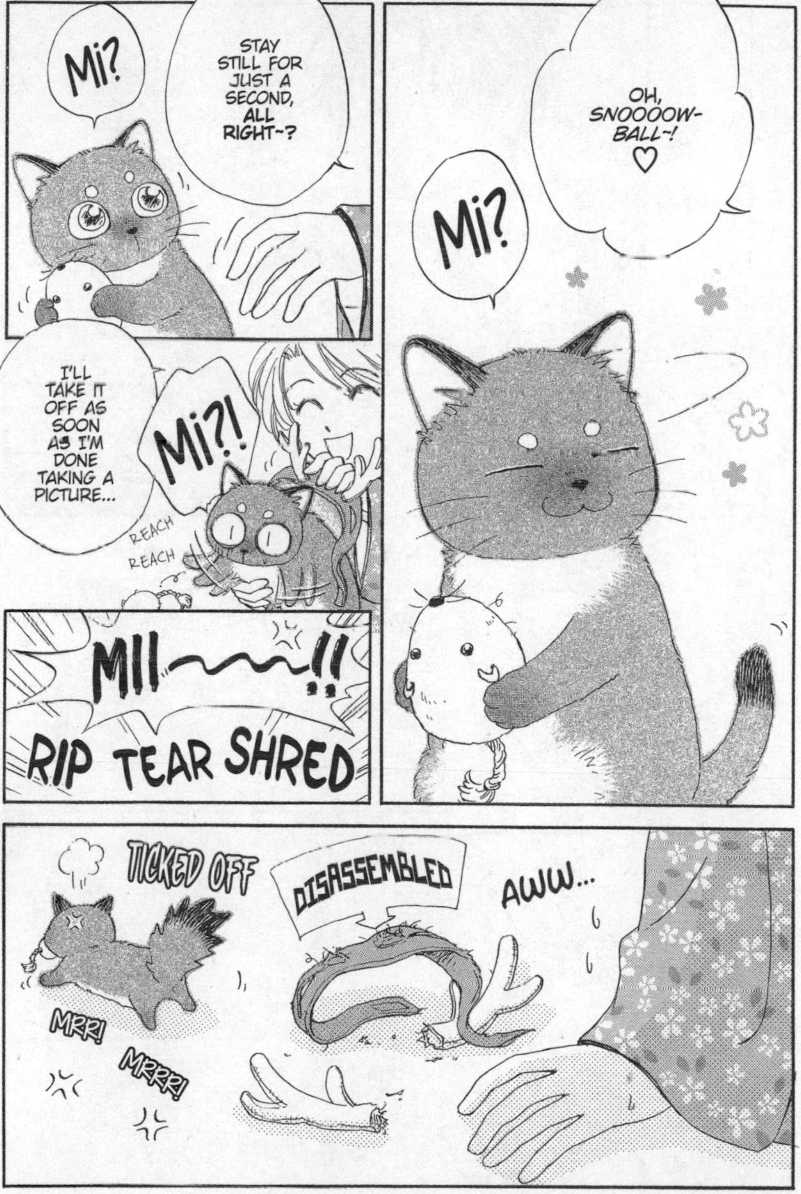
OH, SNOOOOW-BALL~! ♡
Mi?
STAY STILL FOR JUST A SECOND, ALL RIGHT~?
Mi?
I'LL TAKE IT OFF AS SOON AS I'M DONE TAKING A PICTURE...
Mi?!
REACH REACH
MII~~~!!
RIP TEAR SHRED
AWW...
DISASSEMBLED
TICKED OFF
MRR!
MRRR!

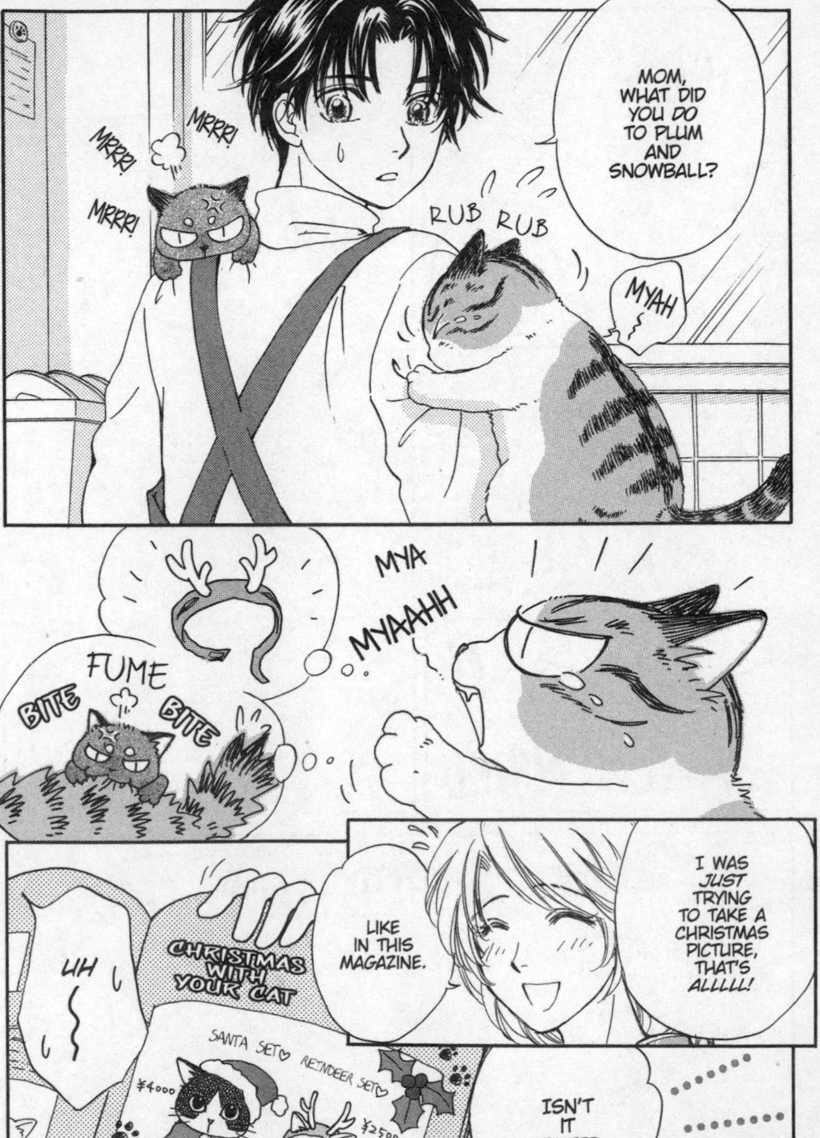
MOM, WHAT DID YOU DO TO PLUM AND SNOWBALL?
RUB RUB
MYAH
MRRR!
MRRR!
MRRR!
MYA
MYAAHH
FUME
BITE
BITE
I WAS JUST TRYING TO TAKE A CHRISTMAS PICTURE, THAT'S ALLLLL!
LIKE IN THIS MAGAZINE.
CHRISTMAS WITH YOUR CAT
SANTA SET♡
REINDEER SET♡
¥4000
¥2500
UH
ISN'T IT CUTE?

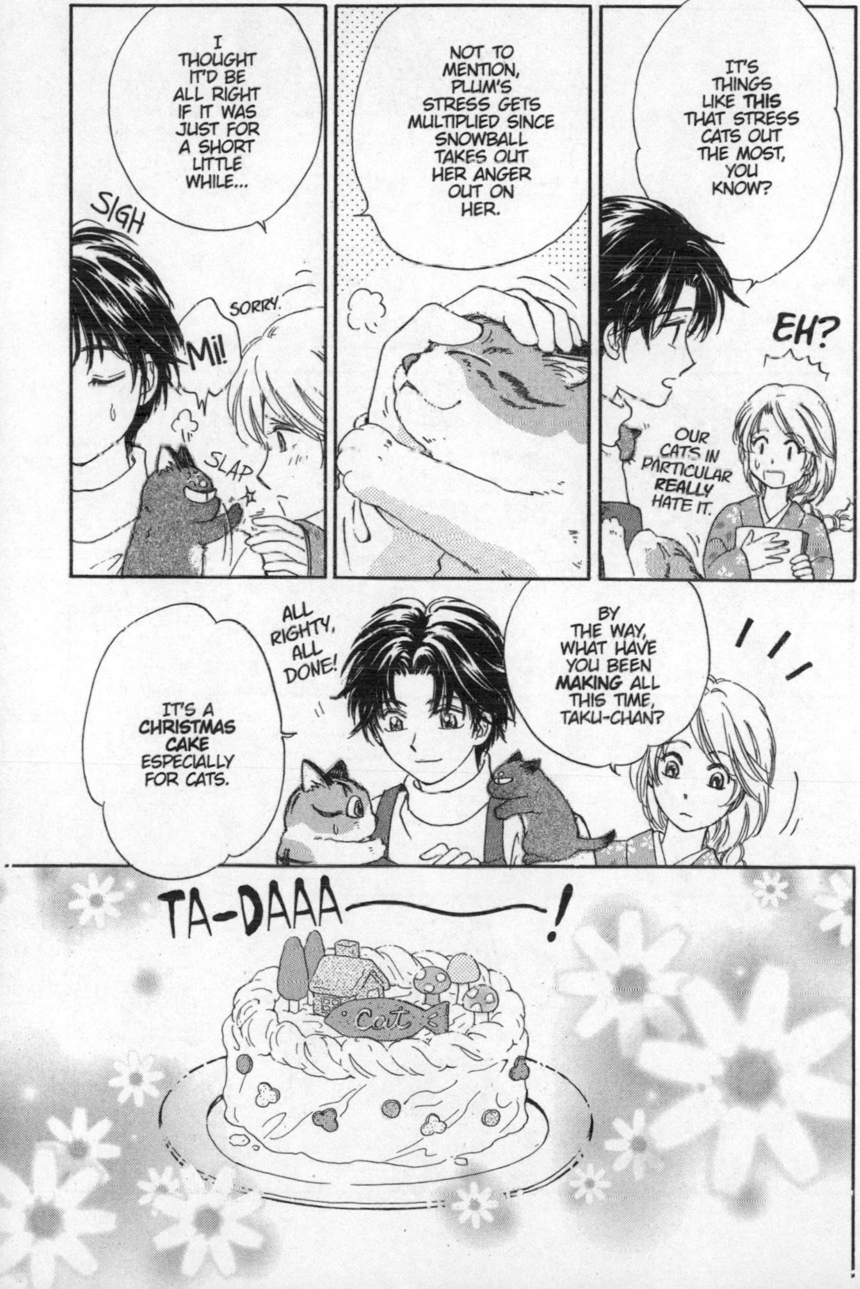
IT'S THINGS LIKE THIS THAT STRESS CATS OUT THE MOST, YOU KNOW?
EH?
OUR CATS IN PARTICULAR REALLY HATE IT.
NOT TO MENTION, PLUM'S STRESS GETS MULTIPLIED SINCE SNOWBALL TAKES OUT HER ANGER OUT ON HER.
I THOUGHT IT'D BE ALL RIGHT IF IT WAS JUST FOR A SHORT LITTLE WHILE...
SIGH
SORRY.
MI!
SLAP
BY THE WAY, WHAT HAVE YOU BEEN MAKING ALL THIS TIME, TAKU-CHAN?
ALL RIGHTY, ALL DONE!
IT'S A CHRISTMAS CAKE ESPECIALLY FOR CATS.
TA-DAAA——!
Cat

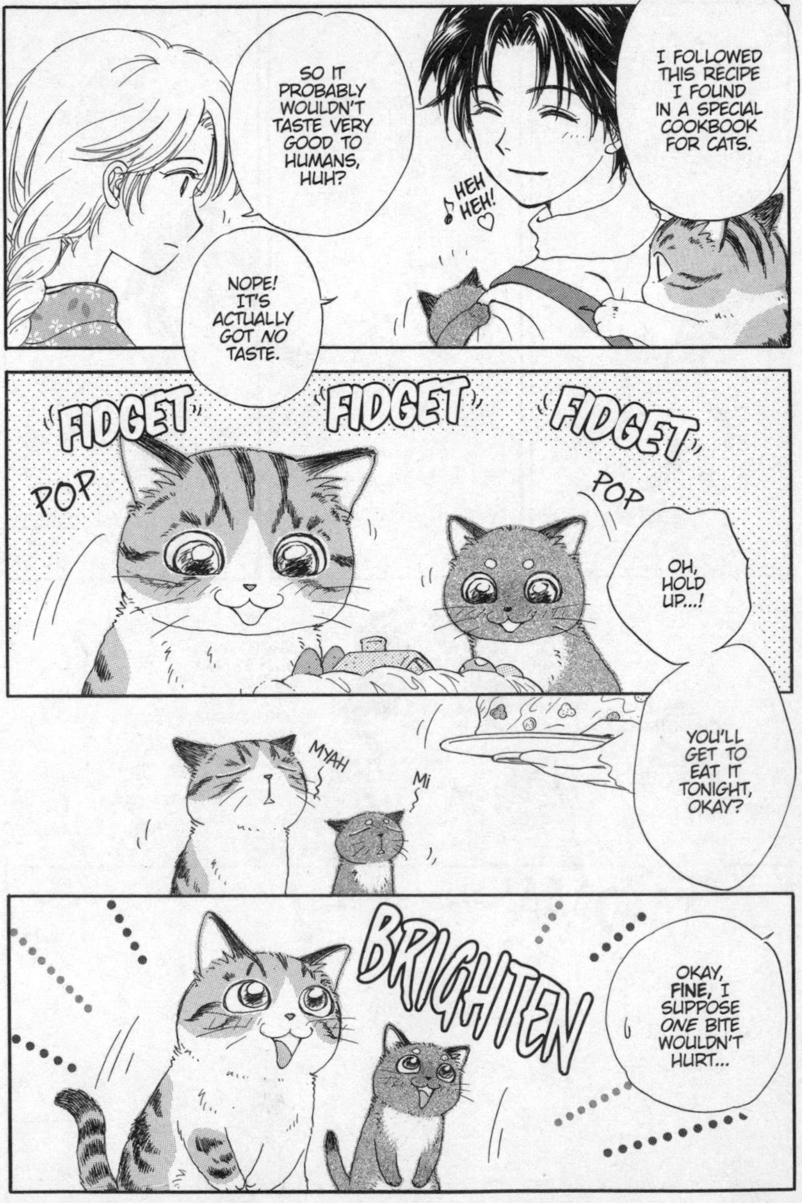
I FOLLOWED THIS RECIPE I FOUND IN A SPECIAL COOKBOOK FOR CATS.
HEH HEH!
SO IT PROBABLY WOULDN'T TASTE VERY GOOD TO HUMANS, HUH?
NOPE! IT'S ACTUALLY GOT NO TASTE.
FIDGET
FIDGET
FIDGET
POP
POP
OH, HOLD UP...!
YOU'LL GET TO EAT IT TONIGHT, OKAY?
MYAH
Mi
OKAY, FINE, I SUPPOSE ONE BITE WOULDN'T HURT...
BRIGHTEN

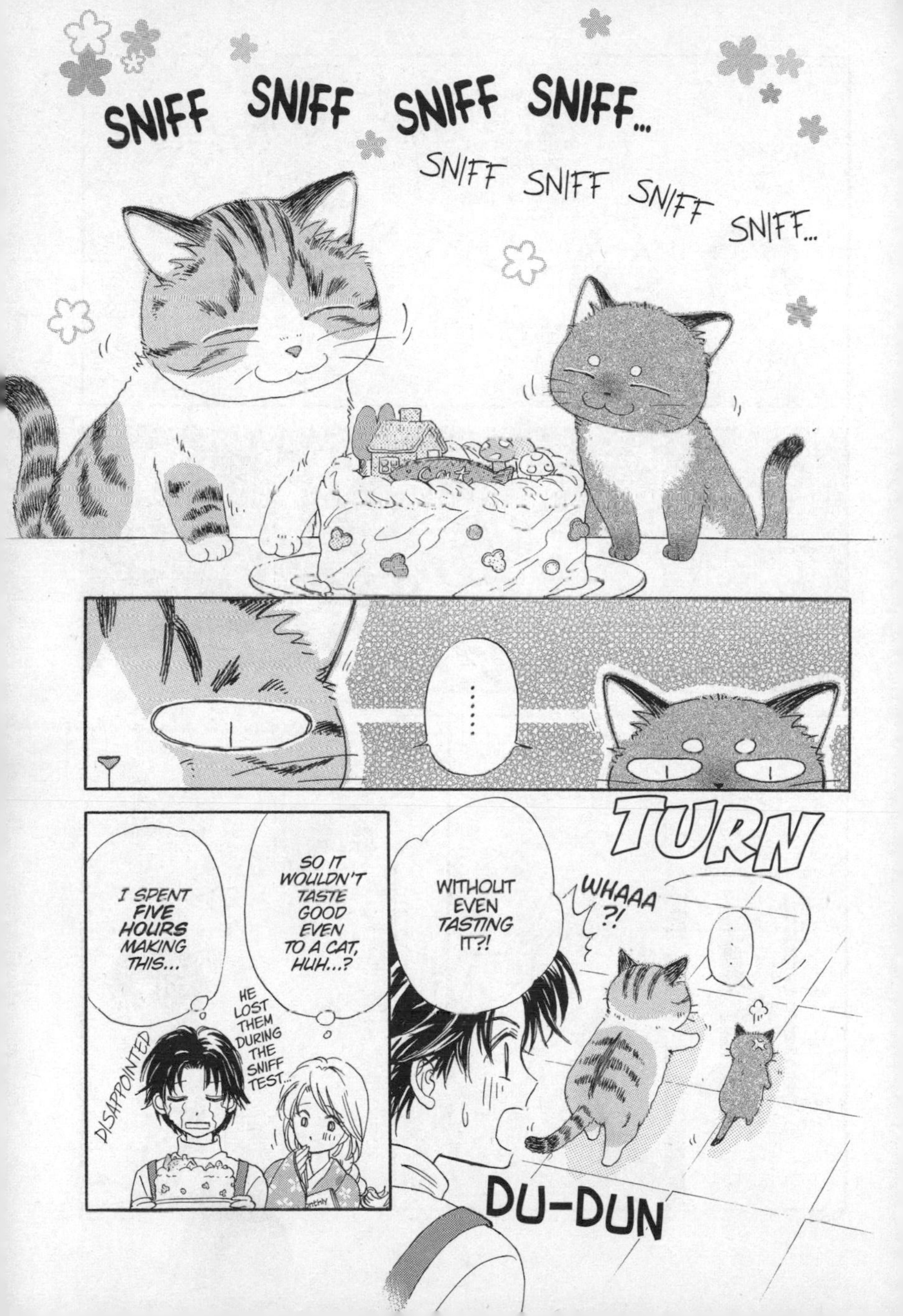
SNIFF SNIFF SNIFF SNIFF...
SNIFF SNIFF SNIFF SNIFF...
......
TURN
WHAAA ?!
WITHOUT EVEN TASTING IT?!
DU-DUN
SO IT WOULDN'T TASTE GOOD EVEN TO A CAT, HUH...?
HE LOST THEM DURING THE SNIFF TEST...
I SPENT FIVE HOURS MAKING THIS...
DISAPPOINTED

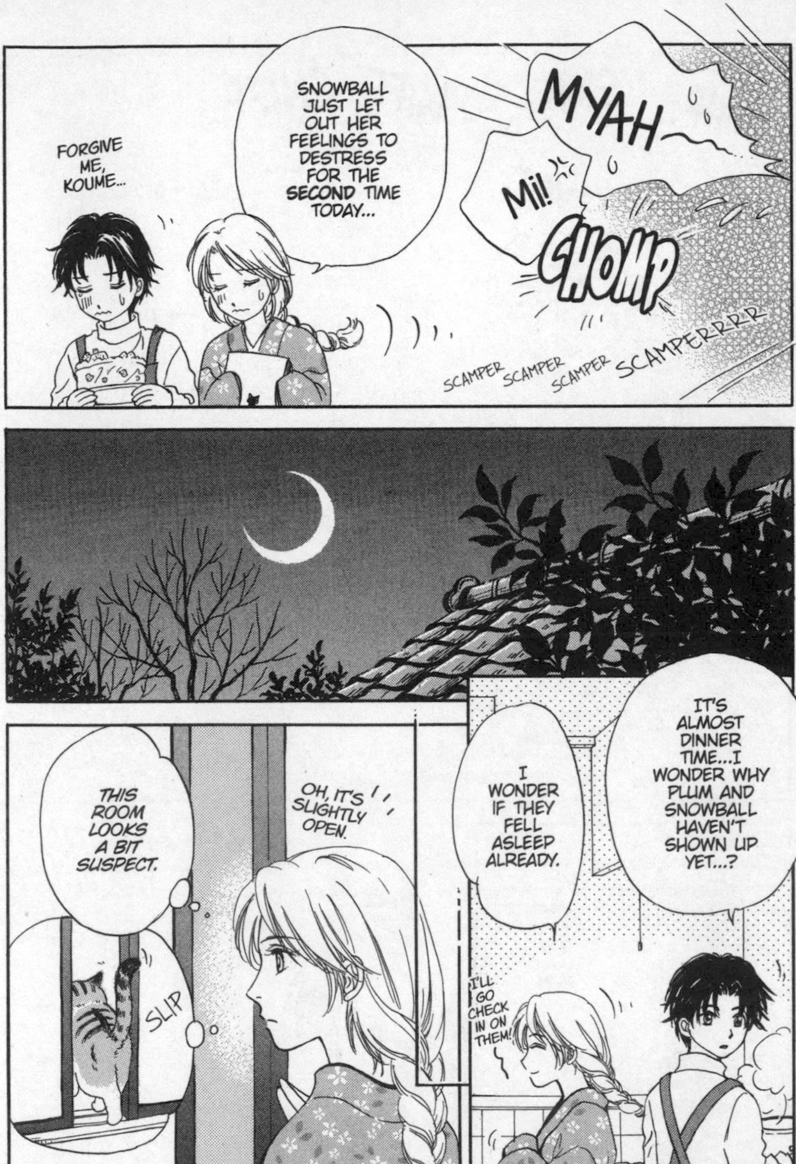
MYAH
Mi!
CHOMP
SCAMPERRRR
SCAMPER SCAMPER SCAMPER
SNOWBALL JUST LET OUT HER FEELINGS TO DESTRESS FOR THE SECOND TIME TODAY...
FORGIVE ME, KOUME...
IT'S ALMOST DINNER TIME...I WONDER WHY PLUM AND SNOWBALL HAVEN'T SHOWN UP YET...?
I WONDER IF THEY FELL ASLEEP ALREADY.
I'LL GO CHECK IN ON THEM!
OH, IT'S SLIGHTLY OPEN.
THIS ROOM LOOKS A BIT SUSPECT.
SLIP

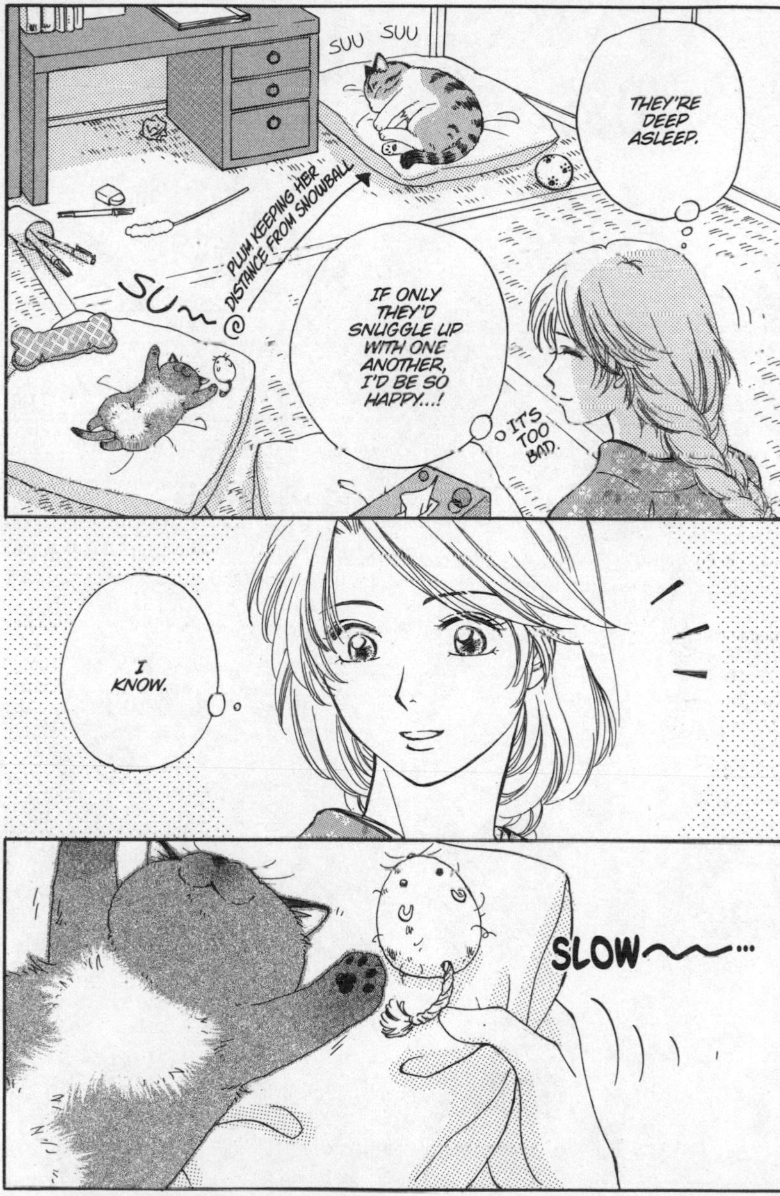
THEY'RE DEEP ASLEEP.
SUU SUU
IT'S TOO BAD.
IF ONLY THEY'D SNUGGLE UP WITH ONE ANOTHER, I'D BE SO HAPPY...!
PLUM KEEPING HER DISTANCE FROM SNOWBALL
SU~
I KNOW.
SLOW~~~...

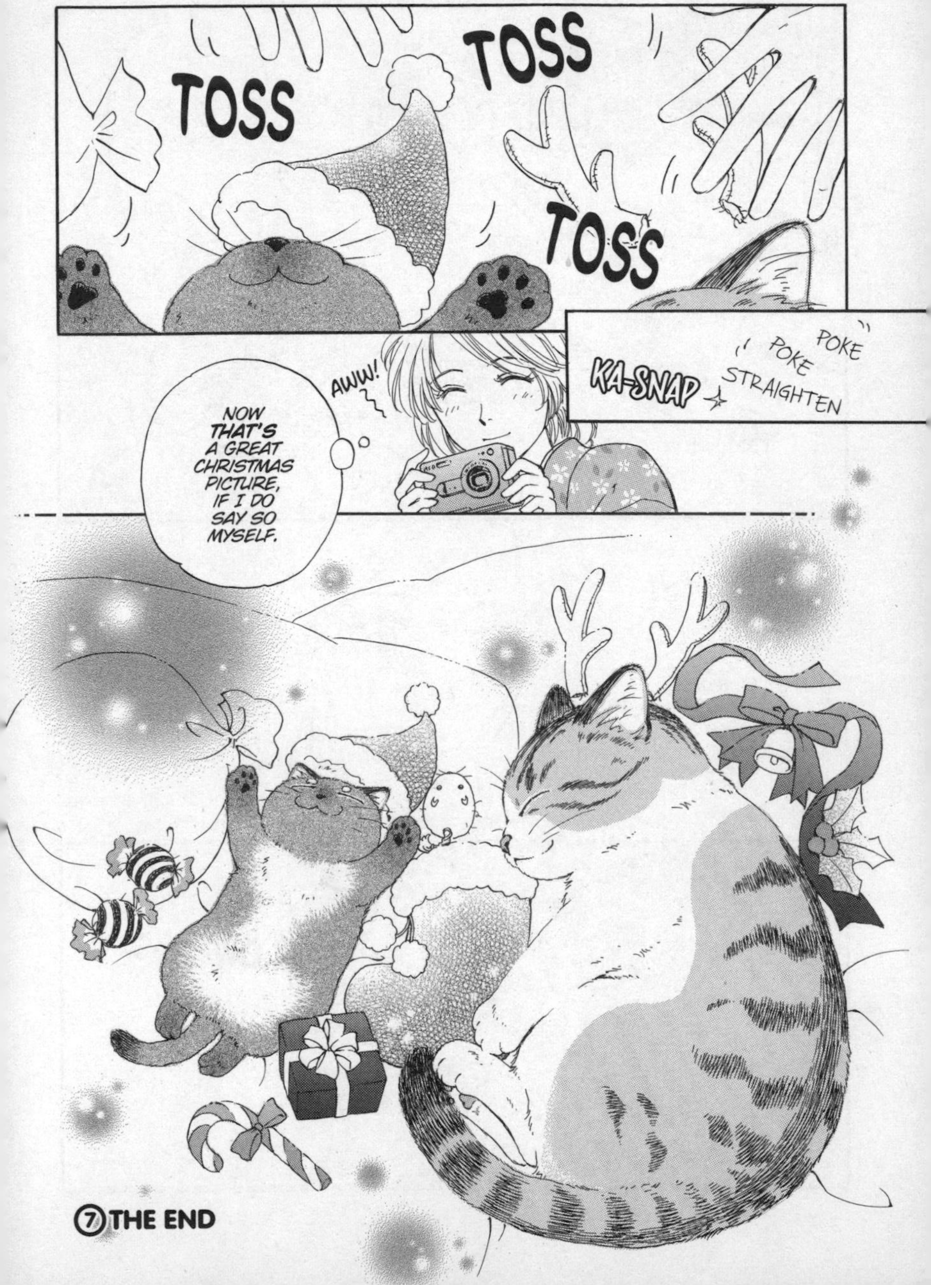
TOSS
TOSS
TOSS
POKE
POKE
STRAIGHTEN
KA-SNAP
AWW!
NOW THAT'S A GREAT CHRISTMAS PICTURE, IF I DO SAY SO MYSELF.
⑦ THE END

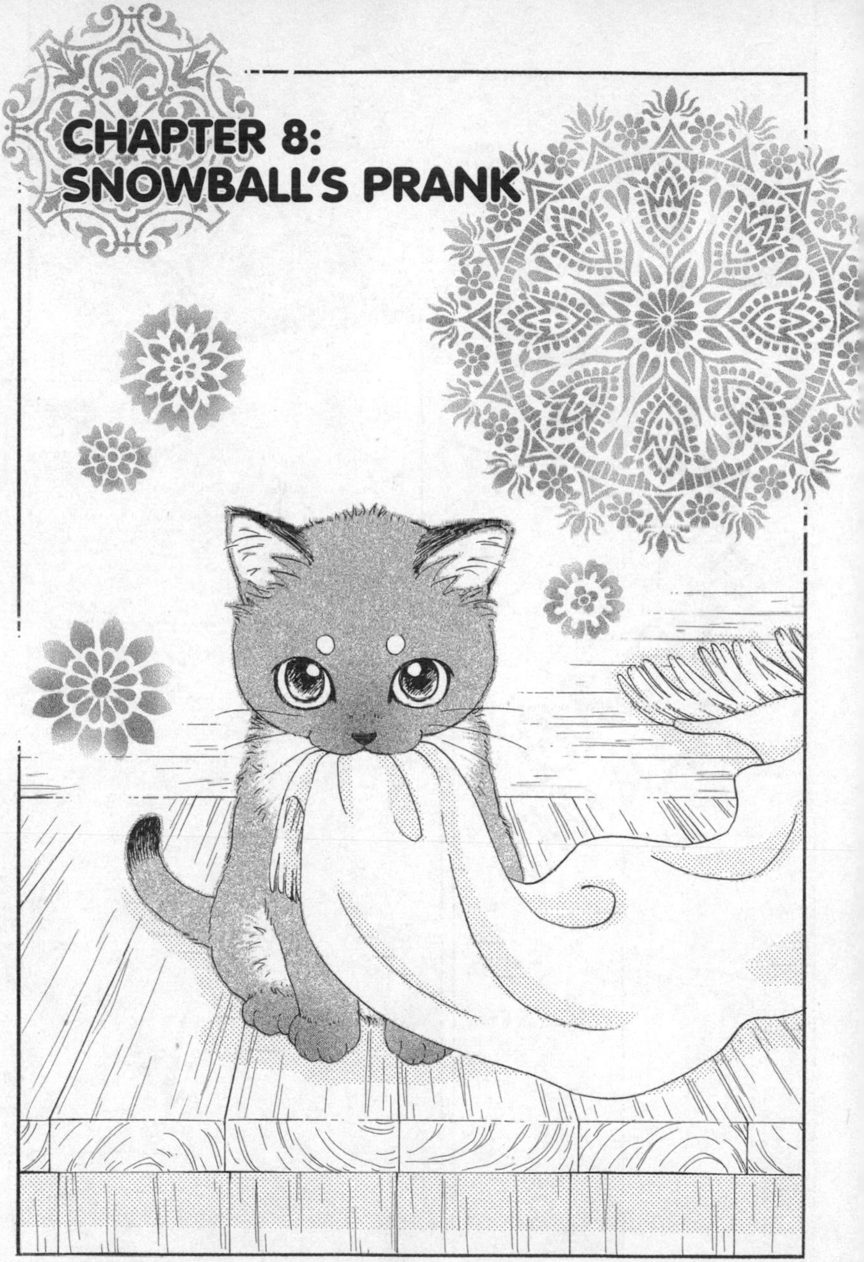
CHAPTER 8:
SNOWBALL'S PRANK

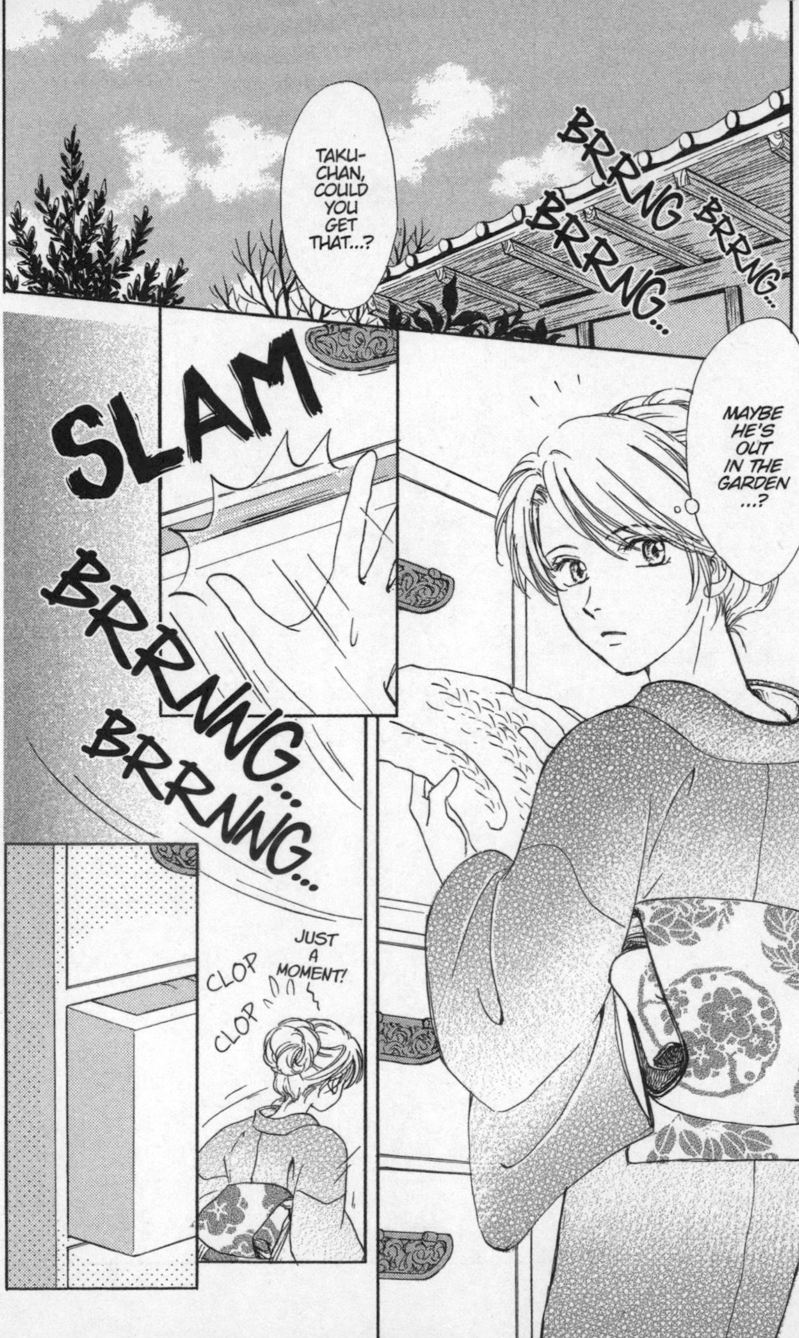
BRRNG BRRNG BRRNG...
TAKU-CHAN, COULD YOU GET THAT...?
MAYBE HE'S OUT IN THE GARDEN ...?
SLAM
BRRNNG... BRRNNG...
JUST A MOMENT!
CLOP CLOP

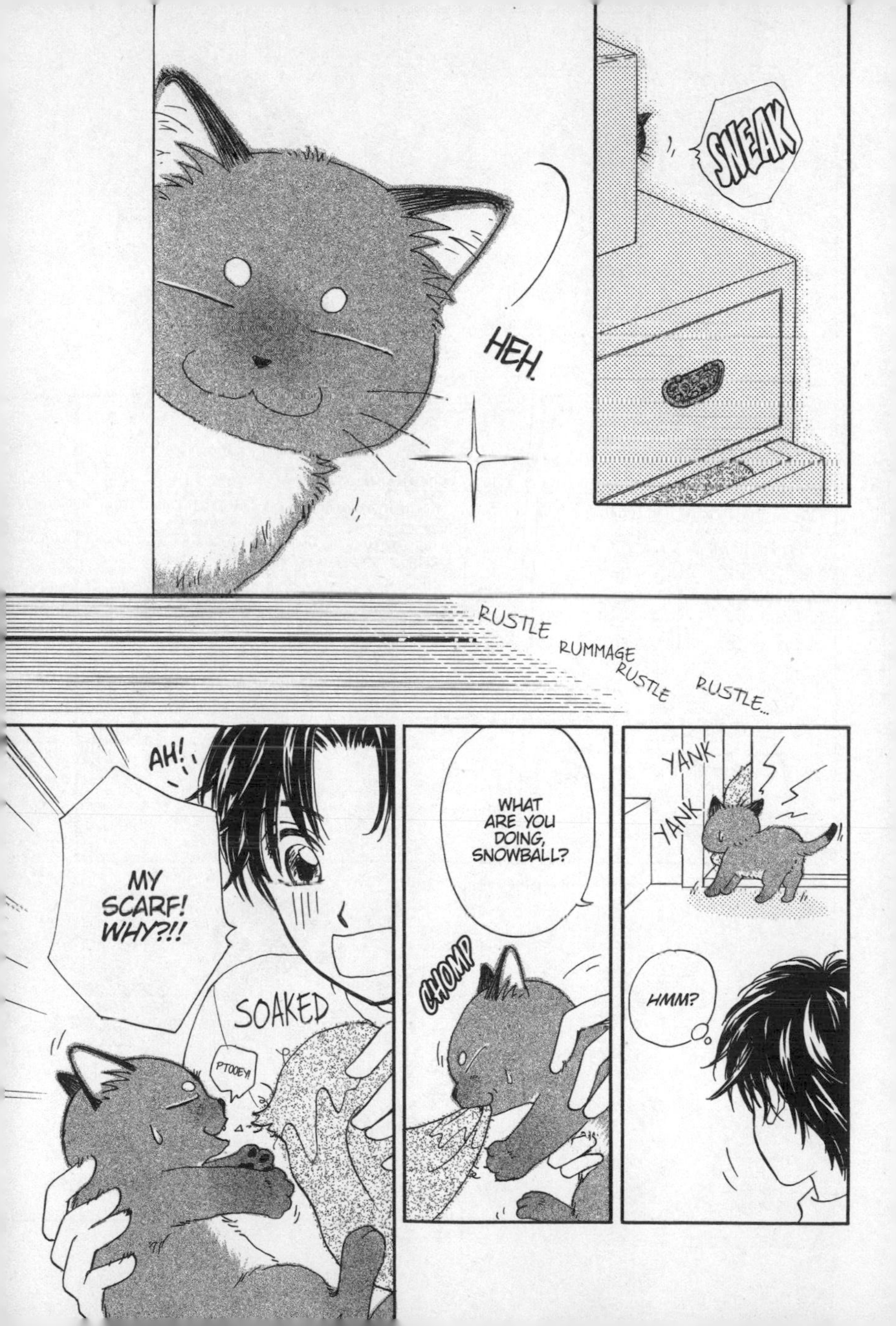
SNEAK
HEH.
RUSTLE RUMMAGE RUSTLE RUSTLE...
YANK YANK
HMM?
WHAT ARE YOU DOING, SNOWBALL?
CHOMP
AH!
MY SCARF! WHY?!!
SOAKED
PTOOEY!

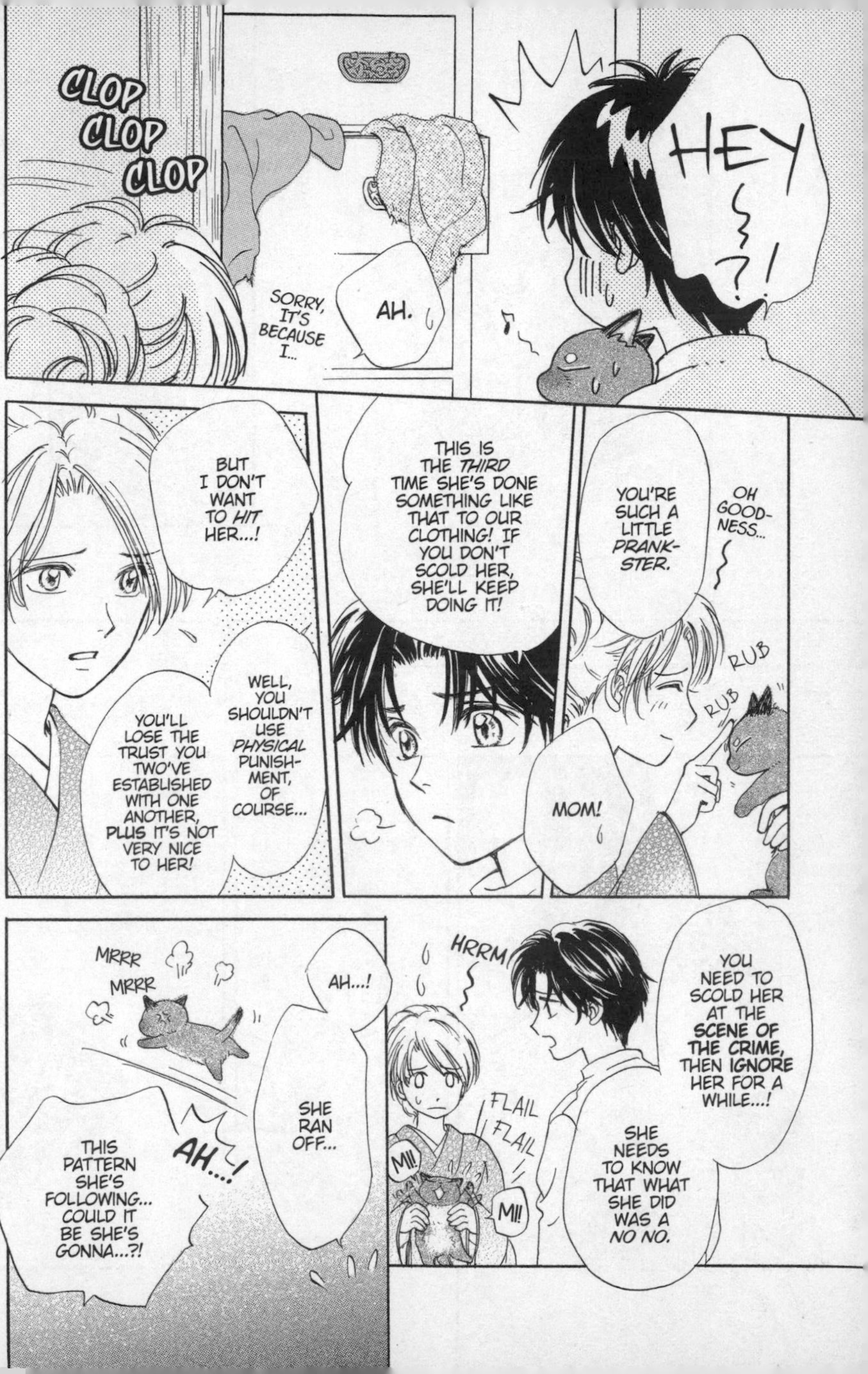
HEY ?!
AH.
SORRY, IT'S BECAUSE I...
CLOP CLOP CLOP
OH GOODNESS...
YOU'RE SUCH A LITTLE *PRANKSTER*.
RUB RUB
MOM!
THIS IS THE *THIRD* TIME SHE'S DONE SOMETHING LIKE THAT TO OUR CLOTHING! IF YOU DON'T SCOLD HER, SHE'LL KEEP DOING IT!
BUT I DON'T WANT TO *HIT* HER...!
WELL, YOU SHOULDN'T USE *PHYSICAL* PUNISHMENT, OF COURSE...
YOU'LL LOSE THE TRUST YOU TWO'VE ESTABLISHED WITH ONE ANOTHER, PLUS IT'S NOT VERY NICE TO HER!
YOU NEED TO SCOLD HER AT THE SCENE OF THE CRIME, THEN IGNORE HER FOR A WHILE...!
SHE NEEDS TO KNOW THAT WHAT SHE DID WAS A *NO NO*.
HRRM
FLAIL FLAIL
MI!
MI!
AH...!
SHE RAN OFF...
MRRR MRRR
AH...!
THIS PATTERN SHE'S FOLLOWING... COULD IT BE SHE'S GONNA...?!

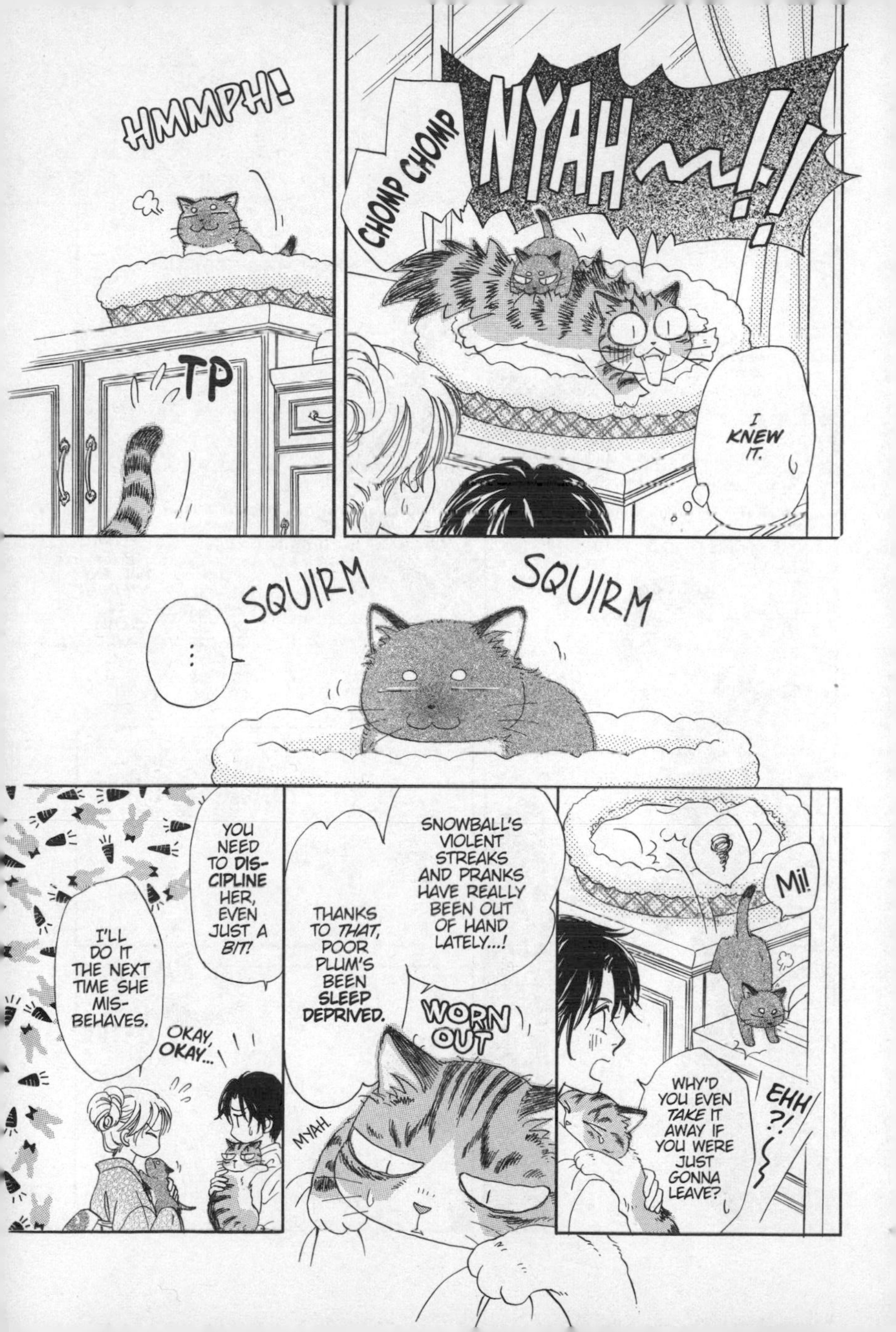
CHOMP CHOMP
NYAH~!!
I KNEW IT.
HMMPH!
TP
SQUIRM
SQUIRM
...
Mi!
WHY'D YOU EVEN TAKE IT AWAY IF YOU WERE JUST GONNA LEAVE?
EHH ?!
SNOWBALL'S VIOLENT STREAKS AND PRANKS HAVE REALLY BEEN OUT OF HAND LATELY...!
THANKS TO THAT, POOR PLUM'S BEEN SLEEP DEPRIVED.
WORN OUT
MYAH
YOU NEED TO DISCIPLINE HER, EVEN JUST A BIT!
I'LL DO IT THE NEXT TIME SHE MIS-BEHAVES.
OKAY, OKAY...

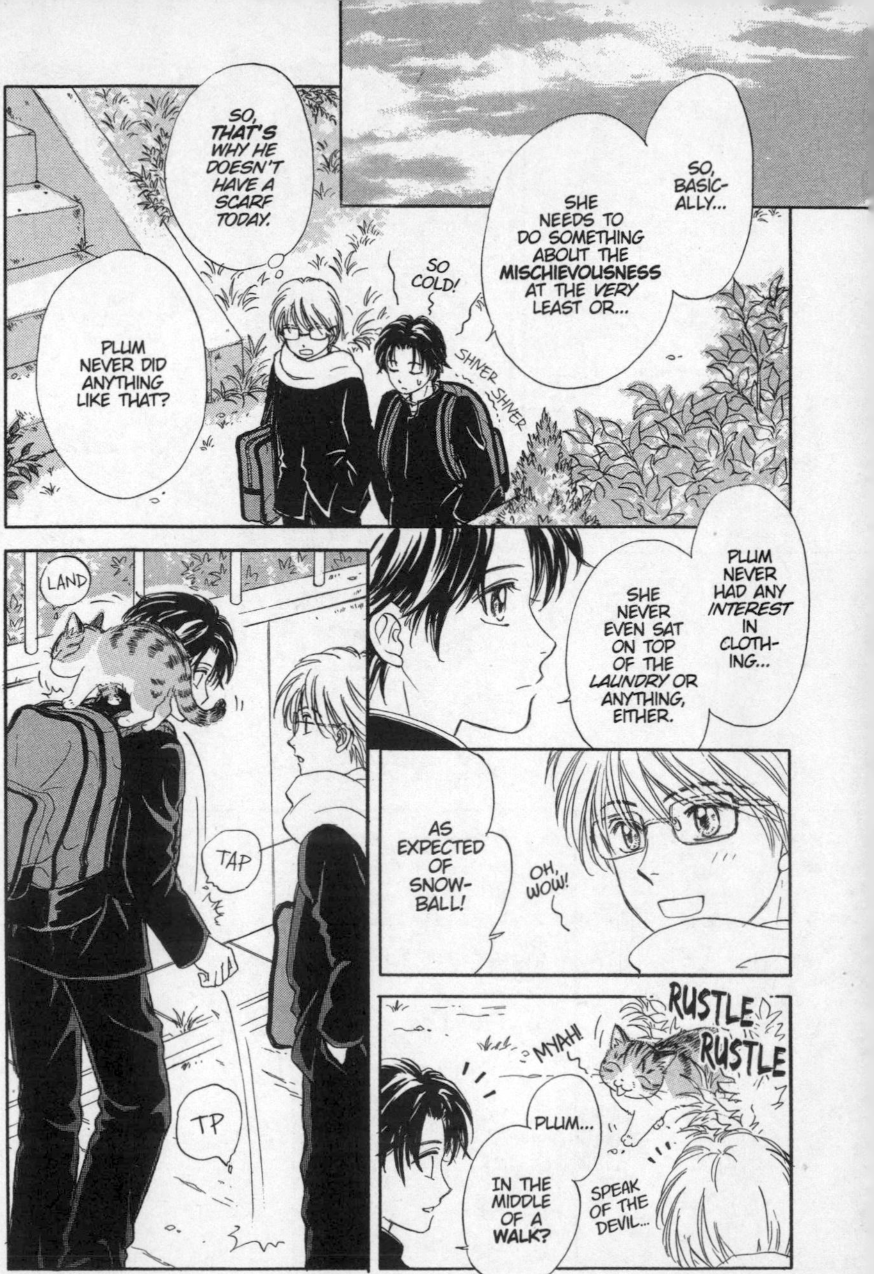
SO, BASICALLY...
SHE NEEDS TO DO SOMETHING ABOUT THE MISCHIEVOUSNESS AT THE VERY LEAST OR...
SO COLD!
SHIVER SHIVER
SO, THAT'S WHY HE DOESN'T HAVE A SCARF TODAY.
PLUM NEVER DID ANYTHING LIKE THAT?
PLUM NEVER HAD ANY INTEREST IN CLOTHING...
SHE NEVER EVEN SAT ON TOP OF THE LAUNDRY OR ANYTHING, EITHER.
AS EXPECTED OF SNOWBALL!
OH, WOW!
RUSTLE RUSTLE
MYAH!
PLUM...
IN THE MIDDLE OF A WALK?
SPEAK OF THE DEVIL...
LAND
TAP
TP

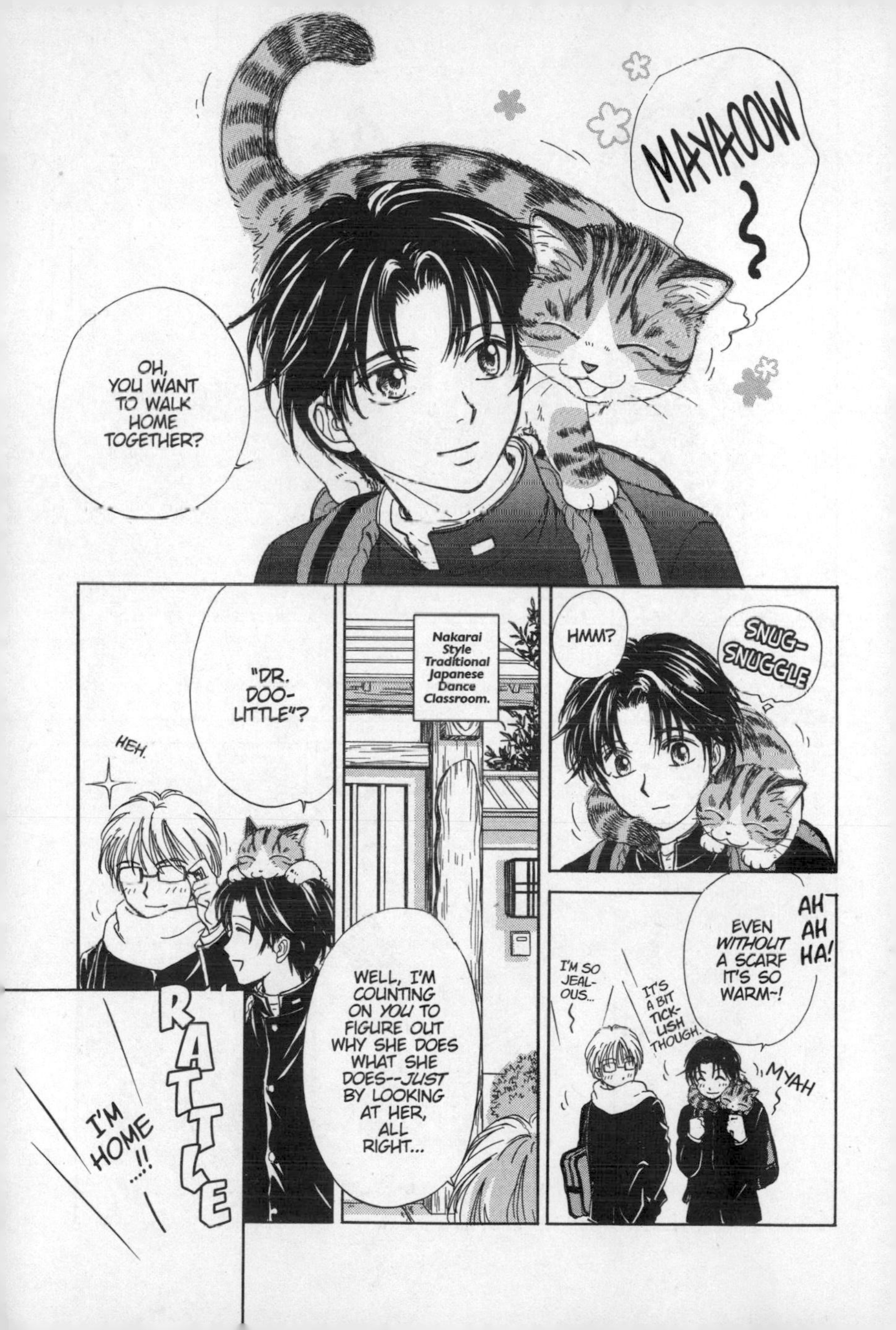
MAYAOOW ~
OH, YOU WANT TO WALK HOME TOGETHER?
SNUG-SNUGGLE
HMM?
AH AH HA!
EVEN WITHOUT A SCARF IT'S SO WARM~!
IT'S A BIT TICK-LISH THOUGH.
I'M SO JEAL-OUS...
MYAH
Nakarai Style Traditional Japanese Dance Classroom.
WELL, I'M COUNTING ON YOU TO FIGURE OUT WHY SHE DOES WHAT SHE DOES--JUST BY LOOKING AT HER, ALL RIGHT...
"DR. DOO-LITTLE"?
HEH.
RATTLE
I'M HOME ...!!

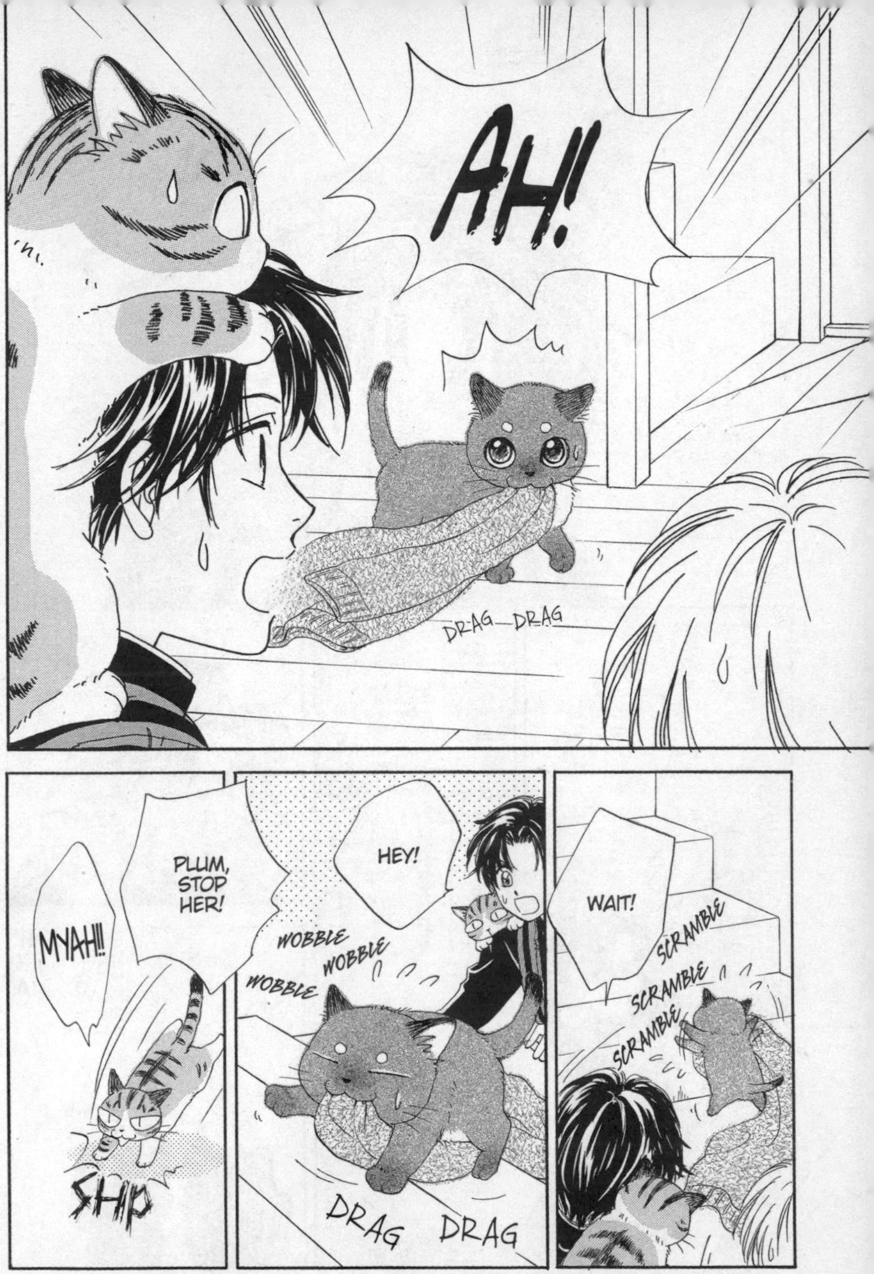
AH!
DRAG DRAG
WAIT!
SCRAMBLE
SCRAMBLE
SCRAMBLE
HEY!
WOBBLE
WOBBLE
WOBBLE
DRAG DRAG
PLUM, STOP HER!
MYAH!!
SHP

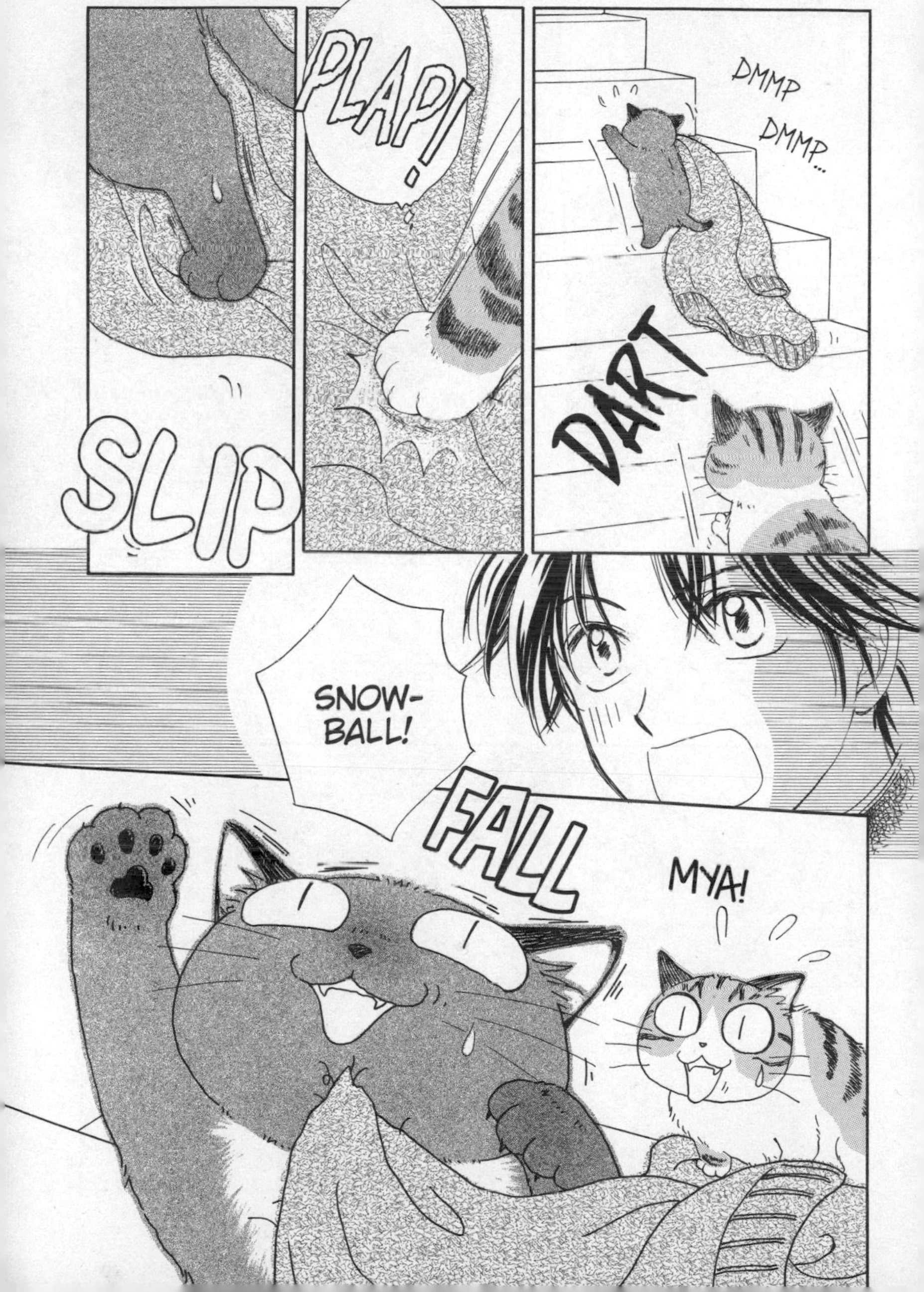
DMMP
DMMP...
DART
PLAP!
SLIP
SNOW-
BALL!
FALL
MYA!

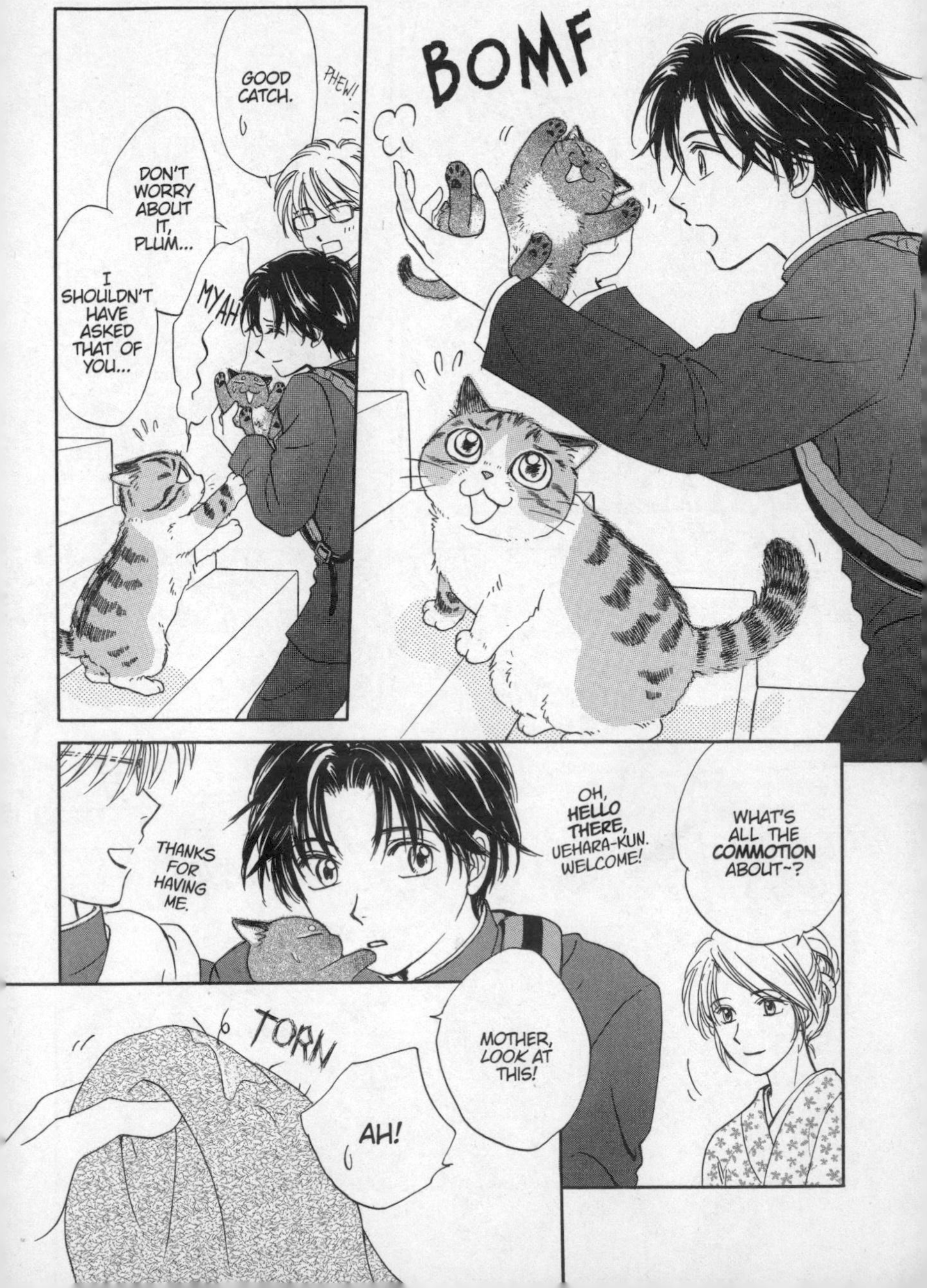
BOMF
GOOD CATCH.
PHEW!
DON'T WORRY ABOUT IT, PLUM...
I SHOULDN'T HAVE ASKED THAT OF YOU...
MYAH
WHAT'S ALL THE COMMOTION ABOUT~?
OH, HELLO THERE, UEHARA-KUN. WELCOME!
THANKS FOR HAVING ME.
MOTHER, LOOK AT THIS!
TORN
AH!

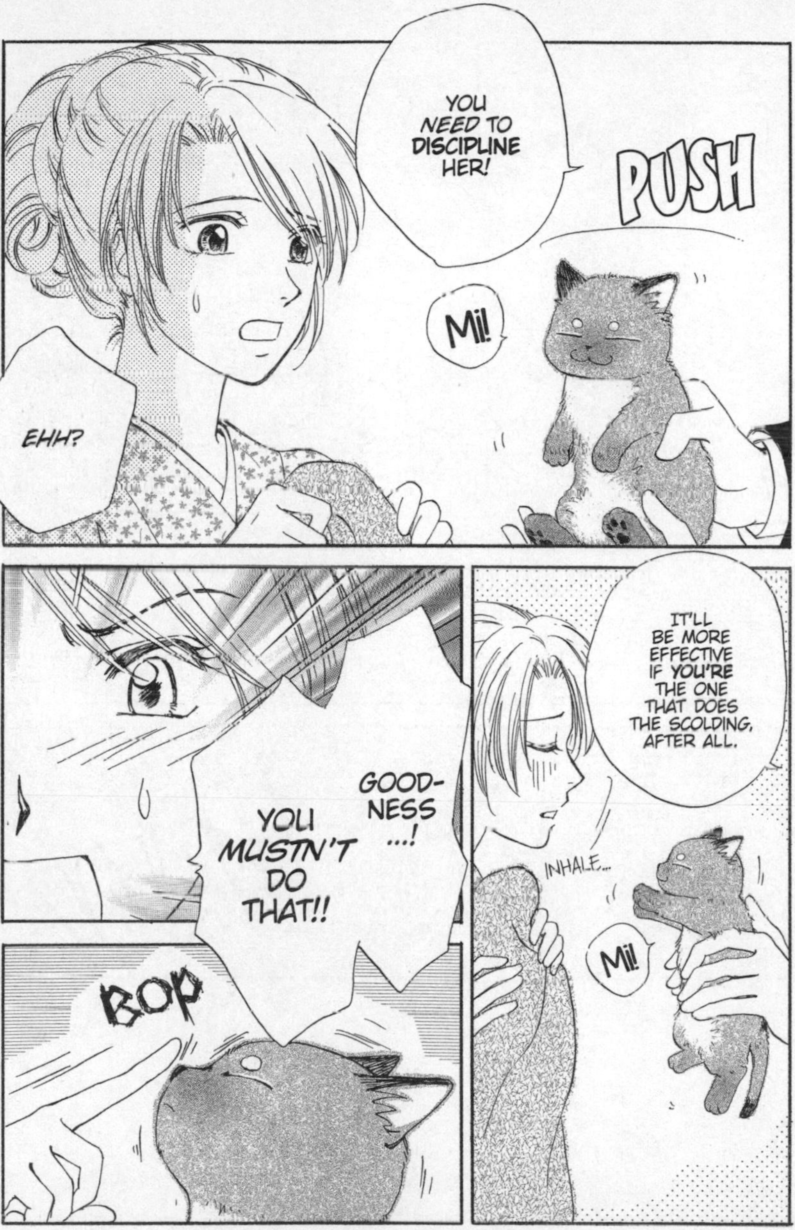
PUSH
Mi!
YOU NEED TO DISCIPLINE HER!
EHH?
IT'LL BE MORE EFFECTIVE IF YOU'RE THE ONE THAT DOES THE SCOLDING, AFTER ALL.
INHALE...
Mi!
GOOD-NESS ...!
YOU MUSTN'T DO THAT!!
BOP

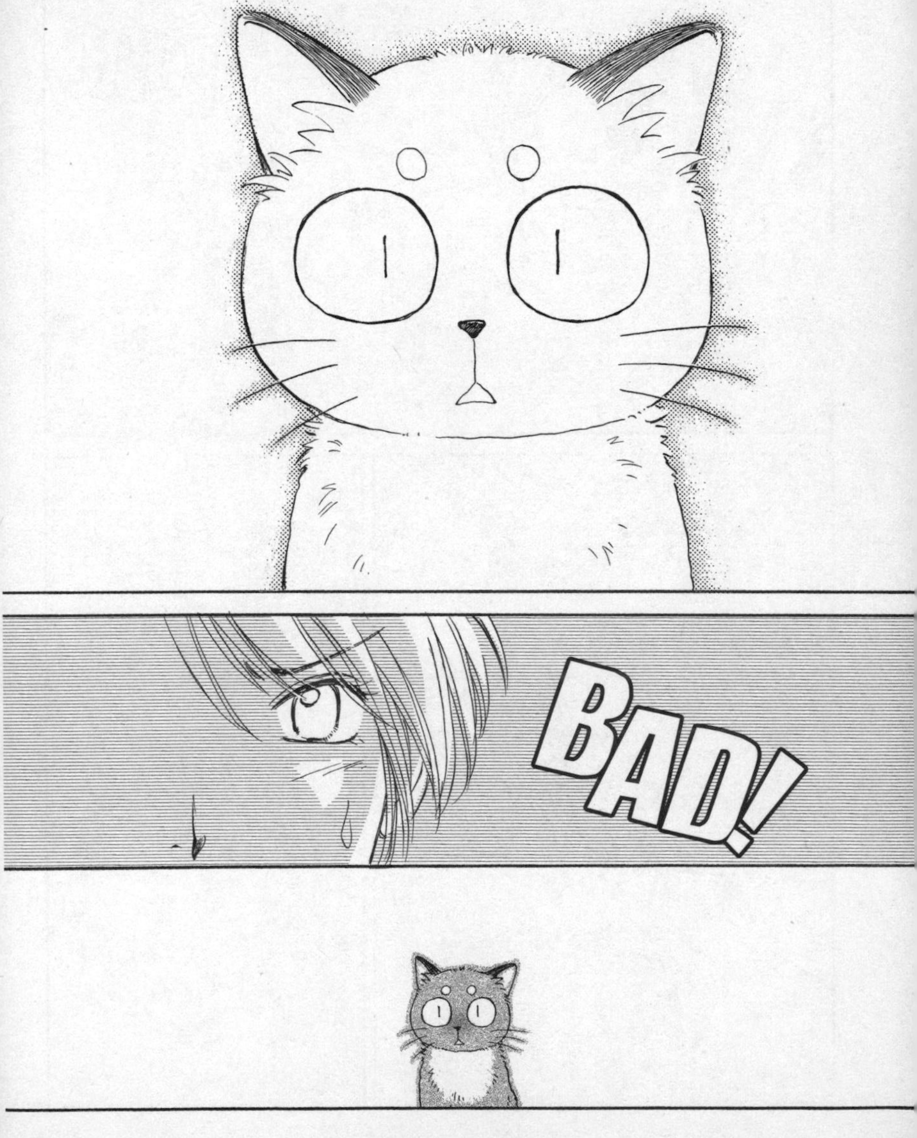
BAD!

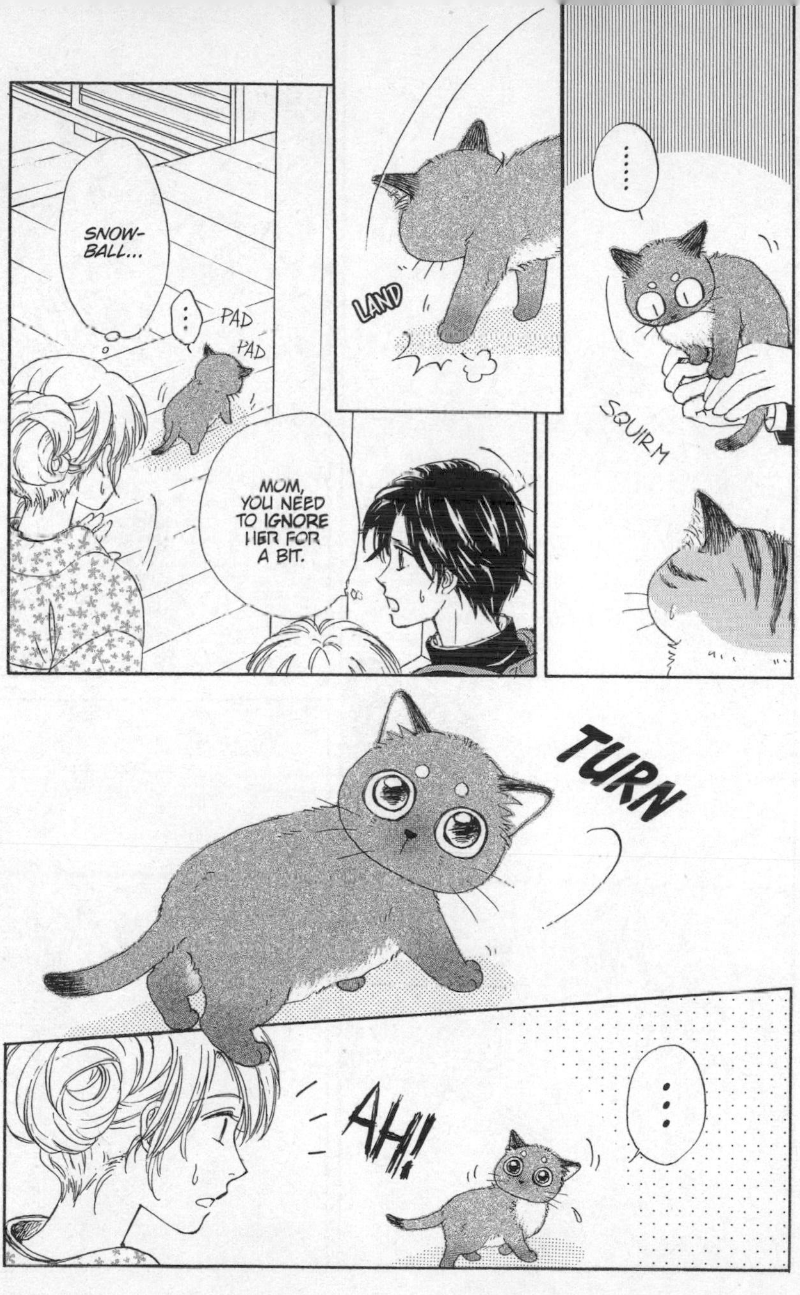
......
SQUIRM
LAND
SNOW-BALL...
...
PAD PAD
MOM, YOU NEED TO IGNORE HER FOR A BIT.
TURN
AH!
...

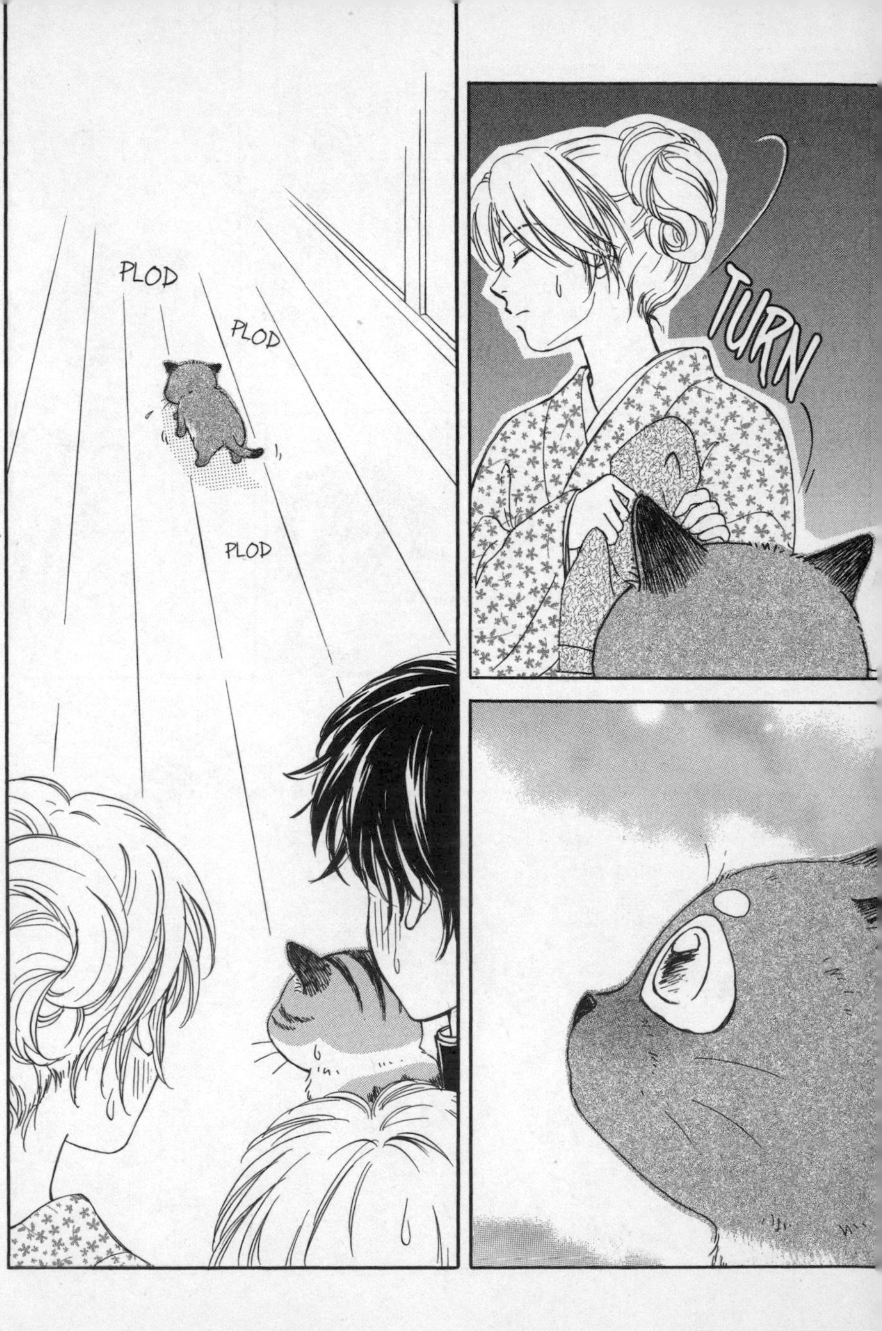
TURN
PLOD
PLOD
PLOD

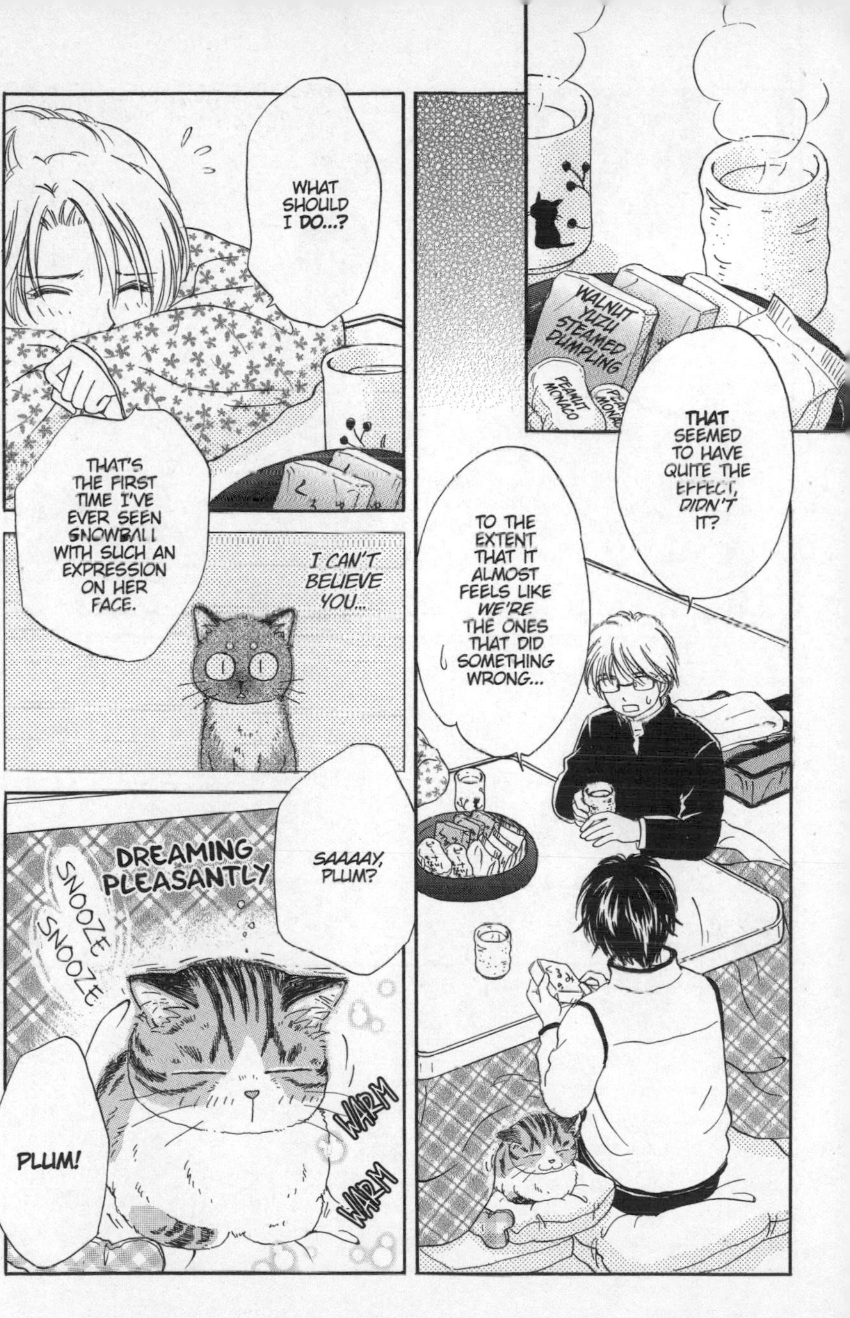
WALNUT YUZU STEAMED DUMPLING
PEANUT MONAKA
PEANUT MONAKA
THAT SEEMED TO HAVE QUITE THE EFFECT, DIDN'T IT?
TO THE EXTENT THAT IT ALMOST FEELS LIKE WE'RE THE ONES THAT DID SOMETHING WRONG...
WHAT SHOULD I DO...?
THAT'S THE FIRST TIME I'VE EVER SEEN SNOWBALL WITH SUCH AN EXPRESSION ON HER FACE.
I CAN'T BELIEVE YOU...
SAAAAY, PLUM?
DREAMING PLEASANTLY
SNOOZE SNOOZE
WARM WARM
PLUM!

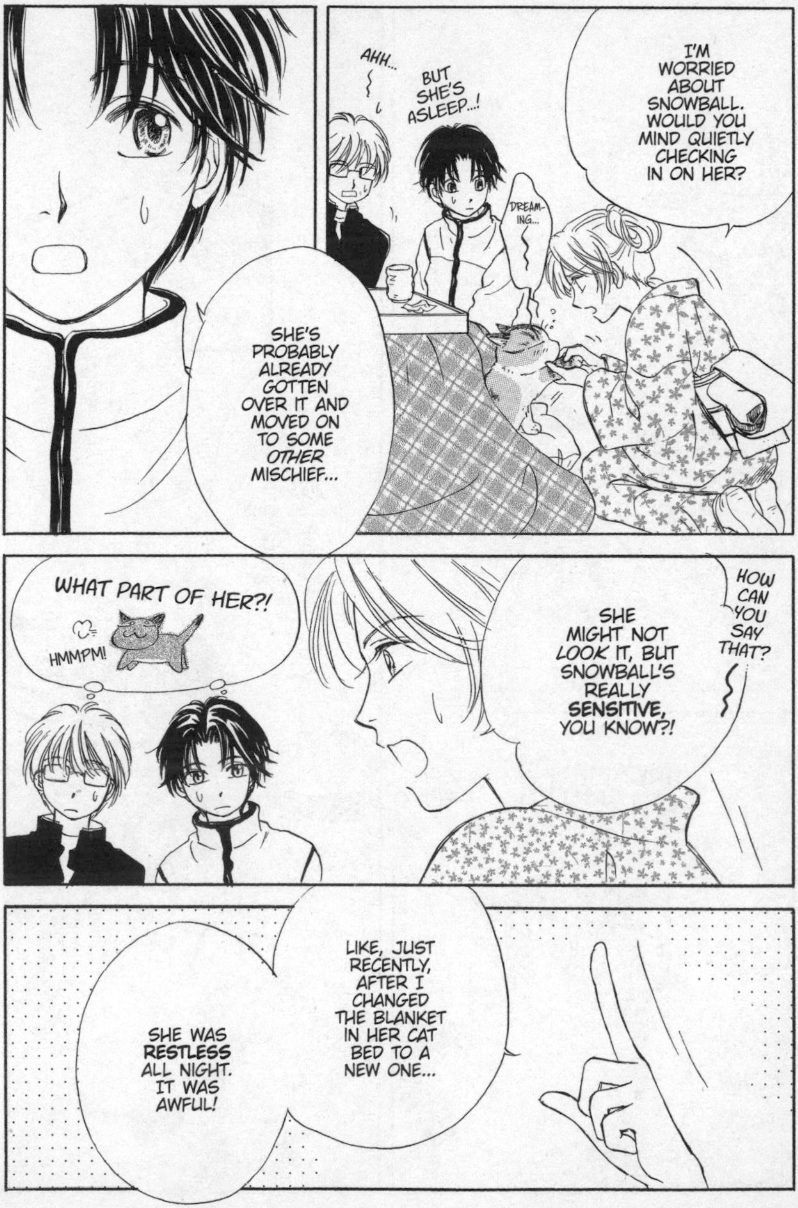
I'M WORRIED ABOUT SNOWBALL. WOULD YOU MIND QUIETLY CHECKING IN ON HER?
DREAMING...
BUT SHE'S ASLEEP...!
AHH...
SHE'S PROBABLY ALREADY GOTTEN OVER IT AND MOVED ON TO SOME OTHER MISCHIEF...
HOW CAN YOU SAY THAT?
SHE MIGHT NOT LOOK IT, BUT SNOWBALL'S REALLY SENSITIVE, YOU KNOW?!
WHAT PART OF HER?!
HMMPM!
LIKE, JUST RECENTLY, AFTER I CHANGED THE BLANKET IN HER CAT BED TO A NEW ONE...
SHE WAS RESTLESS ALL NIGHT. IT WAS AWFUL!

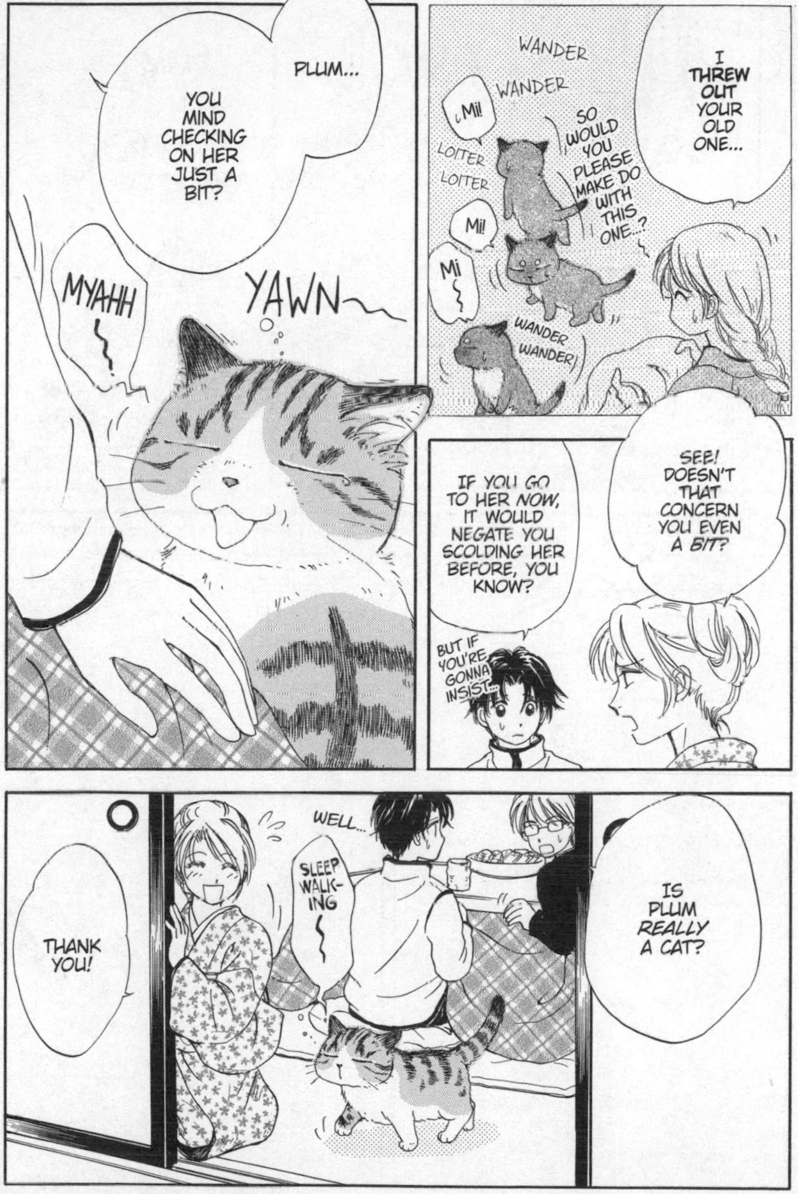
I THREW OUT YOUR OLD ONE...
WANDER
WANDER
SO WOULD YOU PLEASE MAKE DO WITH THIS ONE...?
¿Mi!
LOITER LOITER
Mi!
Mi
WANDER WANDER
SEE! DOESN'T THAT CONCERN YOU EVEN A BIT?
IF YOU GO TO HER NOW, IT WOULD NEGATE YOU SCOLDING HER BEFORE, YOU KNOW?
BUT IF YOU'RE GONNA INSIST...
PLUM...
YOU MIND CHECKING ON HER JUST A BIT?
MYAHH
YAWN
IS PLUM REALLY A CAT?
WELL...
SLEEP-WALKING
THANK YOU!

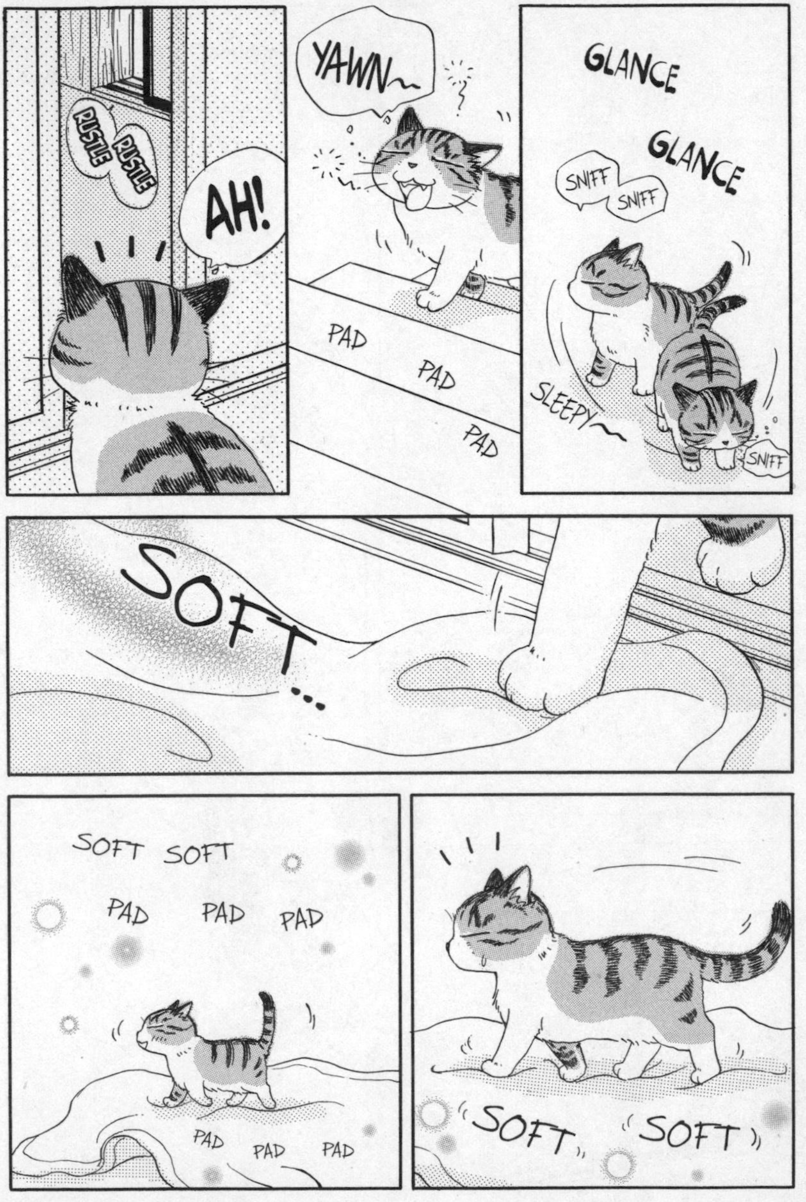
GLANCE
GLANCE
SNIFF
SNIFF
SLEEPY~
SNIFF
YAWN~
PAD
PAD
PAD
RUSTLE
RUSTLE
AH!
SOFT...
SOFT
SOFT
SOFT SOFT
PAD PAD PAD
PAD PAD PAD

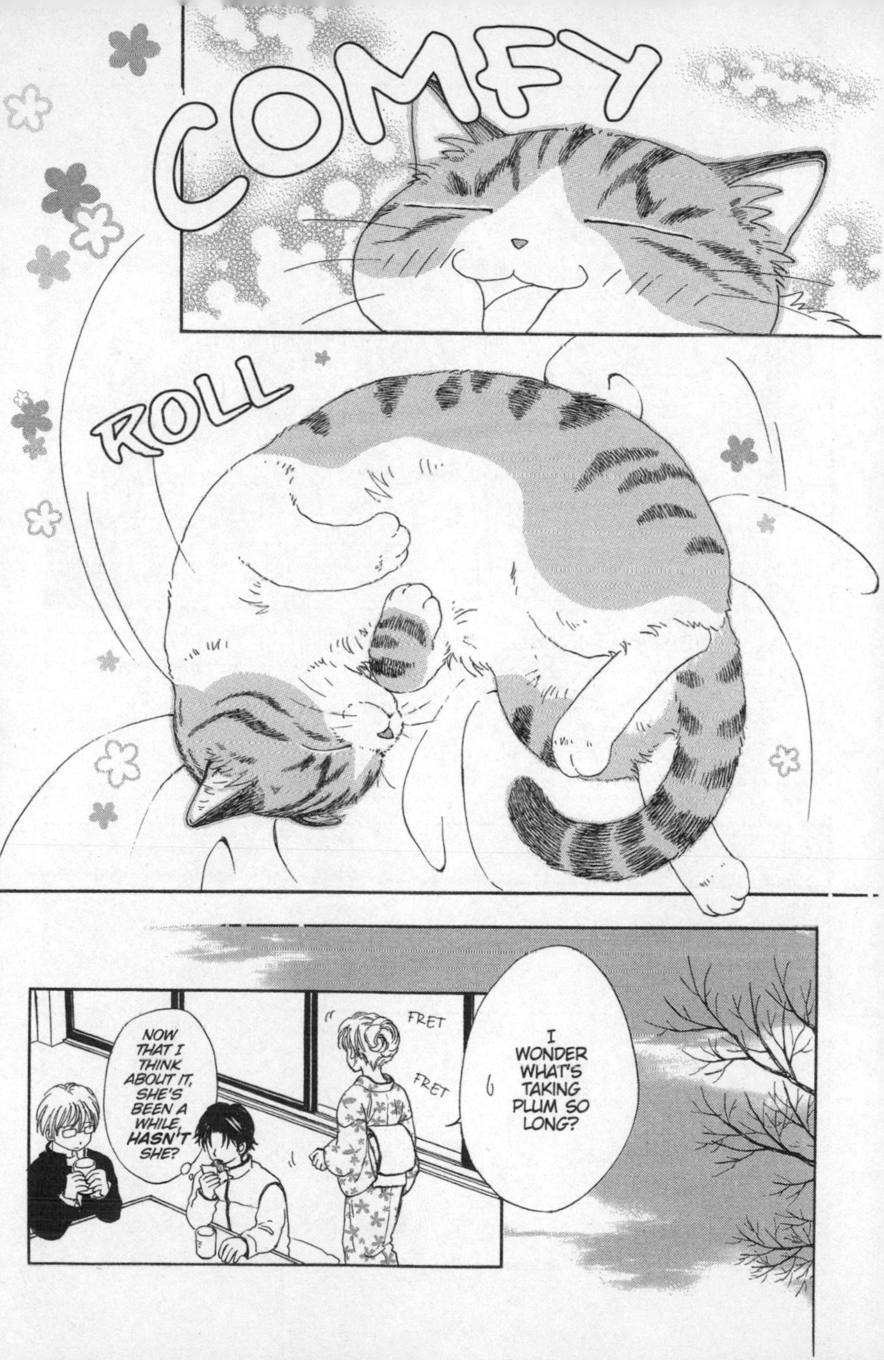
COMFY
ROLL
FRET FRET
I WONDER WHAT'S TAKING PLUM SO LONG?
NOW THAT I THINK ABOUT IT, SHE'S BEEN A WHILE, HASN'T SHE?

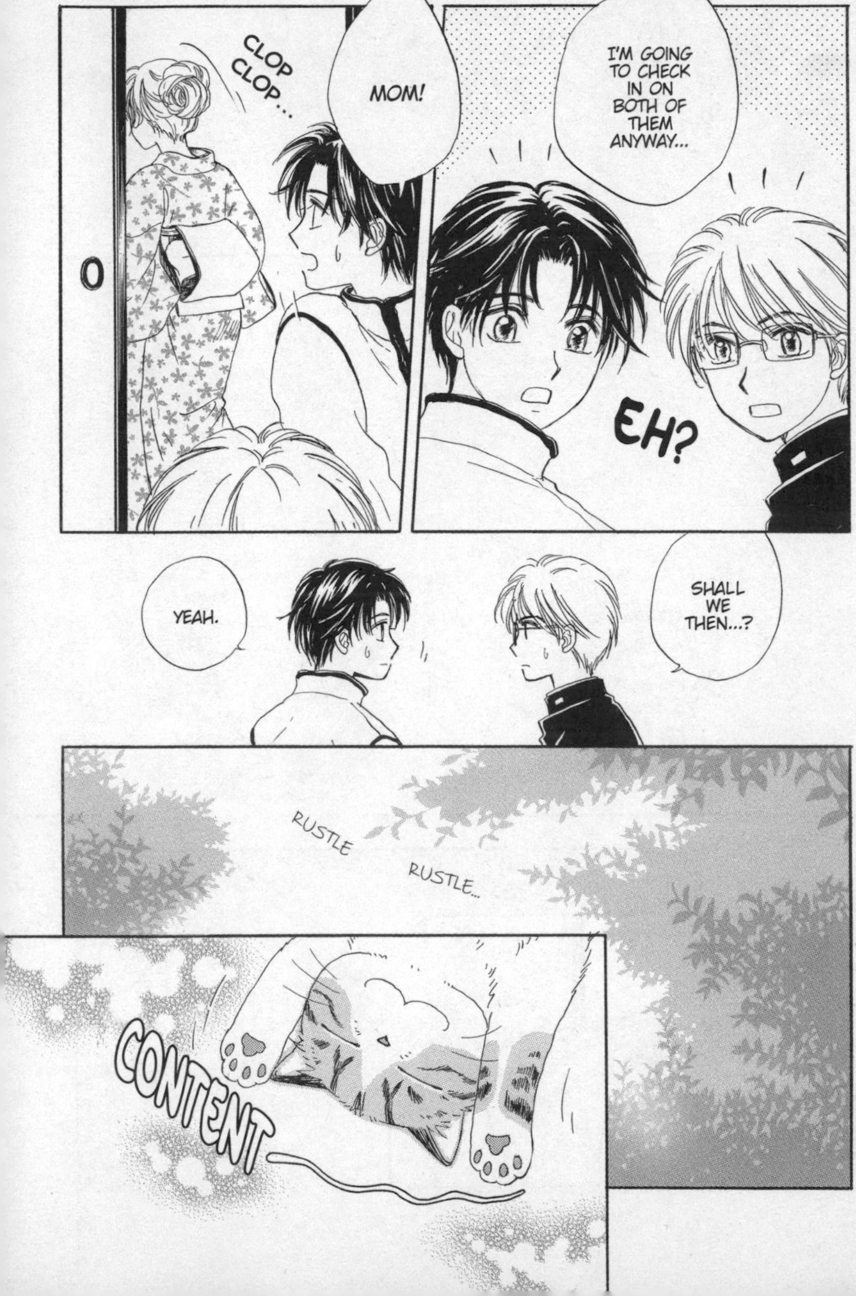
I'M GOING TO CHECK IN ON BOTH OF THEM ANYWAY...
EH?
MOM!
CLOP CLOP...
SHALL WE THEN...?
YEAH.
RUSTLE
RUSTLE...
CONTENT

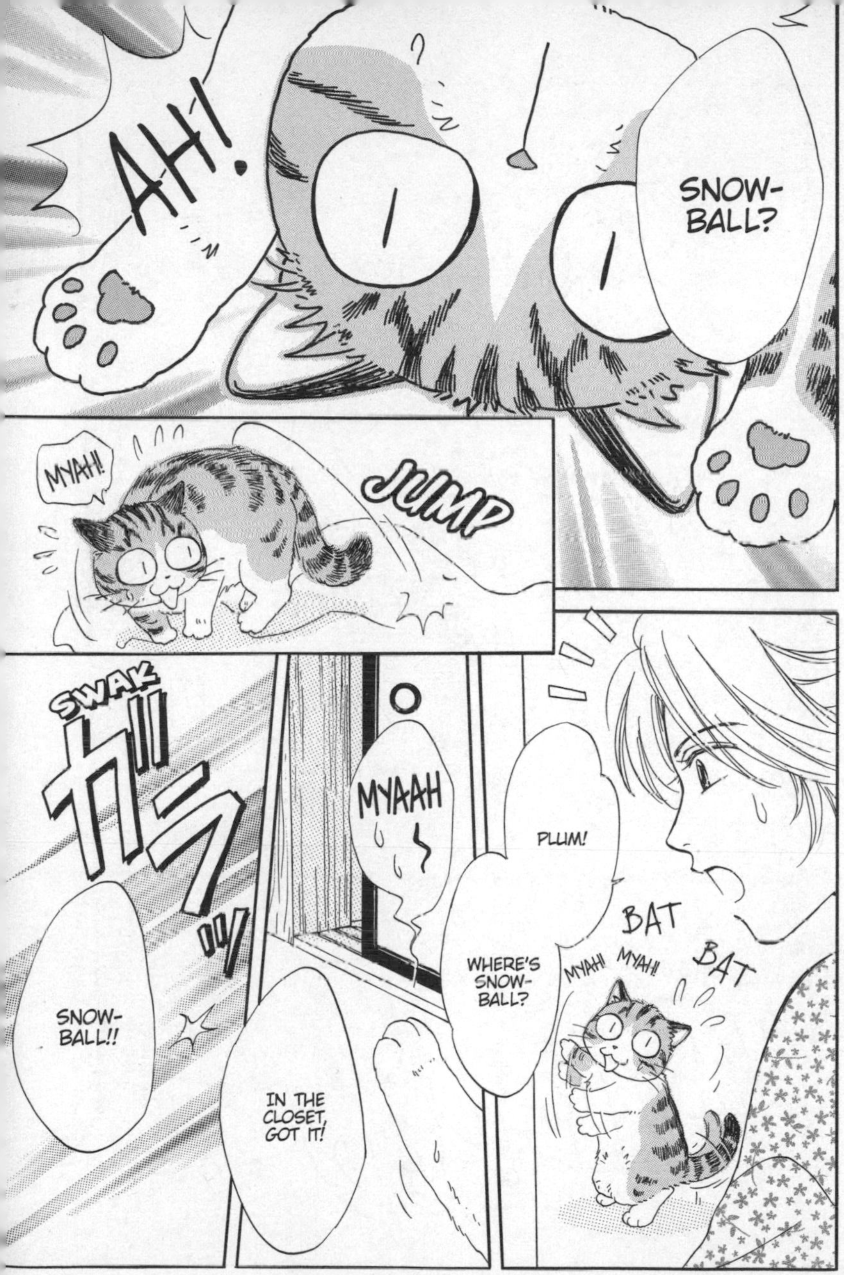
SNOW-
BALL?
AH!
JUMP
MYAH!
PLUM!
WHERE'S
SNOW-
BALL?
MYAH! MYAH!
BAT
BAT
MYAAH
IN THE
CLOSET,
GOT IT!
SWAK
ガラッ
SNOW-
BALL!!

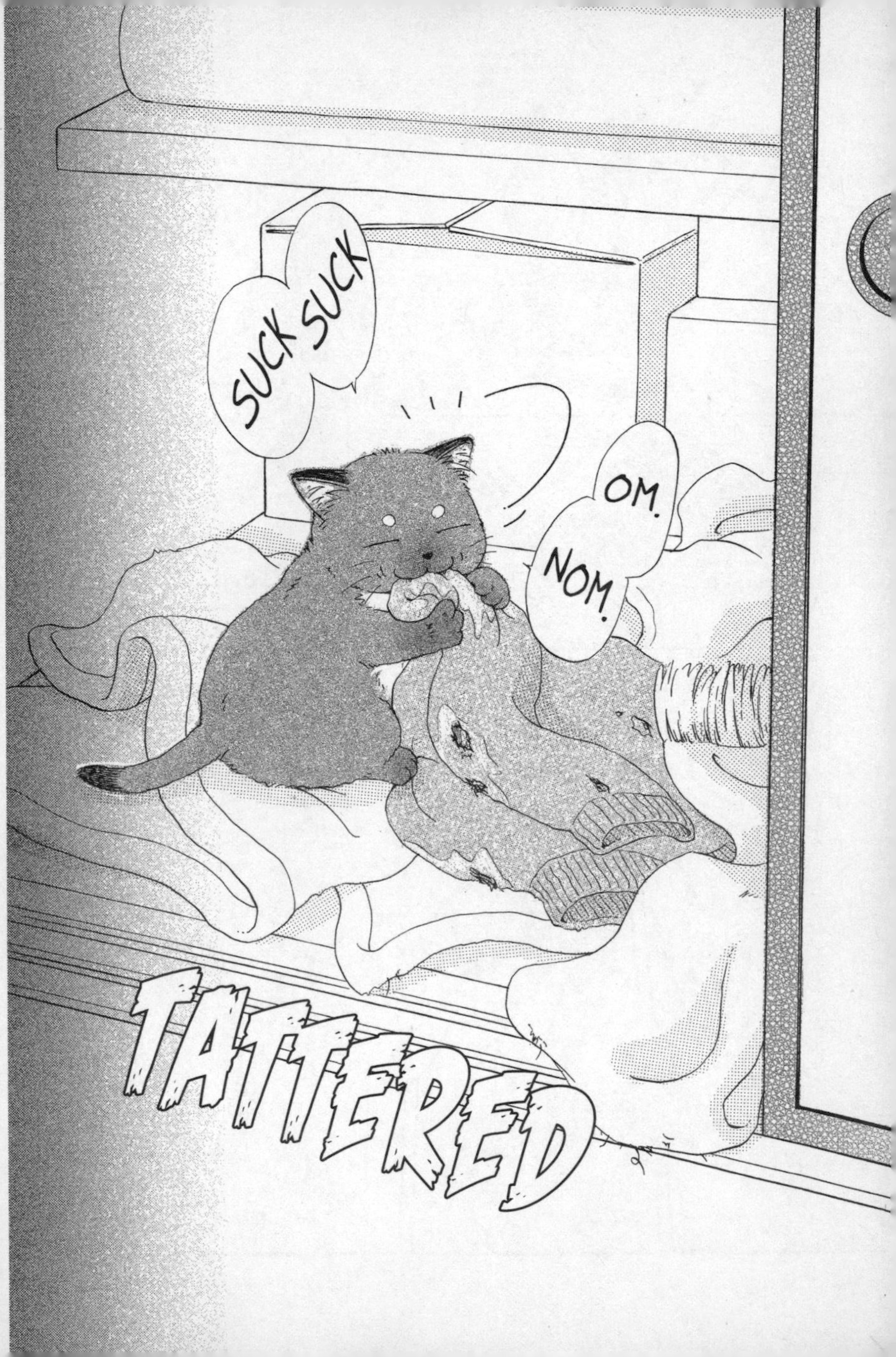
OM. NOM.
SUCK SUCK
TATTERED

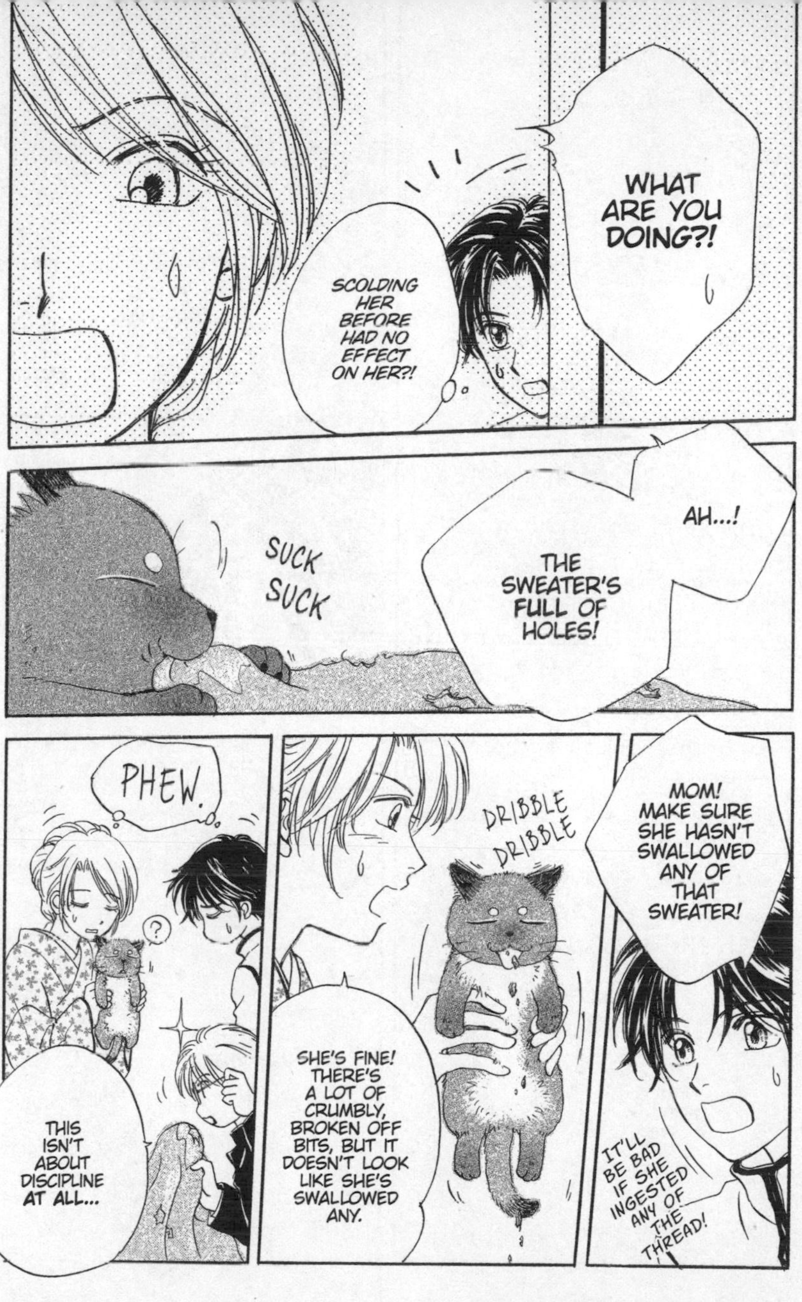
WHAT ARE YOU DOING?!
SCOLDING HER BEFORE HAD NO EFFECT ON HER?!
AH...!
THE SWEATER'S FULL OF HOLES!
SUCK SUCK
MOM! MAKE SURE SHE HASN'T SWALLOWED ANY OF THAT SWEATER!
IT'LL BE BAD IF SHE INGESTED ANY OF THE THREAD!
DRIBBLE DRIBBLE
SHE'S FINE! THERE'S A LOT OF CRUMBLY, BROKEN OFF BITS, BUT IT DOESN'T LOOK LIKE SHE'S SWALLOWED ANY.
PHEW.
THIS ISN'T ABOUT DISCIPLINE AT ALL...

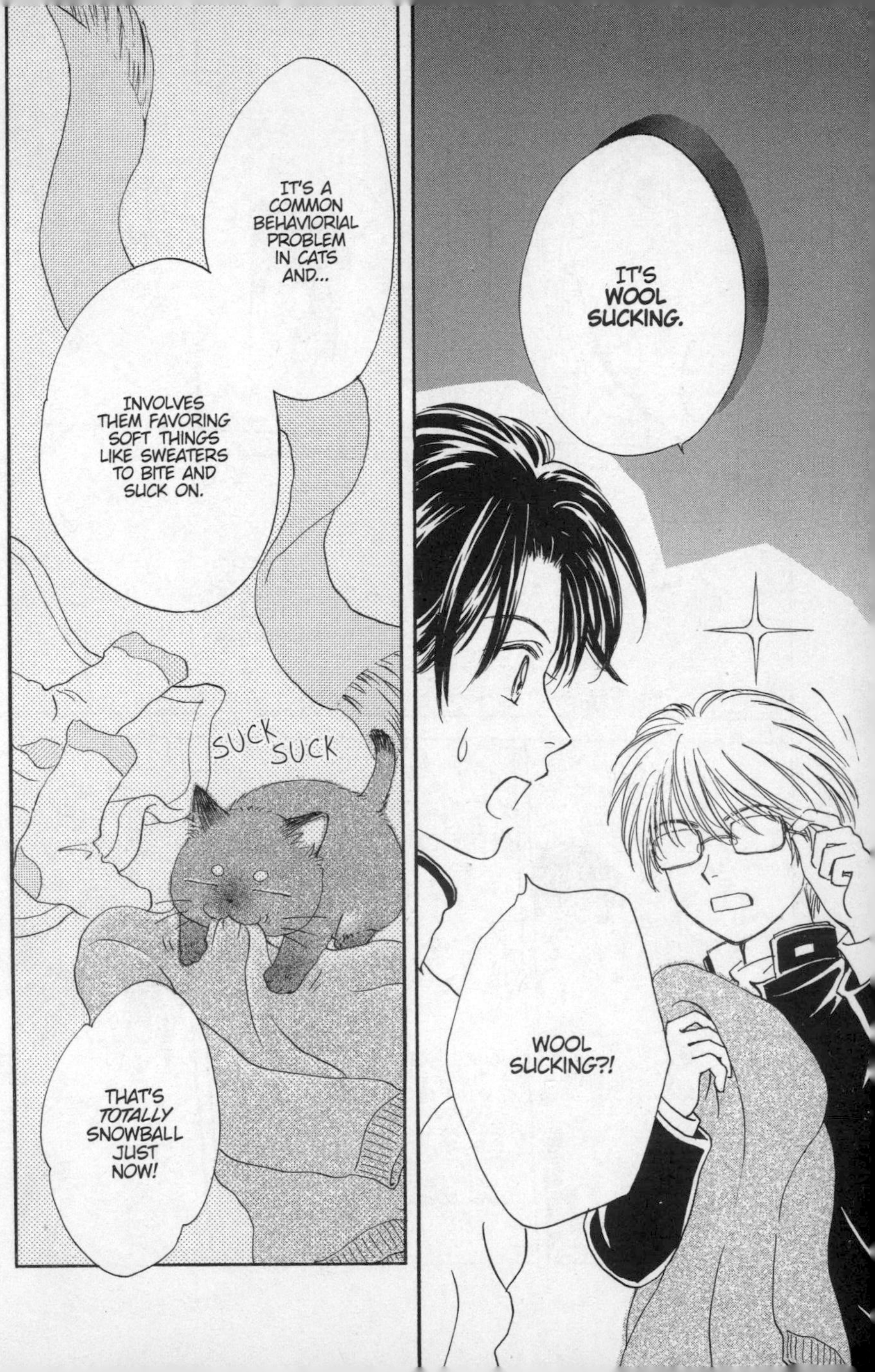
IT'S WOOL SUCKING.
WOOL SUCKING?!
IT'S A COMMON BEHAVIORIAL PROBLEM IN CATS AND...
INVOLVES THEM FAVORING SOFT THINGS LIKE SWEATERS TO BITE AND SUCK ON.
SUCK SUCK
THAT'S *TOTALLY* SNOWBALL JUST NOW!

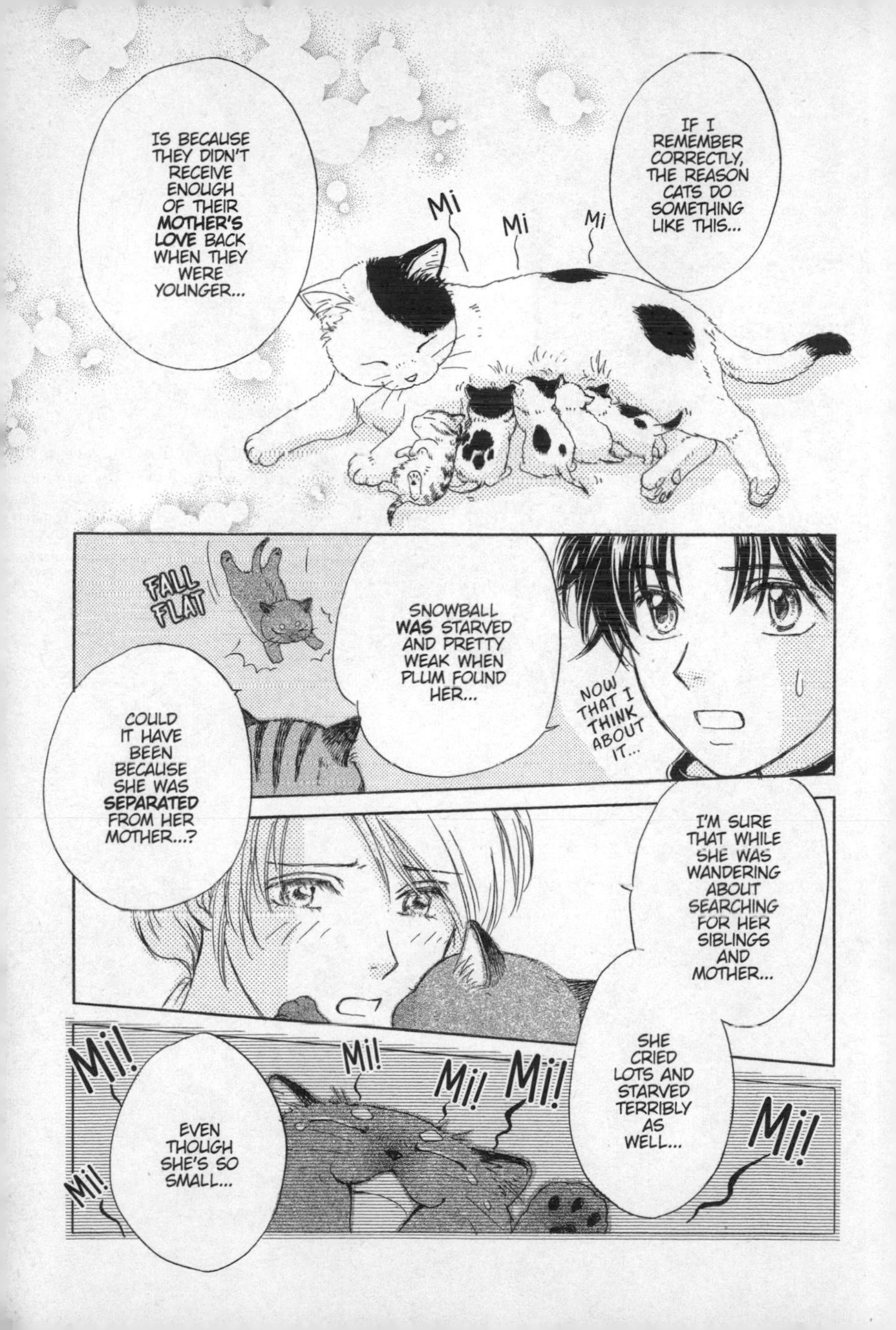
IF I REMEMBER CORRECTLY, THE REASON CATS DO SOMETHING LIKE THIS...
Mi
Mi
Mi
IS BECAUSE THEY DIDN'T RECEIVE ENOUGH OF THEIR **MOTHER'S LOVE** BACK WHEN THEY WERE YOUNGER...
NOW THAT I THINK ABOUT IT...
SNOWBALL **WAS** STARVED AND PRETTY WEAK WHEN PLUM FOUND HER...
FALL FLAT
COULD IT HAVE BEEN BECAUSE SHE WAS **SEPARATED** FROM HER MOTHER...?
I'M SURE THAT WHILE SHE WAS WANDERING ABOUT SEARCHING FOR HER SIBLINGS AND MOTHER...
SHE CRIED LOTS AND STARVED TERRIBLY AS WELL...
Mi!
Mi!
Mi!
Mi!
EVEN THOUGH SHE'S SO SMALL...
Mi!
Mi!

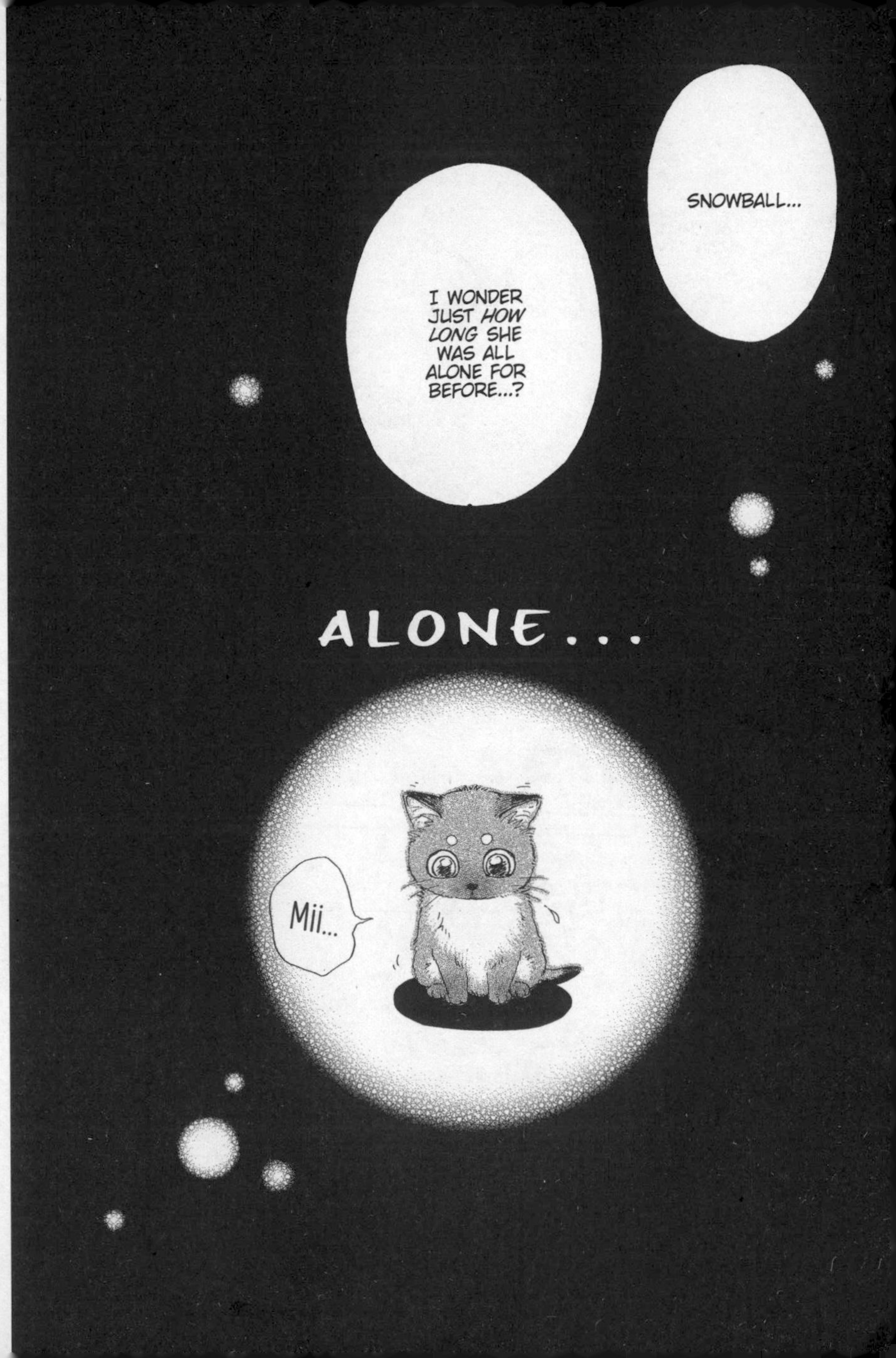
SNOWBALL...
I WONDER JUST *HOW LONG* SHE WAS ALL ALONE FOR BEFORE...?
ALONE...
Mii...

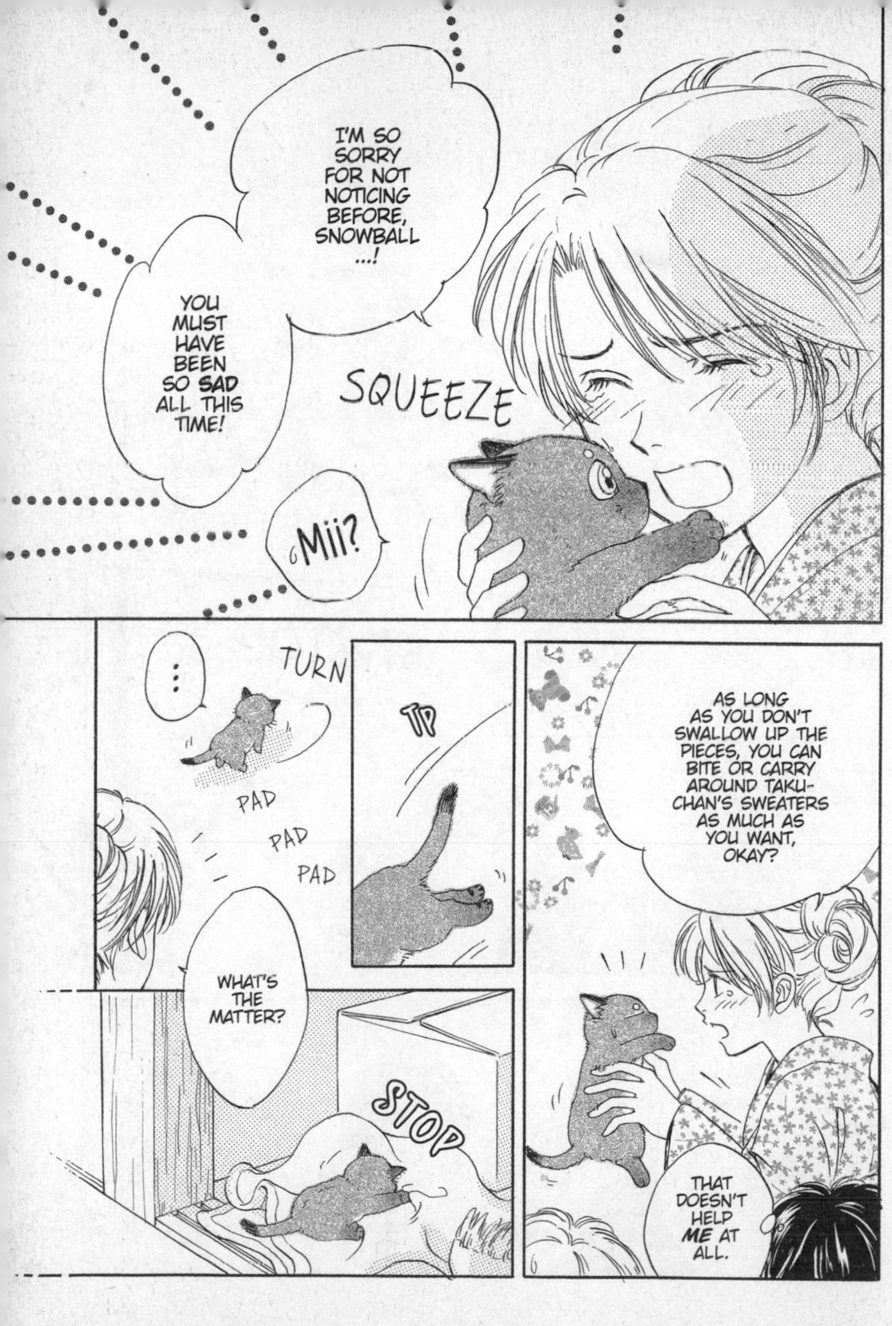
I'M SO SORRY FOR NOT NOTICING BEFORE, SNOWBALL ...!
YOU MUST HAVE BEEN SO **SAD** ALL THIS TIME!
SQUEEZE
Mii?
AS LONG AS YOU DON'T SWALLOW UP THE PIECES, YOU CAN BITE OR CARRY AROUND TAKU-CHAN'S SWEATERS AS MUCH AS YOU WANT, OKAY?
THAT DOESN'T HELP ***ME*** AT ALL.
TP
TURN
...
PAD
PAD
PAD
WHAT'S THE MATTER?
STOP

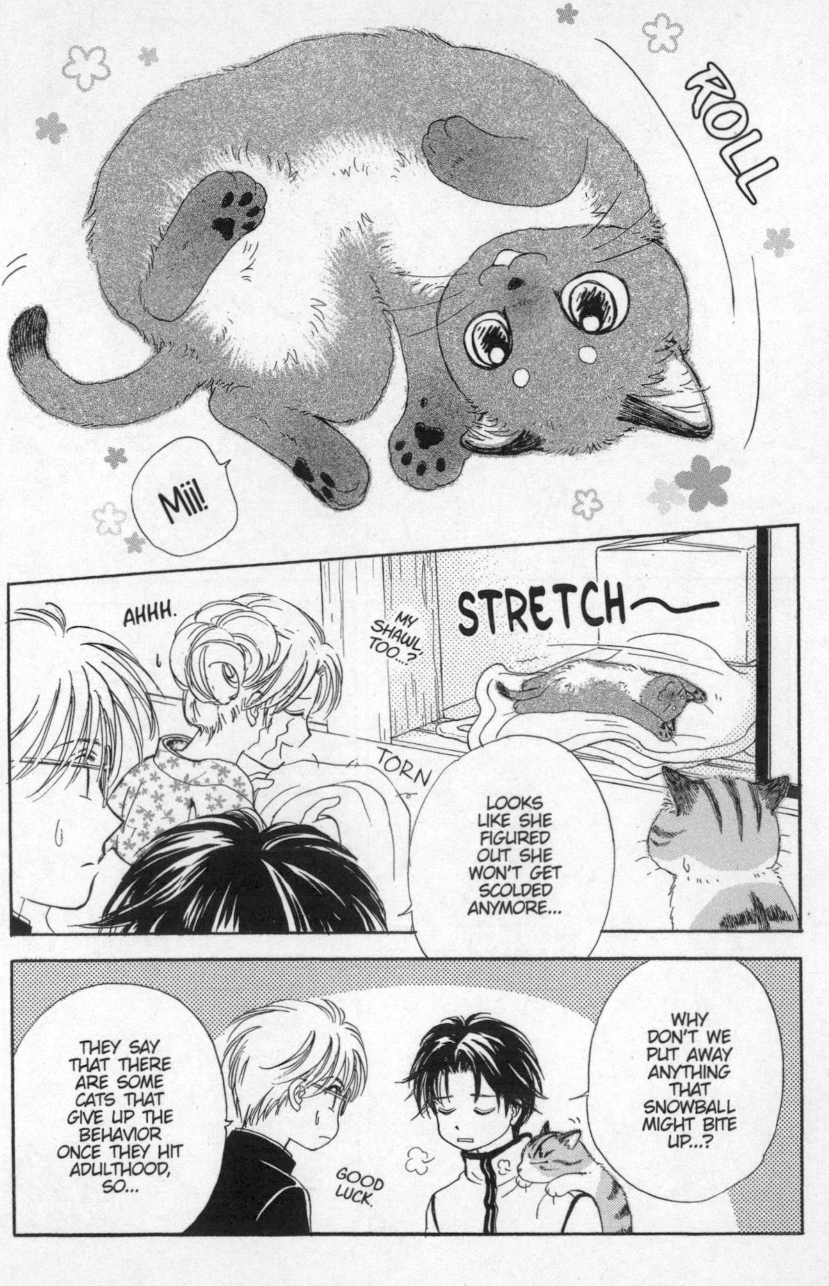
ROLL
Mii!
STRETCH~
LOOKS LIKE SHE FIGURED OUT SHE WON'T GET SCOLDED ANYMORE...
TORN
MY SHAWL, TOO...?
AHHH.
WHY DON'T WE PUT AWAY ANYTHING THAT SNOWBALL MIGHT BITE UP...?
GOOD LUCK.
THEY SAY THAT THERE ARE SOME CATS THAT GIVE UP THE BEHAVIOR ONCE THEY HIT ADULTHOOD, SO...

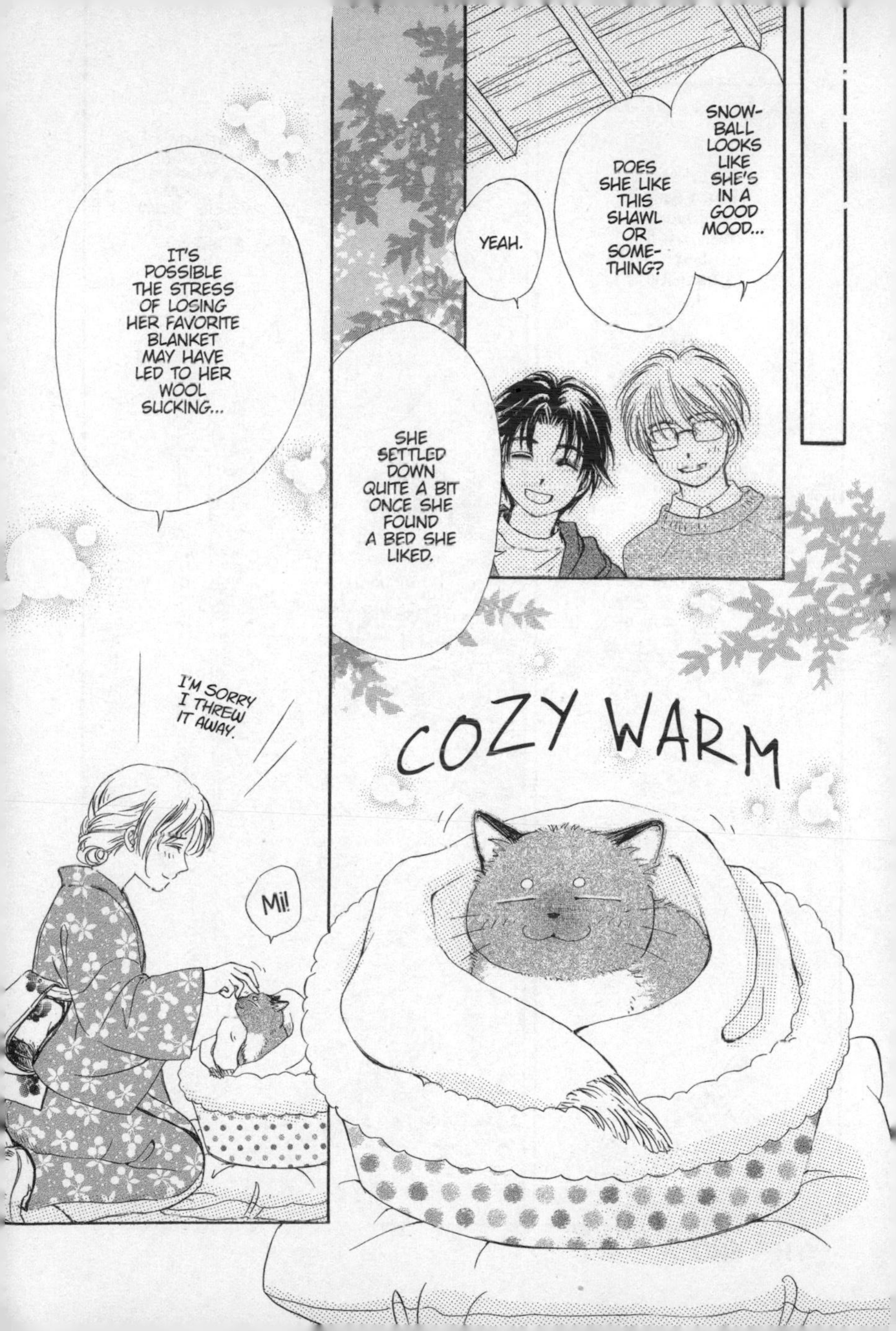
SNOW-BALL LOOKS LIKE SHE'S IN A GOOD MOOD...
DOES SHE LIKE THIS SHAWL OR SOME-THING?
YEAH.
SHE SETTLED DOWN QUITE A BIT ONCE SHE FOUND A BED SHE LIKED.
COZY WARM
IT'S POSSIBLE THE STRESS OF LOSING HER FAVORITE BLANKET MAY HAVE LED TO HER WOOL SUCKING...
I'M SORRY I THREW IT AWAY.
Mi!

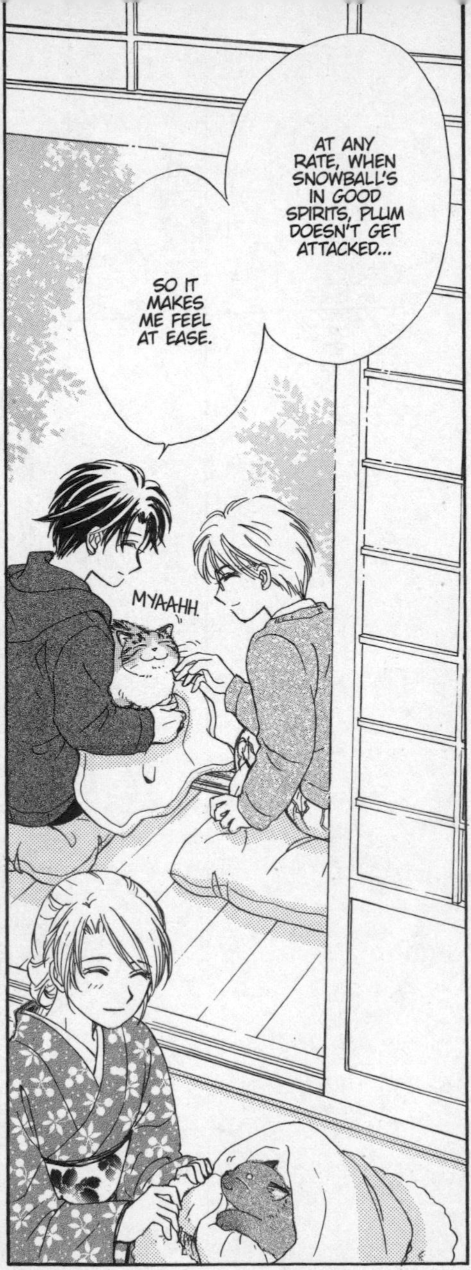
AT ANY RATE, WHEN SNOWBALL'S IN GOOD SPIRITS, PLUM DOESN'T GET ATTACKED...
SO IT MAKES ME FEEL AT EASE.
MYAAHH.

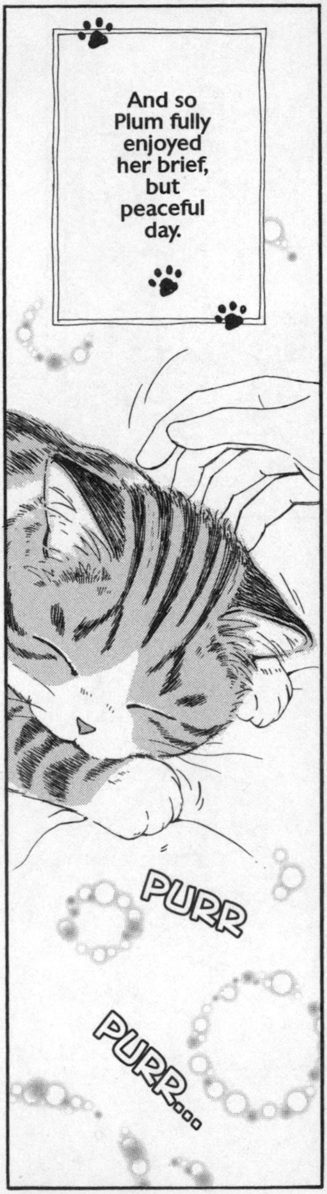
And so Plum fully enjoyed her brief, but peaceful day.
PURR
PURR...

⑧ THE END

STORIES ABOUT MY CAT

This is "Kuu," the little girl who became the model for Snowball.

MORE OFTEN THAN NOT, THE CRY THAT SHE EMITS SOUNDS CLOSER TO A "KURURU" THAN A "NYAH."
PURURU
WAG WAG
SHE HAS A BLACK NECKLACE PATTERN ON HER CHEST.
KUU-CHAAAAN!
PURURU

I took her in about a week after she was born. I wasn't sure of her gender at the time, but her outward appearance was boyish, so for a moment there, she was in danger of almost being named "Gokuu."

She is often restless and doesn't really listen to what you're saying, but when you call for her, she always comes. ♡

WHEN SHE'S SITTING, SHE LOOKS JUST LIKE A BLACK CAT FROM BEHIND.
PURU PURU

She still looks like a kitten despite how much time has passed, and even though she's not a beauty, she's still very cute. ♡

A DOTING PARENT AFTER ALL.

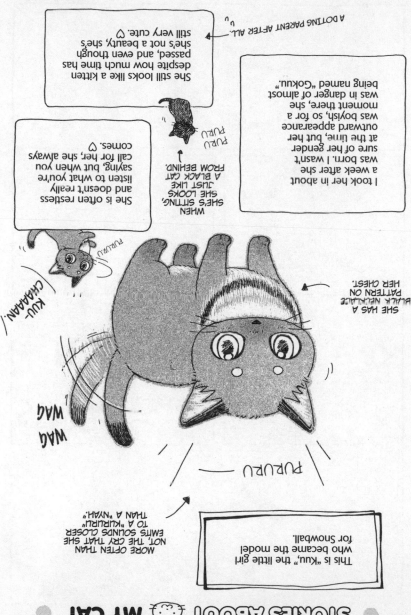

STORIES ABOUT MY CAT

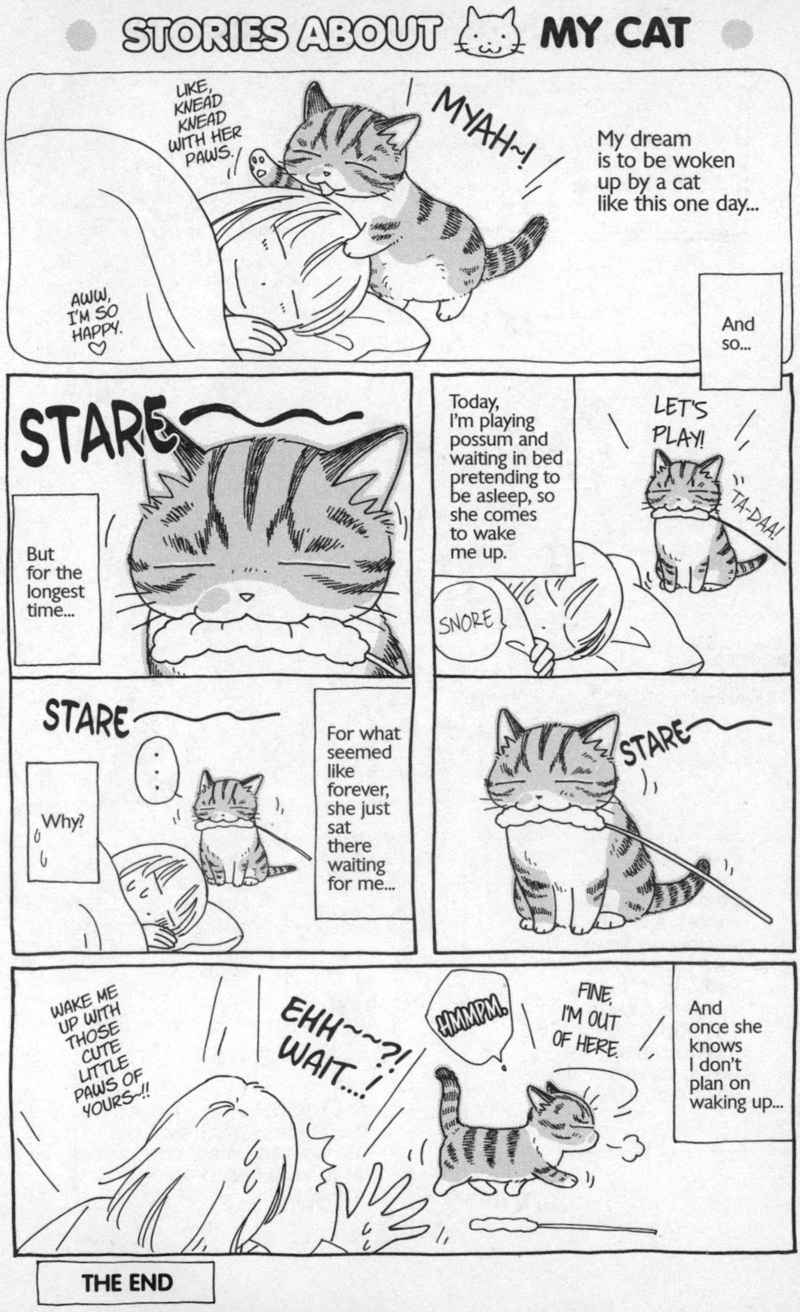
My dream is to be woken up by a cat like this one day...
MYAH~!
LIKE, KNEAD KNEAD WITH HER PAWS.
AWW, I'M SO HAPPY. ♡
And so...
LET'S PLAY!
Today, I'm playing possum and waiting in bed pretending to be asleep, so she comes to wake me up.
TA-DAA!
SNORE
STARE
But for the longest time...
STARE
For what seemed like forever, she just sat there waiting for me...
STARE
Why?
And once she knows I don't plan on waking up...
FINE, I'M OUT OF HERE.
HMMPM.
EHH~~?! WAIT...!
WAKE ME UP WITH THOSE CUTE LITTLE PAWS OF YOURS~!!

THE END

STORIES ABOUT MY CAT

In regards to *Plum Crazy*, there are a number of stories I drew based on real events that took place in my life.

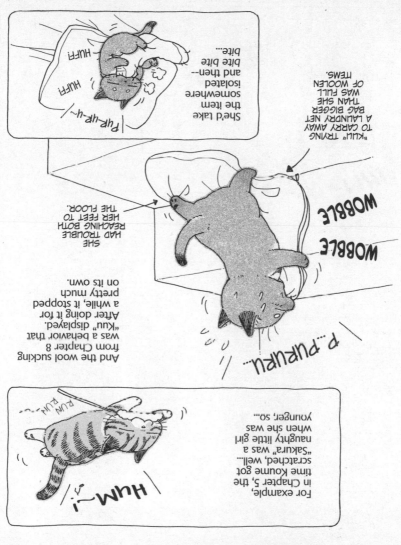

For example, in Chapter 5, the time Koume got scratched, well... "Sakura" was a naughty little girl when she was younger, so...

HUM~!
RUN RUN

And the wool sucking from Chapter 8 was a behavior that "Kuu" displayed. After doing it for a while, it stopped pretty much on its own.

P...PURURU...
WOBBLE
WOBBLE
SHE HAD TROUBLE REACHING BOTH HER FEET TO THE FLOOR.
"KUU" TRYING TO CARRY AWAY A LAUNDRY NET BAG BIGGER THAN SHE WAS FULL OF WOOLEN ITEMS.

She'd take the item somewhere isolated and then-- *bite bite bite...*

PURUR-U~
HUFF!
HUFF!

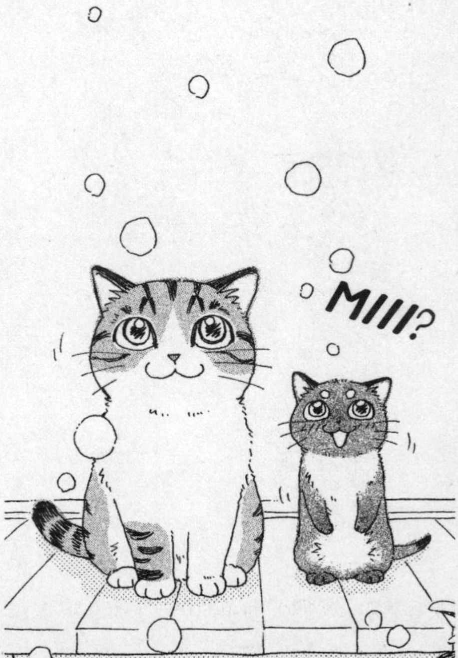
MIII?

plum SHORTS

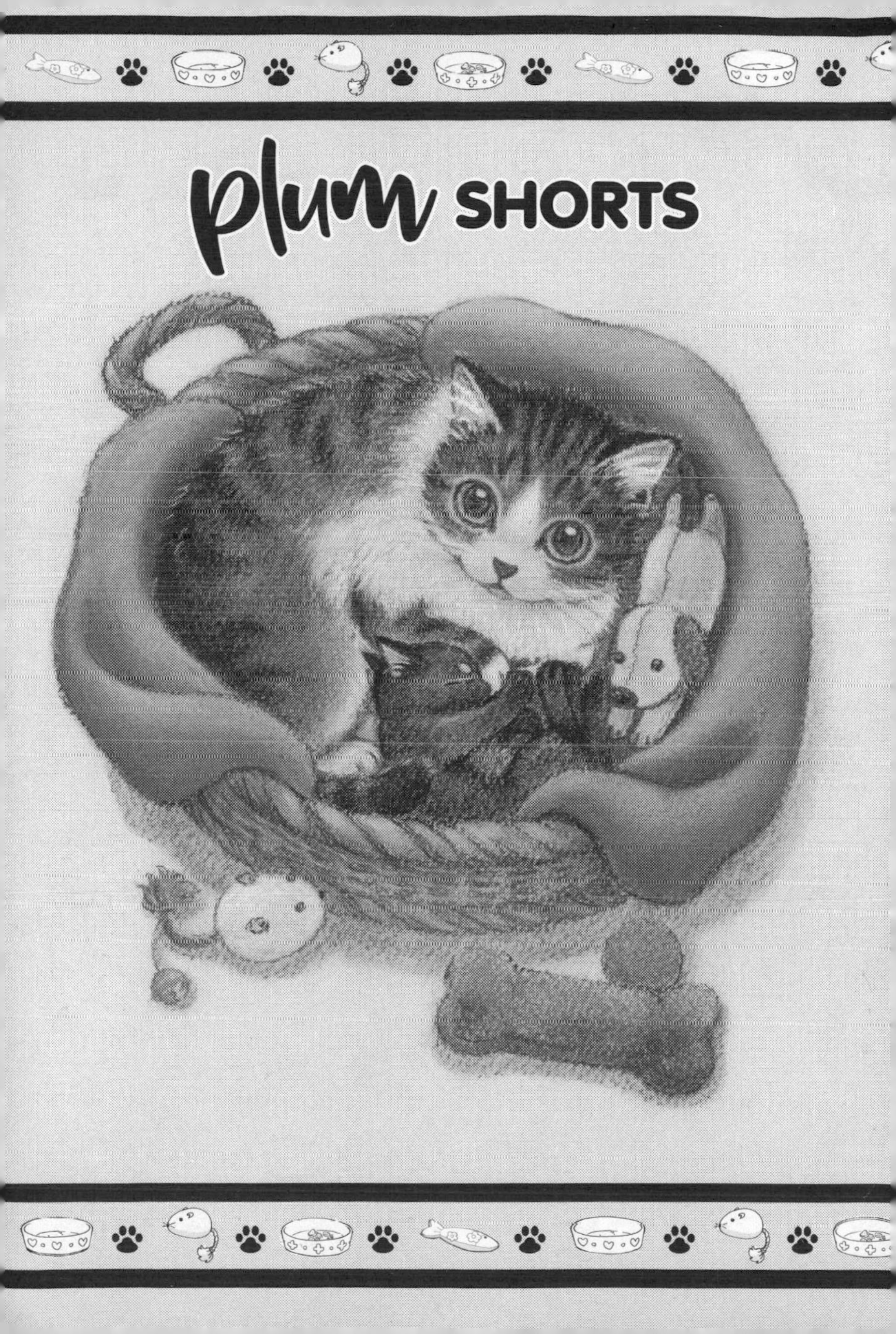

SHORT.1

Koume-san Loves Cleanliness: Part 1

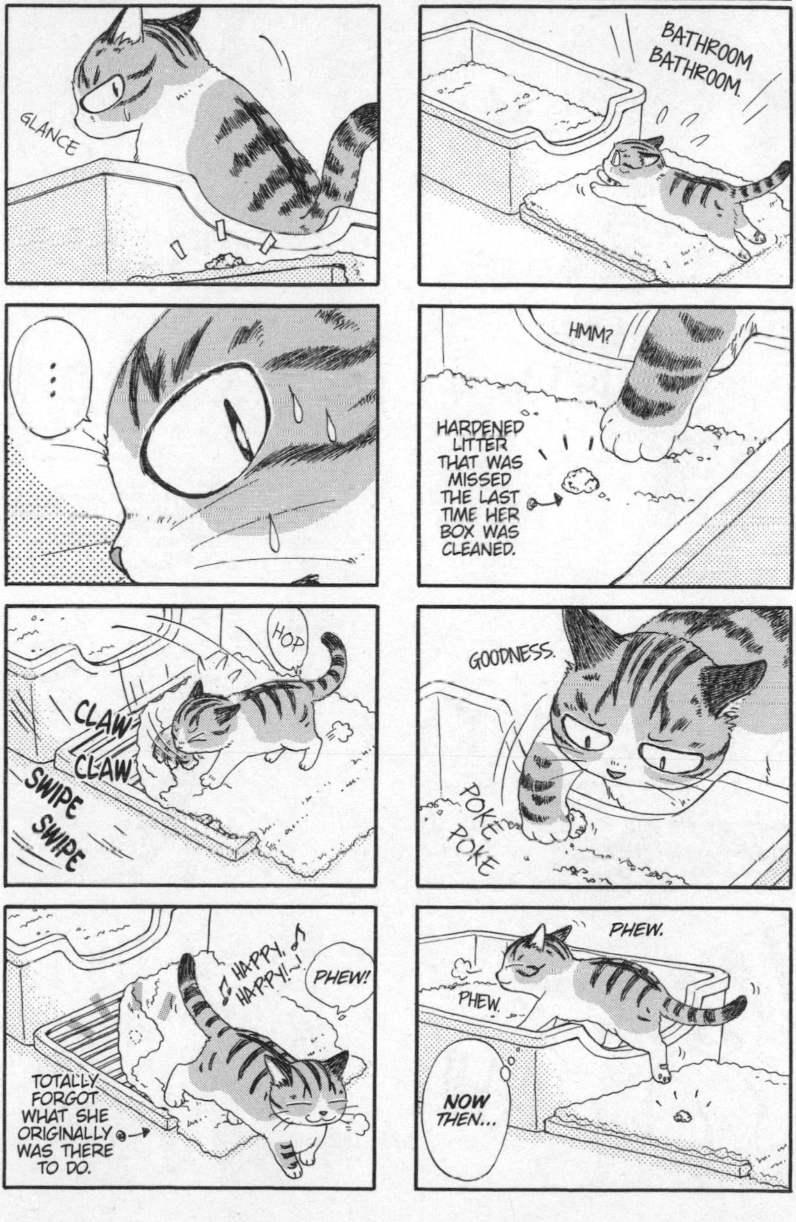
BATHROOM BATHROOM.
GLANCE
HMM?
HARDENED LITTER THAT WAS MISSED THE LAST TIME HER BOX WAS CLEANED.
...
GOODNESS.
POKE POKE
HOP
CLAW CLAW
SWIPE SWIPE
PHEW.
PHEW.
NOW THEN...
HAPPY, HAPPY!
PHEW!
TOTALLY FORGOT WHAT SHE ORIGINALLY WAS THERE TO DO.

Koume-san Loves Cleanliness: Part 2

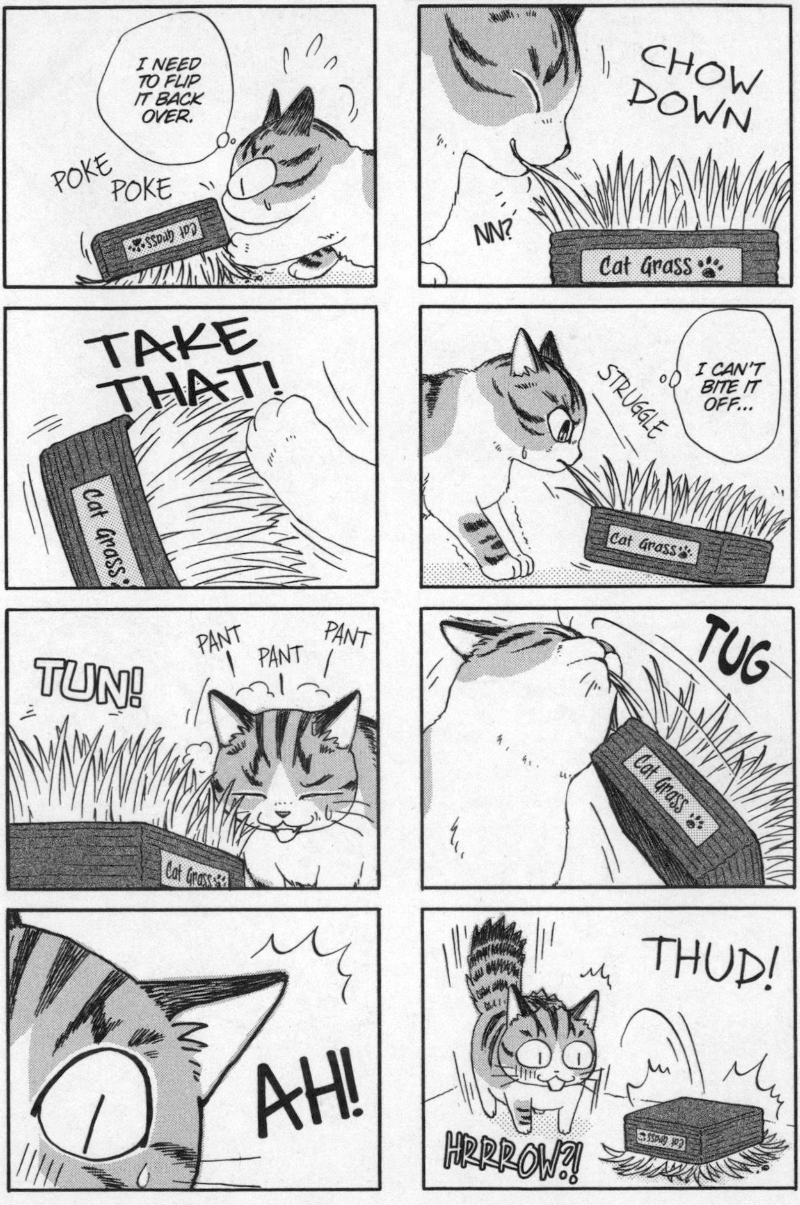
CHOW DOWN
NN?
Cat Grass
I CAN'T BITE IT OFF...
STRUGGLE
Cat Grass
TUG
Cat Grass
THUD!
HRRROW?!
I NEED TO FLIP IT BACK OVER.
POKE POKE
TAKE THAT!
Cat Grass
TUN!
PANT PANT PANT
Cat Grass
AH!

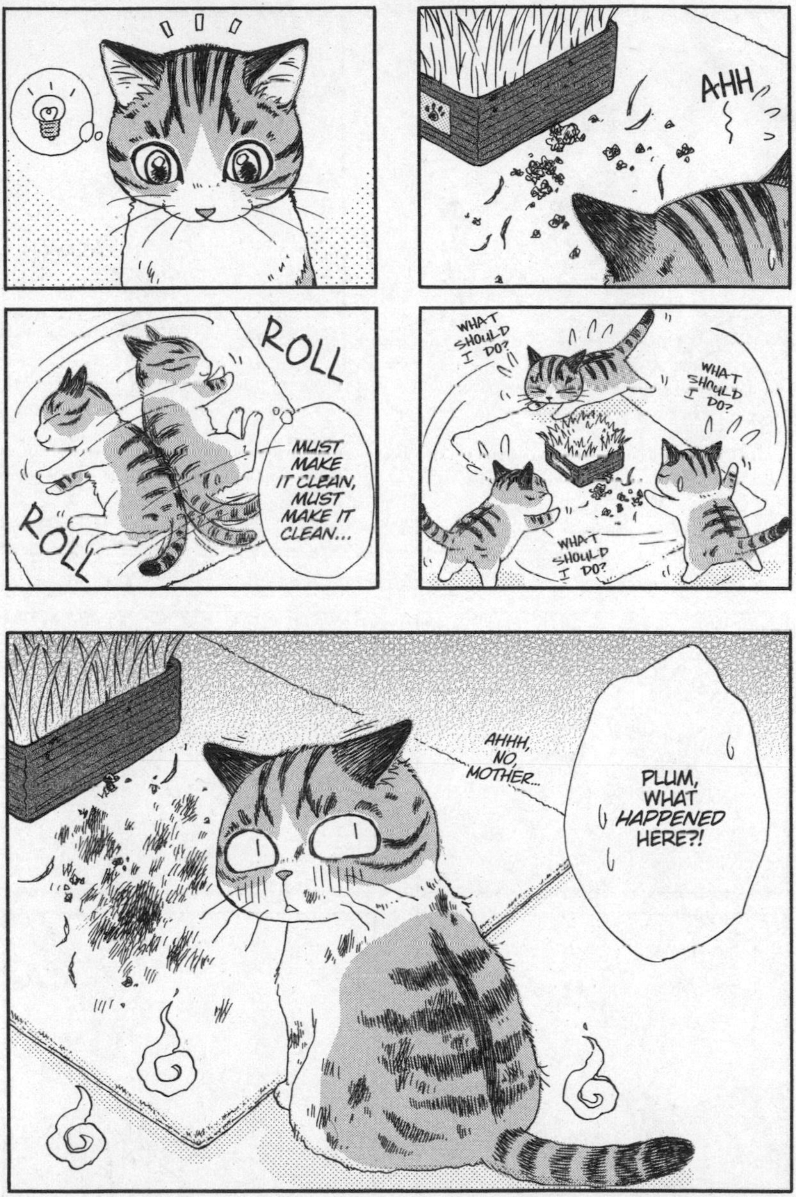
AHH
WHAT SHOULD I DO?
WHAT SHOULD I DO?
WHAT SHOULD I DO?
ROLL
ROLL
MUST MAKE IT CLEAN, MUST MAKE IT CLEAN...
PLUM, WHAT HAPPENED HERE?!
AHHH, NO, MOTHER...

Snowball's Secret

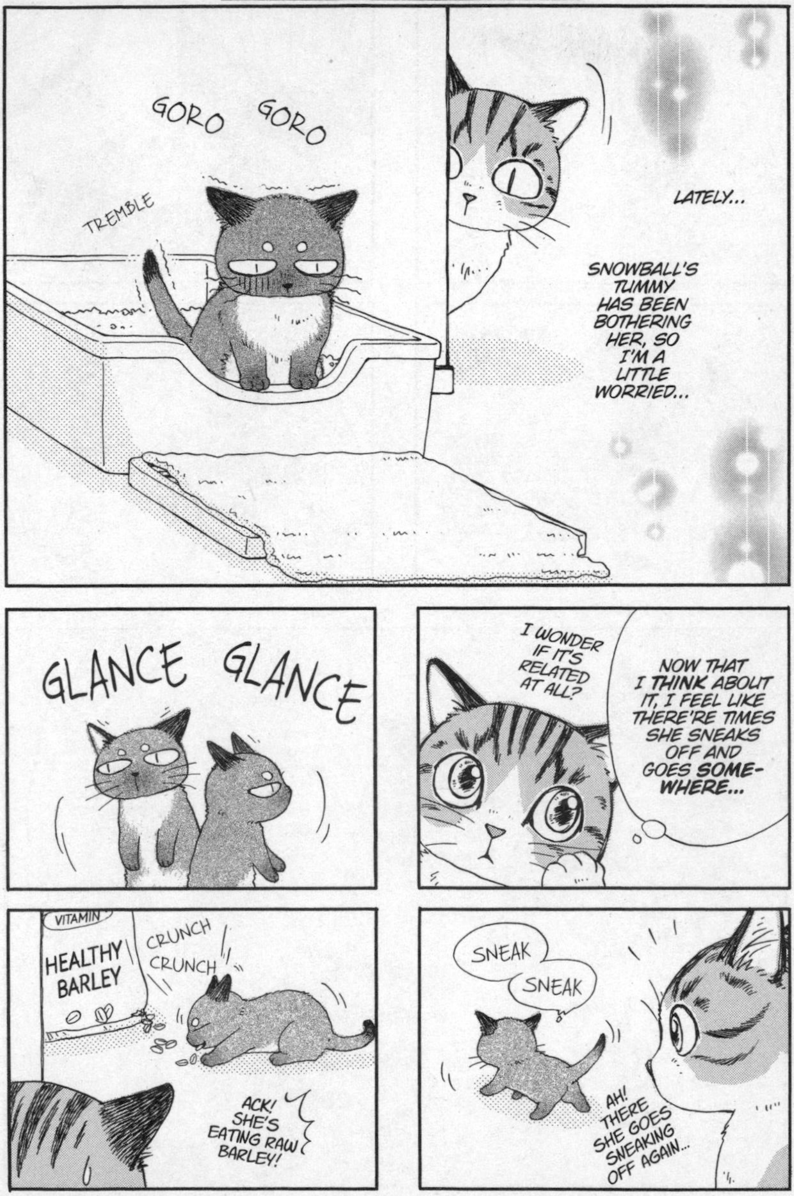
LATELY...
SNOWBALL'S TUMMY HAS BEEN BOTHERING HER, SO I'M A LITTLE WORRIED...
GORO GORO
TREMBLE
NOW THAT I THINK ABOUT IT, I FEEL LIKE THERE'RE TIMES SHE SNEAKS OFF AND GOES SOME-WHERE...
I WONDER IF IT'S RELATED AT ALL?
GLANCE GLANCE
SNEAK
SNEAK
AH! THERE SHE GOES SNEAKING OFF AGAIN...
VITAMIN
HEALTHY BARLEY
CRUNCH CRUNCH
ACK! SHE'S EATING RAW BARLEY!

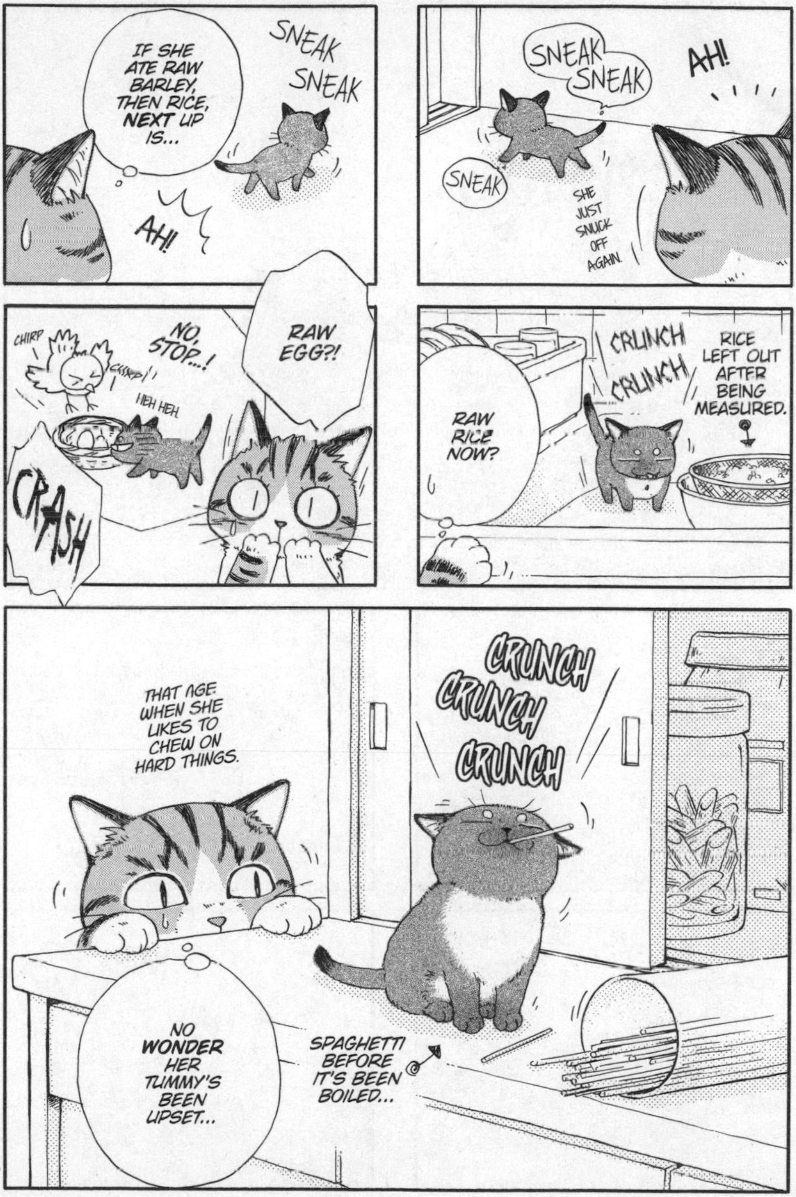
AH!
SNEAK SNEAK
SNEAK
SHE JUST SNUCK OFF AGAIN.
SNEAK SNEAK
IF SHE ATE RAW BARLEY, THEN RICE, NEXT UP IS...
AH!
RICE LEFT OUT AFTER BEING MEASURED.
CRUNCH CRUNCH
RAW RICE NOW?
RAW EGG?!
NO, STOP...!
CHIRP
HEH HEH
CRASH
CRUNCH CRUNCH CRUNCH
THAT AGE WHEN SHE LIKES TO CHEW ON HARD THINGS.
SPAGHETTI BEFORE IT'S BEEN BOILED...
NO WONDER HER TUMMY'S BEEN UPSET...

Plum and Snowball

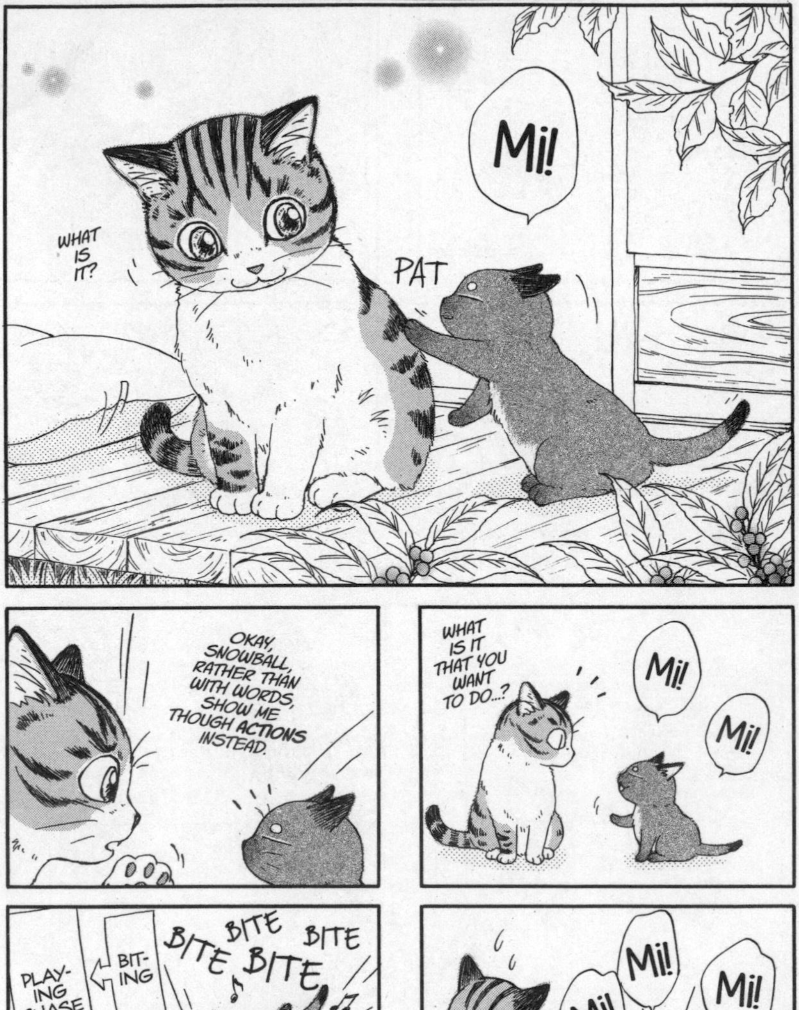
Mi!
WHAT IS IT?
PAT
WHAT IS IT THAT YOU WANT TO DO...?
Mi!
Mi!
OKAY, SNOWBALL, RATHER THAN WITH WORDS, SHOW ME THOUGH ACTIONS INSTEAD.
Mi!
Mi!
Mi!
I DON'T KNOW WHAT YOU'RE SAYING...
BITE BITE BITE BITE
BIT-ING
PLAY-ING CHASE
HYAAAN.

1 THE END

SHORT.2

Plum's Murmurings

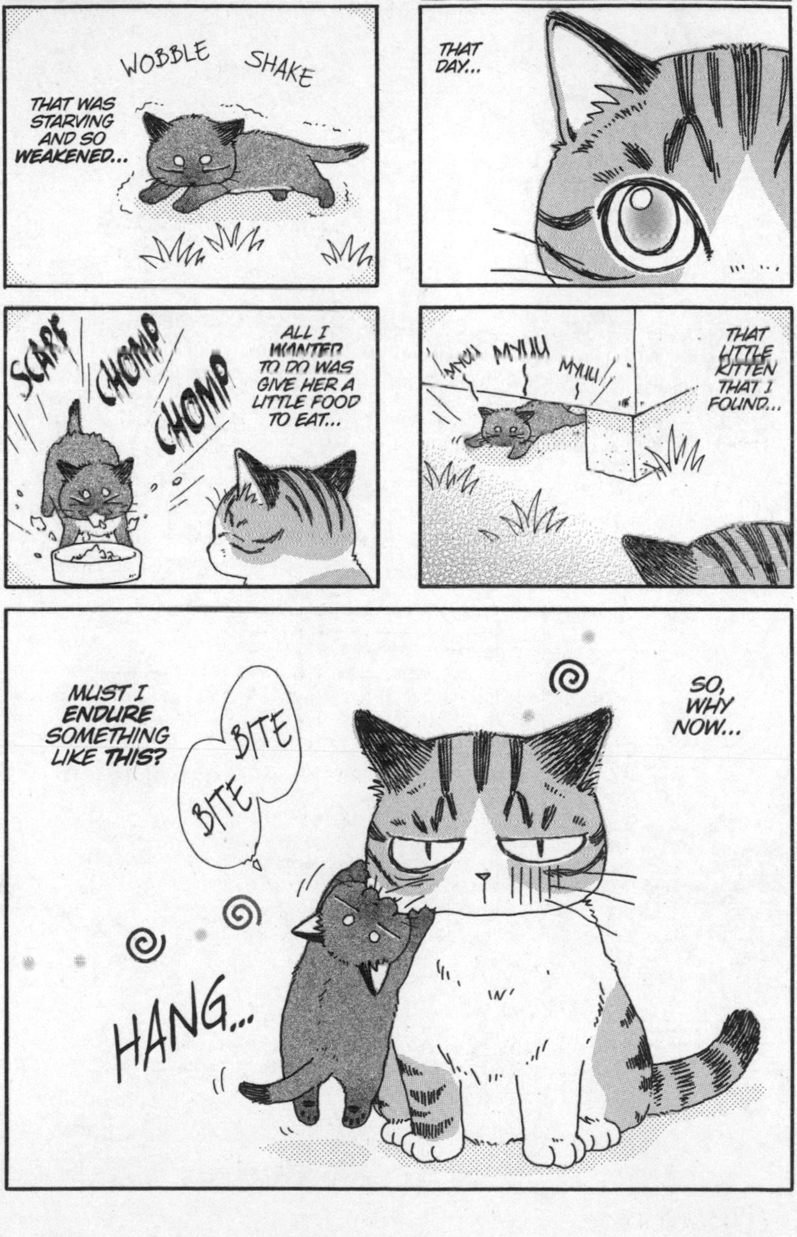
THAT DAY...
THAT WAS STARVING AND SO WEAKENED...
WOBBLE
SHAKE
THAT LITTLE KITTEN THAT I FOUND...
MYUU
MYUU
MYUU
ALL I WANTED TO DO WAS GIVE HER A LITTLE FOOD TO EAT...
CHOMP
CHOMP
SCARF
SO, WHY NOW...
MUST I ENDURE SOMETHING LIKE THIS?
BITE
BITE
HANG...

Plum's Mutterings

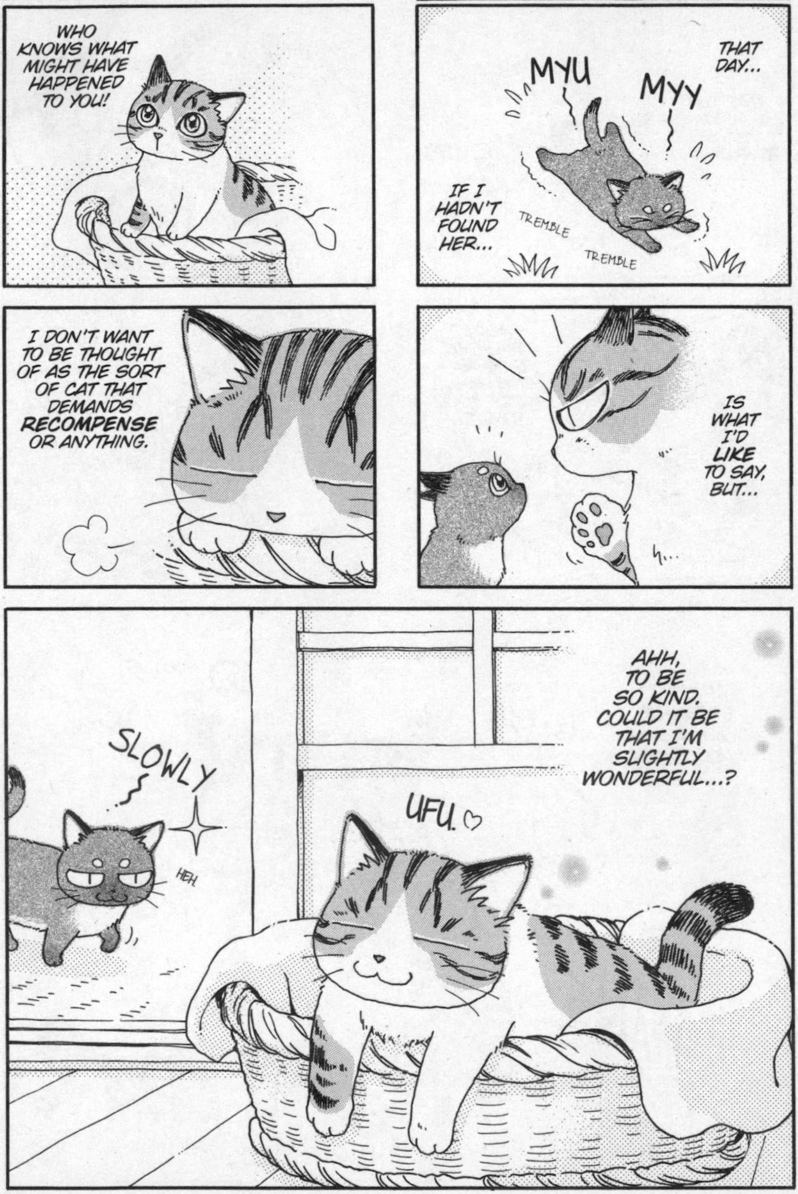
THAT DAY...
MYU
MYY
IF I HADN'T FOUND HER...
TREMBLE
TREMBLE
WHO KNOWS WHAT MIGHT HAVE HAPPENED TO YOU!
IS WHAT I'D **LIKE** TO SAY, BUT...
I DON'T WANT TO BE THOUGHT OF AS THE SORT OF CAT THAT DEMANDS **RECOMPENSE** OR ANYTHING.
AHH, TO BE SO KIND. COULD IT BE THAT I'M SLIGHTLY WONDERFUL...?
UFU.
SLOWLY
HEH

Plum's Grumblings

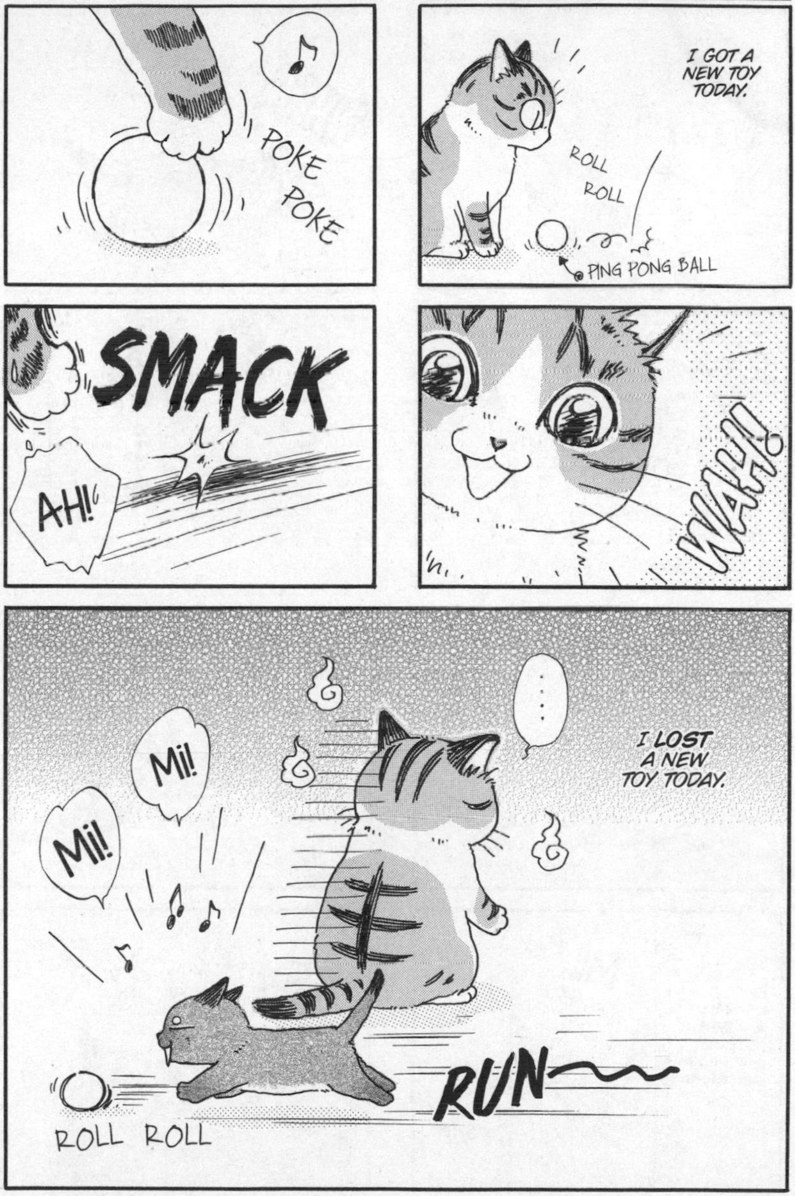
I GOT A NEW TOY TODAY.
ROLL
ROLL
PING PONG BALL
POKE
POKE
WAH!
SMACK
AH!
I LOST A NEW TOY TODAY.
...
Mi!
Mi!
RUN
ROLL ROLL

Snowball's Dangerous Play

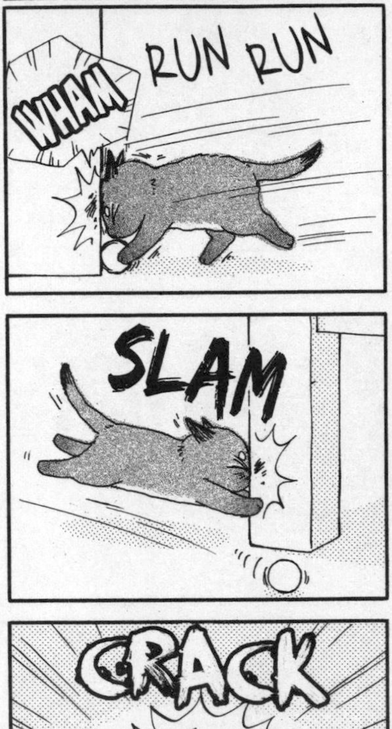
RUN RUN
WHAM
SLAM
CRACK
Mii!
ROLL ROLL
SNOW-BALL...
SO, THAT'S WHY YOUR HEAD'S A BIT...
GLARE

The Usual Time: Part 1

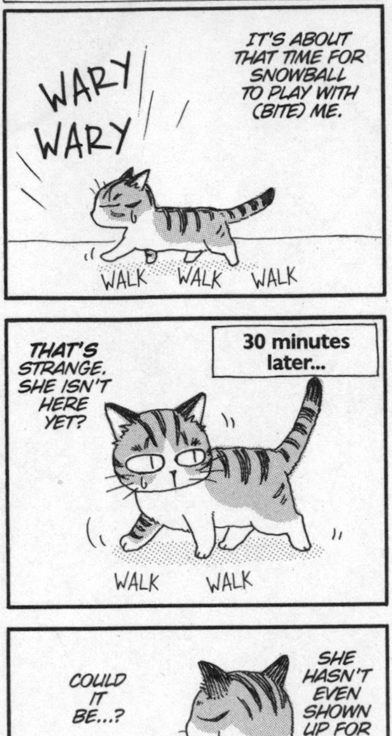
IT'S ABOUT THAT TIME FOR SNOWBALL TO PLAY WITH (BITE) ME.
WARY WARY
WALK WALK WALK
30 minutes later...
THAT'S STRANGE. SHE ISN'T HERE YET?
WALK WALK
SHE HASN'T EVEN SHOWN UP FOR DINNER.
COULD IT BE...?
BURP
RATTLE RATTLE
Mi!
She had been locked in accident-ally.
I KNEW IT.

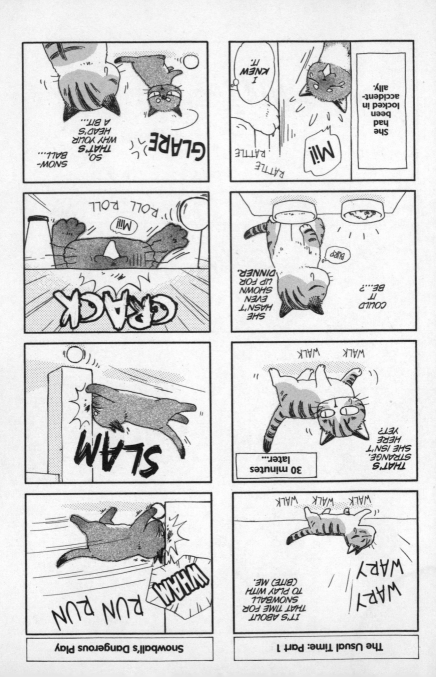

The Usual Time: Part 2

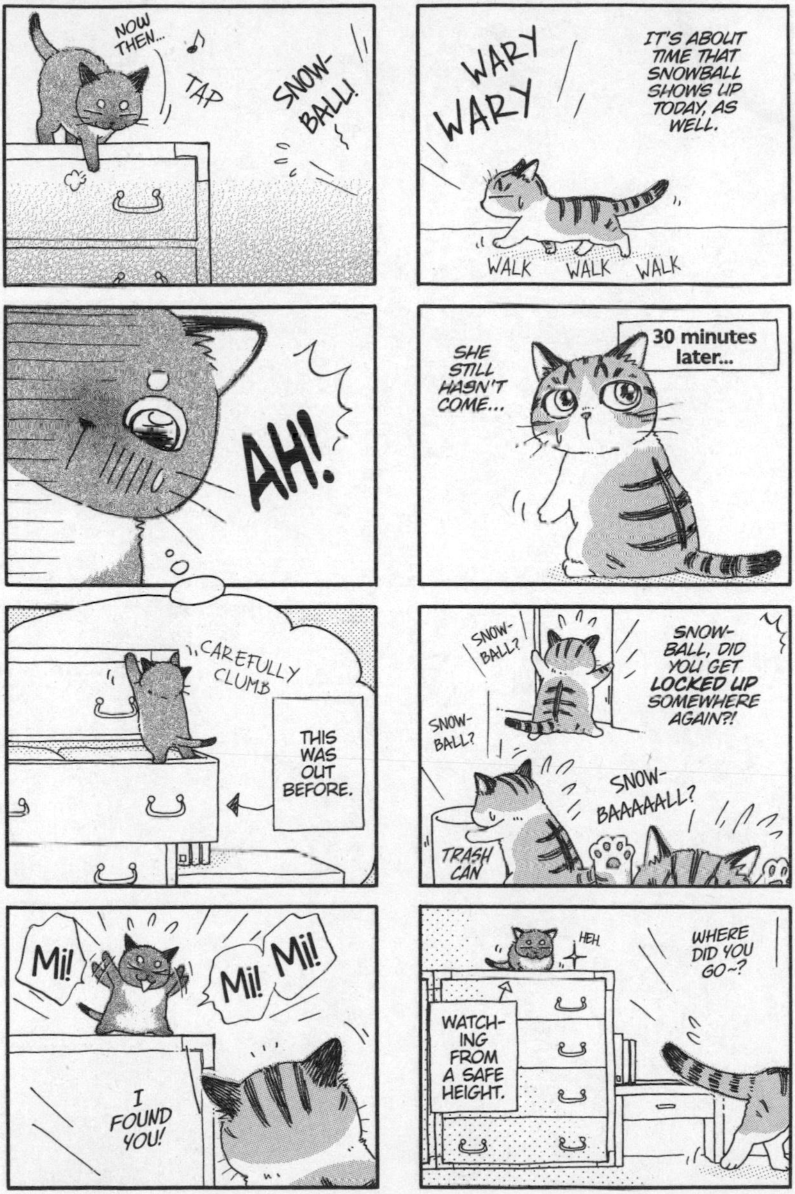
IT'S ABOUT TIME THAT SNOWBALL SHOWS UP TODAY, AS WELL.
WARY WARY
WALK WALK WALK
30 minutes later...
SHE STILL HASN'T COME...
SNOWBALL, DID YOU GET LOCKED UP SOMEWHERE AGAIN?!
SNOW-BALL?
SNOW-BALL?
SNOW-BAAAAALL?
TRASH CAN
WHERE DID YOU GO~?
HEH.
WATCHING FROM A SAFE HEIGHT.
NOW THEN...
TAP
SNOW-BALL!
AH!
CAREFULLY CLUMB
THIS WAS OUT BEFORE.
Mi!
Mi!
Mi!
I FOUND YOU!

Plum Is...

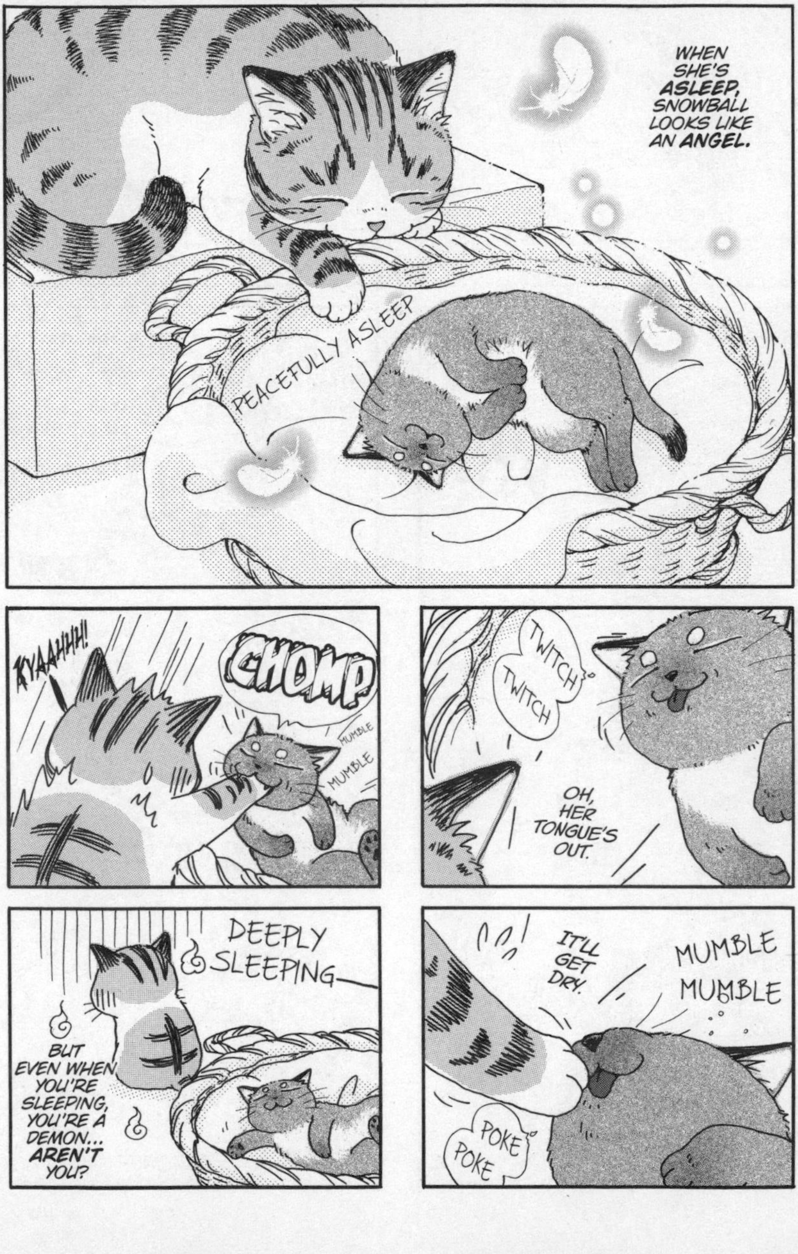
WHEN SHE'S ASLEEP, SNOWBALL LOOKS LIKE AN ANGEL.
PEACEFULLY ASLEEP
TWITCH TWITCH
OH, HER TONGUE'S OUT.
CHOMP
MUMBLE MUMBLE
KYAAHHH!
MUMBLE MUMBLE
IT'LL GET DRY.
POKE POKE
DEEPLY SLEEPING
BUT EVEN WHEN YOU'RE SLEEPING, YOU'RE A DEMON... AREN'T YOU?

Snow Day.

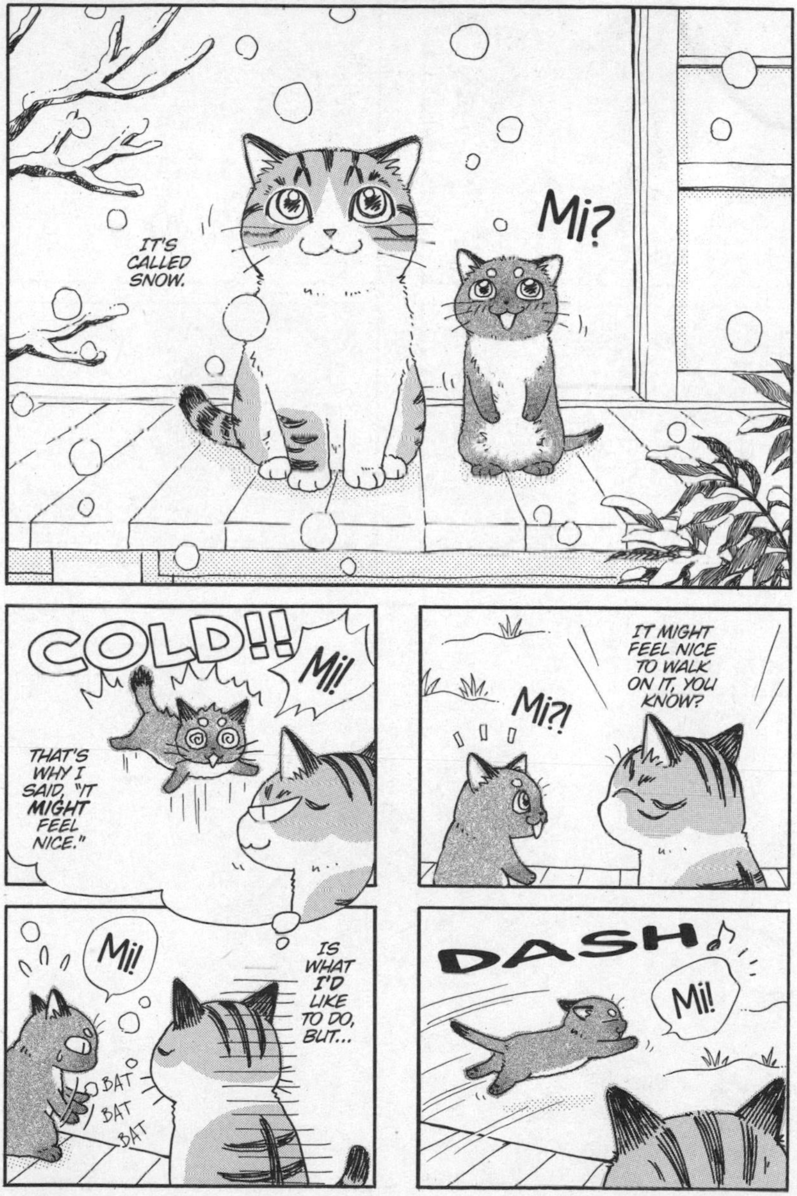
Mi?
IT'S CALLED SNOW.
IT MIGHT FEEL NICE TO WALK ON IT, YOU KNOW?
Mi?!
COLD!!
Mi!
THAT'S WHY I SAID, "IT MIGHT FEEL NICE."
DASH
Mi!
IS WHAT I'D LIKE TO DO, BUT...
Mi!
BAT BAT BAT

After the Snow

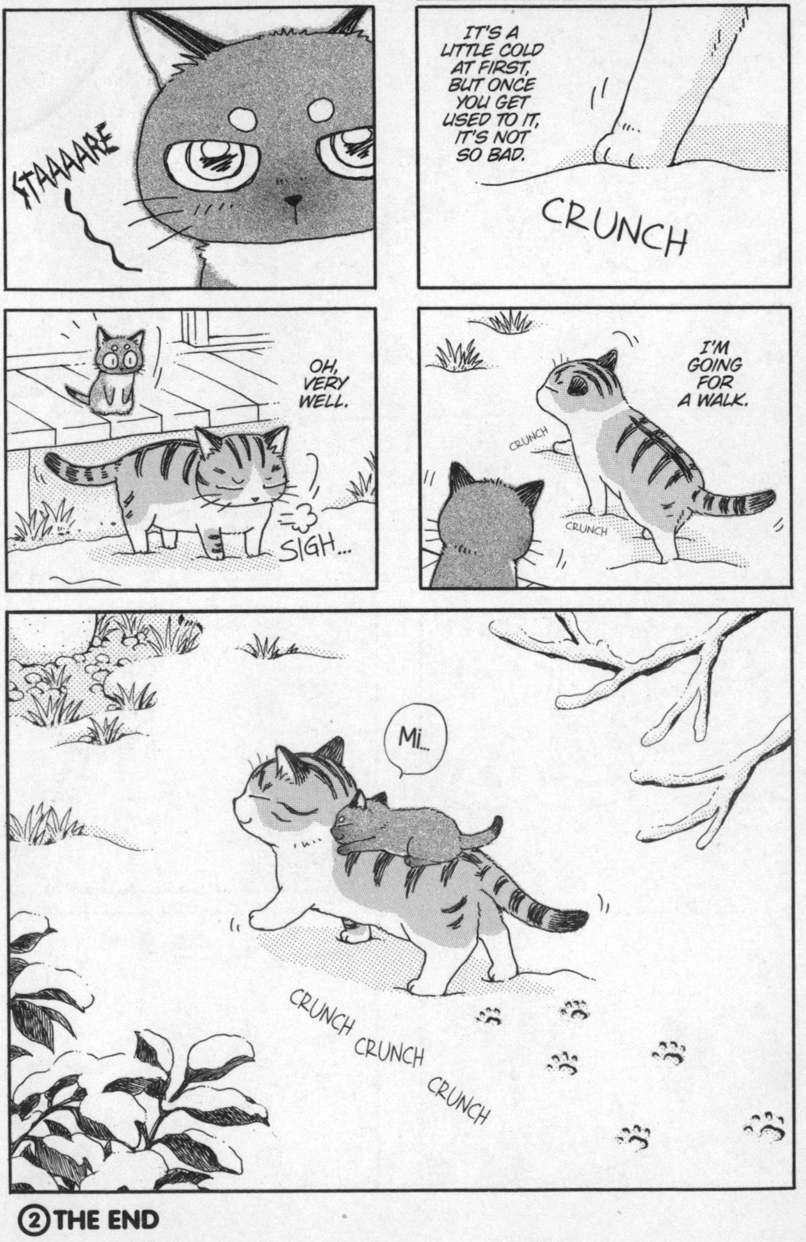
IT'S A LITTLE COLD AT FIRST, BUT ONCE YOU GET USED TO IT, IT'S NOT SO BAD.
CRUNCH
STAAAARE
I'M GOING FOR A WALK.
CRUNCH
CRUNCH
OH, VERY WELL.
SIGH...
Mi...
CRUNCH
CRUNCH
CRUNCH

② THE END

SHORT.3

Snowball's Thoughts

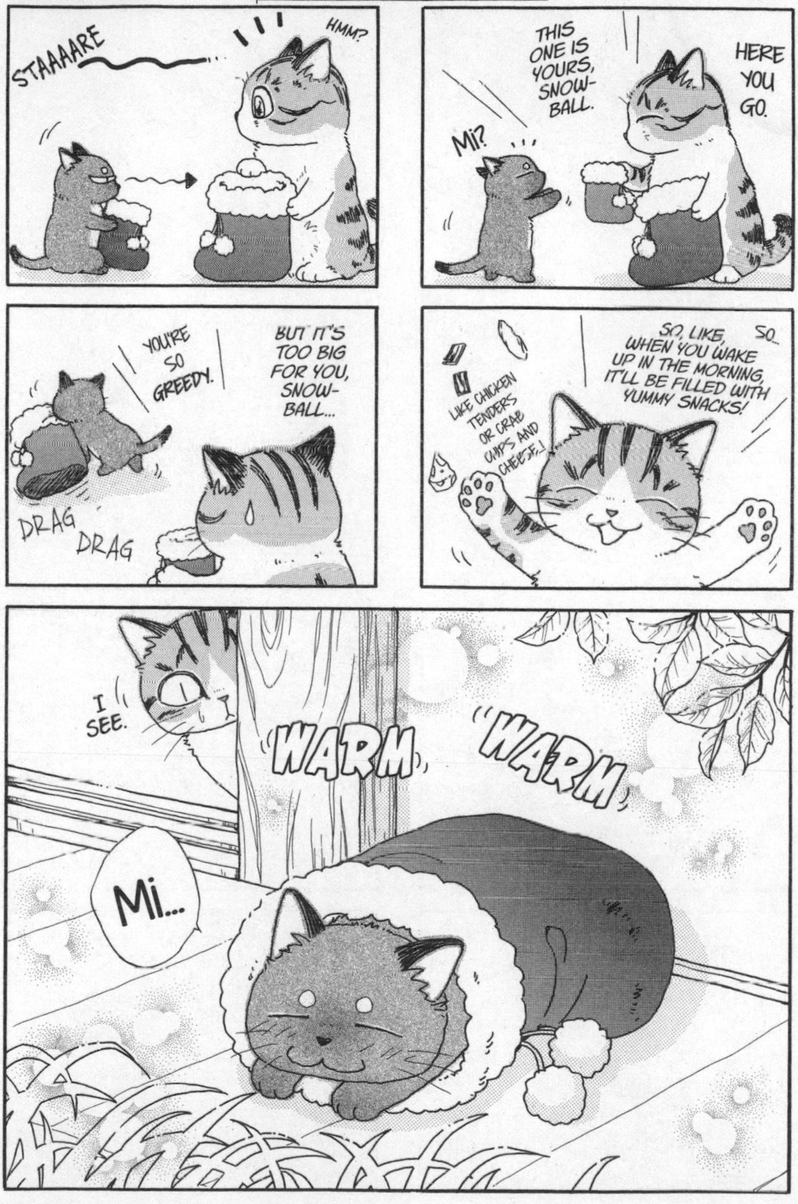
HERE YOU GO.
THIS ONE IS YOURS, SNOW-BALL.
Mi?
STAAAARE
HMM?
SO...
SO, LIKE, WHEN YOU WAKE UP IN THE MORNING, IT'LL BE FILLED WITH YUMMY SNACKS!
LIKE CHICKEN TENDERS OR CRAB CHIPS AND CHEESE...!
BUT IT'S TOO BIG FOR YOU, SNOW-BALL...
YOU'RE SO GREEDY.
DRAG DRAG
I SEE.
WARM WARM
Mi...

A Happy(?) Christmas for Cats As Well

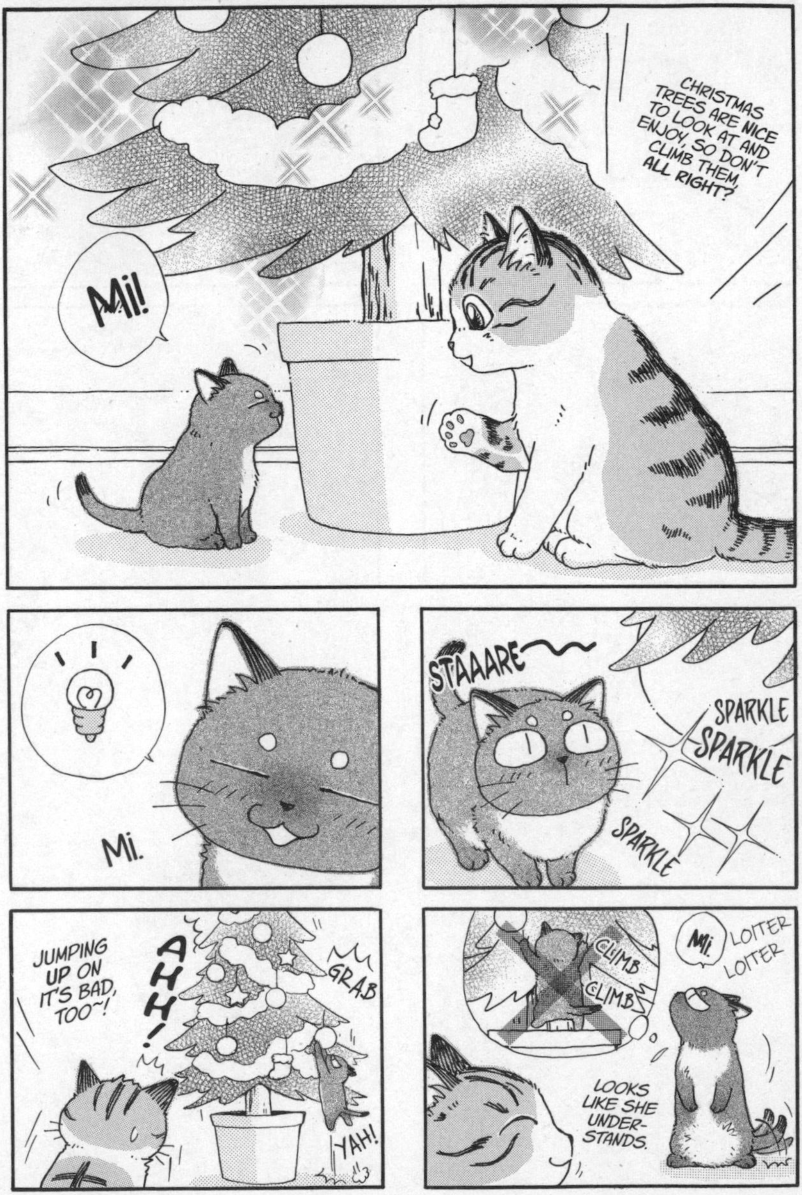
CHRISTMAS TREES ARE NICE TO LOOK AT AND ENJOY, SO DON'T CLIMB THEM, ALL RIGHT?
Mi!
STAAARE~~
SPARKLE SPARKLE
SPARKLE
Mi.
Mi.
LOITER LOITER
CLIMB CLIMB
LOOKS LIKE SHE UNDER-STANDS.
JUMPING UP ON IT'S BAD, TOO~!
AHH!
GRAB
YAH!

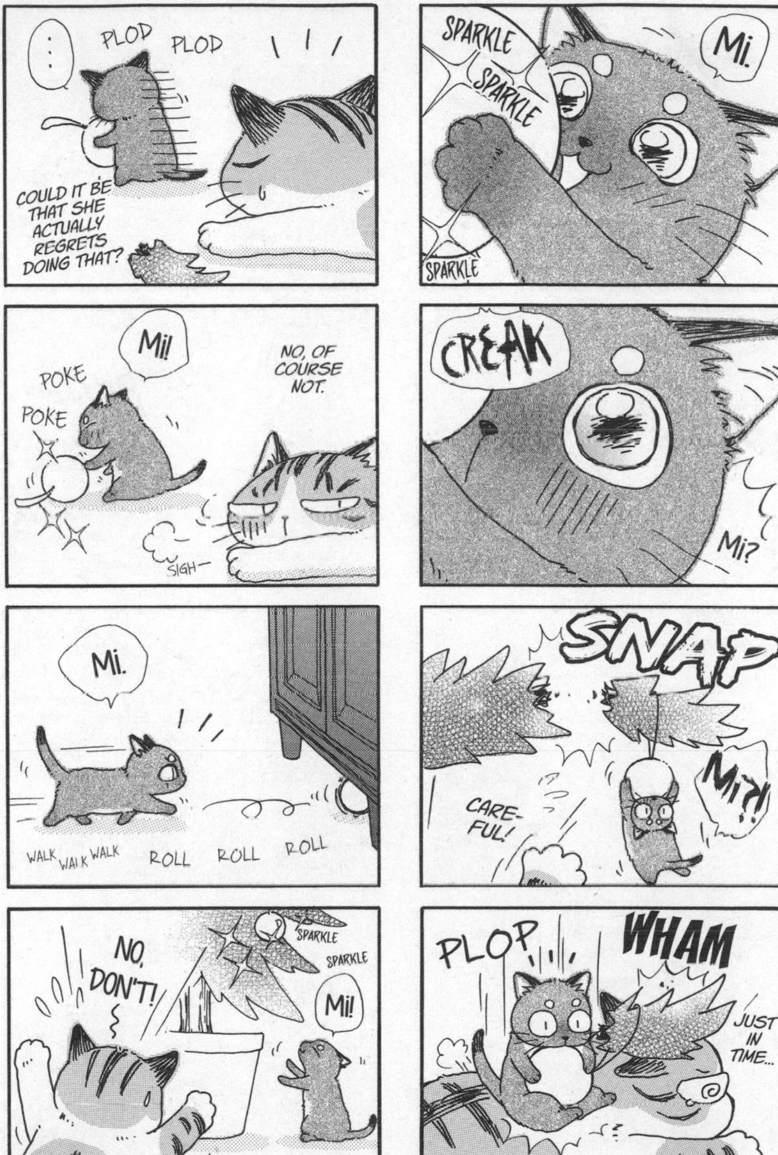
Mi.
SPARKLE
SPARKLE
SPARKLE
CREAK
Mi?
SNAP
Mi?!
CARE-FUL!
WHAM
PLOP
JUST IN TIME...
...
PLOD PLOD
COULD IT BE THAT SHE ACTUALLY REGRETS DOING THAT?
NO, OF COURSE NOT.
Mi!
POKE
POKE
SIGH—
Mi.
WALK WALK WALK
ROLL ROLL ROLL
NO, DON'T!
SPARKLE
SPARKLE
Mi!

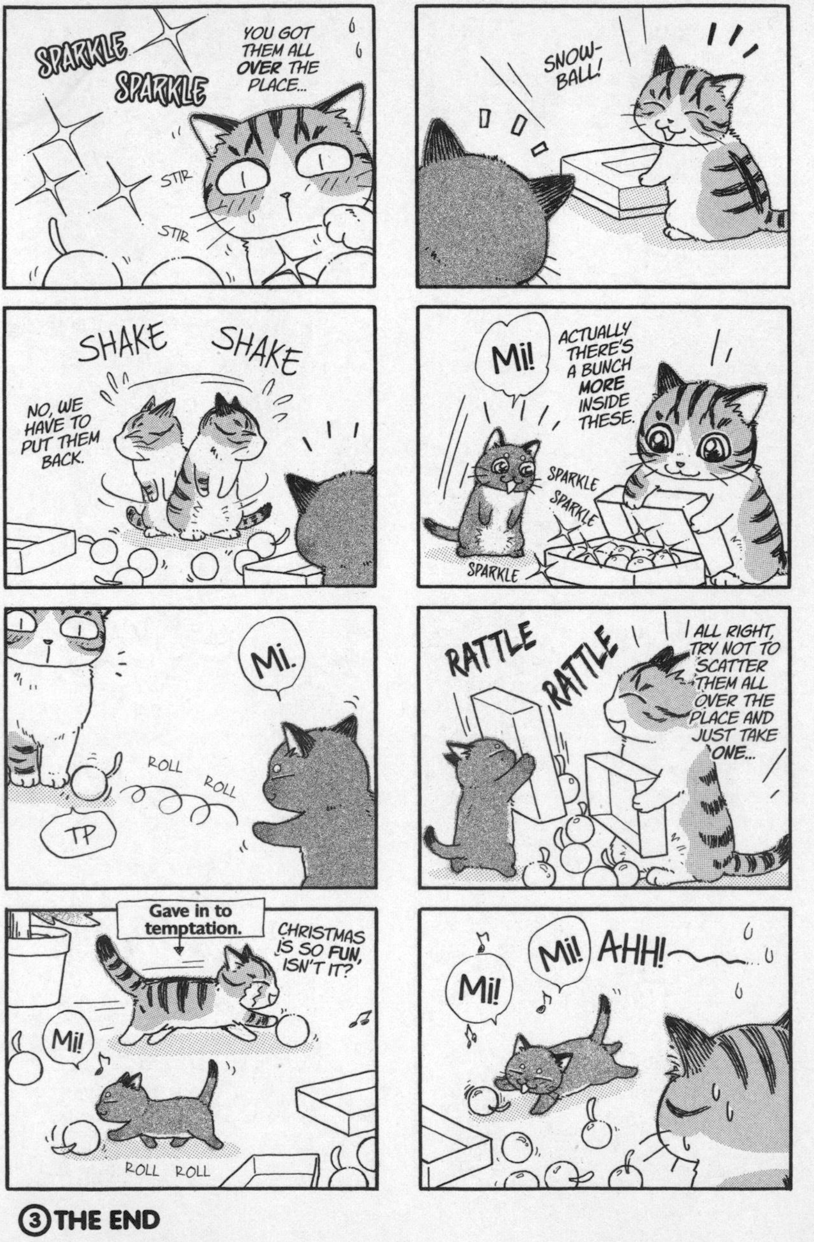
SNOW-BALL!
Mi!
ACTUALLY THERE'S A BUNCH MORE INSIDE THESE.
SPARKLE
SPARKLE
SPARKLE
RATTLE
RATTLE
I ALL RIGHT, TRY NOT TO SCATTER THEM ALL OVER THE PLACE AND JUST TAKE ONE...
Mi!
AHH!
Mi!
YOU GOT THEM ALL OVER THE PLACE...
SPARKLE
SPARKLE
STIR
STIR
SHAKE
SHAKE
NO, WE HAVE TO PUT THEM BACK.
Mi.
ROLL
ROLL
TP
Gave in to temptation.
CHRISTMAS IS SO FUN, ISN'T IT?
Mi!
ROLL ROLL

③ THE END

SHORT.4

Plum and the Kittens

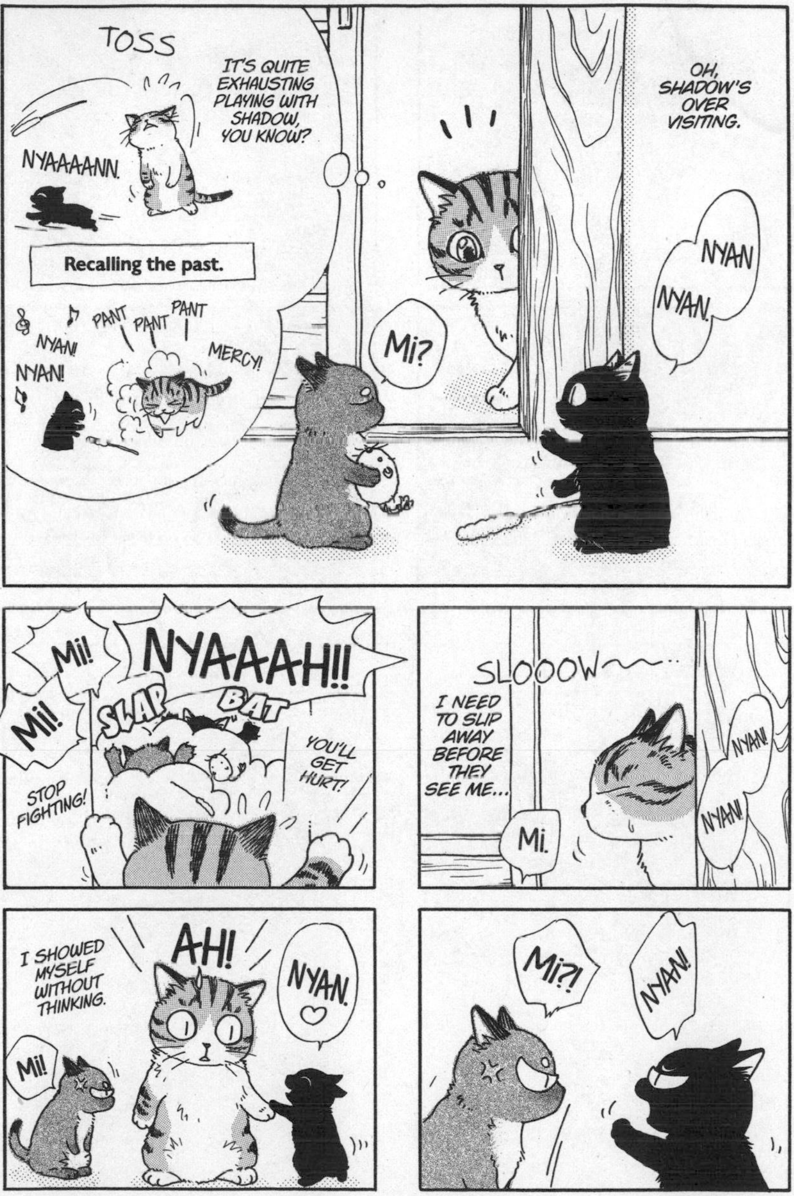
OH, SHADOW'S OVER VISITING.
NYAN NYAN.
Mi?
IT'S QUITE EXHAUSTING PLAYING WITH SHADOW, YOU KNOW?
TOSS
NYAAAANN.
Recalling the past.
PANT PANT PANT
NYAN! NYAN!
MERCY!
SLOOOW
I NEED TO SLIP AWAY BEFORE THEY SEE ME...
NYAN!
NYAN!
Mi.
NYAAAH!!
Mi!
Mi!
SLAP
BAT
YOU'LL GET HURT!
STOP FIGHTING!
NYAN!
Mi?!
NYAN.
AH!
I SHOWED MYSELF WITHOUT THINKING.
Mi!

The Two Kittens' Arguments

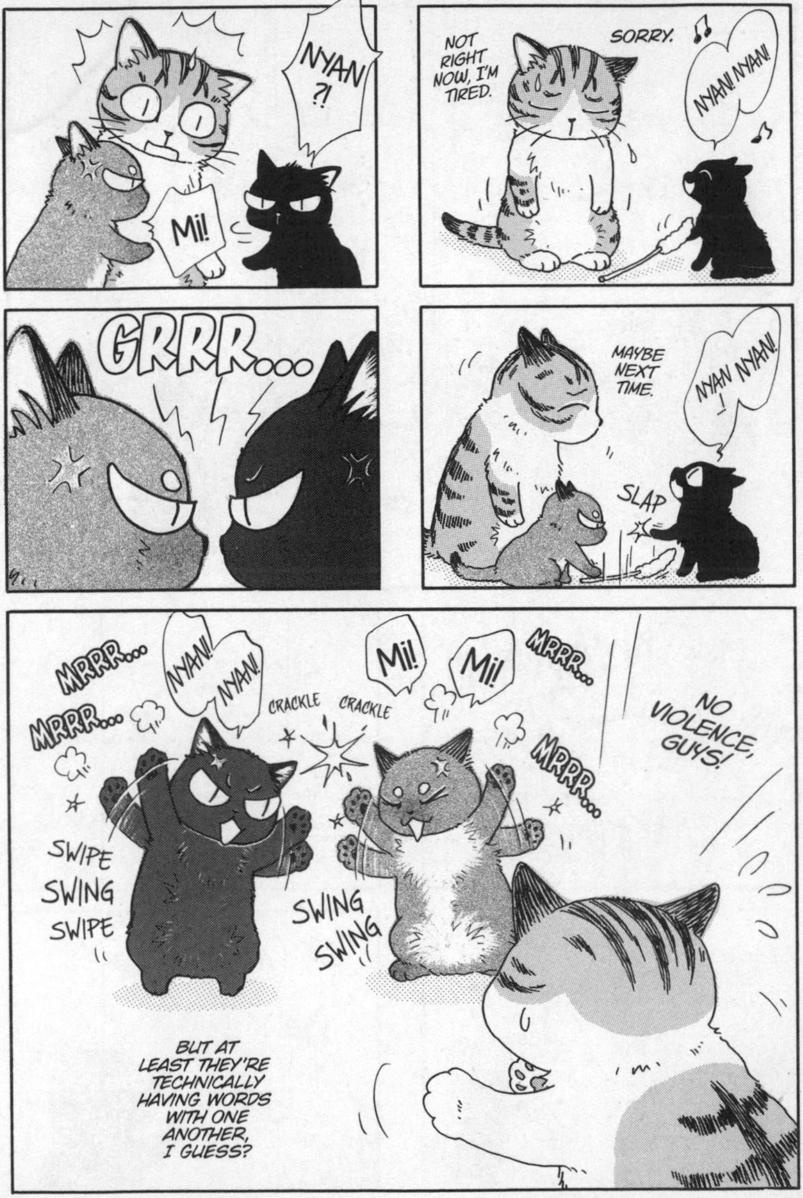
NYAN! NYAN!
SORRY.
NOT RIGHT NOW, I'M TIRED.
NYAN ?!
Mi!
NYAN NYAN! !
MAYBE NEXT TIME.
SLAP
GRRR...
NO VIOLENCE, GUYS!
MRRR...
Mi!
Mi!
MRRR...
CRACKLE
CRACKLE
NYAN! NYAN!
MRRR...
MRRR...
SWING SWING
SWIPE SWING SWIPE
BUT AT LEAST THEY'RE TECHNICALLY HAVING WORDS WITH ONE ANOTHER, I GUESS?

Plum's Reasoning

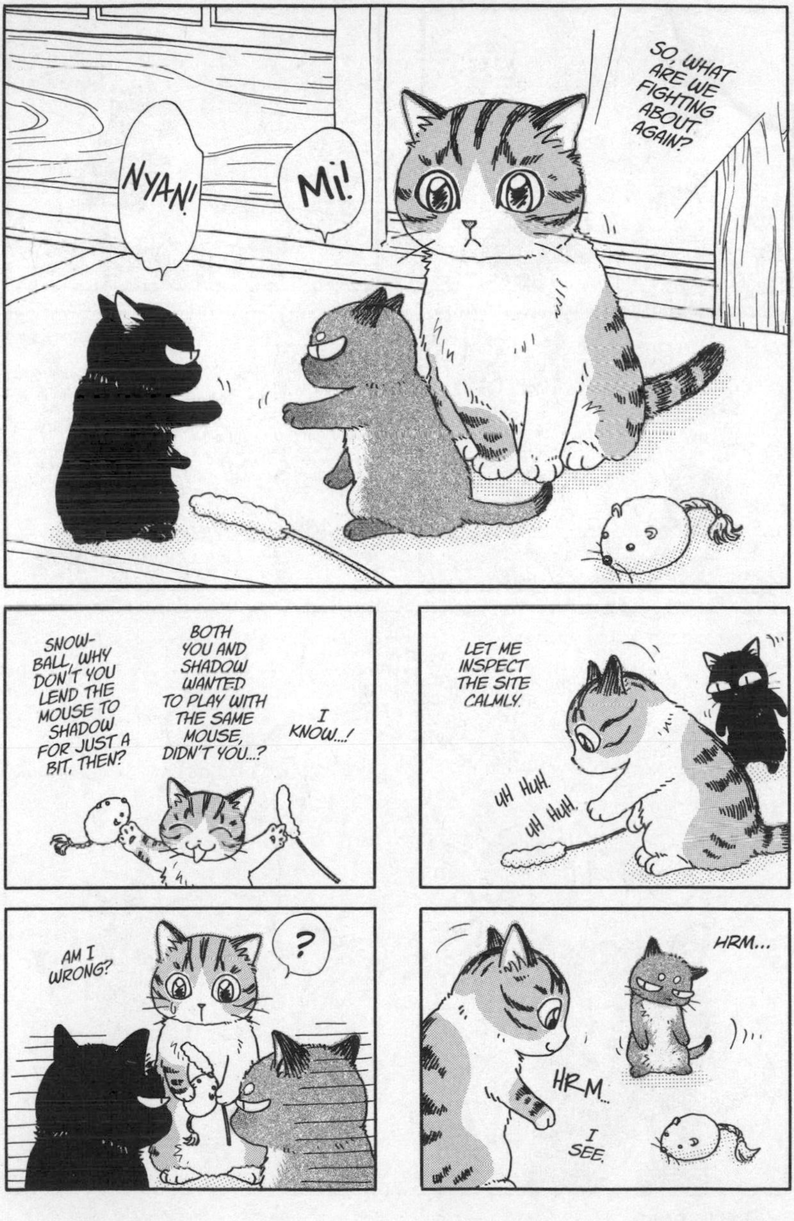
SO, WHAT ARE WE FIGHTING ABOUT AGAIN?
Mi!
NYAN!
LET ME INSPECT THE SITE CALMLY.
UH HUH.
UH HUH.
BOTH YOU AND SHADOW WANTED TO PLAY WITH THE SAME MOUSE, DIDN'T YOU...?
I KNOW...!
SNOW-BALL, WHY DON'T YOU LEND THE MOUSE TO SHADOW FOR JUST A BIT, THEN?
HRM...
HRM...
I SEE.
?
AM I WRONG?

Mi.
Mi.
WHISPER
WHISPER
WHISPER
NYAN.
NYAN.
WEREN'T YOU FIGHTING JUST A MOMENT AGO?
EH?
PLUM'S ODDLY STUPID, ISN'T SHE?
DID YOU JUST NOTICE THAT?
WHISPER
WHISPER
WHAT ARE THEY SAYING WHILE LOOKING AT ME LIKE THAT?
I DON'T UNDERSTAND WHEN YOU ONLY USE "NYAN"S AND "MI"S.
BA-DUMP
BA-DUMP
YOU AREN'T SAYING STUFF LIKE THAT, ARE YOU...?
SAY, SNOWBALL? SHADOW?
EXHALE...
SIIIGH...
WALK WALK
WALK WALK
......
FINE, IF IT'S JUST A LITTLE WHILE, HOW ABOUT I PLAY WITH YOU...?
THE BOTH OF YOU?
SMIRK
Mi.
NYAN.

④ THE END

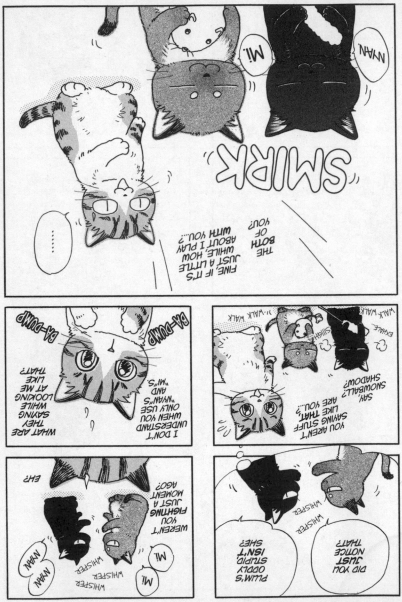

STORIES ABOUT MY CAT

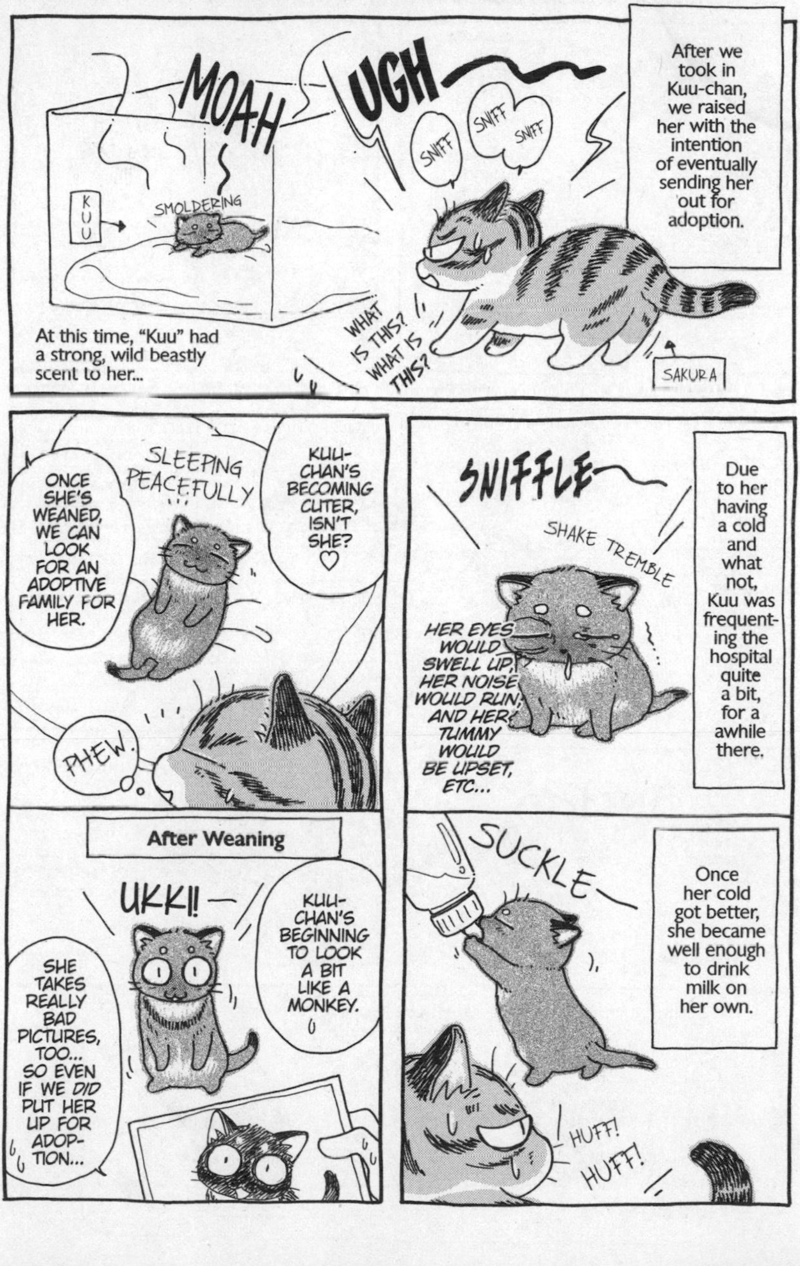
After we took in Kuu-chan, we raised her with the intention of eventually sending her out for adoption.
UGH
MOAH
SNIFF
SNIFF SNIFF
KUU
SMOLDERING
WHAT IS THIS? WHAT IS THIS?
SAKURA
At this time, "Kuu" had a strong, wild beastly scent to her...
Due to her having a cold and what not, Kuu was frequenting the hospital quite a bit, for a awhile there.
SNIFFLE
SHAKE TREMBLE
HER EYES WOULD SWELL UP, HER NOISE WOULD RUN, AND HER TUMMY WOULD BE UPSET, ETC...
KUU-CHAN'S BECOMING CUTER, ISN'T SHE? ♡
SLEEPING PEACEFULLY
ONCE SHE'S WEANED, WE CAN LOOK FOR AN ADOPTIVE FAMILY FOR HER.
PHEW.
Once her cold got better, she became well enough to drink milk on her own.
SUCKLE
HUFF! HUFF!
After Weaning
KUU-CHAN'S BEGINNING TO LOOK A BIT LIKE A MONKEY.
UKKI!
SHE TAKES REALLY BAD PICTURES, TOO... SO EVEN IF WE DID PUT HER UP FOR ADOP-TION...

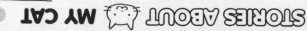

STORIES ABOUT MY CAT

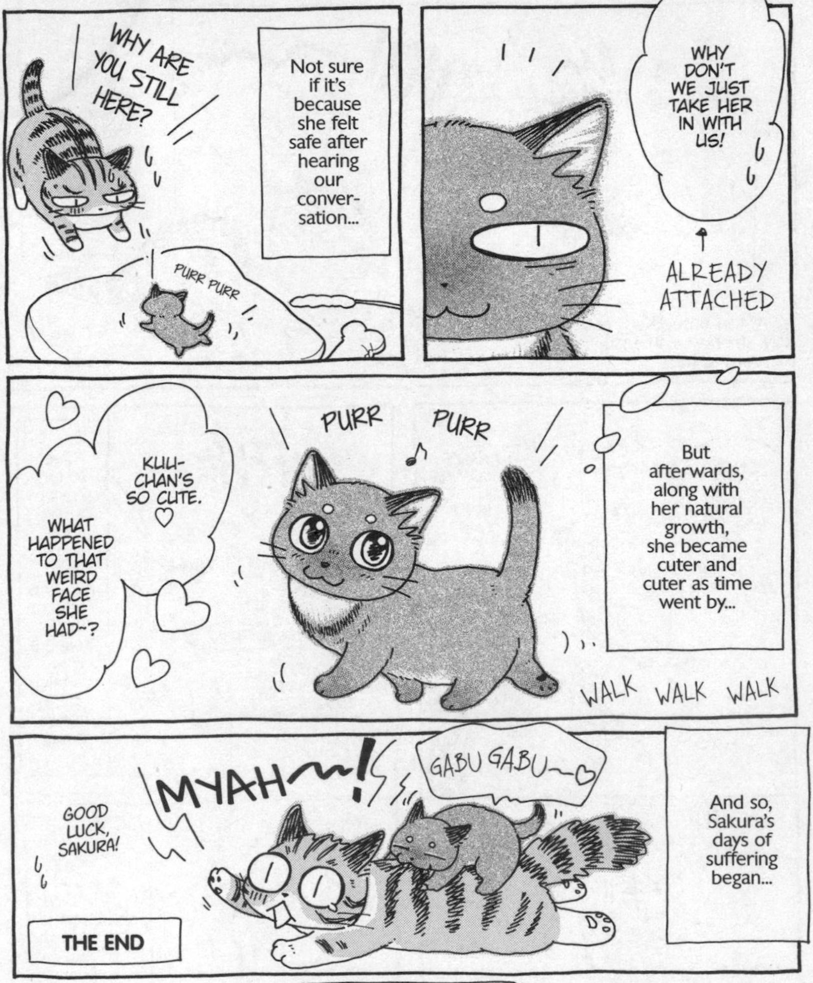
WHY DON'T WE JUST TAKE HER IN WITH US!
ALREADY ATTACHED
Not sure if it's because she felt safe after hearing our conversation...
WHY ARE YOU STILL HERE?
PURR PURR
But afterwards, along with her natural growth, she became cuter and cuter as time went by...
PURR PURR
WALK WALK WALK
KUU-CHAN'S SO CUTE.
WHAT HAPPENED TO THAT WEIRD FACE SHE HAD~?
And so, Sakura's days of suffering began...
GABU GABU~
MYAH~!
GOOD LUCK, SAKURA!
THE END

Author's Musings

THE BOOK FINALLY CAME OUT~!
THIS IS ALL THANKS TO THE EFFORTS OF EVERYONE IN THE EDITORIAL DEPARTMENT, EVERYONE WHO WAS INVOLVED IN THE PUBLISHING PROCESS OF PLUM CRAZY, AND YOU, THE READERS.
THANK YOU SO VERY MUCH.

HOSHINO NATSUMI

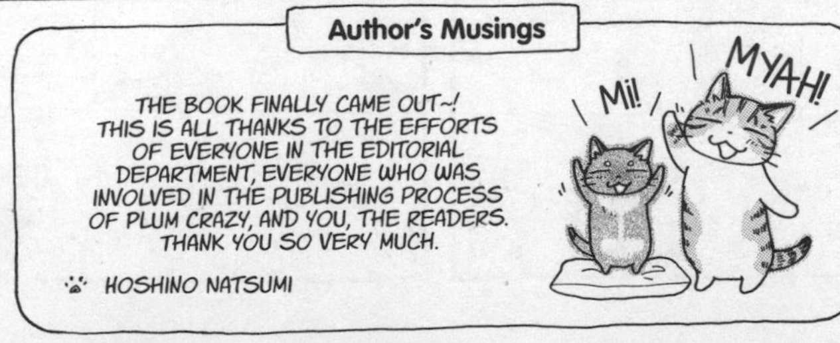
MYAH!
Mi!

Plum Crazy!
tales of a
tiger-striped cat

See you in Volume 2!

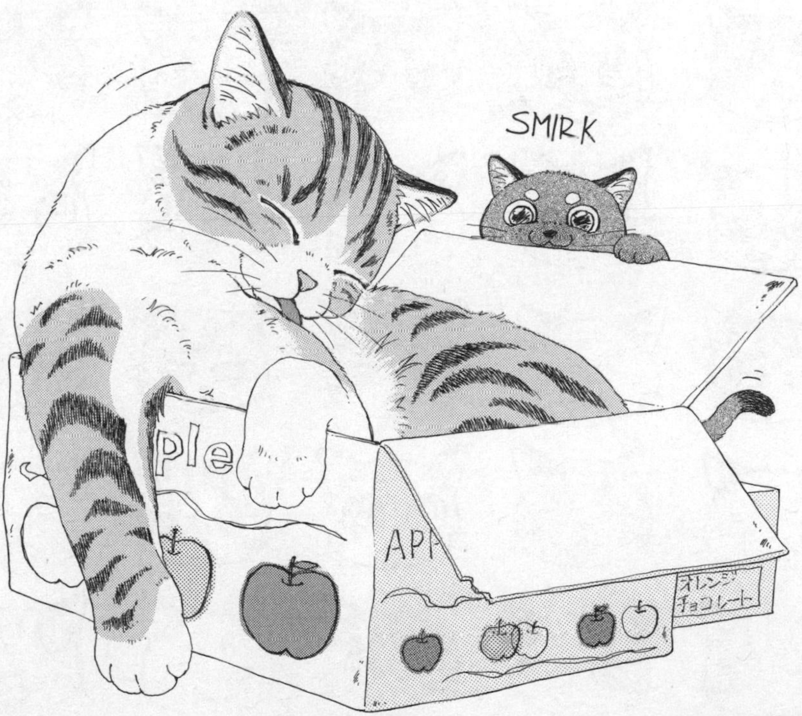
SMIRK
ple
APP
オレンジ
チョコレート

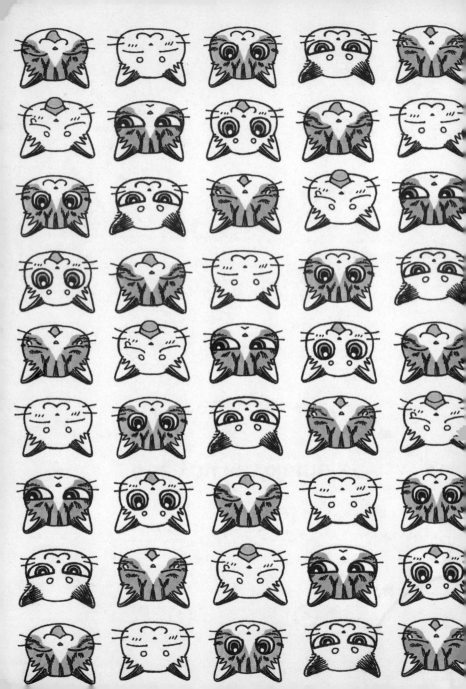

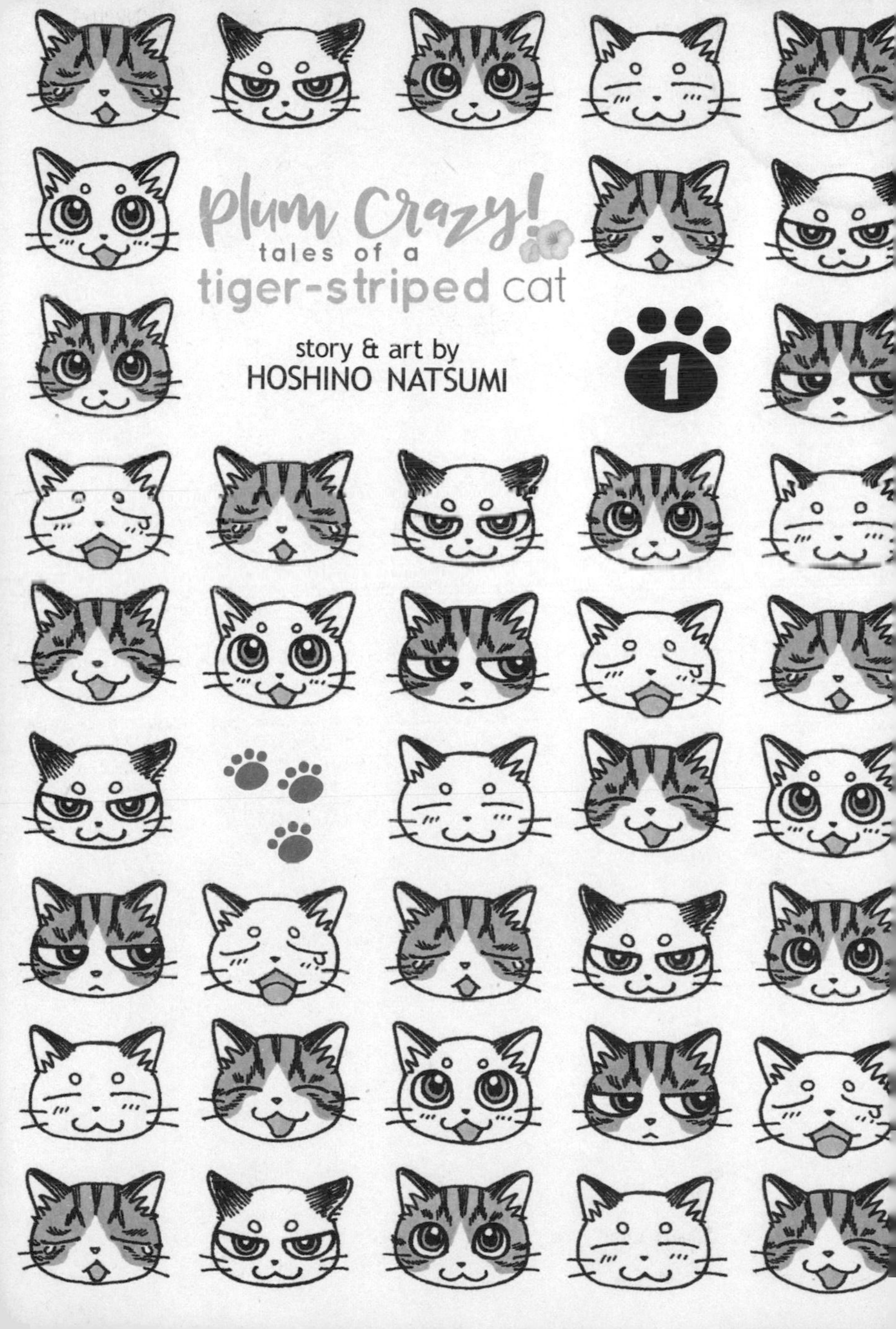
Plum Crazy!
tales of a
tiger-striped cat
story & art by
HOSHINO NATSUMI
1

Plum Crazy!
tales of a
tiger-striped cat

Plum Crazy! tales of a tiger-striped cat

story and art by NATSUMI HOSHINO   VOLUME 1

TRANSLATION
Nan Rymer

LETTERING
Laura Scoville
Will Ringrose

COVER DESIGN
Nicky Lim

PROOFREADER
Kent Clarkson

ASSISTANT EDITOR
Jenn Grunigen

PRODUCTION ASSISTANT
CK Russell

PRODUCTION MANAGER
Lissa Pattillo

EDITOR-IN-CHIEF
Adam Arnold

PUBLISHER
Jason DeAngelis

PLUM CRAZY! TALES OF A TIGER-STRIPED CAT VOLUME 1
© Hoshino Natsumi 2008
Originally published in Japan in 2008 by SHONENGAHOSHA Co., Ltd., Tokyo.
English translation rights arranged through TOHAN CORPORATION, Tokyo.

Seven Seas books may be purchased in bulk for promotional, educational, or business use. Please contact your local bookseller or the Macmillan Corporate and Premium Sales Department at 1-800-221-7945, extension 5442, or by e-mail at MacmillanSpecialMarkets@macmillan.com.

Seven Seas and the Seven Seas logo are trademarks of Seven Seas Entertainment, LLC. All rights reserved.

ISBN: 978-1-626925-28-1

Printed in Canada

First Printing: July 2017

10 9 8 7 6 5 4 3 2 1

FOLLOW US ONLINE: www.gomanga.com

READING DIRECTIONS

This book reads from *right to left*, Japanese style. If this is your first time reading manga, you start reading from the top right panel on each page and take it from there. If you get lost, just follow the numbered diagram here. It may seem backwards at first, but you'll get the hang of it! Have fun!

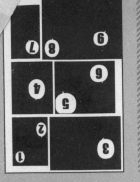